'A view into a bygone world that is as revealing as it is entertaining' *Sunday Telegraph*

'Pure pleasure' *Literary Review*

'Bracing, breezy and often moving memoir' *Spectator*

'A compulsive read' *Glasgow Herald*

'Anecdotes told with artless ease' *TLS*

'Combines the worldly and unworldly in a narrative that by turns amuses, saddens and charms' *House & Garden*

'Licence to thrill' *The Lady*

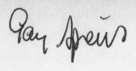

Veronica Maclean was brought up mainly at Beaufort, her family's castle in Scotland. In 1940 she married Alan Phipps, a naval officer, by whom she had a son and a daughter. In 1943 Alan was reported 'missing, believed killed' after a battle on the Greek island of Leros, but cruel twists of fate kept Veronica's hopes alive for many months, and it was not for more than a year that she knew for certain he was dead.

Veronica married her second husband, Fitzroy Maclean, in 1946, and had two more sons by him. Later to be named as Ian Fleming's model for James Bond, 'Fitz' was diplomat, politician, soldier, author and above all traveller: his book *Eastern Approaches*, published in 1949, became a classic, and is still in print today. After the war Lady Maclean supported her husband in his political career, and accompanied him on many adventurous journeys, often making documentary films for the BBC. In the 1990s, with the Balkan conflict raging, she and one of her sons drove a van full of medical supplies and equipment out to Korčula, in the war zone. Yet she still found time to write a bestseller of her own, *Lady Maclean's Cookbook*.

She now divides her time between Strachur, a fine, eighteenth-century house overlooking Loch Fyne, in the Western Highlands of Scotland, and Korčula, the island off the Dalmatian coast where she and Fitz bought and restored an ancient *palazzo*.

Past Forgetting

A memoir of heroes, adventure, love and life with Fitzroy Maclean

VERONICA MACLEAN

review

Copyright © 2002 Veronica Maclean

The right of Veronica Maclean to be identified as the Author
of the Work has been asserted by her in accordance with the
Copyright, Designs and Patents Act 1988.

First published in 2002
by REVIEW

First published in paperback in 2003
by REVIEW

An imprint of Headline Book Publishing

Back cover photograph reproduced by kind permission of FitzGerald Bemiss.

Lines from *Bitter Sweet* by Noël Coward © The Estate of
Noël Coward, reproduced by permission of Methuen Publishing Limited.

10 9 8 7 6 5 4 3 2 1

All rights reserved. No part of this publication may be reproduced,
stored in a retrieval system, or transmitted, in any form or by any
means without the prior written permission of the publisher, nor
be otherwise circulated in any form of binding or cover other than
that in which it is published and without a similar condition
being imposed on the subsequent purchaser.

Every effort has been made to fulfil requirements with regard to reproducing
copyright material. The author and publisher will be glad to rectify any
omissions at the earliest opportunity.

ISBN 0 7553 1025 X

Designed by Ben Cracknell

Typeset by Palimpsest Book Production Limited,
Polmont, Stirlingshire

Printed and bound in Great Britain by
Clays Ltd, St Ives plc

Papers and cover boards used by Headline are natural, recyclable products
made from wood grown in sustainable forests. The manufacturing processes
conform to the environmental regulations of the country of origin.

Headline Book Publishing
A division of Hodder Headline
338 Euston Road
London NW1 3BH

www.reviewbooks.co.uk
www.hodderheadline.com

Dedication

For

Laura	*Jake*	*Margaret*	*Alexander*
Rose	*Jemma*	*Katharine*	*Johnnie*
Caspar		*Charlotte*	
Adam		*Diana*	
Benjie			

Maud, Florence, Arthur, Betsy and Jack, Scarlett and Clementine

If one day you, my grandchildren and great-grandchildren, plus all my Fraser great-nephews and -nieces, should want to understand the complexities of the Lovat family, and the richness and diversity of its ramifications, you need go back no further than my own four grandparents. The rest is ancient history, and I shall try to minimise it in these pages, even though I hope they may possibly arouse in you a curiosity about the past, and the part our ancestors played in it, for, after all, those ancestors are as much yours as mine.

This book, though, is not about the distant past, only about my own life – the life of an ancestor who has lived a very long time, in which a lot has happened, some of it happy, some sad.

I have called it *Past Forgetting*, after the song in Noël Coward's *Bitter Sweet*:

> *Time may lie heavy between,*
> *But what has been*
> *Is past forgetting.*

When I asked my son Charlie, who is a real writer, how I should begin, he said, 'Tell it as it was,' and that is what I have attempted to do.

My Family

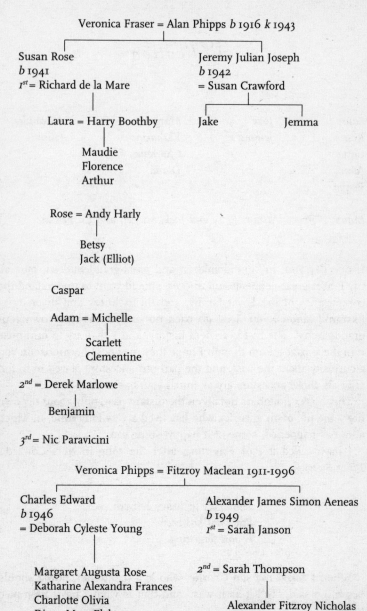

Veronica Fraser = Alan Phipps *b* 1916 *k* 1943

Susan Rose
b 1941
1ˢᵗ = Richard de la Mare

Jeremy Julian Joseph
b 1942
= Susan Crawford

Laura = Harry Boothby

Jake   Jemma

Maudie
Florence
Arthur

Rose = Andy Harly

Betsy
Jack (Elliot)

Caspar

Adam = Michelle

Scarlett
Clementine

2ⁿᵈ = Derek Marlowe

Benjamin

3ʳᵈ = Nic Paravicini

Veronica Phipps = Fitzroy Maclean 1911-1996

Charles Edward
b 1946
= Deborah Cyleste Young

Alexander James Simon Aeneas
b 1949
1ˢᵗ = Sarah Janson

Margaret Augusta Rose
Katharine Alexandra Frances
Charlotte Olivia
Diana Mary Elektra

2ⁿᵈ = Sarah Thompson

Alexander Fitzroy Nicholas
Johnnie

Contents

Acknowledgements

First of all I would like to thank my wonderful editor, Duff Hart-Davis, who cut more than one hundred pages from my manuscript (almost) painlessly, and made it a better book. My thanks also go to Sheila MacPherson, Drusilla Fraser, Mme Sessa and Zivan Filippi in Korčula – who made sense out of my scribbles; Jamie Maclean who spent hours copying and re-copying them; Jeremy Phipps who researched the battle of Leros and his father's citation; General Vladko Velebit, Sir Alexander Glen and Professor A. Pravda, who all improved my version of Jugoslav history; Eleo Gordon, who was the first to encourage me, and Margaret Bemiss who was the last to do so; and finally Jim Gill, my supportive agent, throughout.

1

BEAUFORT

I WAS BORN IN LONDON ON 2 DECEMBER 1920, A SEVEN-MONTH BABY who was made even more puny by catching whooping cough three months later – but as soon as I was considered strong enough to travel, I was taken up to Beaufort, my parents' home in the eastern Highlands of Scotland, where I flourished. Beaufort was more than a huge pink sandstone castle built on a bluff above the River Beauly; it was also a way of life that has now entirely vanished. For me and the other children of Simon and Laura Lovat, it was, quite simply, paradise.

My first memory there is of waking up as usual in our night nursery and registering the familiar hump of my brother Hugh in his nearly grown-up bed on one side of the room, and then – oh, horrors! – a totally unfamiliar figure in the brass bed that our Highland Nana usually occupied beside my cot; a figure with two thick, carroty plaits framing a yellowish face which bore, if not a scowl, then at least a very severe expression.

Worse was to come. Mary, our cheerful nurserymaid, entered the room looking subdued and nervous, and deposited not, as was her habit, three cups of strong black tea and four Rich Tea biscuits (two for Hugh), but three glasses of *fruit juice* beside the stranger's bed.

'Drink up your nice juice, Master Hugh,' said this ogre. 'No more of your nasty tea in *my* nursery! This is *good* for you.'

Nanny Hodge had been engaged by my mother to replace Nellie Cameron, our much-loved, easy-going nanny from the glens, who had been carted off to hospital with suspected TB. Considering that my mother had nursed her own mother through the first stages of tuberculosis, and had founded and now supported the charity that ran three sanatoria in the Highlands, she was somewhat vague about her children's health. She must at least have been aware of the danger of infection, but she never fussed about our health or her own, bore pain stoically, and was quite fatalistic where illnesses were concerned.

Nanny Hodge stayed with us for six months, in spite of our vigorous complaints, the chief of which were that she gave us stewed prunes and no porridge for breakfast, that she made us eat spinach, and that she was *English*. But at the end of that time Nana's health had been improved by direct intercession with the Almighty, and she was back in her brass bed once again, the strong tea and Rich Tea biscuit regime re-established. Our prayers had worked! And I can still remember them, curious and gabbled though they were: 'God bless Dada, Mama, Shimi, Hugh and Magdalen [my brothers and sister]' – sometimes a dog was added – 'look after us all, make Nana better, and thank you for a lovely day' (this gratitude would be sometimes withheld). Then at a great pace: 'Eternal rest grant to Uncle Hugh and Uncle Charles, Uncle Percy, Uncle Boy [all killed in the First World War], Father Bernard Vaughan, Queen Alexandra, Nellie's father and Ina [Nana's relations]. Make me a good little girl and bring back Nana *soon*!'

By the time Nellie returned, Hugh had been moved to a room of his own, and the new baby, Diana Mary Rose, occupied my cot. Hugh was just eight, a strong, wilful child with an inventive mind, a warm heart and a hot and explosive temper.

'I think Hugh is getting to be BW [Beyond Women],' my mother mildly observed, having found a note on her pincushion one evening:

War declared on Lady Lovat after failed negotiations.
Signed, H. Fraser, HQ, The Nursery, 17 hours, 22.8.1926.

The negotiations had been about Hugh's bedtime. His phraseology was culled from his favourite book, a horrific boys' annual, *circa* 1916, given him by a tenant farmer's wife, with pictures of Nurse Edith Cavell tied to a stake being shot by a German firing squad, and Kaiser Bill and German soldiers bayoneting Highland prisoners. Hugh had also, in a moment of sibling jealousy, threatened to 'blow up the baby' by standing in front of the night nursery fire with a handful of cartridges he had found in Shimi's bedroom – *and* he had stuck needles into my mattress when I, unwittingly, disclosed the whereabouts of our secret bomb factory.

Yet in spite of these peccadilloes he remained my dearest companion and hero, and I would have done anything to prevent his being sent away to school, which is what BW meant in our family. The bomb factory was anyway really my parents' fault, because they had given Hugh a magnificent chemistry set for his birthday, with phials of different coloured powders, some labelled *Sulphur,* some *Magnesium.* We had heard my godfather, the author and poet Maurice Baring, talk about the Russian Revolution, and we had discovered at Beaufort the perfect Dynamiters' Den, an abandoned staircase between two floors where a new bathroom now cut off access.

Hugh collected all the old powder horns, relics of the Jacobite rebellions of the '15 and the '45, that lay about the Castle, and emptied their contents into envelopes. Creeping into our hidey-hole through the back of a cupboard, he would lay a trail of gunpowder on the steps and then light a fuse which would blow up the tin soldiers he had arranged in groups, or at least cause them to fall over.

'German soldiers are all right,' he would say, 'and sometimes Grenadier Guards, but *never* Highland soldiers.' I'm afraid Hugh at that time was a racist as well as a potential murderer.

Fortunately, the gunpowder was old and weak and never produced much of a bang, but I do remember a sulphur powder trail from one of the phials that made pretty yellow-green smoke and a horrible smell. It was the smell that proved the dynamiters' undoing. Shimi, Magdalen (nicknamed Tookie) and the older cousins wheedled and tickled the secret out of me.

In those happy years I was so much Hugh's shadow that I was called 'Me-too', for I was forever trying to jump the gap between our ages and follow him at all costs. He, being rather clumsy and not very brave, would use me as an agile guinea pig as we roamed round the Castle roof or on the rocks above the river.

'You go first,' he would say, 'and if it's safe, I'll come too.'

Up I would go, for he was very persuasive; he even persuaded our much older but credulous sister Magdalen that she could with perfect safety parachute off the Castle's tower holding an open golfing umbrella. Fortunately, this manoeuvre was forestalled by Uncle Alastair, who met them on their way up.

About that time my father was made Under-Secretary for the Dominions in Stanley Baldwin's government, and this meant longer spells for him in the Ministry and House of Lords, moving his family down to London and renting various town houses in the capital. As children we hated London and the loss of our glorious freedom at home, but to London we would go on the sleeper train that left Inverness at four fifteen in the afternoon and arrived at Euston at seven o'clock the next morning. We children and Nana were crowded into a third-class, four-berth carriage, but our parents travelled first-class. A top-hatted station master in a frock coat always saw us off.

We rented houses in Upper Grosvenor Street, then Onslow Gardens and then a huge corner house which is now a club in Bryanston Square. It had a beautiful long drawing room overlooking the square, and here my mother would hold her charitable meetings in aid of the Cecil Houses or Homes for the Homeless, as well as grand dinner parties. Hugh and I misbehaved continuously in Hyde Park, creeping up on unguarded prams while nannies gossiped on park benches and making off with them with wild whoops and what we imagined was the MacGregor battle-cry.

Hilaire Belloc was a frequent visitor, and so was Edwin Montagu, 'Cousin' Venetia's husband, who was one of my mother's more ardent cavaliers. But one day Montagu found Belloc's new book, *The Jews*, in her sitting room, inscribed with an affectionate dedication from the author, and he never set foot in the house again.

Venetia Stanley and my mother had known each other from their youthful hunting days in Lancashire, and Venetia was one of the many honorary cousins who peopled my world. I remember her as a rather formidable lady with a large, flat face, sensible brogues and lots of little yapping dogs at her heels. Now that I have read Uncle Henry Asquith's letters to her, written during the height of the Great War, when he was Prime Minister, I cannot think why he was so besotted.

The return journey to Beaufort for the summer holidays was just as exciting for Nana as it was for us. When the sleeping car attendant brought us our tea-trays and Marie biscuits, and snapped back the carriage blinds, we would begin counting the stations that brought us ever nearer to home: Dalnaspidal, Dalwhinnie, Newtonmore, Kingussie, Aviemore, a long stop; Moy; then a pause, and at last the long train would shunt backwards into Inverness station.

Monsignor Ronald Knox – a close friend of the family – perfectly caught the excitement of those journeys in a somewhat unflattering poem he wrote for me:

> *The signal is down for Veronica's train,*
> *And the signalman's face is distorted with pain,*
> *And the signalman's wife cries 'Alas and alack!*
> *We shall have no more peace now Veronica's back!'*
>
> *Large meetings of protest, we hear, have been held*
> *In Struan, Kincraig, Dalnaspidal, Dunkeld;*
> *And the monster petitions, if strewed in her path, 'll*
> *Extend all the way from Dunblane to Blair Atholl.*
>
> *The folk of Dalwhinnie, Carrbridge, Aviemore,*
> *All clustering round at the signalman's door,*
> *Ejaculate: 'Pull up that signal this minute,*
> *And stop the dashed train, for Veronica's in it!'*
>
> *Alas for Tomatin, woe's me, Newtonmore!*
> *The twin locomotives rush on with a roar.*
> *Pitlochry, Kingussie are pleading in vain –*
> *The signal is down for Veronica's train!*

To keep the lengthy back passages at Beaufort swept, to cut kindling, stack and carry logs, to produce oil lamps for every room in the Castle when the electricity failed (which it quite often did, as we made our own with a turbine that depended on the river's height and therefore was famously *un*dependable), to clean the boots and polish the steel knife-blades by turning the handle of a large wooden drum – to do all this there were two 'odd men', Willie the Moon and Hugo Morrison.

We all loved Willie, with his innocent blue eyes, his gentle ways and sweet smile, his sporting talents and his childlike enthusiasm; but he did not have quite the seminal effect on the younger children's lives as he had had on Shimi's, for Hugh and I were not Mowgli creatures like my elder brother, or true hunter-gatherers, as he had been. Though Willie took us fishing on the Beaufort burn and showed me the place where wild lilies-of-the-valley grew in the Beech Wood, a lovely overgrown plantation between the Castle and the river, I never bonded with him as my elder brother had done, or learnt from him the talents and wisdom of the true naturalist. In fact I always found it difficult to thread a wriggly pink worm over the barb on the hook of my first fishing rod; but if Willie would perform this disagreeable task for me, I happily joined in our fishing and the burnside picnics, feeling the thrill of that first nibbling tug, and jerking the fat little trout on to the bank, then roasting them on a biscuit-tin lid over the camp-fire that we carefully built within a circle of protecting stones.

And I remember Willie teaching us how to tell the difference between brown trout and salmon parr; the latter we would always unhook and throw back into the burn so that they could continue their kindergarten life, which would one day lead them to the great river, the open sea, the North Atlantic feeding grounds and eventual return to their home waters, probably to end up as a salmon cutlet in the dining room of the Castle. This we took for granted, for we were all river children.

No one could forget Mrs Willie's birthday teas at Brae Cottage, the bees at the bottom of her tattie patch, the silver pennies of honesty in the front garden and the pink wobbly jelly that was always the centrepiece of the table's spread. Shimi also remembered her famous admonition: 'Press the je'el. It'll nae keep!', which became a family catch-phrase.

Occasionally I was allowed into Willie's lamp room, with all its moon-shaped, opaline globes, gleaming glass funnels and blue-and-white-striped lamp wicks, and smelt the heady mixture of paraffin, engine oil, damp leather and tobacco; indeed, the smell of paraffin unlocks a whole web-site of memories for me, as many as any elegant French tea-cake did for Proust.

When Willie died, Maurice Baring wrote this poem about him:

> *If you're wanting a job to be done well and soon,*
> *The man who can do it is Willie the Moon.*
> *He works all the day and he gives of his best,*
> *But now he is surely in need of a rest.*

It's no use a-calling; he's far, far away,
He's trimming the lamps on the wide Milky Way.
All the pipers in Heaven will strike up a tune
Of welcome to Willie – dear Willie the Moon.

The other 'odd man', Hugo Morrison, was married to our head laundrymaid and used to delight in teasing poor Nana, whose delicate feelings he frequently outraged. 'Here's a lamp for your LAVATORY,' he would announce with a demonic grin, when once more we had been plunged into darkness, well knowing that the word offended her, and rolling it round his tongue. But he had his good points too: he also adored Rose, our beloved toddler, and he knew exactly at what period of the lunar cycle one should plant tatties, and what the weather would be like on Saturday. We regarded him as something of a medicine-man/prophet.

Hugh eventually departed to Gilling Castle, the preparatory school for Ampleforth Abbey College, and Rose turned from a chubby baby into a gentle little girl with my mother's big, sad eyes and dark curly hair, who loved flowers and said of one of my mother's rock plants: 'It's too sweet to pick.' One summer holidays she fell in love, no one quite knew why, with one of the Home Farm dairy cows called Doreen.

Nursery discipline followed a regular pattern at Beaufort, and when the older children were in the schoolroom, the younger ones were taken by Nana or the nurserymaid for an afternoon walk, Rose in a pushchair and me on my sturdy brown legs or sometimes on a reluctant Shetland pony called Tiny. Our destination was usually the garden, half a mile away from the Castle, which my mother had created within the high walls of an ancient cattle pound (in the seventeenth and eighteenth centuries the clan's beasts had to be guarded for fear of cattle raids or blackmail from our wilder neighbours), or alternatively the Home Farm, a regular township of byres and loose-boxes, stores, stables and dairy, which lay beyond.

There was always something to do and see at the farm: turnips to be chopped, sacks of oats and molasses and silage to be mixed into feed; great shire horses being ridden back to their stables by the ploughmen, with sparks flying from their hoofs as they turned into the cobbled yard. Sometimes, if the head cattleman or grieve was about, we would be allowed a glimpse of one of the prize Shorthorn bulls through a loose-box door. 'Stand back, lassie, he's nae safe, this one,' said its minder, and I would tingle with fear to see the great square head, the glaring eye and pale-pink ringed nose of Culrossie Royal King, the progenitor of generations of champions.

Then there was the milking byre and the dairy. Everyone who worked for us was entitled to free milk: the tin cans, large, middling and small, would be left outside the dairy by the children on their way to school and then collected after the evening milking. No doubt by today's standards the rich, creamy milk was full of germs, for our herd was not tuberculin-tested, and the milk was unpasteurised; but if memory is accurate, it tasted all the better in its natural state.

Inside the cool dairy the milk lay in huge, polished steel pans on slate tables, and sometimes we were allowed to skim it for the yellow cream on top and pour this into the butter churn, which was a round wood-and-brass barrel on wheels, turned by hand. The rules of the dairy were strict, but they were concerned more with the quality of the Beaufort butter, which was uniquely delicious, than with health.

Along both sides of the long dairy byre stood the cows, with their names printed in black letters above their heads, chewing their feed, licking salt blocks and waiting patiently to be milked. Doreen, Rose's first love and obsession, was a small, neat Jersey cow with large eyes and long eyelashes. Every day we had to visit her and bring her the most unlikely presents: a sprig of thyme, a flower that Rose loved that grew in the courtyard, a paper bag of salt.

In our day nursery there was a speaking-tube that communicated with my father's bedroom immediately below, and it was very unfair of Shimi to 'moo' up it so that little Rose would rush to its mouthpiece and think she was talking to Doreen. Worse still, when we were next in London, riding on a bus, a brother pointed to an Oxo advertisement and told Rose that while she was away Doreen had been made into Oxo cubes. My mother spent hours persuading her that this was just a poor-taste joke and horrid tease.

Fortunately, before long Doreen's image faded and Rose's need to love was redirected. Her next passion was for black babies. A sermon at Eskadale, our parish church, had convinced her that a mere half-crown would save a black baby from paganism and possible perdition, and also buy it a pair of shoes, so all her pennies and prayers from then on were spent on saving African infants. I think we all expected her to become a missionary nun in a teaching or nursing order. Her vocation must have started when she was four, or perhaps even earlier, for she would lead her elder siblings down the nursery passage to a small, bare, curtained recess which gave on to the main staircase and make them kneel down and close their eyes and wait. Then she would say in a whisper, with her eyes shut and with perfect certainty, 'Now we're in heaven and you can say your prayers.'

Unlike my little sister, I was neither gentle nor holy, and once disgraced myself spectacularly at the farm. A modern silo or concrete tower had been built to my father's specification for storing winter feed. It was fifty feet high, with a ladder of spaced metal rungs. Up this I climbed one summer afternoon, with great difficulty, as the rungs were too far apart for my short legs, suddenly to find myself in the company of several cheery farm-hands who were trampling down the sweet-smelling green fodder as it was tossed up to them from a hay wagon below.

Jumping in to help them, and seeing that they had removed their shirts, I tossed off my own jersey and kilt and, the pitchforks being too heavy for me to handle, began dancing with gay abandon, while the men all cheered and began clapping. I think I even sang. Unfortunately for me the grieve had followed me up the ladder and now thundered, 'Come oot o' there, you wee houri, ye're stopping the men working.' This was reported to my mother, who was inexplicably cross.

'Showing off like that in front of men and dancing and singing!'

'I only sang Dada's favourite song, "Ho-ro, my nut-brown maiden",' I protested, 'and I had my knickers on.'

But for some reason she was not mollified.

In spite of my unwittingly provocative behaviour, I did not lose my virginity in the silo, but I may have a year or two later – to a bicycle, of all things. I had tried to show off again, this time on a boy's rusty old bicycle I had found in an outhouse, and I was riding like mad round the courtyard of the Castle when its seat tipped up and the point hit me smack between the legs. I fell off in front of a lot of grown-ups and burst into tears, because it hurt.

Far more alarm was shown than usual. I was carried up to bed, and old Dr Macdonald was sent for to examine me, which he did by taking my pulse. What he said to my mother I don't know, but a good many years later I was sitting next to Eric Dudley at a dinner party and he asked me if I had been embarrassed on my wedding night.

'What do you mean?' I answered rather frostily.

'Well, I was there when you had that accident on a bicycle, and we all wondered.'

So did I, but I told him sharply it was none of his business and turned to speak to the man on my other side.

Within the courtyard at the front of the Castle, my mother had made a second garden, with square flowerbeds, two lawns and flagstones whose interstices were crammed with small bulbs and creeping plants. She was weeding these one day, helped by Rose, who had just begun to walk, when the over-ebullient Benjie, our beloved Old English sheepdog, bounded up to them and would have knocked over the baby if she had not snatched her up. This unbalanced my mother, and she fell on her hip, fracturing it and her femur. Once the damage had been dealt with, she was nursed at home, tied up like a parcel for six weeks in a splint, which was both very uncomfortable and boring.

Luckily she had a new neighbour to entertain her. Compton Mackenzie had recently rented and moved into Eilean Aigas, one of the nicest houses on the Lovat Estates, which was built on a small island about half a mile square in the middle of the River Beauly upstream of the Castle. It had a romantic history, and 'Monty' loved islands, and had just begun to adore Scotland. He was a friend of Eric Linklater, who first brought him to Beaufort, and he was like no one else I had ever met.

The son of Edward Compton, the Edwardian actor-manager, and of a Highland mother of rather sketchy Mackenzie origins, he was the brother of Fay Compton, the actress, and already a well-known author – *Sinister Street*, *Carnival* and *Guy and Pauline* having broken new ground among the romantic novels of the day. He offered to come and read aloud to the invalid, and my mother wisely accepted. Monty chose extracts from *The Pickwick Papers*, and he read standing up, walking around her bed and acting the parts. It was so funny that poor Moo (as we called my mother) nearly fell out of bed with laughter, splint and all, and occasionally had to beg him to stop.

'When I was a child,' he told us, 'I used to listen to my father rehearsing Dickens doing his readings before he started out on his American lecture tours, and I remember *exactly* how he did it.'

When Moo was well enough to start walking on two crutches, my father decided it would be wiser for her to convalesce at Stronelairg, our shooting lodge at the head of Loch Killin in Stratherrick, rather than at Beaufort, where she would inevitably be plagued by summer visitors and all the cares of hostess and housekeeping. It also meant that they would have to cancel the Stronelairg letting for August, and that he could be with her and for once enjoy the grouse shooting and later the stalking which he so loved. And so the whole family moved up to Stronelairg for the summer and autumn of 1928, for nearly six months of pure bliss.

Up till then my education had been decidedly patchy. Sophie Bühler (always known to her pupils as 'Zellie'), my mother's old German governess, had taught me to read and write and to speak reasonable French. This she did by her own rather strange method, which one can only call osmosis. Every day during the post-prandial hour of 'children's rest' that our family still considered obligatory, she would read aloud to me while I lay on my back in her bedroom counting the flowers on the 'remontant' wallpaper and counting the minutes until I was able to get up and escape to freedom. She would read *Les Malheurs de Sophie*, *Un Bon Petit Diable*, *Pauvre Blaise*, *Sans Famille*, *La Roche aux Mouettes* and other classics of the Bibliothèque Rose, in a heavily accented, quavering German voice – and apart from this and perhaps ten minutes of French vocabulary at morning lessons, that was it.

In two months I could understand the stories, and very soon afterwards speak French. What a pity that the system was not also used to teach me German; but perhaps the memories of the war-to-end-all-wars were still too recent and too terrible for anyone to suggest it.

The next governess, 'Mousy', was as ineffectual as her name conveyed, and I hardly remember her. So it was decided that I should soon start sharing lessons with my first cousin, Irene Stirling, who lived at Keir, near Dunblane, and whose brothers, like mine, had left home and were misbehaving variously at Gilling, Ampleforth, Oxford and Cambridge. Our terms would alternate between Beaufort and Keir, and we would be taught by Irene's governess, Mademoiselle Marie Philippe (another 'Zelle'), who was said to be a paragon. But first there was Stronelairg, and the MacFarlane schoolroom and comparative freedom.

Stronelairg was our favourite shooting lodge. It stood at the top of Stratherrick, where ten miles of a single-track glen road ran out and the hills began. It wasn't only the lodge, or the wilderness, or the sport which we loved, or the peaty bath water which looked like Guinness with a head on it when the burn was in spate (and made your skin feel like silk when you emerged slightly darker than when you got in), but the MacFarlane family, who lived there and who were our friends.

As a sergeant in the Lovat Scouts during the First World War, Archie MacFarlane had won the Military Medal for supreme courage and had been decorated on the field – a rare distinction, even for a Highland soldier. After the war my father had made him head stalker at Stronelairg. He revelled in his work and became one of the best stalkers in all Scotland (and also one of the most feared). Archie was known for his stern discipline and rich vocabulary: if a tenant rashly shot at and wounded a beast when he shouldn't have done so, he would be cursed – no matter who he was – in English and, when the English expletives ran out, in Gaelic, which I am told has a much richer and fruitier vocabulary.

If ever there was a happy man whose job was his hobby, it was Archie, and one could say the same of Mrs MacFarlane, although her hobby was having babies. She would open the wind-battered door of their sturdy, granite-built house, and just one look at her beaming, rosy, bonny face, so like the other little faces crowding round her or peeping out shyly from behind her skirts, was welcome enough, and she would immediately ask us in.

'You must be starving with the cold, you poor moichens! And how about a bite? There's a batch o' scones on the girdle and a pot of tea on the hob. It'll be no trouble, mind, no trouble at all.'

Mrs MacFarlane's work was the ten fine, curly-headed bairns she had borne Archie over the years. Strong, beautiful children with resounding names: William, Mary, Archibald, Clarissa, Georgina, Robina ... For many years a baby had turned up 'as regular as clockwork', Archie would say with a wink, and if it was a boy, it would be christened with the name of the previous season's shooting tenant. If a girl, it would be named after the tenant's wife. Mrs Mac was always on her feet again by the Glorious Twelfth, ready to provide perfect packed lunches or those tremendous stalking teas for which she was famous.

In those days our County Educational Authorities favoured a 'pupil-teacher' system for bringing enlightenment to the remote glens and islands where there were too few children to justify the building of a school. The 'pupil-teachers', or students in their last year of training, would lodge in one of the parents' houses and teach in an extra schoolroom that could be built on to it. Though they may have lacked experience, they certainly made up for it in keenness and dedication, and in a vocational idealism that had not yet been blunted and was deemed compensation enough in their hard and poorly paid profession.

A Miss McArthur had recently come to lodge with the MacFarlanes, and that happy summer term I had the good fortune to be taught by her in their little schoolroom. There were nine of us: four MacFarlanes, me, and two pairs of shepherds' children from further down the glen who walked four miles to and from the schoolroom every day, except when they 'managed' a lift with the mail van. Our ages ranged from six to twelve and, I think, sometimes a MacFarlane baby would be allowed in to scribble contentedly with crayons in a corner as long as it kept quiet.

Any illusions of superiority I may have had when I first entered that bare little room were soon dispelled. The MacFarlane children knew a good deal more than I did in every subject except French, which they had just begun, and the older ones had even started Latin, which to me seemed the height of intellectual achievement. We had a bell in our schoolroom which Miss McArthur rang at nine o'clock when morning lessons began, and we rang at twelve thirty when we were dismissed.

As soon as that bell was put back on her table, we tore out of the classroom as if someone had shouted 'Fire!' It was then a race, a wild stampede across the green and down to the bridge, into the almost-dried-up bed of the burn, hopping from stone to stone with incredible speed and agility till at last we reached our destination – the one deep pool by the waterfall which was all that an unusually sunny June had left of its swift brown waters.

The high cliffs of rock and bracken shut out the sunlight on two sides, and lower down through the bared peat of the crumbling bank you could see the black bones of ancient tree roots. Here there were huge granite boulders and shelves of rock over which we hung for hours at a time – gently feeling for the fat brown speckled trout that slept below, nose in, tail outwards, dreaming perhaps of dragonflies and spate waters; gently, gently you felt, your arm plunged deep into the icy water, gently, slowly, till you knew that your delicate, searching fingers were touching something more solid than water and your pulse quickened and your heart began pounding so loudly that the trout must surely hear it, and your fingers began stroking gently, gently, till your arm ached like a tooth with the coldness of it, and you slowly began changing the position of your hand, but slowly, gently, stroking and turning, until *whoomph!* – you suddenly clutched with all your might, throwing your arm and your whole body back in one fleet movement; and sometimes, not very often but *sometimes*, there would be a greeny-brown, opaque yet shiny little fish with a dark cream belly and red spots on his dappled side, gasping there in the heather beside you – and a distinct, strange, fishy smell in the air.

A trout caught this way made me inordinately proud, and however small it was I would take it back to the lodge kitchen, to Mrs Grady, our housekeeper-cook, always known as 'Geggy', and tell her I'd got something to 'help out' the breakfast; and sure enough, it would turn up next morning, to my intense pleasure, sitting all alone in a silver entrée dish with a lid, and I would generously halve it with whomever I loved best at the moment, and then sit back and watch with beady eyes while the recipient ate it, making quite sure he or she appreciated every morsel.

The Stronelairg school experiment went off so well that my mother seriously thought of continuing it, but there were the practical difficulties of distance and the long, hard and sometimes snowbound winters – and perhaps she had not altogether liked the calluses that were beginning to show in my sensibilities as well as on my bare brown feet.

We had not been long back at Beaufort before a letter arrived for my mother from MacFarlane, a tear-stained, pathetic letter, telling us briefly that Georgina, the merriest and sweetest of all his children, had fallen when playing in our waterfall pool and, striking her head against a rock, had stunned herself. The smaller children had not been strong enough to pull her clear, and by the time they had raised help, the pretty, vivid, dancing little Georgina had drowned.

2

BLOODSTOCK

THE PARADISE INTO WHICH I WAS BORN, EXISTING AS IT DID in the uneasy peace and social change between two world wars, was due largely to two factors: first, geography (for the remoter Highlands were still in a time-warp, twenty to fifty years behind everywhere else); and second, the character of my parents and grandparents, a genetic fusion of four remarkable yet entirely dissimilar families – the Frasers, the Welds, the Listers and the Tennants – who came together through marriage and made their descendants a force to be reckoned with.

The Frasers of Lovat

The Frasers, originally Fresel or Friselli, descended from a family of adventurous knights (some would say carpet-baggers) from Anjou, who arrived in Scotland in the eleventh century and settled at Castle Oliver in Peeblesshire, and around Keith in East Lothian. They slowly climbed, through Church and marriage, into positions of authority at the court of Robert the Bruce, who had much the same antecedents. They fought at Halidon Hill, where three brothers were killed, then again at Durham, where another died of his wounds. The elder and senior brother, Sir Alexander Fraser, married the Bruce's sister and became Chamberlain of Scotland. His descendants, the Frasers of

Philorth, settled in Aberdeenshire and in the Middle Ages became a feudal family outside the Highlands.

The Frasers of Lovat, who descend from Alexander's younger brother, Sir Simon Fraser of Brotherton, acquired rich lands around the Valliscaulian priory of Beauly. Through marriage to a Bysset heiress, and then to a de Fenton of Beaufort, these Frasers consolidated their territory, gradually spreading westwards into the glens of Inverness-shire, and embracing Gaeldom as they did so.

Before long a large clan formed round the powerful incomers, and they in turn adopted the language and ethos of their Celtic neighbours, intermarrying or fighting with other clans until their lands stretched from the east to the west coasts of Scotland. Their chief was always, and still is, called Simon. ('Shimi', which was my brother's nickname, is derived from 'The MacShimidh', the Gaelic for 'Son of Simon', a title held only by the chief of the clan.)

This clan system only existed in the Highlands, on Sir Simon Fraser of Lovat's lands and among his descendants. It was never adopted by their cousins at Philorth, which not only lay the other side of the Highland Divide, but was further separated by an entirely different history and culture. It is therefore quite wrong, historically and factually, for *all* Frasers to consider themselves part of the clan, as some have come to do, encouraged no doubt by the glamour of the name and the commercial interests of the tourist business.

In 1737 the Simon Lovat who became known to the English as the 'Old Fox' was one of the first clan chiefs to join the Association of Jacobite Support, which backed the exiled King James. From the safety of Rome, James had made him Lord Lovat of Beauly, Viscount of the Aird and Strathglass, Earl of Stratherrick and Abertarff, Marquis of Beaufort and Duke of Fraser – quite enough for an upwardly mobile Highlander to be getting on with! But alas, in 1745 the Old Fox found he had backed the wrong side, and after the Prince's defeat at Culloden, he fled to Loch Morar, was captured by the Duke of Cumberland's Redcoats, imprisoned, and in 1747 beheaded on Tower Hill. Instead of getting the dukedom (promised again by Bonnie Prince Charlie) and the magnificent new castle for which William Adam had drawn up plans, the Lovat family saw their lands sequestrated, and Castle Downie (or Beaufort, as it was later called), which had been sacked and burnt in 1715, crumbling into ruin. They retained only one smaller castle – Moniack – which had survived both the '15 and the '45.

Lovat's two sons, Simon and Archibald, eventually retrieved their lands and influence by raising regiments for the Hanoverians. In 1759 Colonel (later General) Sir Simon's 78th Fraser Highlanders scaled the Heights of Abraham and captured Quebec with General Wolfe; and later the Fraser Fencibles fought with Wellington in the Peninsular War. Simon's half-brother, Colonel Sir Archibald Fraser, also commanded the Fencibles, and in peacetime became Consul-General in Algiers. Both brothers were Members of Parliament for Inverness, and Archibald steered a bill through Parliament which redressed the cruel anti-Jacobite and anti-clan laws passed by the Whigs after Culloden (no bearing of arms, no wearing of Highland dress, no singing or dancing in public places, no Catholic education). By so doing – some say – he 'saved the soul of the Highlands'. But the Lovat attainder to the United Kingdom barony, which their father had collected in his less-than-admirable wild youth, when he kidnapped a Murray heiress and held her prisoner, remained, and was not raised until 1857 – and then only at Queen Victoria's express wish.

Unfortunately, neither of these Frasers left heirs to succeed them, and the next Lord Lovat came from a collateral branch of the family, the Frasers of Strichen in Aberdeenshire, who had branched off the main line in the seventeenth century and had been converted to Catholicism.

We can only surmise the feelings with which the new MacShimidh embraced his inheritance in 1815. He was then only a youth, and the step upwards and sideways, from his family's possessions in Aberdeenshire to the governance of the vast estates and the duties of clan chiefdom, as well as, eventually, a seat in the House of Lords, must have seemed a mighty one. Yet Mormand Tam, as he was called, after the hill above Strichen, seems to have had the energy and shrewdness to survive it.

We have two versions of his character. The hagiographic one by his Fraser descendants portrays him as 'Thomas the Improver', Tenth of Strichen, Twelfth of Lovat, celebrated for reclaiming the western end of the Beauly Firth and turning its marshland into rich pasture, revered for rebuilding crofts devastated by war, poverty and neglect, for settling his dispossessed Chisholm neighbours on good land above Beauly, for setting his face against the Clearances, for building churches and

Catholic schools (it would seem) almost by the dozen, and for giving land for the site of a Benedictine abbey at Fort Augustus.

But there is another, less attractive portrait of the Strichen Frasers, revealed a few years ago in the published diaries of an exceptionally talented but penniless daughter of a Buckie fisherman, who used to bring her father's catch up to the family mansion and was courted by the eldest son, until the romance was firmly quashed by his less romantic but perhaps more realistic parents.

Thomas, or Mormand Tam, my great-grandfather, had married Charlotte Jerningham, the daughter of Lord Swinnerton-Stafford of Swinnerton, in 1823, and I have a belt, somewhat elastic and revolting, made of her family's plaited hair, with an inscription on the underside of the gold buckle – 'To the Lady of Lovat from her parents and brothers dear', the names of boys in one column, girls in another, and a butterfly beside 'Mary', signifying, I imagine, her early demise.

Thomas and Charlotte's eldest son Simon, my grandfather, eventually married Alice Weld-Blundell, of Ince Blundell in Lancashire, in 1866; they had three surviving sons and five daughters, the two elder Masters of Lovat having been rather carelessly lost as infants by Granny Lovat on some of her more adventurous early travels on the Continent. Grandfather Lovat died on the hill in 1887 after a particularly good day's grouse-shooting with his neighbour Mackintosh of Mackintosh. It was a fitting end, and, though he mourned him, one appreciated as such by his eldest son, my father, who succeeded him at the age of sixteen.

So, in 1887, my father, Simon Joseph Fraser (later KT, CB, DSO), the sixteenth Lord Lovat in the UK peerage, became hereditary chief of the Fraser clan and the twenty-third MacShimidh. With the Lochiel of his day and Mackintosh, he was the last of those patriarchal chiefs who still regarded their clansmen and the crofters on their estates as their children – which is exactly what the Gaelic word 'clan' means – and, more importantly, their responsibility.

The Welds

The Weld family fortunes and possessions were once almost as widespread and diverse as those of the Frasers. Although Lulworth Castle was their primary seat, together with the land surrounding its famous Dorsetshire cove, the Welds had spread through well-planned marriages to several fine houses and estates in other parts of England. They were an old Catholic and Royalist family, and Lulworth was a Royalist stronghold during the Civil War.

In 1839 one of the Welds married a Blundell, bringing new blood and money into our family. That union also doubled its Catholic consciousness, for the Blundells were an equally ancient recusant Catholic family who, when the Reformation came, had remained loyal to the Old Faith. They were related to almost every other old Catholic family in England (they all pronounced it 'Cartholic'), but to my mundane mind the most interesting and enterprising Blundell was the one known as 'the Collector', who made the eighteenth-century Grand Tour to Italy with circumspection and brought back some remarkably fine Renaissance paintings and some good Roman sculpture, for which he built a delightful miniature Pantheon in the gardens of Ince Blundell, his Regency home near Aintree. To these treasures he added a couple of Stubbses, some romantic Richard Wilson landscapes and many Old Master drawings.

Alice Weld-Blundell and her brothers must have grown up surrounded by aesthetic beauty, but though she was well educated by private governesses and tutors, and the boys went to Stonyhurst, art and the humanities seem to have made little impression on them. Their interests lay elsewhere, and were mostly religious, intellectual or sporting. In two generations this extraordinary family produced so many nuns, priests and monks, including a bishop and two cardinals, that the direct line dwindled to one childless great-uncle and one old maid, and then died out.

My grandmother Alice, on the other hand, produced eight healthy Fraser children, with only one nun among them; and yet, once they were grown up and safely married, she too entered a convent. All I can remember of Granny Lovat is a wizened little face framed by her nun's coif, bright, intelligent brown eyes and a surprisingly strong and emphatic voice, behind a latticed wooden grille. By the time she died, aged ninety-eight, she had very nearly one hundred descendants.

As a young bride she had adapted to the rigours of her new Highland life amazingly well, even surviving the midges and rain of a romantic but surely impractical honeymoon on an island in Loch a'Mhuillidh, at the top of Glen Strathfarrar. She then lived with the eldest of her children – Simon, Maimie and Ethel – in the small house built for the government commissioner who had administered the Lovat Estates when they were sequestered; but plans for a new Beaufort had long been considered, and she entered into them with enthusiasm.

Alas, the drawings that William Adam had made for Old Lovat of the '45 were rejected, and the family called in the architect who had designed Lord Stair's house, Lochinch, in Galloway – one of the largest and most hideous in all Scotland. His designs for Beaufort were almost as grandiose and just as impractical, but he died before they could be realised, as did the next architect. Indeed, the stop–go building of Beaufort, due to moribund architects and periodic lack of funds, lasted fourteen years, and it was only in 1882 that the family finally took up residence in their enormous Victorian Gothic castle above the River Beauly.

By that time my father, the young Master of Lovat, was being poorly educated by the Benedictine monks at Fort Augustus Abbey School, where he spent most of his time playing shinty (a Highland game vaguely resembling hockey) and hooky: deer-stalking with the local poachers, often on his own land. Later he was better taught at the Oratory, a Catholic school in Birmingham recently founded by Cardinal Newman.

Until 1791 the penal laws against Catholics had disbarred them from running their own schools or from going up to Oxford or Cambridge, and their further education had usually continued in the universities of Belgium or France. Although these restrictions had been lifted by the Reform and Catholic Emancipation bills of 1825 and 1829, no Catholic peer had attended either of the old universities since Stuart times.

In the 1880s Cardinal Newman thought my father should break this more-or-less self-imposed taboo. Cardinal Manning, the Arch-bishop of Westminster, disagreed, as was to be expected, but Alice

Lovat – an independent thinker and like all Welds a born polemicist – entered into the controversy with relish, confounding her antagonists with her robust arguments in a three-cornered correspondence that was later published. She wrote many other books, among them a life of the Blessed Julian of Norwich, and edited an anthology of religious poetry. Indeed, 'she was always writing or praying', one of the aunts told me, and, as soon as it was possible, she handed over the housekeeping at Beaufort, first to her eldest daughter, Maimie, and then to her second-youngest daughter, Peggie, the two middle ones having escaped into early marriages.

And so my father went up to Magdalen College in 1892, and spent two of the happiest years of his life at Oxford. He was rusticated for going too far in one of the many rags he initiated, for locking George Bernard Shaw into a don's room when he was supposed to be giving a lecture, and for shooting a fallow deer in the college grounds. His academic career was not distinguished; but he did achieve a little maturity and sophistication, and he made good friends who remained his allies and became his strongest supporters in later life.

The Listers

My mother's paternal grandmother, Emma, Lady Ribblesdale, was born Emma Muir of Rowallan and Caldwell, in a large, square eighteenth-century house on the Ayrshire coast. Her family had been border reivers (robbers!), Covenanters, soldiers and politicians, and her father was a classical scholar of note. She thus came from a highly educated and deeply religious background, and according to those who knew her as a girl, it was not only her perfect profile and golden hair, but the fineness and sensitivity of her mind, that made her something of a classic herself.

In 1853, aged twenty, she married the third Lord Ribblesdale, who owned Gisburne and Malham, two fine estates in Yorkshire, some beautiful pictures and a racing stable which he had latterly bought cheap, racehorse, stock and saddle, together with its rather dubious trainer, from his cousin General Peel, a nephew of the former Tory Prime Minister, Sir Robert Peel.

It was a bargain that ruined him, because hunting and the turf became the ruling passions in his life, and led to his behaviour becoming, to say the least, erratic and irresponsible. For five years he and Emma lived together at Gisburne in perfect harmony, and my grandfather Tommy, Martin and Sissy were born there. Then, in 1858, something happened – I do not know what. Ribblesdale sold Malham, let Gisburne and decamped with his horses to Fontainebleau in France, leaving his wife and children in the care of her own family.

In France he painted with the artists of the Barbizon school, stag-hunted happily in the forest, and raced. Six years later his family joined him, and they all lived together again in a *dépendance* of the Hôtel de Ville of the little town. Two more children were born, Reggie and Adelaide. When Tommy was old enough he was sent to Harrow, and spent his holidays under the care and tutelage of his step-grandparents, Lord and Lady John Russell. When in Fontainebleau, he painted, learnt to ride and hunted with his father, with whom he developed a close but short-lived relationship. The Franco-Prussian War brought this happy period to an end, and Emma returned to England with the children, followed – but not for long – by Ribblesdale. He quite soon left again for France and his horses, and in 1876 Emma received news of his sudden death, 'from a long illness bravely borne' – but of which no account had been heard of or recorded before.

Tommy, my grandfather, succeeded his father, becoming the fourth Lord Ribblesdale when he was only twenty-two and serving as a subaltern in the Rifle Brigade. He resigned his commission, and only a few months later announced his engagement to Charlotte Tennant (always known as 'Charty'). According to her sister Margot, 'he was the finest-looking man I ever saw' – a verdict corroborated by the American portrait painter John Singer Sargent, who said he 'never tired of painting Lister *bone*'. Tommy and Charty had met at a ball in London; a brother officer in his regiment, who saw them waltzing together, asked if she was his sister, to which he replied, 'No, thank God!'

Emma, on returning from France, had settled with her younger children in a small dower-house at the gates of Gisburne, which was still let. Charty's father, Sir Charles Tennant, was fortunately tremendously generous, and he adored his daughters. When they married, he is supposed to have settled a handsome dowry and a house in London on each of them. He must also have paid off the Gisburne mortgage, for before long Tommy and Charty were able to move back into the big house, and when they did, all the bells in the village rang.

Emma's diary, which she started keeping at Fontainebleau, and her letters convey the closeness that existed between herself and her children. Few mothers can have had such selfless devotion from their sons, and vice versa, or such *fun*; but they also show, in a modest and understated way, how well the family knew the principal actors and movers in the Establishment of that time – the quite small oligarchy that ruled Great Britain and the Empire. This became even more evident after Charty's marriage to Tommy, when he, too, began to play a part in public life.

Lord John Russell had been in turn Home and Colonial Secretary, Prime Minister and Foreign Secretary, and it was in his London house that Grandfather was introduced to the politics of the day, heard clever, witty conversation and met statesmen who would later influence his own career. It was through the Russell connection and the Tennants' friendship with Mr Gladstone that Tommy became a lord-in-waiting to Queen Victoria and accepted the entirely ceremonial position of Master of Buckhounds.

This was a comfortable sinecure, whose main duty was to lead the formal procession down the royal racecourse at Ascot, which started, and still starts, the week's racing every June. He rode a spanking chestnut hunter called Curious, who made the most of the occasion, as some horses do; and when he appeared, the Cockneys in the crowd would cuff their youngsters and cry, 'Wake up, 'Enry, it's started, and 'ere comes the Ancestor!' The nickname which they gave him somehow stuck, and became the one by which he was universally known.

Tommy Ribblesdale, the very antithesis of my Fraser forebears, was tall and elegant, fastidious, liberal-minded, witty and cultured. He was the embodiment of that romantic fictional character, the English Gentleman, and ever since Sargent painted the magnificent portrait of him, which now hangs in the National Gallery in London (and even makes a brief appearance in the first *Harry Potter* film), he has been acknowledged as its prototype – somewhat misleadingly, for it was not at all what the family thought of him.

The first part of the Ancestor's life was very happy. As well as being a Privy Counsellor and the Liberal Chief Whip in the House of Lords, he was made a Trustee of the National Gallery and the National Portrait Gallery in London, and became an Alderman of the London County Council. He had just enough money to get by, a beautiful wife who brought him a great deal more, and a wide circle of interesting and talented friends. He lived in a delightful house in lovely country, had his own pack of hounds and hunted whenever he wished. He adored his elder children: the clever, intellectual Barbara; the dashing and handsome cavalry officer, Tommy; the brilliant young Socialist and diplomat, Charles, who joined the Labour Party while still at Eton; and then the dear 'Dolls', my mother Laura and her sister Diana, who arrived almost together after a long gap, and were both born and brought up at Gisburne.

But there was a streak of melancholy in his nature, and perhaps too great sensitivity. When his elder son, Tommy, was killed on active service in Somaliland in 1904, the blow shattered the whole close-knit family. Perhaps he took it the hardest of all, not having the strong faith and Tennant fortitude which sustained his wife. So when Charty died of tuberculosis in 1911, and then Charles, on to whom all his paternal hope and love had been transferred, died of wounds in a hospital ship off Gallipoli in 1915, my grandfather sank into a deep depression from which he never really recovered.

He retired to the rooms he had long rented in Rosa Lewis's Cavendish Hotel, in Jermyn Street, and was nursed back to a modicum of health by her unfailing kindness and Cockney wit. He then amazed his children by suddenly declaring his intention of marrying a rich American socialite, Ava Willing (only *too* willing, according to Rosa), the widow of John Jacob Astor, who had recently been drowned in the *Titanic* disaster. Ava already had two children, Vincent and Alice Astor, and no doubt was an adequate mother to both of them, but her stepchildren-to-be felt sure that she was all wrong for Grandpapa, and they were soon proved right. After a brief try at English country life, and then a London season which he hated, and during which she made few friends, she proposed taking him to New York, where her social standing was more secure and she could show him off. But Grandpapa refused to follow her, and the brief marriage fizzled out.

I glimpsed Ava, Lady Ribblesdale, only once, a lonely but elegant figure in a large black hat, carrying a parasol, on the private railway station at Badminton. The youngest Doll, my aunt Diana ('Dimbo'), by then Lady Westmorland, hurried her children and me past her to the farthest end of the platform, saying, 'I don't want to talk to that person,' and, intriguingly, not explaining why.

Years later Brooke Astor, who had married Vincent, the Astor son, and made that congenitally unhappy man happy, told me she had often visited his mother when she was very old and bedridden. One day Ava said she would like to give Brooke 'something special', and asked her maid Jeanne-Marie to bring out her jewels. A tray-load of beautiful leather boxes, representing, perhaps, the stepping-stones of the old lady's long life, was put at the end of the bed. But when, with pleasurable anticipation, Brooke and Jeanne-Marie opened them carefully, one by one, they found that almost all of them were empty.

The younger Lister children had been brought up in the same enchanted world as their parents; and although they lived a relatively simple country life at Gisburne, their parents' friends, many of whom were leading lights in that rarefied coterie known as 'the Souls', would frequently come to stay. As the Dolls, Laura and Diana, grew up, they would hunt, course greyhounds and climb mountains; they would bicycle, play tennis and go on reading parties in the long, lazy summer vacations with the children of the Souls; and they would fall in and out of love.

There were visits to the Horners at Mells, the Charterises at Stanway on the edge of the Cotswolds, the Wyndhams at Clouds in Wiltshire, and to lovely Clovelly, the Manners' house near Bideford, in Devon, nestling in its woodland park of bluebells and wild garlic above the steep, cobbled street of the old fishing village. There they would enjoy swimming and sailing, Devonshire cream, schoolroom teas and long, intimate discussions in the famous Twinnery, which would continue far into the night. But there the arguments would often be more robust and perhaps more cynical than those of the previous high-minded and romantic generation.

In the letters and memoirs of that time there are one or two snapshots of my mother. John Manners at Clovelly wrote: 'I do wish Laura would not *languish* so'; and Edward Horner, watching her disappear through the doorway of her parents' house in Green

Street after a ball, besought her: 'Oh, don't go! Lovely pink Laura, *please* don't go!'

When, aged nineteen, she married my father, Simon Lovat, she left England and that world of hunting and fun, of politics and culture and elegance, as well as of close family ties, to bury herself in the Highlands of Scotland with a man twenty years older than herself and of a different religion and ethos. It was a singularly courageous act, but the Listers and Tennants had never lacked courage – and she must have been very much in love.

The Tennants

The Tennant genes are so strong that they are still evident in my children and grandchildren, and it would be invidious to leave out of this memoir a short account of their primary source.

My maternal grandmother, Charty Tennant, was the third daughter of Sir Charles Tennant by his first marriage. She was brought up at The Glen, a none-too-beautiful Victorian baronial home he had built in the hills above Inverleithen, in Peeblesshire. He bought the four-thousand-acre moorland estate when he became a partner in the St Rollox Chemical Works in Glasgow, the successful family business built up by two generations of Tennants from its humble eighteenth-century start in the bleaching fields near 'honest Auld Glenconner's' farm in Ayrshire. It prospered, and provided Charles Tennant with a solid base on which to build a worldwide business empire and a new fortune.

Born a little quicker, more punctual and thrusting than his rivals, he was said in the City of London to be 'not on the make, but on the pounce'. He was what today would be called a tycoon, a hugely energetic and dynamic man, whose genius was many-sided and whose fortune was enormous. A supporter of Gladstone, Home Rule and the Liberal Party, he was a generous host to whose unconventional home came many of the most intelligent and discerning young people, distinguished politicians and famous artists of the day.

In her autobiography, his daughter Margot Asquith described him in honest and remarkably objective terms. 'He suffered fools not at all', she wrote, and she went on to explain his dynamism and intractability:

He could not modify himself in any way; he was the same man in his nursery, his school and his office, the same man in church, club, city or suburbs, and was as violent when he was dying as when he was living . . . He was essentially a man of action and a man of will. He made up his mind in a flash, partly from instinct and partly from will. He had the courage for life, and the enterprise to spend his fortune on it . . .

He was always happy, because his nature turned out no waste product . . . He took his own happiness with him, and was self-centred and self-sufficient, for a sociable being the most self-sufficing I have ever known.

Charty was much the tallest, the quietest and the gentlest of the Tennant sisters – yet once, when her husband was about to make a political speech in the country, she telegraphed to him: 'Mind you hit below the belt!' According to Margot – complacent as always – Charty was

in some ways the most capable of us all, but she had not Laura's genius, Lucy's talents nor my understanding. She had wonderful grace, and less vanity than anyone that ever lived, and her social courage was a perpetual joy. She rode as well as I did, but was not so quick to hounds nor so conscious of what was going on all round her.

By their unconventionality and 'social courage' the Tennant girls leapt over the formidable barriers of Victorian society as easily as they had leapt over high fences in Leicestershire, and chose their own friends. Most of these belonged to the old aristocracy, who still lived in large and beautiful houses in the hunting shires, and owned equally large and handsome homes in London. Their lives were cushioned and liberated by armies of servants and employees, a condition they accepted as the traditional norm. The men had serious careers in high places, the women had *leisure* – that most blessed of conditions

– to play with and instruct their children, to entertain their friends, to read and improve their minds, to write letters and keep diaries, to visit the dressmaker or their husband's tenants, to organise charities, even to fight for radical causes, or simply to arrange the flowers the gardener brought in every morning.

It is almost impossible today to visualise such a privileged world, and yet it was a world in which culture, talent and creativity flourished, and in which the intelligent seem to have been wiser, more intellectually curious and infinitely better educated than even the richest corporate tycoon or millionaire 'celebrity', surrounded by spokesmen and aides, is today.

The arrival of the Tennant sisters in London certainly caused a commotion. According to their friend Mary Elcho, they were 'quite unlike anyone that London had seen before'. In Scotland, also, they soon took charge. By the early 1880s their mother, who was quiet and retiring and as amazed by her daughters as anyone else, was quite content to hand over the role of hostess to Laura and Margot, and let them entertain as they wished. In the 1880s they would invite such friends as George Curzon, Doll Liddell, Harry Cust, Arthur Balfour, the Wyndhams, Grenfells, Lytteltons and Charterises to stay, and their idea of entertainment was also quite unlike any other.

Mary Gladstone, daughter of the Prime Minister and a friend of Laura, recalled that at The Glen, apart from shooting, which seems to have been serious and left to the men,

> There was a kind of Star and Garter freedom and recklessness of manner and talk; there was no reserve, no restraint, no holy place kept sacred. All day it was one flurry of fun and games and music and discussion; at meals you tore through subject after subject with the rapidity of lightning; retort, repartee, contradictions, capping, flew across the table with a constant accompaniment of shrieks and peals of laughter. Parting at bedtime only meant leaving the elders below; apple-pie beds, sponge fights, fun and frolic, nobody minding whose room was invaded.

On some evenings the two sisters, dressed decorously in bed-jackets, entertained both sexes in their shared bedroom, and art, literature and great ideas would be discussed until dawn broke. The complete and transparent innocence of the girls disarmed scandal, but obviously encouraged gossip, and at one point Laura even wrote a prayer asking God to help her fight against her too-high spirits – for the entire Tennant family were *deeply* religious. On Sundays they all observed the strict Scottish Sabbath and attended Traquair church, to which crofters and shepherds would come down from the hills and where the shepherds' dogs kept close to their masters' plaids, hung over the high box pews that lined the aisle.

That coterie of friends to which Sir Charles's unruly daughters belonged, and which in some ways they brought together, came to be known as 'the Souls'. They were a brilliant group, which included politicians, statesmen, lawyers, dons, poets, artists, intellectuals and dilettantes. Individually they stood on their own feet, but they shared similar moral and idealistic values, and were distinctly different from the rest of late-Victorian and early-Edwardian society. The Souls foregathered simply because they enjoyed each other's company and had the same intellectual interests. Today their mutual admiration may seem a little excessive, but it engendered many lifelong and rewarding friendships, which flourished irrespective of sex or age and broke new ground, confounding Victorian convention.

Margot's stepdaughter, Violet Bonham Carter, summed up their influence rather well. 'Because of the Souls,' she wrote,

> It was no longer fashionable to be dull ... Platonic friendships between men and women no longer caused scandal . . . Fun and freedom was their legacy, and their philosophy of life was founded on Christianity, patriotism and the triumph of optimism . . . The virtue they most admired was courage.

In 1910, shortly after my mother's engagement and marriage, Charty began finally to lose her long battle with tuberculosis, the still incurable and terrible disease that had already claimed four of her father's children. TB was then regarded as so infectious that none of her own children was allowed to nurse her, or they, her husband and her friends to attend her; and after a valiant struggle for survival, played out in various nursing homes in Switzerland and Italy, and finally in a rented villa nearer home, she died a terribly lonely death, with only her faith to comfort her.

I wish I had known her. The description of her I like most was written by Frances Horner of Mells, her best friend:

> *Charty was quite different from her sisters, tall, of a willowy figure and with gleaming golden hair, she had a gaiety of spirit and a transparent nature which made her the most delightful of companions. If you had been set down in a provincial town on a wet Sunday afternoon in the Midlands, Charty would have made it all fun. There are a few men and women who have that particular gift, not common to Northerners, laughter-loving and laughter-provoking.*

Even though Charty had left her home in Peeblesshire when she was nineteen, she definitely took the Tennant spark with her, for she passed it on to all her own children: articulacy and romanticism; an exaggerated sense of drama; strong faith; concern for the less fortunate; and above all a down-to-earth toughness and courage that would serve them throughout life. I consider that the laughter-loving, laughter-provoking Tennant gene has been passed to my own family. Sukie, my daughter, has it in full measure, and I suspect that Diana, my son Charlie's five-year-old, has inherited a whiff of the Old Bart's (Sir Charles Tennant's) determination, and Margot's amazing self-assurance.

3

YOUTH

'DEAR LADY LOVE-AT-FIRST-SIGHT,' WROTE HARRY CUST (WHOM Diana Cooper always believed to be her real father) at the start of his letter to my mother, Laura Lister, when she became engaged to Simon Lovat. He followed this up with perhaps the nicest wedding present ever devised: twenty of his favourite novels in English and French, bound in golden calf (by Rivière, naturally) with their spine-titles stained in gentle greens and blues.

Intelligence, culture and wit lay lightly on him and made him one of the most popular friends of Charty Ribblesdale's circle and the Souls. When my mother emigrated to the Highlands, he became a frequent visitor to Beaufort. He was particularly good – or bad, should one say? – at shameless puns.

'Harry, did you see any duck?' asked my father after he returned from an abortive morning on the Beauly Firth.

'Never a one, Simon. Not even a *mallard imaginaire!*'

My parents' wedding reception was held at No. 10 Downing Street, courtesy of the Prime Minister, Henry Asquith, and his wife, my mother's formidable Aunt Margot. Laura had insisted on following hounds 'for the last time' at Gisburne, and, in spite of her father's warning to be prudent, she had jumped a high hedge and scratched her face, but it did little to diminish the glory of the day. I still have her navy wool riding-habit (she always rode side-saddle) which she must have taken with her to Beaufort in a moment of homesickness, as well as a little beaver-fur hunting waistcoat with so small a waist that, even at fourteen, I could not button it round myself.

The celebrations at Beaufort for the laird's return with his young and beautiful half-Scottish bride lasted a week, and I believe that when they were over she must have felt very lonely, and that she had sacrificed all for the sake of love, leaving behind poetry, music, hunting, laughter, family and above all friends. Beaufort must at first have seemed another world: all those Fraser relations, the discomforts which none of them noticed, the endless sporting activities and, to her mind, the general hideousness of the furnishings, the lack of elegance, taste and style. 'Everything was pitch pine, or painted dark brown, and downstairs the passages ran with RATS! Not a book or a picture in sight' was how she described it to us children.

In defence of truth, it must be said that this was my imaginative mother at her most dramatic, for rodents were highly unlikely under Aunt Maimie or Aunt Peggie's capable stewardship, but it all added to the thrill of renunciation and sacrifice. The library at Beaufort was a typical eighteenth-century collection of rather dull classical and religious books; it had been brought from Strichen by Mormand Tam and, though rarely added to, it did, in fact, contain a Shakespeare folio. There were one or two quite decent pictures dotted around the house, as well as Simon Lovat of the '45's false teeth and spectacles, in a glass case.

By the time I turned up, all the aunts had long since married, Granny Lovat had retired to her convent and my mother had 'done over' Beaufort from attic to cellar at least twice. She had also been converted to Catholicism: first of all out of love and regard for my father and the children she knew she would bear him, and then through the influence of close friends such as Katharine Asquith and Mary Herbert, plus all the pressures of marrying into an old Catholic family whose faith was unquestioned and solid as rock. That faith must have sustained her through the loss of her own mother and much-loved brother during the terrible years of the First World War, but I don't think it was for some time afterwards, not until, during the spells that our family spent in London, she had met Cecil Chesterton and that strange Irish mystic Father Vincent McNab, and observed the strong relationship that compassion, practical charity and humility have to Catholicism, that she was really happy in her faith.

I remember kneeling with Father Vincent at the door of my mother's drawing room in 48 Bryanston Square, holding out my pinny so that the elegant ladies who came to hear him lecture would drop money into it – money that would go to the funding and upkeep of the Cecil Houses in the East End, a Catholic charity and shelter for down-and-outs, which was what people called the homeless in my childhood. What would the politicians of today have thought of us – a balding, knobbly-faced Irish Dominican in tackety boots, kneeling beside a small, fair-haired child successfully begging for a very small redistribution of inherited wealth?

'The poor you will always have with you,' my mother used to quote, for she was also a realist. 'You've just got to see that they are a bit more comfortable.'

Many of her close friends had been influenced by Father Vincent's mysticism, his humble holiness and his ear for poetry. He had converted some of them, causing schisms in traditional Anglican families, as well as influencing much Catholic writing about this time, and my mother was now able to blend her new-found faith with her aesthetic instincts and new friends.

It was in our London drawing room that three famous Catholic authors – Chesterton, Baring and Belloc – posed for their portrait by James Gunn which now hangs in the National Portrait Gallery, and although you could not by any stretch of the imagination call Beaufort a 'salon', my mother's friends who came to stay every summer did tend to write books: R.A. Knox, Desmond MacCarthy, Maurice Baring, E.V. Lucas, Father Martin d'Arcy, Compton Mackenzie, to name but a few. We children knew they were writers because they tended to shut themselves away in various rooms where one heard typewriters rattle and pens squeak if one listened hard enough at the door.

Maurice Baring was our favourite writer. 'Uncle Mumble', as his close friends' children were taught to call him, was not only a courtesy 'uncle' but also my godfather. He was one of the regular visitors who came every summer to Beaufort, and he was different from any other grown-up we knew. Some grown-ups pretend to be like children – which immediately makes children suspicious. But with Uncle Mumble there was no pretence: the barriers between old and young simply did not exist. Looking back, I suppose this may have been because he was an innocent, and as naturally good as any child, and also as perverse; or it may just have been because he appealed to our imagination and sense of wonder.

Certainly among the many unapproachable grown-ups whom my parents asked to stay, he was always accessible, and he would join in any joke or prank we told him about, usually going that little bit further than we dared to ourselves – except when he was writing. Then he would be closeted in the room my mother allocated him, and we were put on a kind of scouts' honour to tiptoe by it and not to yell in the immediate vicinity. He used often to argue with her about the allocation, especially when other authors were competing for peace and solitude. I remember his telling my mother he couldn't write in the Blue Room because there was too good a view, or in the library because people came in to get books (quite untrue), or in the Organ Room because he could hear the servants laying lunch, and that anyway he couldn't write a word anywhere – he was stuck.

My mother would calm him down by telling him the pansies needed dead-heading or that *The Times* crossword puzzle must be finished, and somewhere down one of the long, rambling passages in which Beaufort abounded she would find him a child-proof, view-proof, visitor- and servant-proof haven.

As children we deeply appreciated his more spectacular eccentricities, when he delighted in going what my mother called 'too far'. There was a famous water battle in the big dining room between him and my father, the chosen weapons being soda-water siphons; but when Mr Vickers, my father's former soldier-servant, reloaded my parent with discreetly slipped fresh ammunition, there were cries of 'Unfair! Unfair!' from his own children.

There was the time when home-baked bread rolls first made their appearance at luncheon, and Uncle Mumble demonstrated how Roman emperors would clean their fingers on the dough and throw the crust to their pet dogs. My mother made him 'get down' and pick up all the bits, much to our delight. And once when, after a parental homily about grown-up and elegant table manners, conversation lagged and we all looked glum, he announced in a voice that shook with laughter, 'But I will give ten pounds to the child who makes the *biggest* mess, *now*!' Naturally there were plenty of takers.

It was my brother Shimi who first called our mother Mooswa, after the hero of one of his favourite books, *Mooswa: the Story of a Canadian Elk*, because he thought that she had eyes just like the elk's portrait on its cover and that therefore (as he told her) 'I could never shoot you.' The nickname was soon shortened to just 'Moo' and used by all the family.

My mother's relationship to Shimi was very close – perhaps in many ways too close, because when he married and broke away, neither of them knew how to cope with the emotional upheaval, and it caused many problems. Perhaps the difficulty had been aggravated by my father's absence in war-time during Shimi's formative years; perhaps it was because he had inherited so many of her own and her family's characteristics – Lister looks and elegance, their dash and style and quick wit, and from the Tennants their determination, if not stubbornness, their courage and their capacity for self-deception. Shimi, her first-born and most-loved child, was also, from the moment I can first remember him, almost impossibly handsome.

'Il fait gros vent; j'ai tué six loups,' he would quote, coming into Moo's boudoir, barefoot, with tousled curls like a westernised Mowgli, a dead rabbit in one hand and airgun in the other.

They both loved drama and had an ear for literature. Moo would read aloud to us in the holidays in both English and French, and in this way we met characters as diverse as the great Bayard, 'chevalier sans peur and sans reproche'; 'Pauvre Copette, Vierge et Martyre'; Brer Rabbit and Uncle Remus, Davie Balfour, and Thrawn Janet.

Moo could just about manage the vernacular of Joel Chandler Harris, for we had none of us ever heard old Southern or negro talk, but when she attempted the dialogue of Old Mortality, we howled with laughter, much to her indignation, as she rightly pronounced herself the only Lowlander present, and the only member of the family who could possibly understand the Borders or indeed Sir Walter Scott himself.

My father used to take Beaufort visitors round the Home Farm and show off his prize Shorthorn bulls; my mother would take them to see her garden inside the old high-walled cattle pound. She had been fortunate in finding there a small and docile burn which meandered through its five acres, and a forty-foot-high box bastion at one end of it, which was in fact an overgrown hedge, and which must have given her an inkling of the soil's fertility.

Her herbaceous borders followed the course of the burn and climbed its banks on either side, with a narrow grass path at their foot and espaliered apple trees at the top of their slopes. They were planted in square blocks of colour like a child's paint-box: red, orange, purple, pink and blue, organised to be at their spectacular best in the holiday months of August and September. Behind them lay her lily border, which was entirely white and green, planted with *Hydrangea paniculata grandiflora*, cloudy white gypsophila and huge clumps of the oriental lily *Auratum platyphillum*, the bulbs of which were sent yearly to Beaufort through the diplomatic bag by Aunt Ethel, her sister-in-law, who was the wife of Sir Frank Lindley, our Ambassador in Tokyo.

The lily border was Moo's triumph. Some of the plants would have as many as fifteen flowers on a single stem and give out such heady scent that I would feel dizzy as I walked past them. My mother always planted these bulbs herself, and I can see her now: kneeling by the flowerbed in the old sheepskin jacket she always wore when gardening, and addressing Mr Reid, our head gardener, as she wielded her trowel: 'You see, Reid, there's only one way to grow lilies. You must plant them with *love*,' and Mr Reid, who was a gloomy and inarticulate Aberdonian (but a very good gardener), turning away and looking as if he wanted to be sick.

Yet, when Moo died, no one wept more at her funeral than poor Reid. He didn't like children, and we were rather frightened of him, as he would bellow, *'Get OOT o' there!'* when we tried to steal figs in the greenhouse. But he and Moo worked in perfect harmony and loved each other, as well as the lilies.

My own relationship with my mother was more simple. Until I was about ten, I adored her and in my eyes she could do no wrong, but then came the inevitable loosening of the umbilical cord, and it happened like this.

Before afternoon lessons in Zelle's schoolroom regime, we could run free, and my cousin Irene Stirling and I had taken to the original and highly competitive pastime of arranging flower heads in a mosaic pattern on a cushion and presenting them to Zelle, simply for the pleasure of hearing her say, *'Ah, comme c'est beau!'* and for the creative fulfilment we achieved by accomplishing these miracles of taste. One afternoon I was late, because I had searched further afield for a specially beautiful scarlet flower, and unfortunately Zelle had met my mother and complained of my tardiness.

For some reason this provoked an explosion. Moo called me out and gave me a severe dressing-down without listening to any of my explanations, which, between sobs, must have been incoherent anyway.

But suddenly I stopped crying and said to myself: 'This is unfair. I didn't mean to be late; there was a good reason for it. You shouldn't talk to me like this.' I refused to apologise either to Moo or to Zelle, walked away, was sent to bed, and became in one short hour my own man (or ten-year-old child).

It was a turning-point, and I was quite aware from then on that I had discovered my own identity and would have control of what happened to me in my life. There have been other pivotal moments when I have been equally sure, but it was the awakening of my sense of justice, which had been outraged – 'It's not FAIR' – and perhaps burgeoning egotism that sparked this first one.

Funnily enough, my mother's own sense of justice was, in another way, equally strong. She took her duties as the laird's wife very seriously, and from the surviving letters written to her by my father from the front, I can see that she was already deeply involved in the lives of the families on the Lovat Estates by the time the Great War separated them.

'Will you go and see so-and-so?' he would write. 'Their son has been wounded,' and she would set off, often by pony-cart, to a croft many miles away up a distant glen, to console and bring comfort. That my mother rapidly became a sort of one-woman second front in the battle against poverty and disease, particularly TB, that was waged by the authorities in the Scotland of her day outrages some modern historians, who now call such efforts 'paternalism' and find them 'degrading', but they didn't seem so to the people she and the other charitable lairds' wives helped. The District Nurse Association, founded by Queen Alexandra, the 'angels on bicycles'; the Royal Infirmary in Inverness with its dedicated beds and no waiting lists; and the three tuberculosis sanatoria in the Highlands were all founded and funded and kept in excellent order by the efforts of these ladies and their committees.

After the war, fund-raising and visiting continued to occupy a large part of my mother's life. There were many regulars on her list, lonely old people who just liked the chance to talk, to hear the gossip from the Castle, to receive sympathy plus a box of good food made up by Geggy and, if their backs or legs were sore, the offer of a new mattress, softer pillows, a bedpan or a new kettle. Wincarnis wine was popular, and Kepler's cod-liver oil and malt was found to be beneficial. Sometimes it would be books that were needed most, for Highlanders are great readers and travelling libraries had not yet been established. I think our visits always gave pleasure, and they taught me from an early age about other people's lives and how to communicate with everyone.

The latest district gossip would be heard by my father after Sunday Mass at Eskadale, when he would join the knot of male parishioners who gathered outside the church for a smoke and a blether before everyone set off on the long journey back up the glen. He knew them all and would shake the offered hands, clap a shoulder, crack a joke; and when he heard that old Macdonald, who lived on one of the remotest crofts on the estate, had had a stroke, he suggested that my mother should pay a visit. 'But remember,' he told her, 'Mrs Macdonald comes from the West Coast and hasn't much English.'

My mother set off next day with water-bed, pillows and strengthening soup which Geggy had poured into large Kilner jars and sealed. Johnnie Sutherland, the stable-boy turned chauffeur (for neither of my parents could drive), took her up the long, track-like road to the Macdonald croft in our smart new *décapotable* Chrysler, which had the Inverness registration number ST3, Mackintosh and Lochiel having beaten my father to it as the first local motorists.

Mrs Macdonald came out of her croft wringing her hands and pouring forth a flood of incomprehensible Gaelic lamentations, which nevertheless conveyed both a warm Highland welcome and general hopelessness and despair. It was not the cleanest of houses, and my mother, shocked by the state of the paralysed old man's mattress, immediately decided to exchange it for the water-bed in the back of the Chrysler.

'Nurse will never manage to get up here more than once a week, and he'll develop bedsores in no time,' she told Johnnie. 'Help me lift him off that awful old thing and we'll burn it outside.'

And in spite of the contorted protestations of old Sandy and the wails of his wife, burn it they did, leaving the old man comfortably tucked up on the new water-bed, with pillows at the correct angle behind his head and a bowl of warm soup at his elbow.

'The only trouble,' my father told my mother after the next Sunday's church gossip, 'is that you also burnt the Macdonalds' life savings, which were tucked into his mattress, and which I will now have to replace.'

Besides my mother's crusades for the sick and the elderly, she had another: the Glasgow Orphans. The 'orphans', who were mostly unwanted or unaffordable bastards, were farmed out in those days to foster parents all over the Highlands. There was nothing intrinsically wrong with that, for abortion was regarded as tantamount to murder, and the poor children almost certainly enjoyed happier lives than they would have had in institutions in the heart of Glasgow city. Those who landed with good families and motherly women were often brought up as real members of the family, and even if they did provide cheap labour and seven shillings (35p) a head a week for their keep, they also received some of the affection and all the chances in life of their foster brethren.

But there were a few not so fortunate, and their only safeguard was a system of reports from the local minister or priest and a twice-yearly inspection by an official from Glasgow. My mother's contention was that the parish priests would seldom write an adverse report for fear of losing a parishioner, and that the foster family was always warned beforehand of the day the inspector would visit. She was perfectly right, of course, and although the system was one which propped up the crofting economy and filled benches in the remote but excellent Highland schools, it was flawed.

I am for ever haunted by the story of an orphan who was moved from a happy but dirty foster home in Mull to one that the inspectorate approved of in Dunoon. He was so unhappy there that he ran away and tried to make his way back to the island and the 'family' he loved, but he was too young and it was too far. A perfunctory search was soon abandoned, and many months later the little fellow's body was found by a pile of empty sea shells on the shores of Loch Striven, only a dozen or so miles from where he had started out on his lonely and impossible odyssey.

The Moniacks

My father's brother, Major Alastair Fraser – known to our family as 'the Alligator' – lived with his wife Sibyl at Moniack Castle, and their six children, being of roughly our age, were our constant companions and greatest friends. I never knew until much later that occasionally the Moniacks envied us. It seemed to me that *they* were the lucky ones, because they had all the things in life I most passionately desired: blue Balmoral bonnets, a ghost in their tower, a nanny who helped them make toffee, a mother who took them to parties, pocket money, proper skates attached to boots, and many other advantages.

All things except, perhaps, a river. A river they did not have, and this, it was true, gave us, the Beauforts, a certain edge. For there existed at that time an almost football-team rivalry between the children of the two families, and, as most of my waking hours were spent in or on our river, I knew this to be a great and glorious advantage.

The River Beauly was a living thing, and it ran through our lives and moulded our characters, and taught us many things that only river children know, and for a long time I felt I belonged to it and loved it almost as if it had been a third parent. Our Moniack cousins would often come to play or swim or fish with us on the river, but it was our river, not theirs, and when we talked about it I would feel for the first time that fierce, sweet and happy thrill of ownership, of possession, that saints and aesthetes so rightly warn us against.

The Moniacks lived only six miles away from us if you bicycled by the main road, but first there was the Drive, through three miles of rhododendron and beech-woods and open farmland, to be negotiated. It was crossed and intersected by small brown burns and wooden bridges, and had an atrocious surface, which my father carefully fostered, both to save money and to stop his children driving too fast – for from the age of eleven we all drove whatever we could lay our hands on. After the Drive's lodge there was a public tarmacadamed road which ran uphill for a mile (as you quickly realised when bicycling) but which eventually joined the main Inverness trunk road at a junction called Brochie's Corner, where almost everyone would leave their bicycles and catch the bus. Brochie's Corner was also a great place for dropping off or picking up parcels from the bus: flat parcels of fish, square parcels of groceries, tin milk-cans with wire handles, and bundles of newspapers done up with string were all dropped off for his friends by Jimmy-the-Bus, as its driver was known. In those days you could have left a hundred pounds in notes on the wall against which the bikes were propped, and no one would have touched them.

Moniack Castle, which my father gave to his brother when Alastair returned from Rhodesia with an ailing wife, was a castle too, but a fifteenth-century rather than a Victorian one. It was much smaller than ours, but prettier, and was harled and whitewashed, with stone facings to the windows. The central tower, or keep, was older than the rest of the house and was said to be haunted by our common ancestor, Simon Lovat of the '45, who had lived there after the '15. Some practical but unaesthetic later owner had stuck a glass conservatory on to the front of the house, which my mother said ruined it, but which we children loved, and indeed had many advantages as an all-weather playroom.

In the garden stood a large beech tree, with wide, ground-sweeping branches that we all climbed. It was perfect for beginners; we practised strenuously on it, as if on nursery slopes, developing our sense of balance and our leg and arm muscles, about which we were hyper-conscious and super-sensitive.

'Feel my muscle!'

'It's enormous!'

'Bigger than yesterday?'

'Oh, definitely.'

The tree's lowest branches nearly touched the grass and made such a safe staircase upwards that within seconds you could find yourself high in the heart of the giant, and could look down benignly, with Olympian detachment, on the other children running about like distracted midgets on the lawns far below. There was also a dangerous swing, which I avoided, and two Tarzan-type ropes used mostly by my boy-cousins, who would shin up them like monkeys and swing with simian whoops from one to the other in what, I think, we called 'Giant Strides'.

The grass tennis lawn was nearly always overgrown, but on it we could play tip-and-run and shinty, though never tennis; and there was a small, stubborn Shetland pony called Tinker. Tinker was looked after (by default) and deeply loved by Elizabeth, the small stubborn cousin who was exactly my age – though it was her brother Sandy, a year older, whom I loved the most.

Best of all, there was my Aunt Sibbie, who read aloud to her children every evening in front of the drawing-room fire, who could rival her own sons at cricket or rounders, who waded across hill lochs with us in search of seagull eggs and climbed dangerous gorges after rare wild flowers, and who took the whole noisy brood, including me, to every children's party in the neighbourhood in a famously battered old Chevrolet, dancing all the Highland dances and reels herself with a lovely, lilting grace and always insisting on staying until the last gallop and 'God Save the King'.

Aunt Sibbie was English by birth and an enthusiast by nature, and she fortunately thrived on the romanticism (not to say narcissism) of our Highland family, throwing herself wholeheartedly into it in a way my mother, perhaps more sensitive and, therefore, more self-conscious, could never quite bring herself to do; besides, my mother was half Scottish herself, and Lowland Scottish at that, which made her a little wary of Highlanders and their mystique.

Aunt Sibyl had been born a Grimston, the eldest daughter of the third Earl of Verulam and a cousin of Lochiel's wife, Lady Hermione Cameron. She had been brought up at Gorhambury, near St Albans in Hertfordshire, and kept Uncle Alastair dangling for several years before she agreed to marry him, for she had many admirers; but when she did, it was with a generous heart and complete commitment. They started married life in Rhodesia, where Alastair was a successful mining engineer, but after her health broke down from the climate there they returned to the Highlands and a way of life to which she soon adapted.

Although my mother knew and cared for every crofter's family on my father's estate, and never tired of visiting them, she made fewer friends among our country neighbours and gentry than did my aunt, who was less critical and soon knew every one of them and their family's history backwards. My mother rarely dined out or took us to children's parties, which she thought rather boring and a waste of time and energy; but Aunt Sibbie did, and seemed to love them as much as we children did.

There was only one drawing room at Moniack, from which the children were never excluded (unlike at Beaufort), so it often looked like a battlefield. It contained two desks and two revolving bookcases – with a Sheraton shell rather dubiously decorating the shiny top of one of them – a few battered armchairs, and no other furniture that I can remember, unless one counts the silver-plated Aladdin lamps which had been a wedding present (for there was no electricity) and which, being in permanent danger from flying objects or hurtling bodies, were the subject of much controversy.

My uncle's desk was in a dark corner behind the door. He was totally insensitive to noise, which was fortunate, as he could work at long and complicated County Council audits and reports while all hell was breaking loose around him: but on the other hand, he was positively morbid about draughts.

'There's not one of you knows how to shut a door!' he would suddenly roar above the din, and if you rushed forward in an attempt to placate him, you would be swept aside like some silly, feckless kitten while his large, freckled, ginger-haired hand would shut and re-shut the offending door, which, like all doors at Moniack, was edged with Turkey red felt. When this was done entirely to his satisfaction, he would return to his desk with a sigh and carry on with the education committee's latest accounts; but it was no good, for within minutes an incoming child, unaware of the danger, would erupt into the room like a cannonball, and the vaudeville would start all over again.

My aunt's desk, where she wrote thank-you letters and puzzled over the monthly bills, was in a sunny corner of the big bay window. It was very tidy, except for an occasional pile of choir parts that she had to go over before taking the weekly practice at Beauly church, for she was as enthusiastic about Catholicism as she was about music and clan history, being a fairly late convert.

'If only they'd choose something simple that they could manage,' my mother would complain after a particularly painful rendering of some new Missa Solemnis on which my aunt had rashly launched her choristers. But usually our two families went to churches in different parishes, and we did not suffer from the heroics of the Beauly choir.

Our church was in the parish of Eskadale, away in the glens below the headwaters of our beloved river, and was attended mostly by shepherds and ghillies and crofters' families, but though it was a much nicer church, built, of course, by Mormand Tam in 1827, I can't say that the singing there, though simple enough, was any better.

Uncle Alastair had a great many theories about life in general – some good, some strange but amusing, some positively alarming – and these he would propound to his wife, or to me, or to any visiting friends and relations who would listen, prefaced invariably with the words 'My dear gel', which he pronounced in the old-fashioned, aristocratic way. One theory he held most firmly was that of the 'savage eye'. His six children were all educated at home, and won scholarships to their public schools, and he greatly discouraged their being taught to read at too early an age; though one of them, Ian, was a wunderkind, a child genius, and taught himself to read without anyone's help from the writing on gramophone record labels and jam-jars.

'Once you depend on the written word, you lose your savage eye,' the Alligator would declare, standing as always plumb centre of the drawing-room fireplace, hands slightly raising the back of his kilt, which was so worn and so faded as to be almost colourless, the better to warm his backside. 'It's something small children and all illiterate races have, and it's extremely valuable and underrated. It vanishes the moment you learn to read. That's when the eye becomes lazy: it no longer observes acutely, for the subconscious tells it not to bother – you can always write it down and read it later.'

What *would* he have thought of the Internet?

Uncle Alastair certainly took full advantage of his own children's 'savage eye' period, and few families were such good naturalists or knew so much practical country lore as my cousins the Moniacks. He taught us all local and Highland history, Lovat Scout fieldcraft and gun laws, how to hide, how to pinpoint a position, how to light bonfires and put them out. He also showed us how to crouch like African natives when defecating out of doors, how to drink water on the hill only when it had sphagnum moss in it, how to kill a rabbit as quickly and kindly as possible, and other useful little tricks that served me well in later life.

Morar

Once a year my uncle and aunt would depart from Moniack to visit their friends and relations in the south, having sent their children to the seaside in the care of Nanny Tansy. There was nothing very strange about this – thousands of families all over the British Isles did it – but the seaside we went to was like no other.

Our destination was Morar, on the West Coast, and sometimes Uncle Alastair would drive us all the way there in the old Chevy. As we passed the sites of our clan's battles and the Jacobite Rising, about which we had learnt from D.K. Broster's novels, history would suddenly come alive, and we could almost see our ancestors fighting to the last man at the terrible Battle of the Shirts, or hear Prince Charlie's sigh of relief when he raised his standard at Glenfinnan and heard the skirl of the pipes, and knew Lochiel was coming over the hill to join him – shortly followed, I could later boast, by the Macleans of Ardgour.

The other method of reaching Morar was on the back of Kenny's lorry. The Moniacks' nanny, 'Napoleon' Tansy, would sit in the cab with the youngest Fraser beside her, but eight or nine of us would sit on rugs and old cushions in the back, with an enormous basket of raspberries supplied by Mr Reid.

Like Morar, Nanny Tansy was unique. She came from Nottingham and was related to either Mr Debenham or Mr Freebody (in whose successful London emporium she proudly held a few valuable shares). By the time I came within her range, she had been at Moniack for at least a dozen years and in that time had established herself as a central figure in the family's lives. As well as looking after six children, she could drive a car, row a boat, cook a meal, organise a party, train a nurserymaid, run up a frock, make toffee – in fact there was nothing Napoleon Tansy couldn't do, hence her nickname. She gave my cousins twenty years of love and devotion, and then, moving on to Shimi's children, another thirty years of the same. At Morar she enjoyed herself immensely, for at Camus Darroch Farm or Cross Farmhouse, rented by our parents, she reigned supreme.

The Lovat Estates on the West Coast had dwindled since the '45, but there was land in North Morar and Arisaig which still belonged to my father, and Morar Lodge, above Loch Morar, which was then let on a long lease to the Caldwell family. From the end of the loch a short but excellent salmon river emerged, leapt over a rocky fault and plunged into its brief estuary and the sea. And, of course, there was the usual Lovat church, this time built by my grandfather in thanksgiving for the survival of his two young sons, Hugh and Alastair, who, when little more than toddlers, had launched a loch-side boat, lost the oars, and would have been swept over the falls by the current if Hugh had not seized the branch of a tree and hung on, within yards of disaster, until a ghillie saved them.

Camus Darroch beach, which was ours, was the beach of everyone's dreams, a quarter of a mile of silver sand between two rocky headlands which framed a spectacular panorama of sea and islands outlined sharply against the horizon – Canna, Eigg, Rhum and the distant Cuillins of Skye – a view that, when one first came on it, caught one's throat and made one stand and stare.

The beach was protected by its machair of sand dunes and marram grass, which faded into sea-turf starred with thrift and thyme, the occasional bog asphodel, hawkweed and harebell, upon which the farm's black-faced sheep grazed. You could not see it from the Arisaig–Morar road, and in those days it had not been discovered by tourists and backpackers, so that, except for the Bowmans and Brintons who owned Camus Darroch Lodge and its approach, it was ours and ours alone.

We would set off in the early morning bearing picnic baskets, towels and rugs, set up camp and stay until it was time to put the youngest child to bed, when back we would trail for games of halma, racing demon or acting clumps (a form of charades) in the farmhouse parlour. Then it was time to clear the table and sit down to the delicious supper-cum-high tea that Nanny Tansy somehow always managed to produce. There were lively discussions about plans for the next day, fierce arguments, teasing, clowning, laughter and sometimes tears; but what made Morar special, I believe, was our interaction with the families who lived there permanently and with whom friendships blossomed, alliances were made and teenage romances started – the echoes of which would linger through life.

Mr Caldwell, a professor of Turin University, had married the beautiful daughter of an Australian sheep farmer and they eventually produced three attractive and talented daughters, one of whom married the cartoonist Fougasse, the second Basil Shaw-Stewart, a brother of the brilliant and better-known Patrick who was killed in 1917, and the third a Skye laird. Two sons-in-law were badly wounded in the First World War. Basil's skull had been dented by a piece of shrapnel and was trepanned with a sheet of tin, which he occasionally would let us feel the edges of, while Fougasse had to lie on his back for many months of miserable boredom until Mollie, his young wife, suggested he should draw pictures of the family's jokes.

The Shaw-Stewart boys, another Patrick (known as Pattie), Michael and Jackie, were our age and our greatest allies in every Morar adventure. They came every summer to Traigh, a pretty house above a small sandy beach next door to ours that specialised in tiny, pale-pink cowrie shells like the tips of babies' toes, which were much sought after.

Mr Caldwell was one of nature's true eccentrics as well as being something of a genius; he invented things but was never interested in making money out of his inventions. Luncheons at Morar Lodge were daunting. When he cursed, which he did frequently, Mrs Caldwell hummed, so that conversation went like this:

Mr Caldwell (who fancied himself as a gourmet): 'Oh, God! The damn sole is off, and it's no bloody good covering it with sauce – these Highland bitches can't cook!'

Mrs Caldwell, humming the 'Skye Boat Song': 'Why, dear, do we have to get it sent from Italy? Mallaig has fresh fish.'

Mr Caldwell: 'You know perfectly well you can't get Dover bloody sole at Mallaig.'

Mrs Caldwell, changing her hum to 'Land of Hope and Glory': 'Patrick, pass your grandfather some salt, dear.'

Mrs Caldwell had harebell-blue eyes and a sweet, wistful smile. She would hustle us out of a side door when Mr C. yelled from the wooden shack that was his laboratory, 'Send me one of those bloody useless children. I want someone to hold . . .'

The Bowmans of Camus Darroch Lodge also came to the beach, and we had to cross their farmland to reach it. Their cousin Mr Brinton was a retired Eton beak, and as we lay in the shelter of the dunes he would tell us wonderful stories – tales that always ended at a particularly exciting and dramatic point, when he would stop, get up, shake the sand off his trousers, fill his pipe and say, 'To be continued tomorrow . . . *if* you're good.' Next day, or sometimes two or three days later, he would pick up the story effortlessly, as if he had never stopped it.

One day he asked me whether I would like to meet an old lady who had seen a fairy. Of course I said I would, and the next morning we walked to her croft behind the bay. At first she was shy and not very willing to talk, but her daughter made us a cup of tea, and that eventually got her started. She came from the Outer Isles, and when she was a girl she and her sister Katie had been gleaning in a newly harvested field when they heard singing coming from behind a stook. Katie was too frightened to look, for it was strange, fairy singing, but Mairi was bolder and crept up and peeked over, and there was a 'wee green man' sitting on the corn stubble beside the stook, singing his heart out. She would give no more details, but when asked, 'How wee?' she pointed to the top of her knee – she was sitting down at the time – and that was it. Not another word could we get out of her.

Lobster-potting, cuddy-fishing at night with old John MacDonald, the fisherman who lived with his daughter Annie in a croft at the top of one of the bay's headlands, or sailing with Pattie Shaw-Stewart in his clapped-out boat the *Mary Rose* on hugely perilous journeys to Eigg and Canna and Skye were only some of our activities at Morar. Gavin Maxwell, the Stirlings and some Camerons of Lochiel would visit and were thought glamorous, but it was Pattie with his blond hair, blue eyes and bare brown legs, Pattie with his spirit of adventure and sense of fun who always led and enchanted every one of us – and tragically, like the uncle he was called after, who had given his life in the First World War, it was Pattie who was killed when he was only nineteen in the Second.

Keir

Sharing a governess with my cousin Irene meant that I would spend every other term at Keir, the home of Brigadier-General Archie Stirling, who had married my father's favourite sister Margaret – to us, Aunt Peg. Keir is an enormous house that still stands on a wooded bluff overlooking the carse, or valley, of the River Teith, with fine, romantic views of Stirling Castle on its mighty rock, and of the Wallace memorial monument. Its unique character was given to it by Archie's grandfather, Sir William Stirling, who, having fought under Wellington in the Peninsular campaign, returned to an impoverished Spain and bought many Spanish works of art and rare books.

He then set about remodelling his house and gardens, building a magnificent library at its core, two storeys high, with a wrought-iron gallery all round it, to house his first editions of Cervantes and the works of seventeenth-century Spanish mystics. In a frieze below the ceiling were carved Latin quotations from the classics, and 'Gang Forward', the Stirling family device. On the ground floor a long gallery, lit at each end by windows opening on to the garden, was lined on either side with the spoils of his collection: Augsburg enamels,

Bohemian glass, Spanish majolica and a beautiful head of an Etruscan boy, poised rather shakily on a Corinthian pillar. The main rooms were enriched with El Grecos, Goyas, Zurbarans, Morales, Murillos, a tiny Titian and many lesser paintings. Even the Schoolroom Passage was lined with charming Neapolitan gouaches of Italian views and classical gods and goddesses.

It was all very different from Beaufort, and at first I clung to Mairi, a gentle young girl from the glens whom my mother had sent with me, to look after me and stop me being homesick. The large house full of treasures, Uncle Archie, and particularly the formal meals in the dining room, all seemed terrifying; but soon Irene (Aunt Peg's youngest daughter) and Zelle, our teacher, absorbed me into the routine of the Keir schoolroom, and I spread my wings and grew to love it all.

Zelle – a contraction of Mademoiselle Marie Philippe, and not to be confused with the German Zellie at Beaufort – was a Frenchwoman from the soles of her neatly shod feet to the silvery crown of her head, on which not even one small hair was ever out of place. She was intelligent, quick-witted, fastidious, greedy, frivolous, feminine and, above all, *fun*. A born teacher, with an ear and an eye for beauty, she effortlessly passed on her enthusiasm and her perfectionism to her loving pupils. She was a warm-hearted, religious woman, whose only fault was perhaps her diffidence and self-doubt, which needed our constant reassurances.

Our schoolroom routines at Keir and Beaufort were strictly observed. Lessons started at nine and went on till twelve thirty, with a quarter of an hour's break at eleven for Zelle to imbibe a *café au lait*. Then came lunch in the dining room and free time until quarter to four, when we would return to our desks. Five o'clock tea would also be with the grown-ups, but at six we would be back at work for *ouvrage de main* and *lecture à haute voix*. We were allowed to suck one toffee, and only one (Milady's Devonshire Cream, bought at Woolworths in Inverness) as we bent our heads over drawn-thread work or embroidery. The day ended with Rosary and evening prayers in the private chapel, where we would be joined by the more devout Catholic servants.

Our reading covered a surprising range of adult French literature, and by the time we were fourteen, Irene and I were almost better read in French than in English; but conspicuously absent were the poems of Verlaine, the short stories of Maupassant, and all Proust. Sex was strictly edited out by Zelle – and we always knew when this was about to happen, for she would blush, look confused and turn several pages at once. This, of course, was the cue for Irene and me to creep back into the schoolroom when Zelle had gone to bed and search for the offending passage. In this way we discovered how D'Artagnan had laid bare the branded *fleur de lis* on Milady's heaving bosom. Although interesting, this did not go very far towards explaining the mysteries of baby-making, which had long intrigued and puzzled us.

The little we saw of Uncle Archie was alarming, and although always kindly and courteous to us, he inspired awe. We had breakfast and supper cheerily in the day nursery at the top of the house, but luncheon in the huge, formal dining room, hung with ancestral family portraits, at a long mahogany table loaded with magnificent silver, was a very different affair from the free-and-easy, noisy and often tempestuous meals at Beaufort.

Mr Hughes, the small, pink-faced and silver-haired butler, was surreptitiously – thank goodness – always our ally. Uncle Archie hated what he called 'messy eating', and when Mr Hughes handed us sauces, cream or similar death-traps in silver sauce-boats or jugs on silver salvers, his eagle eye would watch to see if any drop landed on the salver, our fingers, spoon or napkin. The possibility so frightened me that I avoided cream altogether, until Mr Hughes, with a conspiratorial wink and a skilled jerk, would somehow contain the offending dribble and avert the danger.

Aunt Peg, on the other hand, was always approachable, friendly and affectionate. She was a woman of enormous energy, enthusiasm and charm, as well as great stamina. She ran two dairy farms on the Keir estate, and a successful chicken farm. She re-planned and enlarged the formal gardens round the house, creating herbaceous borders, a woodland glen with a clipped yew house in which you could sit, and a glorious terraced rock garden.

She also became President of the Catholic Women's League for Scotland, a huge organisation in the central industrial belt, and she founded and ran, with difficulty and delight, the Highland Home Industries, an outlet and market for garments made by the unemployed (and largely unemployable) inhabitants of the West Coast and the Hebrides. This entailed several visits a year to the Outer Isles, and an annual sale at the Tea Centre in Lower Regent Street, which Queen Elizabeth always opened with *fanfare*. Every able-bodied member of our far-flung clan would gather round Aunt Peg to help dispense (at exorbitant prices) tea and home-made scones, or to man stalls heaped with awkward lengths of homespun tweed and uneven, knobbly pairs of socks. Conversation would go something like this:

Customer: 'I can't find a pair for this hand-knitted stocking.'

Aunt Peg, holding up a much shorter one: 'That's to avoid shrinkage, in case only one foot steps into a bog. It's very useful on the hill.'

Customer, slightly dazed: 'And what are those deep baskets with one handle for?'

Aunt Peg: 'To carry your hens around in, of course. That will be ten pounds. Shall I put the socks in the basket for you?'

It was tragic that when Uncle Archie died his eldest son, Bill, who had played a leading role in the founding and training of Commandos for Combined Operations, after the war frittered away his great inheritance on a variety of enterprises, most of which came to nothing, and that Keir was eventually sold (to an Arab sheikh) in the 1980s. Much the cleverest of the boys was Peter, who became a diplomat but severely compromised his career when, at a ball in Cairo, he tweaked the bottom of his partner, the sister of King Farouk, and whispered in her shell-like ear, 'Now that's what *I* mean when people talk about the British pinching lower Egypt!' She made an official complaint, and there was a rumpus.

But easily the most remarkable and famous of the Stirling family was the next son, David, 'the Phantom Major', who in 1941 raised the Special Air Service, and so launched a concept of guerrilla warfare and Special Forces that would be emulated worldwide. In creating a new regiment, he followed family tradition, for in 1903 my father had raised Lovat's Scouts (later known as the Lovat Scouts), to take on the Boer sharp-shooters in the South African war. They fought with distinction in both world wars, and for two generations remained a central element in our family's lives.

The youngest Stirling boy, Hugh, was only a year older than Irene, and as children the two were as close as I was to my own brother Hugh. On the outbreak of war he joined the Scots Guards, and was killed in North Africa in 1941. David and Bill, who were both in

Cairo, interviewed his soldier-servant, who, though badly wounded himself, had looked for Hugh in vain. Peter joined them, and for the next few nights, while the battle raged round them, the three brothers continued their search; but they never found his body. At first the family clung to the forlorn hope that he might have been wounded and taken prisoner, but that soon evaporated, and his death and unknown grave remained one of Aunt Peg's and Irene's greatest sorrows.

4

BEAUFORT AGAIN

BEFORE THE DEVASTATING FIRE THAT BURNT DOWN NEARLY HALF of Beaufort in 1935, you could divide the great rambling house into three separate areas. Central to our young lives was the Nursery Passage, lined with brightly coloured Medici prints of Old Masters and coffee-coloured Pre-Raphaelite ones. It opened on to the Back Stairs, at the top of which were the servants' quarters, 'The Barracks', a large room in which sometimes half a dozen young maids slept on narrow iron beds as in a school dormitory. Miss Lee, my mother's lady's maid, occupied a sunny bedroom-cum-sewing room next to it and was supposed to keep an eye on its occupants. She also kept an eye on me.

It was a seminal moment in my childhood when I was moved out of the Nursery Passage and into a room of my own, near to Miss Lee's. It was a turret room and it had a window which looked out to the west, over the wooded banks of our river and towards the distant jagged peaks of Sgurr na Lapaich, a magic view of mountains: brown, purple and blue, like some miniature landscape in the corner of a Renaissance painting.

The delight of helping my mother furnish my room was unforgettable. I was given pretty curtains and, for my birthday, a small Queen Anne desk which fitted perfectly into the round turret recess, and a single four-poster bed to sleep in. That bed was my moral undoing, for I used it for a successful scam which lasted for several years and gave me much satisfaction.

'Lights out and no reading after nine thirty' was my mother's strictest rule, and one that I deeply resented. Unfortunately, it was easily monitored by Miss Lee. Every night she would pad down her little passage to see if a light shone under my bedroom door, and go away pacified if it didn't. Furthermore, to frustrate any infringements of the law, my bedside lamp had been removed and the remaining light could be switched on only from the door, too far away for me to operate – or so they thought.

With devilish ingenuity I rigged up a looped fishing line which passed over the rail of the four-poster to the switch, so that the moment I heard an approach, I could jerk off the switch and pull in the line. Result: darkness, and a good little girl sleeping peacefully in her new bed!

The time won by my deception allowed me to plough through all the Brontës, some Dickens and Thackeray, Stevenson, Rider Haggard, Saki, Conan Doyle, all of Sapper (I was in love with Bulldog Drummond), Valentine Williams (I was terrified by Herr Grundt) and most of P.G. Wodehouse before I went to school. 'You must use P.G. as a happy addition to serious reading,' said Monsignor Ronald Knox when he found me deep in a Jeeves omnibus. 'Have one going at the same time as the classics. He writes perfect English, but you don't want to make a diet of it.'

The golden boys of my mother's early youth, who only a few years later would march so bravely and eagerly into battle, were the role models of my own childhood: I prayed for those who had died, and I learned their poetry by heart. They were my heroes, and I fantasised about one day becoming a heroine myself. I even felt cheated at having missed the opportunities for self-sacrifice that the Great War had given them!

At its far end, the Nursery Passage led to the visitors' quarters, the tower bedrooms, the River or Abertarff Room, the Black and White Passage, so called because my mother had carpeted it like a chessboard, and then the Grand Staircase, down which visitors would parade for dinner. Sometimes they would pause, sniffing the pot-pourri in the blue-and-white Nanking China plates that crowned the corner pillars of each landing, or, when they reached the main floor, the leaves and tassels of *Humea elegans* (a very Edwardian treat), the seedlings of which plants were sent to Beaufort every year from Stanway by the Charterises, to be grown in pots in the greenhouse and brought in for 'the Season'.

Outside the double doors of the drawing room stood a table where a much-consulted barometer sat with its quivering needle usually pointing to 'Rain', and where letters were left to be posted or received, and opposite that was a large, carved-wood, tin-lined tank of doubtful origin, in which every year my mother mixed the new crop of dried rose petals for her pot-pourri with orris root powder and sweet-scented oils (the nearest she ever got to cooking), a happy event in which we all participated.

This long drawing room, or Gallery, in which the guests would gather, was two storeys high, with three huge bay windows overlooking the Castle courtyard; in each of these were comfortable sofas and skirted tables on which lay the famous Beaufort game books. These were albums in which generations of devoted Fraser women had recorded game shot on the estate, together with photographs and excellent watercolour sketches of the venues, guns and company. At the far end hung my mother's portrait by Sargent, a demure little girl in a black taffeta dress and white apron, her brown curls escaping from the lacy Dutch bonnet of the Rembrandt period, and the usual artist's pillar in the background. There were good portraits of my Lovat grandfather by George Frederic Watts and of my Jerningham great-grandmother by William Etty.

My mother, like all the Tennants, was musical, and she collected musical instruments, especially keyboard ones, which were scattered all over the house, but it was in the Gallery and on its fine Bechstein grand that everyone played: Uncle Maurice in a cacophony of sound that was vaguely Russian, Auntie Diana singing in her sweet soprano 'Mademoiselle Pirouette', a deliciously witty ballad with which, we were told, she had trumped her rival Coco Chanel's operatic performance in a Paris drawing room. David and Gerald Maxwell, our cousins, would play by ear all the latest ragtime or anything else one hummed to them; and it was here that Moo, a brilliant accompanist, taught her children to sing.

Unlike most of the grown-up rooms at Beaufort, the general effect of the Gallery was rather grand and formal, and it was never used when the family was alone, for then we all congregated in my mother's boudoir, or sitting room, on the other side of the house. The big dining room that overlooked the river was both a formal and a family room, with one enormous table for large parties and a smaller one in the bow of the great plate-glass windows for breakfasts and family meals. The view from those windows was one of the most spectacular in Scotland. The Beauly river flowed peacefully immediately below terraces of well-kept lawns, and the eye could sweep far above and beyond it across the Aird valley to the mountains – Ben Wyvis beyond the Black Isle, Beinn a'Bha'achard and Sgurr na Lapaich in the Western Highlands, a vast and awe-inspiring panorama.

To the right of the dining room and behind the Gallery were three of what estate agents call 'reception rooms', the Organ Room, the library and the billiard room. The latter had never been 'done over' by my mother, so as well as a billiard table (nearly always covered by Hugh's rolling stock of Hornby trains) it contained all the big-game trophies that the Fraser brethren had killed: stuffed heads and stags' antlers – only 'royals' permitted – various gazelles, antelopes and wild sheep, while on the floor lay the skins of tigers and polar bears, with their fierce heads left on and their green eyes permanently fixed in glassy stares. To this room Moo banished all the murderous mementoes of the Frasers' sporting past, and it had now become a peaceful playroom for a younger generation.

There was also a fine collection of beautifully labelled birds' eggs reposing in cotton wool-lined drawers, and a cabinet of all the minerals, including crystal, gold and amethyst, found on the estate, as well as some gradually deteriorating beetles and moths in locked glass showcases, which we were not supposed to touch. Granny's children had been good naturalists as well as killers, and her own brother, Great-Uncle Herbert Weld-Blundell, a seriously good one. He took my father as a young man on one of his Royal Geographical expeditions to the unexplored mountains of Abyssinia, where several new species of bird and butterfly were discovered and named after them.

We children loved Uncle Herbie, who would drop in at Beaufort unexpectedly, usually from some remote and exciting part of the world. He had been to Mecca, disguised as an Arab, and Hugh and I would beg him to give the muezzin's call to prayer. Then he would climb onto a chair in the dining room, close one ear with one forefinger and a nostril with the other, and out would wail: '*Allaaaaaaah,*' to our enormous delight and mystification. I think it may well have started my romance with the mysterious East.

The third and by far the most vibrant part of Beaufort was the Boudoir Passage, which was my mother's domain. Next door to my parents' bedrooms was her sitting room, the very heart of the house.

Two large sofas on either side of a permanently smouldering log fire made it comfy, and a fine Chippendale knee-hole desk from Gisburne was always kept banked with fresh flowers from the garden and greenhouse, so that it smelt delicious. Here she wrote her letters, and here a spinet stood beneath a 'verdure' tapestry, while bookshelves lined every other wall. Old *Punch* volumes bound in faded pink buckram, du Maurier and Leech albums of late-Victorian jokes, the white Gibson Girl sketchbooks, Arthur Rackham, Gustave Doré, Edmund Dulac and Bouté de Monville picture-books in the taller shelves behind the sofa provided me with constant delight, and the old political *Punch* cartoons taught me as much history, geography and world affairs as I ever learnt in the schoolroom.

From the Nursery Passage to the ground floor a second staircase, which opened on to each floor through glass-panelled swing doors, was the one used by children and domestics alike. 'Chase', a simple version of hide-and-seek, was played up and down these stairs and corridors, but at Beaufort there was not much hide – for the quarry was captured, and rescued, by touch. The elected pair of 'He's' would usually separate, chase us all up and down the two staircases, along the passages, in and out of bedrooms; and then, just as they thought they had everyone caught, rounded up and made prisoner on the wide landing outside the Gallery, a crafty, un-caught child would shoot out from a cunning hide, dash in and rescue everyone within sight, and the fun would start all over again.

It was hectic and noisy and exciting; prodigious feats of valour were often performed, especially when the grown-ups joined in. Aunt Sibbie, who was fleet of foot, was said once when hotly pursued by her sons to have leapt the last twelve steps of the Grand Staircase in one graceful bound to rescue a prisoner at its bottom.

Beaufort 'Chase' was bound sooner or later to end in drama, and so it did when the 'He's' were pursuing the fleeing daughter of a fishing tenant. She did not realise, poor child, that the swing door that led to the Nursery Passage was panelled with opaque glass, and, putting up her hand to push, went straight through it. Panic and consternation! We led her, bleeding, into the nearest bathroom, where she dripped into the bath, bits of glass sticking out of her face and fingers. The grown-ups were summoned and took over. My father was furious with us all, as Major Mann-Thomson was a particularly tricky tenant and, quite naturally, not amused. I never knew whether the stitches that had to be put into his daughter's hands and forehead left scars, and can only hope they did not. She was a very brave little girl and kept on apologising for making a mess, which filled us all the more with guilt and remorse. The swing doors, next day, were re-panelled with wood, and Chase was played less often that summer.

At the bottom of the back staircase was the ground floor with its own luggage and backyard entrances, service areas and long passages which were never seen by visitors, and rarely by our elders. It belonged to the servants, and their world was just as important and fascinating to us as that of the grown-ups.

The Housekeeper's Room was the upper servants' domain. It was where they were waited on by the youngest footman or hall-boy, and where they entertained, with much decorum, the valets and lady's maids of the family's grandest visitors, and also where they relaxed during the afternoons and on the rare occasions when they were off duty. At Beaufort only Miss Lee, Geggy and Vickers, our butler, used the 'Room', for, as in most houses of the aristocracy, hierarchy in the household, though self-imposed, was as strict as any that existed upstairs. There were things that were done and simply not done, though in a Highland, and therefore extremely hospitable and convivial, establishment, rules were somewhat lax.

In the Servants' Hall, a barrack-like room on whose walls hung the second-best skulls and antlers of stags killed by earlier sporting Frasers, the atmosphere was a good deal less genteel, indeed positively lively. Bicycling down the long back passages on my Fairy trike, I would sometimes poke my head in at high tea time, to hear Willie the Moon, accompanying himself with two spoons which went *click*, *click*, *clickety-click*, singing, 'Pass me the Bun, the Bap, the Ginger-snap, the COOKIE', a ditty much favoured by the younger house- and scullerymaids, who would giggle and squeak for an encore.

Oddly enough, the hierarchy and *modus vivendi* of the kitchen staff were entirely separate, especially under the reign of Monsieur Darde, my mother's one-and-only, quite short-lived French chef. My memories of him are vague, but my brother Hugh could never forget him.

One day Hugh, not yet dining room-worthy, was scootering down the long passage that led from the kitchens to the serving lift which transported all food up a floor to the dining room, when he espied two sauce-boats of mayonnaise outside the kitchen hatch waiting to be picked up. The hatch was closed, and so he dipped a chubby finger into one of them, 'just to taste', but at that moment the shutter flew up, framing Monsieur Darde's furious face.

'It looked like the Devil, honestly!' claimed Hugh, who had been dragged neck first into the kitchen, sat on a stool and made to eat a whole sauceboatful of the oily stuff.

One day in the summer holidays we had all sat down to luncheon and were happily munching our way through the first course when in came a flustered Kate Chisholm, our near-toothless but much-loved parlourmaid, and whispered in my mother's ear. Moo laid down her fork and begged for silence. 'Simon, Monsieur Darde has disappeared. He was last seen heading for the river two hours ago with a fishing rod in his hand. You must do something about it.'

My father and all the men in the company rose to their feet. 'He must be into something big!' they cried. 'Carry on with the cheese!' and they dashed for the door.

Indeed Monsieur Darde was into something big – a huge salmon that he had lured with a piece of bread on a hook and had been trying to land for over an hour. The poor man was exhausted; yet my father, not wishing to spoil his moment of glory, did not take over but simply offered advice and encouragement.

'*Doucement, doucement, Monsieur Darde!* Bring him into the shallows. That's it, keep the point of your rod up . . .' and so on until the silver monster was neatly gaffed by a visitor and lay gasping at the victorious chef's feet. The fish weighed forty-two pounds.

When Monsieur Darde departed to start a restaurant in Burgundy, he was succeeded by Alice Donnelly, and then by Joan Matheson, who was a character as well as a wonderful cook. She was also extremely pretty and a natural hostess. She held court in the vast and impractical kitchens of Beaufort, which would have made any of today's food writers faint, but from which she somehow produced, with the help of her sister Jean and two other girls, the best food in the north.

Joan and Jean were the children of a crofter up one of the glens who was reputed to have kept an illicit still for himself and his neighbours, and perhaps it was this tradition of hospitality that inspired the Matheson sisters. If you visited the kitchen at eleven a.m.

you would always find a party in full swing. Kenny the lorry driver, a fishing ghillie, a postman, an under-keeper, a gardener, a tradesman from Beauly would all be seated round the huge table drinking mugs of tea and finishing off odds and ends of food on thick slabs of bread known as 'pieces'.

Monsignor Ronald Knox was one of the writers and regulars at Beaufort. The son of an Anglican bishop, and the brother of E.V. Knox, the editor of *Punch,* and Wilfrid ('Dilly') Knox, the cryptographer of Bletchley and Enigma fame, he went to Eton, and it was there that he made friends with my uncle Charles Lister, an equally unconventional character, and the two Grenfell brothers, Billy and Julian. Together they edited the *Eton College Chronicle,* and my mother had a lovely, clowning photograph of them chewing pens, ruffling hair and waiting for inspiration. Only Ronnie survived the Great War, and after conversion to Catholicism and training for the priesthood, he spent a few miserable years teaching in a Catholic preparatory school, before being appointed chaplain to the Catholic undergraduates at Oxford, with a delightful house to live in: The Old Palace, in St Aldate's, just off the High.

The Monsignor Knox I knew as a child was a very grown-up figure among the grown-ups, and he was one of the few who could quell us with a glance or, in my case, with a single lifted finger, which he established as a signal that I was being too noisy or, worse still, *showing off.* He was impatient with children, but they always amused him, and though irritable when they disturbed his writing or the daily completion of *The Times* crossword puzzle, he was never cross for long. And there were other childlike and delightful sides to Monsignor Knox that we appreciated. When little Rose would plan a doll's wedding in the nursery, with elaborate dishes of cake crumbs and lemonade, rose petals and confetti, he would be invited by her to come and dance at it, which he would always do, slowly and gravely, with black cassock swinging, accompanying himself with the tinkly music box inside a pink teddy bear.

Though he said Mass every day in the chapel, usually served by my reluctant brothers, of whose Ampleforth-accented Latin he disapproved, I did not think of him very much as a priest, or holy, until years later I read one of his books, *The Mass in Slow Motion,* and was illuminated by it; so I was considerably startled when one day, in our chapel's confessional box, after I had rattled off my usual lapses, he stopped me and said, 'Veronica, I do wish you could think of more grown-up sins for which I can ask God to forgive you.' From then on I added 'proud and uncharitable' to the list, because I believed then, and still do, that pride and envy are the cause of most grown-up sins and most people's troubles.

Monsignor Knox always came for the Christmas holidays, to decorate the tree that was the central feature of the estate children's Christmas party. For most families, decorating the Christmas tree is a joint effort and fun. For Ronnie Knox it was a challenge, a mathematical exercise, a work of art, a creative process and above all a solo performance. Children might just as well have asked Michelangelo whether they could help him with the Sistine Chapel ceiling as any of us dare to ask whether we could hang one silver ball on Monsignor Knox's tree, or even open the Gallery door to catch a glimpse when he was at work.

On the morning of the Christmas party, Joan and Geggy must have been stretched, for the children's tea was always a good one, and there was still dining-room lunch and dinner to prepare. At three p.m. the first young guests would arrive, crammed into the back of the estate lorry driven by Kenny Smith, our old friend and ally, or by special bus from Beauly, to be dumped unceremoniously by the luggage entrance. Geggy would stand at the door in her white apron and blue-and-white checked dress that reached to her black buttoned boots, directing the older children to the Servants' Hall and the mothers and babies to the 'Room'.

'Too splendid, too splendid,' was Geggy's welcome. 'Come in, Mrs Macdonald, come in, you must be half dead with the cold, and there's a nice fire going in the "Room". Away with you, Duncan and Callum! Off to the Hall, and take wee Jamie with you. You know the way, Mrs Mac. Too splendid, too splendid.'

By four forty the children had eaten and assembled in the inner hall, with the school-teaching Miss Rattrays rounding up their flock like sheepdogs, lining them into a crocodile of whispering, excited, shuffling expectancy. At exactly five o'clock Monsignor Knox threw open the double doors of the Gallery, and to hear that great 'Oooooh!' that seemed to carry up into the roof and the clouds above it made everyone's work seem worthwhile. As the children trooped in, Miss Rattray or Father Geddes, the Eskadale parish priest and a great betting man, proclaimed above the din that he or she would be taking wagers on how many candles there were on the tree. I still have a record of some of their guesses: '150', '500', '983', '1,000,000', scrawled in childish figures in a yellowing copybook.

The presents had all been bought the previous month in Woolworths and Selfridges bargain basement in London, and were, or so the younger Lovats thought, of the most desirable quality; but my mother was rather cavalier in handing them out, and this caused me pain and sometimes trouble, especially if the recipient was a friend.

'Jimmy says he had one like it last year,' I would hiss in her ear, 'and he would rather have the pistol.'

But to no avail, and later I would have to do a little legerdemain to get things right and then be scolded for it. After singing a Christmas carol, then 'God Save the King', and thanking everyone in sight, the children would file out to their transport, clutching their presents and also a bag of sweeties and an orange to sustain them on the long journey home.

Many years later Rhoda Stone, the head keeper's daughter who became my own family's nanny and has stayed with us for over sixty years, told me that when she was eight she once missed a Beaufort Christmas tree party because she had measles. 'The others all went, but I couldn't. I felt it was the end of the world and cried for two whole days, even though my mother stayed with me and my sisters brought me back a present.'

Beaufort had always been famous for its hospitality, and during my brothers' summer holidays, which coincided with the sporting season and general exodus from London, it always seemed to be full of visitors, which suited us children very well, as everyone was much too busy to bother about us or interfere with our activities.

In Gaeldom, hospitality is regarded as one of the cardinal virtues, and to close one's door to the stranger is to risk 'a constriction of the soul'. The Gaelic rune of hospitality explains why, and my mother had it beautifully transcribed and illuminated by an Ampleforth monk, and hung in the front hall.

> *I saw a stranger yester e'en.*
> *I put food in the eating place,*

Drink in the drinking place,
Music in the listening place:
And in the sacred name of the Triune
He blessed myself and my dear ones,
My cattle and my house.
And the lark said in her song,
Often, often, often
Goes Christ in the stranger's guise,
Often, often, often
Goes Christ in the stranger's guise.

In our family, hospitality was a serious tradition, for had not Simon Lovat, in fleeing westward after the defeat at Culloden, exercised it in its purest form? The 'Old Fox' had stopped to rest at Gorthlick, the house of a kinsman whom he knew to be safe (i.e. a Jacobite), and was just sitting down to a quiet evening meal when there was a clatter of hoofs outside the door and up rode none other than the Prince himself, who had had the same notion of seeking sanctuary on his flight to the west. To refuse him entry was against every instinct of a Highlander, and yet to compromise himself by such close association with the defeated Prince would be, quite simply, a death sentence.

Old Lovat, who had dithered so long in deciding whether to support the Stuart or the Hanoverian cause, did not hesitate. He rose to his feet and welcomed the exhausted and desperate fugitives into the house.

The guests whom my parents entertained at Beaufort were not all fugitives; mostly they came to Beaufort because they enjoyed the good food and comfort, the happy atmosphere and the casual sport. The best fishing beats on the River Beauly were usually let to regular tenants, but there was always the chance of an 'off day' or unwanted stretch of water, which the family would seize with alacrity, as well as quite good sport to be had fishing for brown trout in the hill lochs. There would be a few days' grouse-shooting on Farley Moor in August; pheasants and rabbits to bag around the Castle, while from September onwards there would be roe deer stalking, and later excellent red deer stalking on several forests up the glens.

Often quite grand visitors would stop off on their way to their own estates further north. The Dukes of Portland and Sutherland called regularly on their way to Langwell and Dunrobin, and 'Cousin' Winnie Portland (all my mother's old friends insisted on being called 'cousin' to bridge the gap between respect and intimacy, an Edwardian affectation to which we submitted) would arrive from Welbeck with *two* lady's maids: a French one who looked after her hair and jewels, and a Scottish one who looked after her clothes.

Once we had graduated from the nursery and were thought to be *'Salon gefecht'*, we would join the visitors for breakfast and for luncheon in the dining room, but 'coming down to dinner' was quite another stage in the process of growing up. That was an almost unimaginable Elysium.

Dining-room life was not at all formal at Beaufort. At breakfast we helped ourselves from a great bowl of porridge and from a row of silver entrée dishes on a hot-plate on the sideboard. Dining-room food was infinitely better than fare in the nursery, where we lived on a diet of rabbit and salmon, home-grown, cheap and always available, and the occasional treat of mince and tatties.

The conversation was also much jollier. My father would eat his porridge from a wooden bowl, walking round the room and enthusiastically planning the day ahead. When someone asked him to sit down he would answer, 'Not until I've finished my porridge,' and when asked why, he would answer with a twinkle in his eyes, 'A Highland chief never sits down when eating porridge, because of possible emerrrrrgencies!' and he would roll those r's and wink at me and, imagining at least a hundred fierce Macdonalds galloping up to the courtyard brandishing claymores, I would look at my father with round eyes and love, knowing he was the hero who would defend us all.

In his day company was never lacking at Beaufort. He filled the house from cellar to ceiling with a never-ending flood of visitors and friends. He was the most gregarious of men – and what was the point of having a castle with nearly a hundred rooms if one kept half of it empty?

Shimi's Coming-of-Age

In 1932, when I was eleven, my eldest brother Shimi came of age, and in the celebrations that ensued, I understood for the first time a lot of things about my father, the family and our clan. I had always known that my father was what the MacFarlane children and I called 'grand', because people were always telling me so – 'He's a grand man, your father, child. A grand man altogether.' That was one kind of grandness. And I knew he was grand because he gave orders to people of whom I was personally in awe, like Archie MacFarlane or Miss Lee – and quite sharp orders, too, which they never seemed to mind. That was another kind. But that wasn't all.

I had been to an Opening of Parliament in London with Rose, and we had sat in a gallery in the House of Lords, sporting our new coats bought specially for the occasion, and had seen him walk in wearing his peer's robes, all scarlet and white, and he had turned his head and smiled at us, almost winked, as the procession moved past, though all the other peers looked stuffy and solemn. That was another version of being grand, and I had felt proud of him.

I was proud of him, too, when he walked out into the arena at the Northern Meetings (the Highland gathering in Inverness which we attended every year) to present some silver cup or other, with his old, faded plaid over his shoulder and his stick and bonnet with a bit of yew in the silver badge at the side of it.

Not until the coming-of-age, however, did I realise how much he was loved by the people of the Highlands; then I saw that there were hundreds, literally hundreds of men whom he could make happy just by clapping them on the shoulder or saying a few words of welcome. There was something different about him that they all understood and I should have known all along, something that belonged peculiarly to our part of Scotland and to our relationship with him, and through him with each other: a shared pride in our Highland blood, our clan's history and our clan's chief, which bound us together in brotherhood and loyalty.

The preparations for the great event had begun months beforehand, and that summer we children talked of little else.

'Don't go into the kitchen,' I warned Hugh. 'Geggy's making mayonnaise for the luncheon, and it'll curdle if you talk to her.'

'Not again!'

'Yes, she is. She's made gallons of it. I don't suppose she'll ever be able to look mayonnaise in the eye again.'

'Well, that's something,' Hugh admitted. 'Perhaps we won't get it any more. I hate salmon mayonnaise and I hate rabbit. We never seem to get real meat, like at school.'

'They're not having rabbit, silly,' I told him. 'They're having soup, and salmon mayonnaise, and cold beef, and trifle and jelly.' I knew it by heart, as we had written out the beautifully illustrated menus in the schoolroom.

It was typical of my mother, who had agreed with a sigh to trifle and jelly, to insist on the mayonnaise 'at least' being real, without having any idea of the work it would involve. But Geggy, sweet Geggy of the golden hair and innocent eyes, was radiant.

'Too splendid, too splendid,' she would say, bustling round the kitchen with its long wooden table at which you could have sat an army – then, to the moon-faced sixteen-year-old who had ventured to ask if the fat was hot enough, 'Don't ask silly questions, girl. If you want to know if it's hot enough, put your finger in and see!' while over her shoulder – for she had eyes in the back of her head – 'Now don't touch that, Master Hugh, it's for our dear Lord's party.' Geggy always called my father, and then Shimi, 'our dear Lord', which could at times be confusing.

Two days before the great occasion even the kitchen was out of bounds. On the morning, when guests began arriving about ten o'clock, the forecourt and the Castle still looked much the same except for the flags and bunting, but outside the wrought-iron courtyard gates there had been a transformation. Seven enormous grey tents like recumbent elephants covered half the green. Post-and-rope enclosures had been squared off; a new wooden platform for the pipers, gay little booths and long trestle tables had materialised where before our belted Galloways had quietly munched and chewed their cud. There was not a beast in sight – only people. Close on six hundred of them had come down from the glens and the clachans, the small Highland towns and villages, by car and by bus, on bicycles and on foot to converge on our courtyard to celebrate and to feast with their chief and the young Master of Lovat.

On the official programme the luncheon guests fell into three categories: employees and tenants of the Lovat Estates; local dignitaries and ministers of religion; clansmen and clanswomen. On top of this, Beaufort itself and many of our neighbours' houses had been crammed to the rafters with visiting friends and relations.

Before the luncheon there were presentations to be made, on the front steps of the Castle, so that everyone could see. My brother's chief worry was that he would not get through his carefully prepared speeches, two for the presentations and one for each of the tents at the end of the luncheon, before he became what is politely called inebriated and less politely 'fu', under the mounting pressure of toasts and proffered drams of neat whisky that he was bound in all honour to accept – for it is an insult for a Highlander to refuse to drink with a friend.

Yet when he arrived with my father at our tent, the blue-aproned one where the Moniacks and I were helping with the waiting, he was still walking quite steadily, if a trifle pink and self-conscious and perhaps just a little bit 'blurred round the edges', and still carried himself with his usual panache, looking every inch the handsome young laird.

There were sports in the afternoon for the children, and shinty and a greasy pole and caber-tossing for the men. There was piping and there was dancing, tugs-of-war and an endless flow of whisky. There was the first dram I ever tasted, which Mr Martin, our head carpenter, and Bobby Fraser, the village painter, gave me in the bushes behind the kennel door: it made my eyes water and left me gasping, but I gamely declared it was delicious. There was also home-made ice-cream and lemonade, which was a good deal more to my taste.

That night there was a bonfire on a grassy hill near the Castle. It was lit by the oldest tenant on the estate, whom my brother carried up on his shoulders to perform the ceremony. She was a tiny old woman who would see her hundredth year out next birthday, and she was as spry and neat as a little hen partridge. And then there was drinking and singing and piping and dancing until long after I had been sent, protesting loudly, to bed.

Less than a year after my brother's coming-of-age, my father died suddenly of a heart attack. His death in February 1933 marked the end of an era for our family and for many people in the glens and clachans round Beaufort, and much of its glory died with him.

No one who went to his funeral will ever forget it. The night before beacons had been lit on hilltops all over the northern counties, and on that bleak February morning old Lovat Scouts, farmers, stalkers, ghillies and keepers, crofters, tenants, clansmen and neighbours converged before the Castle. So many people walked behind the plain farm cart that was his hearse – the men taking it in turn to pull it – that the cortège had not stopped forming at Beaufort when the head of it reached Eskadale church, four miles away.

In the peaceful churchyard in the hills, above the quiet waters of the Beauly, he was laid to rest, and the strath was filled with the saddest of all bagpipe dirges, 'Lord Lovat's Lament'. It was the funeral of a last great Highland prince.

The inscription on the tombstone that marks his grave is simple, as he wished it. After his name is written: 'Heart of Jesus, Hope of the Eternal Hills, have mercy on him.'

5

L'AGE INGRAT

I WAS ONLY TWELVE WHEN MY FATHER DIED, BUT SHIMI WAS TWENTY-two and would soon leave Oxford to take up a short-term commission in the Scots Guards. Magdalen was nineteen, beautiful, dutiful, and about to become engaged to her cousin, Jack Eldon. Hugh was fifteen, still at Ampleforth, clever and yearning for the excitements of a wider world. And Rose, darling Rose, sweet, grave and gentle Rose, was only seven but probably already knew more surely than any of us where she was going. She had just left the nursery and begun lessons with Zelle.

My father appointed his brother Alastair to act as his senior trustee. His will reads sadly. It said that the estate, in spite of its size, was 'not a rich one'. As my cousin Ian Fraser points out in his own memoir, *The High Road to England*,

> being a chief was not all romance and adulation. The economics of chiefdom were uncertain in the extreme. The elements which went into the original acquisition of these huge properties, upon which the rights and duties of the chief rested, were conquest, marriage and monastic dissolution. But, unlike in the big estates of the Lowlands or of England, there was no coal industry or urban development to finance maintenance and modernisation.
>
> Furthermore, successive London governments had piled costs, taxes and, later, county rates on to the Highland landowners. Because of the Crofting Acts of 1886, enlightened lairds were never able to recover the cost of improvements to farms, crofts and houses

demanded by the spirit of the age. Many chiefs took to the bottle,
more to gambling. Others borrowed from banks and sold off land
when mortgage debts could no longer be serviced . . .

My father's method had been more elegant. He had negotiated a
large loan from the Free Church of Scotland, secured on land – a nice
trick for Scotland's leading Catholic peer! But of course that too had
to be serviced, and now there were no directors' fees or earnings with
which to do so. The result for our family was a grinding change of gear:
retrenchment and economies on every front. At first my mother had no
idea what this meant, but after mildly suggesting, 'No more napkins
at luncheon,' she was rapidly disabused by the lawyers, Major Dewar
the estate factor, and Uncle Alastair; and from then on they bullied her
into establishing a new regime at Beaufort. The huge central-heating
boilers were shut down, and for the next winter or two we put on
outdoor coats to negotiate the Castle's freezing passages. For us it was
war-time, without much sign of victory ahead.

Even the safe and long-established routines of our schoolroom
changed. My cousin Irene Stirling, with whom I had shared lessons,
had already left for Les Oiseaux, a convent in Kent, and first Kisty
McEwen, and then a quiet and studious little girl called Mig Phipps,
daughter of Sir Eric and Lady Phipps, came to share Rose's lessons at
Beaufort. Soon my own fate was decided, and I was sent to join Irene
at Westgate-on-Sea for three gloomy and not very profitable years of
convent education. I hated the idea of school, and had no desire to leave
Beaufort and everything I loved. The day before my departure, I paid
an emotional visit to my river. I sat alone in the little summer-house
above the Cruives Pool and said goodbye to it. I remember promising
it, out loud, that I would return, that I would never abandon it, and that
I would love it till the end of my days. I then walked sadly back to the
Castle and began to pack.

The year before I was supposed to sit my school certificate exams, I
swallowed every cherry-stone I could get hold of, as a school myth had
it that this would produce acute appendicitis and instant removal from
Les Oiseaux. A better understanding of anatomy would have taught me
otherwise, but biology was a science neglected by the nuns.

Be that as it may, immediately after returning to Beaufort for the
holidays, I had to be rushed into the Royal Infirmary in Inverness with

near-peritonitis, and later my heart developed a murmur. I was kept at home for a year, returning to Zelle's happy schoolroom, with a top-up of English tuition twice a week at an excellent day school in Inverness.

While I was recovering in these congenial conditions, the abdication crisis blew up, and Zelle and I would listen anxiously to her radio, the only one in the Castle. My mother was in London when we heard that King Edward VIII would address the nation – so, having consulted Geggy, I summoned the household into the schoolroom and we all listened together to the fateful words of the abdication speech, which now sound so egocentric and wimpish.

I had already formed my own opinion of the King, as our paths had crossed on an earlier occasion. One of my father's regular duties had been to put up and take care of visiting royalty, and the visit most memorable for me had been that of the Prince of Wales. He was to arrive in his own aeroplane from Nairn where, between functions, he had been playing golf, and was due to land at three thirty p.m.

My father had arranged a special netting session at the weir known as the Cruives, on the River Beauly, half a mile above the Castle. The barrier, built across the river in the sixteenth century, impeded the salmon's progress upstream so that they gathered in large numbers below it, and could continue on their way only when the sluice gates were opened for them. Because of an ancient royal grant, the MacShimidh had the right to net these fish and control their progress as he wished.

The netting was always an exciting business – the despair of the current fishing tenant, who had probably been flogging the Cruives Pool all morning without success or even seeing a fish, and the delight of the onlookers, who would often help haul in the nets, full of leaping, slippery silver beauties, which we children had no compunction at all in killing by a hard tap on the nose with short birch-wood clubs, or 'priests', as they were called.

On that special day there were many onlookers, as the young Prince was a popular figure, and the Moniacks, the Maxwells and many other neighbours and friends had come to watch and perhaps to be presented, if my father so decreed. Three thirty came and went without a sign of the Prince or his plane, and at four o'clock my father, none too pleased, lost patience and ordered the ghillies to begin netting.

At four thirty, when everyone on the river was engrossed, a small silver aeroplane was spotted by Nanny Tansy, who had stayed behind in the Castle with the younger children. It circled the green, and then made a graceful landing between two orange drogues set out by the farm-hands that morning.

Seeing there was no welcoming party in place, Napoleon T. did not hesitate, but scooped up two of the babies and dashed out with the other toddlers in tow. When the door of the plane opened and its steps were lowered, HRH found a row of very small children standing at attention, who bowed or curtsied neatly as he shook hands with each in turn.

That same night, fresh from my bath, I was crouched in the secret observation post that Hugh and I had created behind a curtain at the end of the Nursery Passage to watch the grown-ups descend the Grand Staircase in their stately progress from bedroom to drawing room below. Thirty minutes earlier a dressing-gong had been sounded, followed by a more urgent tocsin which announced it was time for dinner, and we found it very entertaining to note the latecomers' behaviour as they hurried down the broad staircase, still chattering, adjusting recalcitrant evening ties, fastening glove buttons, twitching bows and usually blaming each other for being late as they passed by our spy-hole.

Suddenly the curtain behind which I had been hiding was thrust aside and, 'Caught you!' said the Prince of Wales with evident delight.

Remembering the strict instructions of Moo and Nellie, I managed a small bob rather than a curtsy, for I was impeded by the bundle of underclothes which I was still clutching under my dressing gown.

'I wasn't really spying, sir,' I blurted, 'just watching everyone go down to dinner.'

'Ah,' he answered, as if considering. Then, 'How would you like to go up tomorrow? In my aeroplane? I can tell Group Captain Fielden to give you a spin in the morning, if you'd like me to. You might even loop the loop!'

'Oh, yes, sir, please, sir, I'd love you to. There's nothing I'd love better!' In my embarrassment and excitement I dropped my bundle, to be further mortified by HRH handing me back one pair of knickers, navy-blue, cotton, size 2, and one liberty bodice, cotton, white, ditto, with the charming smile and courteous manner that won hearts everywhere and made him so much loved by an uncritical public.

'Well then, it's a deal,' and he continued on his way downstairs, kilt swinging bravely, no adjustments, in the comfortable confidence that everyone would be waiting for *him*.

Of course he forgot about the 'deal' next day, and I waited, booted and spurred, all morning for the call that never came. My confidence in the Prince of Wales, future heir to the throne and Emperor of India and all our dominions over the sea, evaporated there and then, and I was not at all surprised by his subsequent behaviour.

The best memories I have of that in-between time were not of Beaufort or of school, but of exciting visits which added new feathers to my fledgling awareness and widened my horizon. The first, not far from home, was to my special friend Monty, or Compton Mackenzie, on the island of Barra in the Outer Hebrides.

Monty had always liked to live and write on islands, and when he became tired of growing daffodils on Jethou it so happened that Miss Anne Pierpoint-Morgan's lease of Eilean Aigas had just come to an end. So when Monty was driven over to see the Island, he fell in love with it immediately, and then with the entire Fraser family. 'I thought I'd seen a little bit of heaven,' he would tease me, because that Sunday I had worn my new sky-blue angora beret to Mass at Eskadale, and had peered over our family's balcony at the back of the church to view the new tenant of Eilean Aigas in his private box-pew below us.

The story of Monty's youthful elopement and marriage to Faith Stone has been beautifully told in *Guy and Pauline*, perhaps the best of his novels; but their only child's death in infancy affected him so much that he never wrote about it, not even, I think, in his long and rather rambling autobiography. Sadly, too, the marriage broke down, for Monty was an impossible man to be married to, and though friendship and respect remained between him and Faith, there were no children in his life – which is why, I suppose, he adopted me.

Nearly every Sunday, Irene and I would be dropped off at the Island on the way back from Eskadale, to have lunch and spend the afternoon with him and his two secretaries. The older and plainer one, Nellie Boyd, had been one of his innumerable mistresses before his Highland period began, and she had loyally stayed on, but by the time we knew him, she had been supplanted by a sloe-eyed young beauty from the Outer Hebrides, Miss Chrissie MacSween, who could type, speak Gaelic, sing and dance and, in spite of having a Presbyterian minister for an uncle, must have been quite willingly seduced, for she really loved Monty.

Though Monty's love life was complicated and varied, his writing life was simple and serious, though somewhat eccentric. He wrote only at night, by hand, in a small, ill-lit room with no view, lying back in a kind of dentist's chair which had a swivelling desk in front of it, for he suffered from agonising attacks of sciatica, and this position was supposed to ease his pain. Next door one secretary would be in attendance all through the night, and the next day the other secretary would type out his manuscript while he and the first one slept.

But on Sundays he was on holiday, and he seemed to enjoy the fun he dreamt up for us as much as we did, playing classical records, reading aloud to us, or walking us round the Island telling jokes and stories. It was always magic.

Zelle used to disapprove of the visits, which she suspected put unsuitable ideas into my head, but my parents believed in their innocence and welcomed Monty's civilising influence. He stayed at Eilean Aigas only a few years, for he was always restless, and the next island that took his fancy was Barra, which he loved so much that he built a house there; but when Magdalen, Hugh and I visited him, it was still without a roof, and he was staying in the house of 'The Coddy', the famous Barra postmaster, while Magdalen, Chrissie and I lodged with 'The Crookle', a North Bay fisherman, and my brother was sentenced to be put up by Father John Macmillan, the North Bay poet and parish priest. I say 'sentenced' because not only did Hugh have to rise at seven a.m. and serve Mass, but he also had to have breakfast afterwards with Father John, who would read or recite long Gaelic poems throughout the meal, pausing for Hugh's appreciation, or shaking him by the shoulder: 'Poy, poy, was not that peautiful?' It may well have been, but poor Hugh did not understand one single word of it.

'The Crookle' (actually Mr McNeil – for on Barra there were so many McNeils that they had to have distinguishing nicknames) was a much less demanding host, and his wife was a good cook, serving us fresh scallops straight out of the sea, rolled in oatmeal and 'jumped' in butter in a huge frying pan. I shared a brass bed with Chrissie, who took up too much room, and it was the first time I realised that women had pubic hair, which came as a shock. Magdalen had a room of her own.

Monty had arranged for our visit to coincide with a 'Luagh', or traditional 'shrinking of the cloth', a ceremonial and social event in the islands when tweed or blankets woven by crofters on their handlooms are shrunk or tightened by being sprinkled with water and then thumped on a table of rough boards to the accompaniment of Luagh songs.

The evening turned out to be way beyond our expectations. The old girls sat on either side of a long table with bunched-up tweed in either hand, and thumped away in unison, first to the right and then to the left, to the rhythm of the ancient shrinking songs, until they could thump no longer and had to be revived with whisky, after which they picked up the cloth once more and, with the speed of the rhythm ever increasing, thumped away until the beat suddenly doubled, and they fell over the table in utter exhaustion, to the hoots and whistles of an admiring audience. And after the Luagh there was a wonderful ceilidh which lasted to the small hours just before dawn.

Much has been written about The Coddy – his stories, character, insight and knowledge of his island's Gaelic culture, which was already beginning to disappear. I have a vivid memory of his power to enchant on the occasion when The Crookle took us out in his boat to see Berneray, the most southerly in the chain of outer islands, uninhabited, and a great bird and seal sanctuary. The Coddy regaled us with stories about seals all the way over, and when we finally beached below the great cliff that rises straight out of the sea, a storm of protesting puffins and gannets arose, and many fat grey seals with mournful eyes flopped into the water all round us.

'Go on, Coddy,' said Monty. 'You've been telling us how they love music. Go on, sing to them, a proper seal song, mind; a Gaelic seal song.'

The Coddy took up the challenge, waded ashore, climbed on to a thrift-covered rock, threw back his head, puffed out his little chest, and sang a wild, mournful song about a maiden and her seal lover. Whether the sea creatures responded or not, I do not know, but when the singer clambered back into the boat, Monty and I and perhaps even The Crookle had tears in our eyes, and could scarcely see the rotund and cuddly Coddy, who looked so like a seal himself.

It was in 1933 that I went abroad for the first time, when my mother packed me off to France, to stay for a month with Zelle and her brother

Louis Philippe at Lons-le-Saunier, in the Jura, the lower side of the French Alps. Louis was tall and nice-looking; he worked as the head agent of a small insurance company and had three main passions in life: shooting (*'le sport des rois'*!), eating good food and drinking good wine. Every Sunday he would drive us to visit his clients, the small farmers and wine-growers of the Franche-Comté or Burgundy, who were only too keen to feast and fatten us in the hope of obtaining lower premiums for their policies – and what feasts they were!

On weekdays Zelle would wake me with *café au lait* (in a bright blue bowl), a croissant warm from the corner bakery, and sometimes a tangerine on a stalk, with *leaves* on it. Shopping for Louis' evening meal was an education in itself. Our own luncheon was usually charcuterie and a salad, but in the evenings we went in for serious food, and for the first time I became aware that cooking was an art requiring skill and dedication, and that you could improve gentlemen's moods simply by the quality of the *sauce Béarnaise*. When things smelt particularly good, Louis would disappear into the cellar and return holding some special bottle of wine in reverent hands.

Later he was moved to Dijon, and if he was not on the road, he would join us for lunch at a small restaurant in the Grande Place, where I nearly always ordered *escargots* – Pierre, our special waiter, would slip me a dozen instead of the six that were our ration. It was the green, garlicky sauce that I found so delicious, and I still have Pierre's recipe for it.

Zelle always called me her *papillon*, for I was a feckless child, too interested in too many things to be serious about any of them, with great curiosity but poor concentration. During that trip Zelle became my *Maman Papillon*, and Louis accepted the title of *Papa Papillon* with a Gallic shrug (*'Ces femmes!'*) but also with a sweet smile.

The best of all our foreign visits came in August 1934, when Moo took Hugh and me to stay with the Herberts at Portofino.

After our train passed through Genoa and all its tunnels, Moo told us to douse the lights, and sitting beside the window of our *wagon-lit*, she kept taking peeks behind its brown Holland blind, until she suddenly said, 'Now!' and released the catch. Up flew the blind, and there was the Mediterranean. It seemed within yards of us as we hurtled alongside it, sparkling in the sunshine and blue, blue, like no colour I had ever seen before.

The train stopped at Santa Margarita and there Mary, widow of Aubrey Herbert, met us in a battered straw hat, espadrilles and sun-faded linen dress. She looked just right, and her welcome was so warm that Hugh and I were instantly captivated. Also, she treated us like grown-ups, which put us on our best behaviour.

We climbed into a car rather like a hearse, and Mary drove it at breakneck speed, 'like the Italians do, on the horn and the brake, the only way to get anywhere in this country, especially round blind corners', her son Auberon explained to me later. The road ended at Portofino, a fishing village of gently coloured houses built round a church and a cobbled quayside, and dominated by the Casteletto, a medieval castle high up on a peninsula above it, where the rocky mountains come down to the sea. When Mary blew the horn, there emerged from one of the houses the stooped figure of an old man, who took charge of our luggage. She then pointed to a small iron gate and a precipitous, zigzagging track that led up a terraced cliff to its summit high above the village. 'I'm afraid it's a long way up,' she said, 'but you've got good Highland legs,' and she charged off ahead, setting a cracking pace.

Alta Chiara, the imposing nineteenth-century Carnarvon villa, stands at the top of the cliff, with a stupendous view from its windows and its wide, ilex-shaded terrace, which ends in a low stone wall. Beyond that the land falls perpendicularly to the sea, which can be heard crashing on the rocks below.

After a brief but astonishing career in the Balkans and the Middle East that out-Buchaned any Buchan hero, Aubrey Herbert had died in the terrible influenza epidemic that ravaged Europe after the First World War, leaving Mary bereft, with three small daughters and a posthumous son. He also bequeathed her Pixton, a beautiful eighteenth-century house, a large estate on the edge of Dartmoor, and Alta Chiara in Portofino. She told us that one of Aubrey's most endearing traits had been his childish love of pranks. At Portofino he would rush out of the dining room as if distraught, and leap over the terrace wall, shouting, 'I can't bear it any longer!' to the horror of assembled guests. He knew, but they didn't, that on the other side, above the drop, there was a narrow ledge; but as he was extremely short-sighted, it was always on the cards that he would miss it.

Fortunately, Mary (the only child of that great beauty Lady de Vesci, née Charteris) was a young woman of strong character and great courage. Fortunately, too, she was completely unself-conscious and unconventional, so that the way of life in which her family grew up at Pixton and Portofino was startlingly different and wonderfully enjoyable for those who were lucky enough to share it. The girls were clever, cultured and beautiful, with Mary's graveyard sense of humour and their father's love of risk and adventure.

When we arrived at Portofino that summer, Gabriel, the eldest, was about to leave for Spain to drive ambulances for Franco; Bridget was newly married to Eddie Grant, the funniest and most delightful of men, who, riding as an amateur, had fallen off at the last fence in the Grand National and had never, Bridget would say, 'been the same since'. He had a wonderful ear for literature, and sometimes read casually submitted manuscripts for John Murray, the publisher, but an eager careerist and breadwinner he was patently not. Laura was absent in London, being courted by Evelyn Waugh, to the collective dismay of the family, who made unkind jokes about his provenance, looks and habits, though they all agreed he was an exceptionally fine writer.

The other two guests in this now sparsely furnished but grandiose house, which had been built for Lord Carnarvon and a much more luxurious style of entertaining, were Hilaire Belloc and young James Lees-Milne, who had trodden on a sea urchin and spent most of the day lying in a hammock sadly picking at the embedded spines with a pin. Mary's son Auberon, who was much the same age as Hugh and also at Ampleforth, was greatly influenced by Mr Belloc, whose eccentricity, foreignness and romantic, intemperate views appealed to him enormously. Mary herself would stand no nonsense from Hilaire, but I don't know if she realised how strong and wayward an influence he was having on her son, who, among all those women, obviously needed and craved for a father figure.

One morning at breakfast under the ilex trees, Belloc appeared looking dangerously in the dumps. 'I have no friends, no friends at all. I am an old man who is friendless,' he intoned, rolling his r's at the back of his tonsils, as the French do.

'Don't be silly, Hilaire,' retorted Mary from the top of the table. 'What do you think we're all doing, asking you to stay and putting up with your grumps and loving you in spite of them?'

'No friends, no friends, only *acquaintances*,' Mr Belloc repeated, but Mary threw a well-aimed butter-pat at him and he cheered up.

In the evenings, as we sat at the same table under glorious, warm, starlit skies, swatting mosquitoes and looping spaghetti round our forks, Mr Belloc would sing the French drinking songs of his youth, and then, when Mary begged for them, he would softly sing some of his own poems, which ran like music in his head, creating their own tunes – 'Do you remember an inn, Miranda?' or 'Sing to me of the islands, oh daughter of Cuchulain, sing'.

Mr Belloc was godfather to my young sister Rose, and at Portofino he gave Moo the manuscript of this poem that he had written to her when she was a baby:

> Rose, little Rose, the youngest of the Roses,
> My little Rose, whom I may never see,
> When you shall come to where the heart reposes,
> Cut me a Rose and send it down to me.
>
> When you shall come unto the High Rose Gardens,
> Where Roses bend upon Our Lady's tree,
> The place of Plenitudes, the place of Pardons,
> Cut me a Rose and send it down to me.

One day Auberon ordered the village *carozza* and horse to take me to tea with Max Beerbohm, a great honour. When we arrived at his beautiful villa in Santa Margarita, our host was standing in a white suit outside the door. He doffed his panama and said, 'Ah, carriage folk, I see,' then handed me down as if I had been Zuleika Dobson herself!

In England, the house I particularly loved visiting was Mells, near Frome, in Somerset. It was still the home of Lady Horner (one of the last surviving Souls), her widowed daughter, Katharine Asquith, and her grandchildren, of whom Julian ('Trim') was my special friend. Mells was the perfect English manor house, full of ancient beauty, wonderful books and pictures, yet with a simple, almost spartan atmosphere. The bells of the village church were so close that they sounded as if they rang directly above your bed. All the family were musical, and all extremely clever. Lady Horner liked to play intellectual Edwardian games after dinner, with everyone gathered round a huge log fire in the drawing room – an activity thought by some to be intimidating, as it could separate sheep from goats, but it was great fun watching distinguished academics writhe in agony when unable to think of a toadstool beginning with the letter 'D'!

It was at Mells that I first met Donald ('Traitor') Maclean. He was my partner in what was usually light-hearted tennis, but when I served three double faults in succession, and he threw down his racquet in rage and despair and actually *jumped* on it, I took a dim view of his character.

Beyond the orchard was a swimming pool, equipped with an old-fashioned hand-operated mangle, made of iron, with rubber rollers through which we could wring our swimsuits after bathing. Someone had the bright idea of drying my waist-long hair in the same way, and in spite of a good deal of squealing and protest, the ends were fed into the jaws of the machine. But when it was belatedly realised that I couldn't follow my hair, and that if rolled through I would come out flat, frantic efforts were made to disengage me. I would certainly have been scalped, and would have had to wear a turban, *à la* Freya Stark, for the rest of my life, if an old gardener had not come and released the rollers.

Eilean Aigas

In 1935 a stray spark from a small chimney-fire that had burnt some five days previously landed on the dry duckboarding of Beaufort's roof and smouldered; then crept along the whole of one wing until a gust of wind ignited it. The first anyone in the building knew of impending disaster was when two boys who had been playing on the green ran into the courtyard shouting, 'The Castle's on fire!' and by that time the whole wing was blazing. The only reason my home was not burnt to the ground was that the wind suddenly changed direction and blew back over the part that was already gutted.

When I returned from school that autumn, my mother, Zelle and Rose had already moved to Eilean Aigas, temporarily, it was thought at the time, until Beaufort was rebuilt – but when my brother Shimi married Rosamund Broughton in 1938, the wooded island in the River Beauly became our home.

The house was of great charm and uncertain date, and it had a doubly romantic history. It was there in the late seventeenth century that the young Simon of Lovat, in collusion with his father Thomas, brought the Atholl heiress he had kidnapped, and it was there, in a real Mills and Boon scenario, that he ravished her, ripping her bodice with his dirk and ordering his piper to drown her screams. Shortly afterwards her vengeful Murray relations rode up with a small army, but, according to family legend, the reluctant 'bride' was unwilling to accompany them back to the safety of Blair Castle.

The Atholl family, however, had its revenge. Simon Lovat was arraigned before the House of Lords, his title was attainted and his lands confiscated. He spent the rest of his life trying to repair the damage of his youthful folly, pleading his cause first at Stuart and then at Hanoverian courts, and having backed the wrong side at Culloden, he ended it on Tower Hill.

And then, a century later, came the romantic 'Sobieski' Stuarts, two young Polish brothers who turned up in Inverness-shire shortly after my grandparents' marriage, claiming to be the sons of Prince Charles Edward Stuart. Though this was certainly a fable they had been duped into believing, they were Jacobite, Catholic and gentlemen, and they were treated with kindness and courtesy by Simon Lovat, who granted them a lease of Eilean Aigas, where they settled, rebuilding the original house in a slightly continental Victorian version of what they imagined a royal abode should be. The result was charming and it became my home until I married.

The Sobieski Stuarts wore their hair long, in eighteenth-century style and, one being a poet and the other an accomplished artist and designer, they had considerable influence on the Scottish Gothic revival, inventing new 'dress' tartans and coats of arms for Victorian Highlanders and publishing the results. My grandmother curtsied to them when she first called, and every Sunday they were rowed upriver to Eskadale for Mass in a kind of royal barge. There was a painting of them, by the artist brother, which always hung in the library of the Island, but has now, sadly, been sold. They died without issue and are buried in two magnificent tombs in the sanctuary of Eskadale church.

6

COMING OUT

'COMING OUT' WAS THE CURIOUS EUPHEMISM USED IN THOSE DAYS for being taken to as many dances and parties in London as mothers, through their own social connections, could get their daughters invited to, in the hope, of course, that they would meet eligible young men and be taken off their hands. 'Coming out' had nothing whatever to do with its present, more lurid meaning: it simply signified the difference between ending what little education girls of my world were given, and their discreet entry into the marriage market and society. It necessitated living in London from April to August for a year or more, and being presented at Court.

Bella, the fat and lovable cook at Moniack, did not approve of it, and put it to us like this: 'There's her puir Ladyship having to take Miss Fanny a' the way doon to London to find hersel' a maan! Up 'n' doon, up 'n' doon they go, and baack she comes *every year, just the same!*' Fanny was indeed choosy about finding the right man, and she did not marry until 1946, when she fell in love with a second cousin, Colonel Humphrey Weld, and went to live at Chiddock, in Dorset – a happy fate that had little to do with earlier endeavour.

In my own case, it was decided that Moo would share the London flat that the Lister sisters already owned with my aunt Diana Westmorland, who also had a daughter to bring out, June Capel, my favourite English cousin. The Listers had acquired it as a retirement home for Zellie (their old governess), and when she died, they had fortunately kept it on, installing in it two delightful sisters from the West Coast, Mary and Kathy Macleay, who took in lodgers, or 'gentlemen', as they called them. These were soon banished sideways to an adjoining flat; Junie arrived from her home, Lyegrove, and my mother and I moved down from the Island together to start our 'season'.

The seedier end of the Edgware Road was not exactly a salubrious neighbourhood from which to launch a social debut. The flat was on the ground floor of No. 10 Hyde Park Mansions, and directly opposite us lived the mother of Jack Spot, the racecourse gangster; down the road was the 'Rosary' Roman Catholic church, a hotbed of Irish Republican sympathisers, and above us lived two of the poorer violins of the BBC Symphony Orchestra, who practised loudly at inconvenient times, but with whom we made friends. The mansion block had been built in the 1920s of angry red brick that had darkened with age to such a gloomy puce that Fitzroy would always call them the Deep Purple flats.

It was an unconventional background for someone tackling the London season, but, thank goodness, our mothers were not at all conventional: perhaps they were unworldly enough, or maybe just secure enough, not to bother with a lot of its silliness. Their friends, they were sure, would ask their daughters to balls and parties, and if they didn't, too bad. There was no question of giving a ball themselves, as many mothers did on a quid pro quo basis. Luckily for us, their friends all entertained us lavishly, and we were asked to dozens of balls, and to weekend parties before balls, which were even more enjoyable, and at which we met scores of young people our own age who became our admirers, pursuers and quite often our friends for life.

But first of all, we had to be presented at Court – and that, in the muffled words of Miss Dora Keogh ('Kiwi'), Moo's new lady's maid, who spoke with her mouth full of pins as she adjusted a hem and straightened a wavering ostrich feather, was 'a right carry-on'. Yet when my mother was ready to lead us into the waiting taxi (no hired Daimler or purring Rolls for us), Kiwi looked at her and gasped, 'Oh, your Ladyship! You look just like a queen!' Her compliment would have seemed even more flattering had she not added, 'Queen Victoria herself!'

In fact, no one could have looked *less* like the Dowager Empress than my mother did at that time. She was tall and still willowy. She had very large eyes, a nose with a delightfully faceted tip, a pretty mouth and a long, slender neck. She may have been a bit soulful ('languishing' was what her friends had called it in her youth), but she could also be very funny, and had a lovely, clear, unaffected laugh. Having been used to running things for so long in Inverness-shire, where she was regarded practically as God, she had a slightly arrogant and impatient manner in London shops, which used to embarrass me terribly – and, like her father and Tennant grandfather before her, she suffered fools 'not at all'.

Teenagers, I suppose, always find shopping with their mothers agony. I was no exception, but somehow she managed to kit me out with five glamorous ball dresses without blood actually being spilt. I remember a pink one and a white one from Peter Jones that looked like ballerina's tutus from *Swan Lake*, and cost only £15 each, and one absolutely lovely dress from Worth that Uncle Mumble gave me as a godfatherly present – a huge ice-blue satin skirt with a tiny waist and black lace top. I was allowed to choose one dress myself, and insisted on an unbelievably hideous purple chiffon creation, with a Carmen Miranda bunch of flowers on one shoulder (fruit, too, if I remember rightly); but Moo, wincing visibly, took out her chequebook and paid for it.

She probably enjoyed the first weeks of our new life as much as I did. She resuscitated old friendships, visited great houses once again, and entertained with her usual flair in the flat's tiny dining room a motley collection of old admirers who had not had time or money enough to come and see her in Scotland: General Adrian Carton de Wiart, Sir Ronald Storrs, Freddie Alhusen and Princess Marthe Bibesco among them. But soon she became bored and restless, and longed to return to Rose at Eilean Aigas and the garden she was beginning to make there. 'You'll promise to ring up twice a week, won't you, darling?' she said as she left. 'Remember, *no* nightclubs, and always come back to the flat with friends – *never* on your own.' With that she fled north, leaving Mary Macleay to feed us and Kiwi to dress us and attempt to control our night-life.

In the daytime this was done most effectively by the ward sisters of St Mary's Hospital, Paddington, for our mothers had enrolled us on a pre-probationer training course at the hospital, and we worked there every day from eight a.m. to three p.m. The course was really a splendid way for the hospital to get ward-maids for free – indeed, to be *paid* for training them; but for us it was a good way to do something useful which we enjoyed: to become experts at making beds with hospital corners, to tuck in draw-sheets without a wrinkle, to fill hot-water bottles without scalding ourselves (or the patients), to empty bed-pans, measure urine and sterilise the bottles, polish floors the *right* way, and cheer up patients as we took the tea-trolley round.

Not only did it keep us out of trouble: it made us love both hospitals and nursing. The mini-dramas in our wards, the gossip in the ward kitchen, the mild flirtations with our housemen and student doctors gave us a lifelong affection for the profession, and admiration for the wonderful nurses, ward sisters and matrons, whose dedication and skill were in no way matched by the pitiful wages they then earned.

At lunchtime there was no provision for feeding us, so we would scoot into Praed Street, just round the corner, where we tried out pubs until we found one that advertised 'Soup, Steak-and-Chips-and-Peas, Apple Pie – 1s. 6d.'. 'Bloody marvellous,' as Fred Emney, our favourite comedian, would say.

I cannot remember who gave the first ball I went to with Moo, but I shall never forget the dinner party before it. Our host was Baron James de Rothschild, and he lived in a very grand house. His face looked like a piece of smoked haddock, but he was so kindly and courteous that one hardly noticed. The table was the most elegant I had ever seen: snow-white linen, with huge silver bowls of pink Malmaison carnations down its centre, magnificent candlesticks and sparkling crystal. The food was perfection, too.

My mother had told me that I was bound to be asked to dance by the men who sat on either side of me at dinner, and I chattered away to them, hoping to make a good impression; but alas, when the time came to leave for the ball, they both excused themselves, one saying he had a gammy leg, the other that he never danced. Dear James saw us off from his front door and said that I looked 'like a snowflake' in my new evening cloak, run up that morning by Kiwi from some left-over ostrich feathers, with a pink satin lining.

Half an hour later in the ballroom of some grand house I sat gloomily on a gilded bamboo chair beside my mother, shut my eyes and prayed for a partner. None came, and – worse still – when a rather dashing soldierly-looking man did approach, he said, 'Laura! How lovely to see you!' and asked *her* to dance – *and* she accepted!

Shocked by this betrayal, I prayed again, rather harder.

'Why have you got your eyes shut?' said a voice in front of me. I opened them, and saw a young man with eyes turned down at the corners, like a spaniel.

'I'm praying for a partner,' I answered truthfully, and was immediately whisked off my chair and danced round the room by Robert Cecil, and then by all his friends, for the rest of the night.

'You know we've been asked by Lady Salisbury to stay at Hatfield for a ball next month,' said my mother on the way home. 'That was her grandson you were dancing with.' I was drunk with delight at not having been a wallflower after all, and already halfway to falling in love with my very first partner – so all I could think of to say was, 'Oh, good!'

Robert was not my only cavalier during that dizzy summer. My brother Hugh was already in his second year at Balliol, and a rising star in the debating and political firmament; he shared a flat with David Ormsby-Gore (Robert's cousin), Julian Amery, Julian Oxford and Simon Wardell, son of the editor of the *Daily Express*. Jakie and Michael Astor were also at Oxford (Robert had just left), and there were many weekends when Junie and I would be driven down from London to join them (once by David Wills at 100 m.p.h. in an open-top sky-blue Lagonda) – or else one of them would come to London to take us out.

Michael Astor was very much in love with Junie, who was only just recovering from an unrequited and unsuitable passion for a married man. Michael, or perhaps his brother Bill, kept several fine hunters in Leicestershire. Wishing to please Junie, he lent her his favourite horse for a day with the Quorn, and his new Bentley in which to drive herself back to London, where he planned to give her a slap-up dinner and propose. Fine horsewoman though she was, she had the misfortune to stake the horse over a difficult jump, so that it had to be put down, then crashed the Bentley on her way south (it was a total wreck), and arrived at the rendezvous late, and in tears. When Michael patted her on the back and proposed, she burst into tears once again, and then, with an anguished sob, turned him down, and fled.

In spite of flirting outrageously with all our young men, we always tried to avoid embarrassing proposals, as we had no wish to embroil ourselves in marriage – yet. One day I was visiting Hugh in Oxford when a mysterious letter marked 'Private – By Hand' was delivered to me. It was from a Mr Riddle, whom I hardly knew and could only just place as someone I had danced with once, at a ball. He asked if he could give me tea in his college rooms at four p.m. It seemed rude to refuse, so round I went and sipped politely at a cup of Earl Grey, until I was startled and horrified to see him go down on one knee and blurt out a proposal of marriage. I don't know exactly what I answered, but it evidently pained him, and, feeling ever more guilty and awkward, I backed out of the room.

Young Maurice Macmillan, Harold's son, was in his last half at Eton, but this did not stop him coming up to London quite often and taking me out to a nightclub called The Nest. At just eighteen, he was very good-looking and far more sophisticated and worldly-wise than me or any of our university friends; and, not being in the least in love with me (we just liked to dance, and were both very good at it), he proceeded to teach me, in a preceptorial way, some of the facts of life.

'You see those two pansies over there? The one with the crew-cut is the *top* queen. The other's his lover.' I thought I knew all about pansies, because Auntie Barbara Wilson's sons Martin and Peter were a constant source of anxiety and despair to the Lister sisters in the Deep Purple flat. But I was not sure what they actually *did*, so this was interesting, and something new. 'And those two women,' Maurice went on, 'the fat one and the thin one. I expect they're lesbians, because they're only dancing with each other.'

'What's a lesbian?' I asked – and I was treated to a dissertation on female sex and the island of Lesbos, a subject which Zelle and Lamé Fleury had never taught me.

Of course I shouldn't have been at The Nest at all, and whenever Moo rang up to say, 'Darling, I hear you're being a bit *wild*. Are you going to *nightclubs*?' I would answer, 'Only to the Bird's Nest, Moo. It's very tame and quiet, and friends go there all the time.' I became adept at cutting my poor mother off the Kiltarlity line in the middle of her next sentence.

In a way it was true. The Nest belonged, or half-belonged, to a gentle, déclassé queer called Ulrick Browne, whose family owned half of Ardnamurchan, in Argyll, and who had set up the club with his strange partner and mentor, Alma. She was ugly, half-Russian, old enough to be his mother and probably a retired brothel-keeper, but she had considerable charm and that Slavic, all-embracing humanity that I have always found irresistible. The two loved each other, and I think he married her at the beginning of the war, but, sadly, he was killed in the Italian campaign, and I never heard of Alma or The Nest again. Drink and drugs were certainly indulged in by some of her clientele, but the small black band was the best in London.

Our house party at Hatfield had been enormous fun. 'Gomma', as all her grandchildren called old Lady Salisbury, had put me in the dressing room that communicated with my mother's grand bedroom. When Moo dragged me away from the fun, which was still going on well after midnight, she fell into a well-earned sleep, little realising that my room had an escape route via a closet, and that Robert was waiting for me at the bottom of it. We continued the party in the great yew maze below the west terrace, and someone, having stolen poor Kathleen ('Kick') Kennedy's shoes, threw all the left-footed ones into its centre, with Kick hopping about on one leg, laughing and protesting. Everyone loved Kick, to my mind far the nicest of her family.

My later meetings with Robert's relations were not so successful. One day we drove down to Eton to visit his Uncle Linky, Lord Hugh Cecil, who was then the Provost, and after tea he asked me if I would like to come to evensong in the college chapel. Prompted by a kick from Robert, I said I would love to. It was the first time I had ever been to a service in an Anglican church, and I was at a loss as to how to behave. The nuns had told me that one might attend, but not take part in, Protestant worship; and although my instinct, in that great building, with the fine music and the beautiful words of the 1662 Prayer Book and the Authorised Version, was to join in and love it, I somehow felt that this would be a betrayal of what I believed in. So I sat on my hands and never moved throughout the service. Linky noticed, as of course Robert did too, and it was only then that we began to realise that a perhaps unbridgeable gulf would keep us apart in the years ahead.

The best ball of the summer was given by 'Cousin' Nancy Astor, the first woman Member of Parliament, who came from Virginia and was an old friend of my father. She gave the party for all her children, but the chief organisers were her sons Michael and Jakie, who were wild, funny and enormously attractive. They danced beautifully and were up to every kind of mischief, especially when their mother was absent from Cliveden on her parliamentary duties in Plymouth or Westminster. For the ball they brought over from New York two bands of which no one in England had heard the like. The main one, the first to play big-band jazz, had Louis Armstrong as its leader and trumpeter, and the second, much smaller, had Benny Goodman on clarinet. The two played alternately at either end of the huge ballroom, and it was sensational.

One day at luncheon Lee, who had been the Cliveden butler for many years, announced that this time the boys had gone too far. 'I'm sorry, my Lady,' he announced, 'but my nerves can't stand it any longer. I'm giving you my notice, and I'm leaving.'

'That's perfectly all right, Lee,' answered her Ladyship calmly. 'I quite understand. Tell me where you're going, and I'll come too.'

Of course Lee stayed on to a ripe old age, and the boys tried, for a time, not to misbehave.

The summer passed, and I returned to the Island with promises from my new friends that they would join me there in September for the Northern Meetings. The men in our house-party for my first Highland ball were Robert Cecil, Andrew Cavendish and my brother Hugh. It was rather lamentable that there should be so many penguins (non-kilted dancers) in our midst, but it couldn't be helped.

After the ball I drove Robert over to look at Beaufort and the river.

'There it is!' I exclaimed. 'Isn't it the most beautiful house you've ever seen?'

He looked at the Castle calmly. 'Well, no – at least, not to my mind. You see, I don't really like Victorian baronial architecture. I suppose I prefer the real thing, in France.'

Scales fell from my eyes as I looked at Beaufort objectively for the first time. 'It's the sixth castle that's been built here, and it was much better before half of it was burnt down,' I answered rather crossly, and we drove on.

Notwithstanding our aesthetic, ethnic and religious differences, and although Robert and Andrew cut poor figures when confronted by our whooping, leaping, spring-heeled Highland neighbours in their velvet doublets and lace jabots, we all had fun, and when they left there was scarcely time to draw breath before I joined my Moniack Fraser cousins in Skye for another two nights of dancing at the Portree Gathering.

On the second night in Skye we danced almost until dawn, so that there was no time for me to change out of my ball dress before dashing for the MacBrayne ferryboat that would take me to the train at Kyleakin for the start of my journey south. A sailor took my luggage and said he had put it on board, and I had a cloak to keep me warm, so I had no worries as I ran up a gangplank just as the ship cast off. I sat on a bench with my back to the warm funnel and dozed off. The sky was turning a faint pink, and one could just see the dark and jagged outline of the Cuillin range on the horizon.

An hour later I woke with a start. There was no land in sight, and we were steaming northwards at a good speed. I looked for my luggage in vain. 'Squeaky' Macdonald, the captain, was sympathetic. 'You've got on the wrong boat, lassie. But never fear. After Stornoway we turn south again, and ye'll be back at Kyleakin by Tuesday morning.'

I groaned, for the Sabbath had only just dawned.

Squeaky lent me a pair of enormous flannel pyjamas that went twice round my waist, and a seaman's jersey, and I settled down to enjoy the voyage – there was nothing else to do. Squeaky was a great raconteur, happy to have a wide-eyed captive audience, and with his Gaelic-inflected syntax and high Hebridean voice he kept me enthralled.

One highlight of the journey came when we had called at Stornoway and were casting off from the quayside. A young Glaswegian mother who had just come aboard leant over the rail and shouted at her in-laws, who were busy tucking their newest grandchild into a pram: 'Well, cheery-bye-bye! Ta for the visit, and mind and postcard me when Baby can say "Banana"!' Told and retold, it soon became our family's stock form of farewell.

My next destination was Holker, the Cavendish home in Cumbria, and when I arrived there in the evening *sans culottes* things were a bit awkward. The large house-party was just sitting down to dinner. I knew only Jean Ogilvy, Robert, and Sibyl Cavendish, and I felt pretty silly and insecure as Lady Moira looked up, smiled and said, 'Ah! Here's the girl who travels *really* light – in fact with no luggage at all!' But then she added, 'Don't worry, my dear. Come and eat. It may well arrive tomorrow, and meanwhile we can lend you a nightie and a toothbrush.' She sat me between Robert and Sibyl, and all was well.

That was my first experience of Holker, one of the nicest, most welcoming and hospitable houses in the world. Of course my luggage did *not* arrive next day, and Robert, Jean and I set off for Ireland – and a week's visit to the Lansdownes at Derreen in County Kerry – with a curious trousseau of garments that the company, but mostly Jean, had kindly lent me. Poor Jean was seasick throughout the crossing, and since she was at that time a Christian Scientist, Robert and I teased her mercilessly. 'Remember, it's all in the mind! You can rise above it!' But at the word 'rise' she would rush to the nearest porthole, and *whoosh!*

No one minded much about clothes at Derreen. It was like Morar, only more elegant. Sweet Lady Lansdowne, who loved young people, presided. Charlie Lansdowne and Kitty and Ned took us fishing and lobster-potting. There were donkeys and pubs and soft Irish voices, fishermen and jaunting-cars. Killarney was then unspoilt by incomers and tourists, and wonderfully beautiful. We had a glorious time, and I forgot all about my errant suitcase.

At that time the residence of the United States Ambassador in London was a very large house in Prince's Gate. It needed to be, because in holiday time Ambassador Joseph and Mrs Kennedy had eight children living at home. Big Joe was a large, beefy, ignorant bully, as Yankee-Irish as they come, who hated the British almost as much as he hated Communism, but who was rich and successful and an astute politician. Mrs Kennedy must have been much nicer, even though she had the ugliest voice I have ever heard, like a duck with laryngitis, for her children loved her and she was devoted to them. I have often wondered why, back-handers and Irish votes notwithstanding, her husband was appointed to the Court of St James at that particular time (we now know that he was corresponding personally with Hitler) – though I am glad he was, because his children became great friends of our family, and we would not have known them otherwise.

We danced and joked with little Joe and Jack, but my friend was Kick, and one day she asked me to lunch. 'It's not a party, just the usual family bun-fight, so you'll have to fit in.'

I hope I did, but I found it all very unusual. We sat at a long table, with places for the parents at either end. The Ambassador was late, and joined us halfway through. Eight young Kennedy backs straightened immediately, for they knew what to expect.

'Joe, Jack, Bobby – let's hear it! How ya doing?' – and one by one they got up and stood, more or less at attention, giving details of their height, weight, bowel movements, school grades, church attendance and anything else they could think of, while their father slurped his food, saying, 'Good, good,' at intervals, but occasionally pouncing on what seemed to be a misdemeanour. The girls got off more lightly, but also reported in detail to their formidable parent. After the inquisition was over, he picked up a *New York Herald Tribune* and read it for the rest of lunch, while we continued talking, but *pianissimo*.

7

WAITING
FOR WAR

OLITICS, ESPECIALLY INTERNATIONAL AFFAIRS, STILL MEANT
nothing to me, but Hugh and, I'm sorry to say, my mother,
who was extremely right-wing, were fascinated by events in
Germany, and by the appearance in England of Sir Oswald Mosley
and his blackshirts, as well as by the Civil War in Spain. Moo even
wrote a letter to the *Inverness Courier,* our local newspaper, putting
her anti-Communist, Catholic views. She was surprised when it
was published under the headline LADY LOVAT, THE POPE AND
FRANCO – you will please note the order.

In 1938 she and Hugh visited Munich and stayed with the
Montgelas, the aristocratic Bavarian family with whom she had learnt
German in her teens. They were taken to a Hitler Youth rally in
Nuremberg and heard the Führer speak – apparently an unforgettable
experience. But it was not until Dr Stefan Zeissl, a gentle, intellectual
Jew of the Viennese musical establishment, came into our lives that
she fully understood the dreadful realities of Hitler's rise to power and
the nature of the Third Reich. After the *Anschluss* in March 1938, when
German troops marched into Austria, Stefan was arrested and briefly
imprisoned in Dachau concentration camp, because he had been a
member of the bodyguard protecting the Austrian Chancellor, Kurt
von Schuschnigg, who had tried to oppose Hitler's demands; but he was
allowed to emigrate with his small daughter, while his wife, an Aryan,
remained in Austria. Frau Zeissl happened to know our neighbours,
the Munros of Foulis, who nobly promised to look after and bring up

the little girl until it was safe for her to return to Vienna; the task of ensuring Stefan's well-being and safety somehow fell on us. Officially he was a Jewish refugee, still thought of as a friendly alien, and until war was declared he was able to work in London; but he spent most of his holidays in Scotland to be near his nine-year-old daughter.

He brought with him to the Island a lot of music and metaphysical discussion, a great deal of laughter and endless drama. We all loved his outsize presence, his zany jokes and childlike affection. We tolerated his anger and despair, which at first we thought were exaggerated, but later realised were all too real.

Junie and I were too busy polishing floors and making beds with hospital corners to go to many lunch parties; but when Debo Mitford one day asked me to her parents' house, I accepted, curious to see what this unusual and much-publicised family were like at home. For the past couple of years the newspapers had been full of her sister Unity's infatuation with Hitler, and they had reported her elder sister Diana's marriage to the British Fascist leader Sir Oswald Mosley.

It turned out that Debo was the only member of the family present, and she had cooked lunch herself, with skill and efficiency. There were three other friends; the food was delicious, and it was a merry party. Then, in the middle of the veal fillets and *épinards en branche*, the telephone rang next door, and we heard her clipped, businesslike voice answer it. 'Oh – that was surely a bad mistake, wasn't it?' And then: 'Oh yes, very serious, I should say . . . How much did you say? . . . No, no. *Double* that, and I might accept.'

As she came back to the table, looking very pleased, she announced, 'I've just made two hundred pounds! Those idiots at the *Daily Blank* have published a photograph of *me*, thinking it was Unity, under a nasty headline. They've just realised their mistake – and they had the cheek to offer me only a hundred quid!'

We were all vastly impressed by such financial acumen, and by her coolness in dealing with the press, of whom we had been taught to beware – but Debo was obviously used to it. Before we left she took us up to her mother's bedroom to collect our coats. It was a pretty room and round the walls were attractive pastel portraits of Lady Redesdale's six daughters as children, beautiful, blue-eyed and blonde: six, except that one portrait had been taken down and lay with its face to the wall. Having ticked off Nancy, Diana, Decca, Unity and Debo, I asked, 'Who's that one?'

'Oh,' answered our hostess, 'that's the Woman' – as if that explained it all. We collected our coats and said our goodbyes.

The Woman, also known as Pamela Mitford, eventually married Professor Jackson, one of the great eccentrics and scientists of my generation; and this led me to consider that if poor Unity had realised her dreams, Lady Redesdale's sons-in-law would have included Adolf Hitler, Sir Oswald Mosley, one of the inventors of the atom bomb and the Duke of Devonshire – a somewhat mixed bag, but possibly all charismatic in their own way!

The autumn of 1938 was the time of Neville Chamberlain's visit to Hitler in Munich when he promised he had brought us back 'peace with honour', and a deep division of opinion opened up in the Foreign Office, in Parliament and in the country. Robert's father, 'Bobbity' Cranborne, Anthony Eden, Duff Cooper and, of course, Winston Churchill were on one side: they were totally opposed to appeasement, believing that Hitler should be challenged immediately (Duff resigned from the Government over the issue, as did Vansittart, head of the Foreign Office). The Londonderrys, the Kemsley branch of the Berry family, and to some extent the Astors were for caution, veering dangerously towards conciliation, while among our own friends at least two of the Mitfords positively supported the Führer and his 'fight against Communism'.

Two years earlier Diana Guinness (*née* Mitford) had married Oswald Mosley in the home of Dr Joseph Goebbels, the German propaganda minister, in Berlin. Her sister Unity had been present, and Hitler had attended the wedding breakfast in the Goebbels' lakeside villa. Unity had afterwards taken up residence on the fringes of Hitler's court.

That summer my romance with Robert had become far more serious. We were very much in love, and longed to get engaged, but for a Cecil heir to give a solemn commitment to bring up his children as Roman Catholics seemed unthinkable, and both our families felt the problem to be insurmountable.

Although I had probably first fallen for Robert's looks and his lazy, quite unconscious charm, I had come to love him more and more because he was so genuinely honourable and good. When he confided both his sorrows and his ideals to me, I felt privileged, for with most people he was very reserved. He had both Cecil and Cavendish wit and intelligence, and a huge amount of *joie de vivre*, as well as wonderfully informed taste in someone so young. Once, we drove down to Hatfield after a ball in London to stop and look across a ride at the great Tudor building lying peacefully in the moonlight, and he told me that of all his family's possessions, this was the one he loved most, the one to which he felt dedicated and which he was determined to save for posterity.

One day we were both summoned to No. 1 Arlington Street, the Salisburys' house in London, and there old Lord Salisbury, Robert's grandfather, gently explained to me what the breaking of the family traditions and renunciation of their historic position as leaders of the Anglican community really meant. He did not ask me to give up my religion and convictions, which he respected; he merely asked us both to wait for a year and to avoid each other's company for that time, as much as possible. I held back my tears and thanked him, because he had been so courteous and kind, and obviously loved Robert, and also because he had convinced me of the importance of our decision for other people's lives as well as our own. We both promised to do our best about not meeting, and to wait a year.

And yet, however good my intentions, I still longed to marry Robert, and one day I joined a strangely assorted company on a pilgrimage to St Patrick's Purgatory on Lough Dergh, in County Donegal, to pray for the miracle that would resolve our problem. The sanctuary is on an island in the lough, which is supposed (though I doubt it) to have been visited by an early Celtic saint, and includes a large monastery and church. For three nights and two full days my cousin Sally Hardwicke, Mademoiselle Go-Go Schiaparelli and I followed a crowd of Irish pilgrims round six or seven small rock gardens or 'graves', named after early Irish saints, who had never actually been there, dead or alive. Barefoot and hungry, mumbling the requisite prayers, kneeling and rising from what, I think, were specially sharpened stones, we eventually came to rest in the lough itself, where we threw up our arms and renounced the 'world, the flesh and the devil'.

This was enjoyable, and somewhat soothed our aching feet and knees; but after a short communal meal of dry toast and black tea in the women's refectory, it was back to prayer, and we repaired to the gloomy church for an all-night vigil, relieved only by a scolding sermon and some bad singing. Next morning, still fasting, we again heard Mass, and by this time we felt on a kind of plateau, far above man's earthly struggles and more in touch with heaven. The sensation may have been produced by lack of food, but one source was certainly the real and tangible faith of so many good people all round us, some of whom were spending their only holiday of the year, some even their honeymoon, on the island.

A series of boats and buses brought us back across the lough, and me to the gates of Mount Stewart, where the Londonderrys had asked me to stay the weekend. I arrived at what I hoped would be nearly bedtime, because my fast would not end until midnight; but alas, dinner was late that night, and I was shown into the dining room and sat down next to Cousin Charlie, and had to refuse a series of delectable puddings and desserts and fragrant coffee, all waved under my nose. No one knew where I had come from, and I pleaded travel sickness as an excuse for not eating. You can bet I was first down to breakfast next morning!

Illyrian Spring

In the early spring of 1939 I was allowed to join my Moniack cousins Fanny and Sandy Fraser and an Oxford friend of Sandy on an exciting botanical expedition to Dalmatia (I think it was a kind of sop for not having let me try for Oxford myself). In our schoolroom days three of us had collected wild flowers and had been prize-winning members of the British Wild Flower Society, so we knew a bit about the subject; but we had also read Ann Bridge's much-acclaimed book, *Illyrian Spring*, and this had fired our imaginations. The idea of motoring across Europe, down the enchanted Adriatic coast, swimming in warm waters, visiting ancient monasteries and possibly driving up into the wild mountains of Montenegro thrilled us all.

The Alligator generously lent us his Chevrolet, and we set off with high hopes. Our expedition lasted a month, and apart from the moment when we turned the car over in the Swiss Alps, and when we found the Montenegrin passes blocked by snow, so that we could not reach Četinje, it all went according to plan. We spent Easter in Dubrovnik and saw the splendid theatre of Passion Week there, attending both the Catholic and Serbian Orthodox ceremonies. We also witnessed the surprise arrival of King Zog and Queen Geraldine from Albania, with what was supposed to be a week-old Albanian princeling (he was actually six months old: it was an early example of successful political spin). The royal family were fleeing from Mussolini's soldiers, who had just invaded their country.

It was disappointing that the road from Kotor to Četinje was closed; but this turned out a major blessing, for we decided instead to visit one of Dubrovnik's neighbouring islands, and we chose Korčula. So I have been able to crow, ever since, that *I* was the first to discover Korčula, at the age of eighteen, without any help from Partisans or my future husband.

It was a brief but happy visit: we learnt some local songs, visited the Franciscan monastery at Badia, and loved it all. We stayed for two nights in the Hotel Korčula on the quayside, where we were plagued by mosquitoes, and when I stood on the old-fashioned washstand in our room to swat one of the brutes, I unfortunately cracked its marble top. Next morning we absconded without paying for the damage, and I have felt guilty about it ever since. The other day, sixty years on, I offered to make good my debt, with interest, but the proprietors refused: instead, we celebrated Fitzroy's honorary Korčulan citizenship and our many years of friendship with several glasses of rakia.

By early 1939 there were quite a few Germans about, all wearing identical heavy-duty belted mackintoshes that must have been general Gestapo issue, and all obviously spying out the coast and quizzing its population. We did our best to confuse them, but on our way home even I woke up to the existence of international tension. When Sandy went back through the Austrian–Jugoslav frontier to post his Dalmatian hotel key, which he had inadvertently brought with him into Austria, he was grilled, accused of espionage and threatened; but what really shook him were the maps on the wall of the Austrian guardroom which clearly showed plans for the Führer's impending *Blitzkrieg*. At least half of Europe was coloured dirty brown and marked '*Deutschland*', with arrows pointing at the heart of Belgium, France and the Balkans.

*   *   *

At that time our circle of friends included a group known as the Liberal Girls, among whom were Laura Bonham Carter, Mary Asquith of Clovelly, Gay Margesson and Clarissa Churchill. They were mostly a bit older than me and were intelligent, attractive and well-educated, *having been to university*. Though they all became my friends later on, I was jealous of this and doubly jealous of Clarissa, the most beautiful of them all, as she was also fancied a lot by Robert.

It was through one of them that I met Philip Toynbee, whose father was the historian Arnold Toynbee, and whose mother was a Howard of Castle Howard. He had been sacked from Rugby just before his final exams, but had been taken in by the Ampleforth monks, probably because of his cleverness and his academic background and no doubt also because his mother had recently converted to Catholicism.

At Oxford he became a Communist rather than a Catholic (he told me, when he left the Communist Party three years later, that the two faiths were very much alike and he couldn't stand the discipline of either). When I met him he was drifting round London mostly living in rooms in Charlotte Street, the fashionable end of Bloomsbury, beginning to write, but still absorbed in left-wing politics. He taught me Communist Party songs, one of which went like this:

> *Long-haired preachers come out every night*
> *For to teach us what's wrong and what's right.*
> *But if you ask them for something to eat,*
> *They will answer in voices so sweet:*
> > *'You will eat, by and by,*
> > *In the glorious land beyond the sky*
> > *Work and pray*
> > *Live on hay-ay*
> > *You'll get pie*
> > *In the sky*
> > *When you die.*
> > IT'S A LIE!

The last line had to be shouted with terrific fervour. I didn't believe a word of it, but it was fun pretending to be a revolutionary.

Philip introduced me to the works of Auden and Isherwood: he read T.S. Eliot and Firbank aloud to me, and also Henry James's *The Turn of the Screw*, which sent me shivering into his arms. We would lunch at Schmidt's or a cheap but delicious Charlotte Street restaurant called the Étoile, and he sometimes took me to his local pub at the end of the street, where the poets Rabindranath Tagore and Dylan Thomas would be either declaiming or drunk, or both.

I met other clever people on my trips to Oxford, but, though I was bedazzled and entranced by this newly discovered intellectual life, short visits to the dreaming spires could not make up for my lack of learning, and I was never really part of the undergraduates' world, only an onlooker. Yet the boxes of curiosity and glimpses of beauty that were laid up in my empty head, labelled 'To be opened later', were very much part of my growing-up.

There were two young dons at Oxford whom I often met with Trim Asquith: Isaiah Berlin and John Sparrow. Isaiah used to come with us to high-brow concerts given by, I think, the Pro Arte String Quartet, and whisper sibilantly in my ear about the troglodytic qualities of all quartet musicians.

'You see the viola player's legs? They're at least a foot shorter than either yours or mine.' He used to make me shake with suppressed giggles instead of looking rapt as I should have, and the rest of the audience did.

Trim had discovered the Players' Theatre at the back of Charing Cross station, where thespians who were 'resting' or beginning their acting careers would perform burlesque music-hall songs under the direction of Mr Leonard Sachs, a Jewish musical genius. You had to be a member to get in, so as not to break some union or civic by-law, but you could bring as many guests as you wanted to and the show was known as *Ridgeway's Late Joys*. It was not expensive, so once word got around, it was crowded every night.

Mr Sachs sat at a table covered by a red velvet cloth, in a prominent position by the side of the stage, a gavel, a glass and the only bottle of wine in the house in front of him, and he would introduce the singers so enthusiastically that the audience would be in hysterics before the curtain rose.

'The one, the only, the greatest diva you will be likely ever to hear this side of Cricklewood [cheers], our own, our exquisite, our *unparalleled* nightingale [more cheers], Miss Joan STERNDALE *BENNETT*!'

Then he would bang with his gavel, up would go the curtain, and Miss Bennett would burst into song. The programmes, mostly resuscitating Victorian music-hall numbers, were a real joy, and the talent was of high quality, drawn from amazingly varied sources. There was a lovely man who sang gentle songs between a long rambling monologue – an academic who by day transcribed medieval manuscripts in the British Library. One of his songs went:

> *We're about to have a baby,*
> *And I'm to be the Pa,*
> *Tra-la-la* [I forget what]
> *Or if a Lady Baby,*
> *It will look like its Mama.*

I have always thought of female infants as Lady Babies ever since.

Most people knew that John Sparrow was homosexual, but I don't think I did, and he used to take me to the ballet in London and try out on me his ideas for new librettos. I thought Uncle Maurice's fairy-tale *Forget-Me-Not and Lily of the Valley* would make a wonderfully romantic ballet, and John suggested it to Frederick Ashton, a mutual friend. One day, as our friendship progressed, he brought patterns of pinstripe material and asked me to choose one for the new suit he was ordering; but such relative intimacy came, alas, to an abrupt end. From nursing by day and dancing by night, I was very short of sleep, and during a gala night at Sadler's Wells, when the proscenium lights turned low and the first ballerina flitted across the stage, I committed the unpardonable sin of falling fast asleep. He never asked me out again.

When Maurice Baring moved from Cheyne Row to Half-Way House at Rottingdean in Sussex, we sometimes used to visit him, and during the last summer before the outbreak of war my mother rented Enid Bagnold's (Lady Jones's) pretty Georgian house there, facing the duck-pond on the green. I didn't see much of Mumble that summer, and I only half-realised that my mother, Enid, Diana Cooper, Katharine Asquith and other devoted friends were all supporting him in the first stages of the dreadful illness that changed his life, imprisoning him within a nerve-racked, shaking body and tragically bringing to an end his career as a writer, the thing he cared about most.

Junie and I signed on for a new nursing course, this time to be trained as first-year VADs at the Royal Northern Hospital in Hammersmith. Our work now proved much more interesting and demanding, and off duty, we weeded out the debs' delights from our circle, making real and lasting friendships. Even with the threat of war on the horizon, there were many grand balls that spring and summer, and the grandest of all was the one given at Blenheim by Bert, the tenth Duke of Marlborough, and his long-suffering wife Mary, for their daughter Sarah. It was in July, and the magnificent Vanbrugh palace, its lake and terraces were spectacularly floodlit. Between dances couples wandered round the parterres and flowerbeds, which were lit by Chinese lanterns, and among them strolled musicians in Tyrolean costume, singing *gemütlich* Austrian songs. But to me this homely entertainment seemed to strike a wrong note: the palace deserved better, and grander, and it needed to be viewed from a distance.

Julian Amery and I escaped, and he drove me, rather erratically and in slalom fashion, in and out of an avenue of young lime trees. Then we stopped and looked back. I countered the Tyroleans by singing a Dalmatian sailors' song that I had learnt in Korčula, and he responded with '*Ochi Tcherniya*' ('Black Eyes') – for although still in his last year at Oxford, he was already fascinated by Balkan politics and espionage, and he had just returned from Jugoslavia, where he had been taught a little about both by Sandy Glen, our man in Belgrade.

We drove back to the ball feeling emotional and patriotic, ready to take on Germany, Hitler and all comers. But then, we were very young and pretty silly. It did not occur to us that if the Führer had dropped a bomb on Blenheim that night, he would have wiped out half the future War Cabinet, and a goodly part of the Establishment – such was the narrowness of the oligarchy that ruled our country before the Second World War.

In September that year the Northern Meeting ball ended dramatically. The long lines of dancers, their kilts and velvet doublets mingling with the scarlet or green mess dress of the soldiers and the sober blue of the Royal Navy, had just broken up as the men began leading their tartan-sashed and laughing partners down to supper, when there was a roll on the drums commanding silence, and an announcement was made over the Tannoy: 'Will all naval officers and regulars of the Highland regiments report for duty immediately.'

A buzz of consternation swept through the ballroom as the soldiers and sailors took leave of their girls and quickly disappeared. We felt as if we were attending the Duchess of Richmond's ball before the battle of Waterloo.

In every family in the land options were debated and plans made, abandoned and re-made as the war that now seemed inevitable crept ever nearer. Suddenly there appeared at Eilean Aigas an unexpected and not entirely welcome visitor: young Prince Frederick Hohenzollern, grandson of the late Kaiser, and a committed Anglophile. I had danced with him once or twice in London and had probably vaguely asked him to look us up if he ever visited the Highlands, but I scarcely knew him.

He came with a letter from the Duke of Buccleuch: 'Please be kind to Prince Fritzi. He is desperate not to be sent back to Germany, and can't stay here any longer as Drumlanrig is evacuating to London. Good luck!'

Everyone looked at me as if I were Mata Hari, but in the next few days we began to feel very sorry for the shy, rather boring and extremely polite young man. The German Embassy would ring him daily to urge him to return to Germany, and we would hear his agonised, *'Nein, nein, das kann nicht sein,'* as he argued on the only and very public telephone, in our dining room.

Finally my mother said to him, 'Sir, I really believe you should go back to London, but I see no need for you to report to your embassy. I'm sure you must have friends in our Foreign Office who will advise and help you.' This he did. He was interned in England for the duration of the war, but eventually emerged, married a Guinness heiress and had three beautiful daughters.

My brother Shimi and his lovely young wife Rosamund were living in the re-roofed but still unfinished Castle. Rosie was awaiting the birth of their first child, Simon, who was born a week after war was declared. Shimi was a major, and second-in-command of our family's regiment, the Lovat Scouts. Magdalen was at Longwood, her new home near Winchester, also expecting a baby, and Hugh had just come down from Balliol. He had left Oxford in a blaze of glory. As President of the Union he had organised the debate that reversed the Union's previous conclusion that 'This University will not fight in any future war'. He had helped Quintin Hogg win the Oxford City seat for the Tories, and he was obviously now destined for a political career. We had all really known this ever since, at the age of six, he had stood on a soapbox in the courtyard at Beaufort and shouted, 'Three cheers for Hugh Fraser!'

8

WAR: PINNER
AND PAIN

AUNT MOULLIE, WHICH IS SLANG GAELIC FOR MURIEL, WAS THE youngest of my father's sisters. Her vocation to become a nun and a nurse was clear and certain: and when she was twenty she joined the Society of St Vincent de Paul and began her training at St Thomas's, then the best teaching hospital in Britain, but her health broke down under its rigours and she had to go back home. Undaunted, she returned two years later and passed all her exams; then, having heard that Professor Sir Roderick Jones had started a hospital in Liverpool which dealt specifically with bone diseases, she finished her training with him.

After two years she knew enough to become matron in charge of a new hospital, St Vincent's at Pinner, just north of London, which would deal solely with orthopaedic patients. Within a few years she not only ran the hospital, but had created a kind of hospital kibbutz, where cured but unemployed and often unemployable ex-patients ran workshops, laundries, kitchen gardens and even a successful farm, for as well as being a superbly efficient and determined nurse, she was a country girl at heart.

Curing bone disease is a slow business, often taking two to four years or more. As much of the illness was tubercular in origin, the hospital was divided into warm wards and open wards, where the patients' beds were lined up in arched wooden pavilions open to the elements, which, especially in winter, made for chilly nursing. Money was always short, and St Vincent's was ever grateful for unpaid voluntary help. Aunt Moullie's large clan of nieces and cousins had nearly all done their stint on the open wards at Pinner, and in the autumn of 1939 it was Irene's and my turn.

When I arrived at the beginning of September, I was appointed to one of the boys' wards, and had bed-bound and walking cripples to look after. There was no political correctness in those days, and in Aunt Moullie's vocabulary a cripple was a cripple, meaning simply a patient who could not walk normally and whom she was determined to care for and help. The active ones ran about in leg-callipers and hopped on crutches, while the bed-bound ones, poor mites, were mostly strapped to the cruel, immobilising padded frames that were part of their post-operative cure. They lay on their backs for months on end, and had to be washed and fed and amused and comforted while they waited for their bone-grafts to grip. But they nearly all recovered eventually, which was a huge advance on all previous orthopaedic techniques.

Many came from the poorer parts of the East End, and a cheerier, wittier, naughtier bunch of kids it would be difficult to find. They taught me rhyming slang and East End doggerel songs (the chorus of one went 'More, more for the undertaker!').

The hospital had already been issued with gas-masks in cardboard boxes, and on 3 September 1939, although Mr Chamberlain's ultimatum to Hitler had not yet been answered, Aunt Moullie ordered a gas-mask practice to try them out. The result was chaos, but very funny. None of the masks fitted, some were without straps, and the children thought their first Christmas presents had just arrived. Some, though, choked and sobbed and nearly asphyxiated themselves.

There was a wireless in the staff room, and almost as soon as we had put the gas-masks back into their boxes, we heard the Prime Minister tell us, 'And as a consequence, we are now at war with Germany.' Ten minutes later we heard our first air-raid warning, but the horrible wail of the sirens did not panic Aunt Moullie.

'Let's wait and see what happens,' she told everyone. 'They're probably just practising too. Meanwhile, carry on with lunch.' As usual, she was right.

That afternoon I was off duty, and for the first time travelled on the Bakerloo line to London. It was like a dead city. Sandbags were piled in doorways and brown paper strips were pasted over every window; huge grey barrage balloons floated in the sky over Hyde Park. No shop was open. Our flat was closed and locked. I couldn't think of anyone to visit, so I bought an evening paper to read on my return journey. Suddenly I realised it was *Sunday*. War can be very disorientating.

For the next four months I nursed at Pinner by day and, if I was not on late duty, caught the six fifteen train up to London, returning at dawn on a milk train, having dined and danced and partied all night. London was far from dead: in fact, it was heaving with friends. Nearly all now appeared in uniform, looking unfamiliar but much more glamorous.

'I chose the air force,' said Simon Wardell, tossing back his golden locks. 'The uniform's so much more becoming, don't you think?'

Robert, like all his family before him, was a Grenadier, a second lieutenant, and he told me that as such he could no longer ride in a bus. Philip turned up as a temporary officer in the Welsh Guards, and some other friends, the more artistic ones, had followed Victor Cazalet into the Artists' Rifles, which was bursting with talent.

We no longer visited The Nest, but switched to that old Edwardian haunt the Café Royal in Regent Street, where one could drink and talk and toy with an ice-cream for ages without being asked to pay; or, if my friends were rich enough, to the underground Café de Paris, further down the street, where one could dine and dance and be entertained by brilliant cabaret artistes. Beatrice Lillie was the stage name of Lady Peel, who would sing witty songs lampooning all the fads and fashions of the moment. Camp old Douglas Byng was another star, and would appear in a chiffon toga, singing:

> *I'm Doris, the goddess of Wind,*
> *And I don't care a* puff *when I've sinned.*

Then there was the great Hutch, who sang Cole Porter's 'Night and Day', and 'I've got you under my skin', in a velvet baritone; and once Marlene Dietrich glided down its famous staircase in a gold spangled dress and long white fox-furs, singing in that inimitable, husky-harsh, don't-care voice that could suddenly turn intimate and sweet as honey, 'Oh, see what the boys in the back room will have'.

One night Philip came to say goodbye to me at King's Cross. He was only mildly drunk, and had begun an argument about the advantages and disadvantages of marrying me (he did this to a different girl nearly every week). It became so involved that he got into my carriage to carry on with it, and it was only at Potters Bar, when I finally convinced him there were endless *dis*advantages, that he got out of the corridorless train in a huff, leaving me alone with a likely rapist, with whom I played a kind of frightening musical chairs until we reached the next station.

That winter brought lots of enemy air-raids, and the sirens were always wailing. My mother, who had come back to the flat to see how we were all getting on, told Hugh and me of her plan for survival.

'You see, darlings, when the alarm starts, I just get into a taxi and ask the cabbie to drive round and round Hyde Park. They're so kind and so clever, and moving targets are *much* more difficult to hit!'

It was no good explaining: she was sure she had found the answer.

One afternoon, though, Hugh and I had a terrifying experience. The sirens had started, and we were about to walk up Edgware Road to tea with Moo in the Deep Purple flat. Suddenly we were rounded up by police and air-raid wardens. 'You can't be out on the street during a raid!' they yelled, and pushed us into the open doors of the Marble Arch tube station. There was no room, and more and more people were being herded in behind us. Hugh saw to his horror that at the bottom of the moving staircase people were beginning to fall, and he grabbed me by the hand and rushed me into the mouth of a 'No Entrance' tunnel. We were lucky to find an exit, and ran all the way back to the flat through side streets with sticks of bombs landing just behind us. They destroyed houses in Cumberland Place, with a few casualties, but many more people died in the tube stampede.

The Lister Sisters

This was the time when the long-suffering wives of my two 'wicked uncles' would come up to London to lunch with their sister Laura and pour out their perennial worries. Auntie Barbara Wilson fretted about her son Peter, who longed to join Sotheby's, which she couldn't afford (in those days you had to 'buy yourself in'), and Auntie Dimbo Westmorland agonised about her daughter Junie's love life, as well as about Burghie, her immensely elegant and sweet-natured third husband, who had once more succumbed to a bout of heavy drinking.

As for Peter, after a good deal of moaning and drama, I heard them agree that each sister should contribute a few hundred pounds towards granting him his wish – a move that eventually led to Sotheby's making millions through the 'poor boy's' business acumen, and earned Peter himself a fortune and a villa in the South of France.

Dimbo's problems were more intractable. Although she often threatened Uncle Burghie with banishment from Lyegrove, rows always ended in his being allowed to stay on. She had less control over Junie, who was hopelessly embroiled in an affair with Anthony Chaplin while working as a cryptographer at Bletchley. Whenever Dimbo confronted him about his intentions, he would make solemn vows that he would very soon divorce his wife Alvilde, from whom he was separated, and marry June – but the promises never came to anything.

It was about this time, too, that old Queen Mary paid Dimbo a visit. At the beginning of the war she had moved (with a staff of sixty) from London to Badminton, and had taken up residence there until such time as hostilities should cease. The Westmorlands were good neighbours of the Beauforts, whose home she had invaded, and to lessen the strain on them Dimbo invited the old Queen to tea and to a personally conducted tour of the famous Lyegrove garden. Young David, back from Eton on long leave, was told to watch out for the visitors' arrival, and hovered in the hall. When the Queen descended from the royal barouche, wearing her immaculate tulle toque and carrying a white lace parasol, David gave her his arm and politely offered to take it from her. But she held on to it firmly. There was a slight struggle, and, to his amazement and delight, out of its frilly folds fell a small pearl-handled revolver.

Queen Mary glared at him. 'One of these days they're going to try and kidnap me, you know. And if they do . . .' the old lady's jaw tightened, 'I mean to take one with me!' With which she gave David a defiant and somehow regal sniff and walked into the house.

My Auntie Barbara could also be very determined, and whenever we met I was rather alarmed by the sharpness of her wit and the firmness of her opinions. Grandpa Ribblesdale got her exactly right when he wrote to the Dolls in 1907:

> *Lady Wilson is at last better and now looks like nothing on earth . . .*
> *In spite of her indisposition, her spirit is not quenched. She is now*
> *fighting with (1) her parish council, (2) the rural district council,*
> *(3) the Duke of Devonshire, over their responsibilities for the repair*
> *of a few yards of road. She has notified the Duke that he must*
> *walk over her dead body before she will yield. Whether or not the*
> *nobleman will do so has not transpired.*

Auntie Dimbo was a great deal tougher than her delicate appearance suggested. No one could have suffered more tragedies in life, but, as her son Julian Fane wrote, she was sustained by 'a kind of jocular stoicism that recognised, and mocked, the machinations of fate. The word "jolly" was substituted for the word "tragic" – "Dear old X has been run over by a bus. Jolly, isn't it?" . . . "A jolly old massacre . . ."' Catastrophe could produce giggles, and sometimes laughter would ward off tears.

A major and final blow now befell her when her trusted solicitor, a salt-of-the-earth Yorkshireman, shot himself and was found to have embezzled almost half her fortune. She carried on living at Lyegrove, but in very reduced circumstances. Deliciously pretty, feminine, flirtatious and funny, Aunt Dimbo was perhaps more lightweight than her two sisters, but nevertheless a very courageous woman.

One evening that first winter of the war, by a strange trick of destiny, all the three men I have loved came together at a cocktail party given by old Lady Salisbury in Arlington Street. Her grandson Robert was there, of course, but the party was for a young naval officer, Lieutenant Alan Phipps, whose ship had recently returned to home waters after three years in the Mediterranean. His mother, Frances, had told Gomma that he knew scarcely any young people in London, so Robert suggested the party, after which twenty or so of our friends went on to dine and dance at the Café de Paris. Fitzroy Maclean, then still in the Foreign Office, came with Zara Mainwaring, but neither he nor Alan talked or danced with me that evening, though I was faintly aware of them both.

Other intimations of our destinies also went unnoticed – for by then there was no Nellie Cameron to read the tea-leaves at the bottom of my nursery cup. One evening Robert took me to a heavyweight championship boxing match at Olympia, and with a fellow-officer came a young and merry Irish girl with masses of golden-red hair, green eyes and a delicate, heart-shaped face, slightly spoilt by outsize yellow dangling ear-rings. She was only seventeen, and as she told us how she had just started nursing at Salisbury Hospital, she bubbled over with excitement, friendliness and *joie de vivre*. She was Mollie Wyndham Quin, the girl whom Robert – had he but known it – would one day marry, and who would – had *I* but known it – become my best friend. We watched Len Harvey knock out Jackie Doyle in the first round, then saw Mollie and her escort into a taxi, and went our different ways.

Aunt Moullie was having trouble with the air-raid wardens, because of the starched and folded white napkin that all Sisters of Charity wear on their heads. 'Sister Theresa,' they begged her, 'will you please not go outside at night when there is an air-raid on? The searchlights pick up your – *ahem* – head-dress, and it shines out in a very dangerous way.'

'I'm so sorry, officer,' Aunt Moullie answered dutifully. 'I won't do it again.' But she loved watching the night skies and the air battles over London, and from then on she would creep out with a black umbrella held over her offending coif, peeping upwards from under its brim.

Robert and I were seeing a lot of each other again, either in London or sometimes at Boofy and Fiona Gore's house at Hemel Hempstead. The war was our excuse for breaking pledges. Who knew if each meeting might not be the last? And who knows what might have happened if fate had not intervened?

At Pinner I had become a theatrical impresario, as well as a nocturnally absconding nurse. Our Christmas revue had taken a month to prepare and rehearse, and on the first night, as I came off stage, having sung 'My Heart Belongs to Daddy' like a proper trouper, in fish-net stockings and a borrowed silk top hat (to yells of approval from the young villains of my own ward), I was handed a telephone message marked *URGENT*. Would I please come to Room 23 of Sister Agnes's nursing home, in London, as Lieutenant Cecil wished to speak to me?

Between acts, as soon as I possibly could, I rang, and was told by a frosty night-nurse that 'Lord Cecil' had had a severe accident, and could not speak, as he was under sedation. I was in agony. I couldn't leave immediately, and next day I would be on duty. I didn't dare ring Robert's mother, and I imagined him dying without a last word. Finally I escaped from Pinner and rushed to Beaumont Street, in Marylebone.

There was very little I could see of poor Robert as he lay prone. On his way back from our last evening together he had run his car into a stone bridge, breaking his nose, his jaw and other bones. Now he was wired up and bandaged all over. I sat on his bed and we held hands, and then just what I prayed wouldn't happen *did* happen: in walked his parents, and his mother, Betty, looked at me with cold eyes and said icily, 'I thought nurses were told *never* to sit on patients' beds?'

I leapt up like a singed cat, smiled weakly at everyone, and left. Robert's father Bobbity came out with me to the anteroom and patted my shoulder, but said nothing.

At Christmas I went home, practically in mourning, for I knew it was the end of our love affair. I took to my bed with sinusitis and then bronchitis. I remember dear, clumsy old Stefan upsetting a jug of boiling friar's balsam, which I had been inhaling, all over me, just to add to my misery.

Robert had once told me that he would send me a family brooch or locket with 'It's better to have loved and lost than never to have loved at all' engraved on it. I thought he might have sent it then, or a letter, or even a Christmas card. But nothing came. Cecils are taught from birth to be cautious, and never to commit themselves on paper.

9

THE MAGINOT LINE

IN JANUARY 1940 AUBERON HERBERT'S ELDEST SISTER GABRIEL, who had been a heroine in the Spanish Civil War, was going out to France to join a mobile ambulance unit which was due to move up to the Maginot Line, and my sensible mother asked if she would take me with her as a VAD. Though some parents might have questioned the wisdom of such a plan, it was an inspired idea. Moo was a warrior who had no scruples about pressing her children into active service. She thought that the many families who were sending their loved ones to safe countries abroad showed both selfishness and defeatism, and said they reminded her of rats. We all felt elated when Queen Elizabeth announced: 'The children won't leave without me; I won't leave without the King; and the King will *never* leave.'

As I was being seen off at Inverness station, a special train pulled in, and Moo recognised Winston Churchill, wearing his Admiralty peaked cap and a jaunty air, getting out of a carriage to stretch his legs. Since he was an old friend of hers, she took me over to be introduced.

'This is my daughter Veronica, Winston,' she said. 'She's just going out to France to nurse the wounded. Would you be kind enough to give her a safe-conduct note, in case she gets into trouble? It could well save her life.'

As usual, my mother was being melodramatic, but Winston, who liked that sort of thing, gazed at me tenderly and immediately wrote on a piece of paper headed 'The Admiralty, Whitehall': 'To whom it may concern: I should be personally grateful if every assistance is given to Mlle Veronica Fraser, who is joining a mobile ambulance unit . . .' and so on, signing it 'Winston S. Churchill'.

I would give anything in the world to have that scrap of paper today, but it was left in my suitcase in a hotel in Neuilly when we went up to the front, and was lost forever with the fall of France.

Our unit, I found, consisted of an amalgamation of doctors from the American Hospital in Cannes and society members of the French Red Cross, all volunteers, as well as various volunteer drivers, both French and British, with a scattering of Parisian Mexicans, including the Yturbe brothers, who became great friends. I was thrown in at the deep end with all of them, but luckily one of my fellow VADs turned out to be Daisy de Brogli, daughter of Daisy Fellowes, the Parisian hostess and Singer sewing-machine heiress. 'Little Daisy', as she was called, was my age, and she took me under her wing and installed me temporarily in her flat. I was soon drinking in Parisian life in great gulps.

There was only one real drawback. My mother had failed to make any financial arrangements for me, either being too vague or thinking I would be supported by the unit; so, once my travel money ran out, on days and nights when I wasn't asked out by my new friends, I virtually starved. I learnt to live on a pot of yoghurt and a plate of onion soup a day – but even that cost money, and soon I was down to yoghurt.

Then I remembered that Maurice Baring's brother, also known as 'Uncle Hugo', was something or other in the Bank of Westminster, in the Place Vendôme. He turned out to be head of it, and I was soon ushered into his presence at the top of the building in a lovely, un-officey room looking out over plane trees towards the Ritz Hotel on the other side of the square.

When I explained my dilemma, he immediately opened an account for me, put some money into it, gave me some cash, made lots of jokes and took me to lunch at the Ritz. There he made me promise that I would call in at the bank once a week 'to regulate my financial position', which I did.

On those occasions he would ring a bell, and a uniformed bank official would come in, bow and hand him my passbook, which he would carefully study. If my account was overdrawn, he would reach in his pocket and produce the necessary to bring it back into credit, and then say, 'Well – that's that. Now let's go and have some lunch, and you can tell me all the gossip.' I looked forward enormously to these financial transactions.

Our movement orders were constantly expected, and constantly delayed. The unit was supposed to move up to the Maginot Line in the New Year, then in late January, then in February. One rumour suggested that the delay was being caused by the fact that our uniforms were not ready. These were being made for us, free of charge, by no less a couturier than Lanvin, and our team-leader, Madame du Luart, kept changing her mind about the style.

There were lots of jokes. I was christened 'la femme fatale' because I had unwisely told Daisy about my broken heart. There was also much impatience, and finally Gabriel, fed up with the waiting, left in a huff. But soon afterwards everything was ready, down to the last bandage and button, and orders came through that we were to be inspected the very next day by Madame Pétain on the Champ de Mars, before moving out of Paris and setting off for the north, with General George and the 4ième Armée.

In the morning the unit formed up in position, but I had been given the unenviable task of announcing to the President's wife that we were ready for inspection. I was rehearsed by a friend, who told me, 'You simply go up to her apartment, knock on the door, salute, and say, "Madame la Présidente, les estafettes vous attendent", and then lead her down to her car and its outriders.'

It didn't sound too difficult, and my salute was admirable, but unfortunately I forgot the word estafettes and inadvertently substituted estapettes, which I had heard recently (it means 'gigolos'). The general's wife gave me a queer look and swept downstairs to her waiting cortège. The inspection then took place as planned. We were told to reassemble at dusk, given our positions in the convoy, and at last we were off – but I was never allowed to forget my gaffe.

Driving at a snail's pace, the speed of the slowest vehicle in the huge and composite cohort which we joined, was a bit tedious in daytime, but when dusk fell and we arrived in a small town or village, we would take the place over and bivouac for the night. The maréchal des logis would stride up and down the line of vehicles with lists in his hands, shouting out orders, and we would tumble, stiff-legged and nervous, from our lorry-cabs to search for the quarters he had allocated us. Sometimes we would be received with friendly enthusiasm and asked to share the family's supper; but as we drew nearer to Metz, our hosts became less pleasant, and we would unroll sleeping-bags and eat our rations in their parlours or bedrooms in gloomy silence.

It took four days to reach our destination, a small *château* outside a village whose name we never knew because all the signposts had been removed or blanked out, for we were only a dozen kilometres from the Maginot front-line defences, roughly where the British and French armies met and overlapped. Because of this, the sector was often probed for weaknesses by the Germans on the other side of the line, and we had to deal with casualties from the moment we set up shop.

The wounds were often severe, as the two sides sat glowering at each other on either side of a barrier that did not really exist, and in that early stage of the war there were no casualty clearing stations, so that we would sometimes receive amputation or multiple-wound cases. It was to one of these that, shortly after we arrived, I behaved so badly and irresponsibly that I shall never cease to regret it.

Corporal Balls had been brought in after being blown up by a mine; his right leg was shattered and would have to be amputated below the knee. The poor lad was desperate about it, for he loved football and knew he would never be able to play again. As we prepared him for the operation, he begged me to be with him when he woke up, even if I was off-duty. I promised I would, and then wheeled him down to the theatre to be anaesthetised.

That afternoon, while he was in theatre, a small contingent of Seaforth Highlanders happened to pass through the village, and, hearing that a Scottish VAD was nursing at the *château*, two officers called in. They were two of my oldest friends, Pat Munro of Foulis and Colin Mackenzie of Farr, and they bore me off for tea and gossip in their temporary mess. Time flew, and when I looked at my watch, my heart sank, for I knew Corporal Balls would be back in my ward, alone, possibly conscious and miserably contemplating his bandaged stump. In fact when I came to his bedside, he had been sedated and was only just conscious, but he looked up and said, 'You promised . . .' and a tear slid down his cheek. I felt awful, and still do whenever I think of him.

In the convalescent rooms were two bearded giants from the Foreign Legion. They were due to be released in a few days' time, but this meant they would miss *la fête du régiment*, which was due the very next day, and they pleaded with the doctors to sign them out early. The doctors were adamant that they could not go until a specialist had seen them. When I looked in and found the room unnaturally tidy, I became suspicious of their plans, so, as a precaution, I removed their khaki trousers from a cupboard and told them to be good boys and go to sleep. An hour later, when I checked again, I saw to my horror two empty beds: the curtains were blowing, a sash window was open, and knotted sheets were tied to a shutter. The legionnaires, *sans culottes*, were on their way, and I must say, I couldn't help cheering for them.

Hitler planned to attack the Maginot Line on 6 May, and our commandant's husband, Le Comte Laddy du Luart, who was high up in the French War Ministry's intelligence department, must have known of the deadline, and warned his wife, for just a week before it she sent for me and another young French VAD and told us we were dismissed! We must return to Paris, or wherever, *immediately*, she said, as she could no longer be responsible for any girl under the age of twenty-one. I pleaded to be allowed to remain, but she was stony-faced, and told us that transport had been arranged, and we were to leave that very afternoon. There was nothing for it but to pack up and go.

On 30 April 1940 Paris was in turmoil. Half the population seemed to be loading cars, besieging ticket offices, queueing on station platforms. I went straight to Uncle Hugo and asked his advice. He told me that without the unit my position was hopeless, and that I must go back to London and review it. But how? He gave me a letter to General Hugo, Victor's grandson, who was in charge of civil evacuation. After three days of queueing I reached the General, who read the letter slowly, then reached for a chit, which he stamped. 'I hope, mademoiselle,' he said with a charming smile, 'that next time you come to Paris, it will be in happier circumstances. Meanwhile, *bon voyage!*'

The aeroplane that took off from Neuilly was very old, and at one point there was a grinding noise, and it turned back as if to re-land, then changed its mind and flew to Hendon, where we landed safely on 4 May. In spite of my disappointment, I was overjoyed to be with the family again. Rose was doing lessons with Mig Phipps at West

Stowell, her home near Marlborough, so Moo and Kiwi were back in the Deep Purple flat.

On 6 May the real war began, and we held our breath as the German *Blitzkrieg* swept over Belgium and northern France, and the British Expeditionary Force retreated slowly to the Channel ports. The Highland Brigade were bottled up at St Valéry, and many of our Scottish friends were taken prisoner. It was a terrible time, with nothing but bad news from every side.

Junie was still decoding ciphers at Bletchley Park, and her romance with Anthony continued to keep the Lister sisters busy worrying. Irene was at Pinner, doing serious nursing, but hoping soon to become engaged to George Jellicoe, of whom she was seeing a lot. All my other friends were in uniform, or doing some useful form of war work.

Abandoning hope of rejoining the ambulance unit, I volunteered for the Motor Transport Corps, which I thought would be the best bet for returning overseas. Dressed in khaki overalls, we drilled in London squares and spent many of our waking hours under the bonnets of trucks and lorries, learning the mysteries of the internal combustion engine. At night we gathered on a rooftop, where some of our officers must have been in charge of a searchlight or listening station. As the fighting drew nearer, we could hear the boom of big guns across the Channel quite clearly.

One day I was able to visit Trim, who was with a training battalion at Folkestone, waiting to go overseas, and there the guns sounded even louder. Yet we spent a happy afternoon picnicking on the cliffs above the harbour. His gas-mask case was full of the wild flowers he had collected on the downs, the gas-mask absent. 'You'll never make a soldier!' I chided, and he smiled. We said goodbye, and he went back to his lines, and I to my rooftop in London. Two days later the evacuation of Dunkirk began.

The civilian French who escaped with our armies were rounded up and put in a transit-camp-cum-temporary prison at Olympia, in West London, until they could be sorted out, and any German spies (invariably reported to be dressed as nuns) arrested. 'Look at their feet,' I was told. 'If they have too big feet, apprehend or report them.'

I had volunteered to interpret and to help feed the refugees, who were a woeful sight. Nowadays we are inured to seeing the thousands of tragic displaced and dispossessed people that the twentieth century has spawned, but in 1940 it was shocking. So many families had been broken up, and so many cared only whether their sons, husbands or fathers were still alive. I must have written hundreds of letters that week, and filled in a thousand forms, for many of the people were peasants, bewildered by their transportation to a strange country whose language they couldn't even speak.

One evening I was taken out to dinner, and afterwards to the Four Hundred nightclub, by a young Free French officer who called himself Michel Coulon, though that was not his real name. When we said goodnight and goodbye, he asked me to marry him, for he was going back to join the Resistance in southern France, and he said it would make him happy to know he had someone to return to. It was a very sad moment. I never saw him again, and it was only too likely that he was eventually betrayed and shot by the Gestapo.

10

ALAN I

Alan Phipps, brother of Mig, who had done lessons with Rose, was also a survivor from Dunkirk and was on 'survivor's leave' when I met him, for the second time, at the end of July 1940. His destroyer, HMS *Ivanhoe,* had received a direct hit on its last crossing, but had managed to limp into port and was now being refitted at Chatham dockyard. It had done its bit, sailing day and night for five days without respite, and had evacuated over six thousand soldiers from the beaches.

He seemed to me not only a hero, but by far the most attractive of an attractive family. He had light-coloured eyes in a tanned face, a wide mouth, a delightful grin and very thick dark hair. He also had a quick wit, with just a touch of zaniness, enormous courtesy and great charm. Though only two inches taller than me, he was strong and fit, and gave the impression of being very alert and alive, fearing nothing and ready for anything. He was hugely generous, self-deprecating, sensitive and totally without vanity – but that I learnt later. I found him irresistible.

We went out every night together for a whole week, at the end of which he proposed to me, sitting on a bench in Regent's Park, with searchlights combing a sky which still managed to be full of stars. As he had barely a month of leave, our engagement lasted only a fortnight, and the speed of everything drove our parents wild. My godfather Maurice Baring gave me my wedding dress, and Worth's Madame Marthe, who had made my coming-out one, was delighted and fitted it in record time.

We were married in the Church of the Assumption, behind Regent Street, on 12 August 1940 by Father Vincent McNab, now a very old man, with Alan's brother William, aged five, to hold my train, wearing a white sailor-suit from Gieves with a real bosun's pipe, which he occasionally blew. Since Alan was first lieutenant, or number one (second-in-command) on *Ivanhoe*, and very popular, his sailors pulled our car on ropes halfway down Regent Street. Then at the party we gave in rooms near Tite Street for the entire ship's company, his coxswain stood on a chair to drink our health and told us solemnly, 'You must always remember who is the captain and who is number one,' after which cryptic remark he called for 'Three cheers, lads!', fell off the chair, and then ordered 'Another three!' from a recumbent position on the floor.

Alan's parents, Eric (always known as 'Pike') and Frances Phipps (known, no less mysteriously, as 'Brown'), joined forces with Moo to give us a lovely reception in Sargent's old studio flat in Tite Street. Pike had rented it when he retired from the British Embassy in Paris, where he had been Ambassador from 1937 to 1939, and it had an iron staircase which led down from the great studio room to a garden below, so there was plenty of space. It was nice to think that my grandfather Ribblesdale had often visited it, and perhaps even been painted there.

By then Maurice Baring was nearly bedridden at Half-Way House in Rottingdean, and since he had met Alan as a midshipman in the battleship *Queen Elizabeth* when he went on summer cruises with his friend Admiral Fisher, he was doubly delighted by the wedding. We had promised we would visit him before we went north, so that was where we started our honeymoon.

His illness had been diagnosed as *Paralysis agitans* (now called Parkinson's Disease) and he was very shaky. Nevertheless, he and his devoted Australian nurse, Jean Neill, had a delicious dinner waiting for us in his willow-patterned, book-lined sitting room, and after it we talked happily until nearly midnight. Then Mumble said, 'Well, you must both be tired, so I'll say goodnight. Nurse will show you to your room. Sleep well, my dear ones, and thank you for coming.' It was a very gentle and civilised start to our married life.

Shimi and Rosie had lent us their Aston Martin for the second part of our honeymoon, and we drove over to Morar and stopped to thank them at Lochailort, where Shimi was training his future commandos; but he was out on the hill and we couldn't find Rosie. We stayed in Cross Farm, between Arisaig and Morar, as I had always vowed I would, looked after by Annie MacDonald, old John's daughter (whose house on the headland of Camus Darroch Bay was given a steeple when *Local Hero* was filmed there many decades later). Alan passed the test by loving it all. We sailed over to Simon Lovat's island in Loch Morar (Alan showing off) and fished in the pool below the falls (Veronica showing off), and I even caught a small salmon for supper.

I had very little idea of what it would be like to be a naval officer's wife in war-time. Indeed, I had very little idea what a first lieutenant's life was like anyway. 'You've got eyes that crinkle at the corners, as if you are always looking out to sea,' I told Alan lovingly. 'It's the gin!' was his answer, which didn't get me much further. But gradually he opened up and told me about Dunkirk.

What was still troubling him was that on one of his trips back and forth from *Ivanhoe* to the long line of men wading out from the beach to be evacuated, a soldier had suddenly panicked and rushed the whaler of which he was in charge, and was about to be followed by others. Alan had stood up and fired his revolver into the air and shouted, 'Stand back, or you'll sink us!' but still they came, and he had shot again, this time at the soldier, who had fallen back into the water. He didn't know whether the man was alive or dead, but it stopped the stampede and they pulled away with yet another boatload. Next time he went over, there was no sign of a wounded or dead soldier, so he imagined another boat might have pulled him out, or that he had indeed drowned.

Alan wrote well, and loved writing, and he was very proud when one of his articles was published in the *Weekly Review* of 25 July 1940. It gave a vivid idea of life on destroyers at that time, and he showed it to me:

We have done, like all destroyers, a bit of everything. There have been survivors, shivering with cold, that we have picked up many miles from land. We have wrapped them up in warm blankets and put them to sleep in some willingly vacated sailors' hammocks. There have also been quite a lot of German prisoners, who could

*not understand why our sailors were so kind to them, giving them
cigarettes and warm food.*

*We have escorted convoys, we have patrolled the coasts and the
Channel. We have screened the Battle Fleet. We have seen the calm,
warm Mediterranean, and have rolled and pitched and tossed in
the wide Atlantic. For days on end we have shivered in the Arctic
Circle, while the seamen's mess-decks have been partly under water
and spray has drenched the lookouts and gun crews.*

*We have spent long nights closed up at action-stations watching
in the inky blackness for a sudden E-boat, and when day broke
watching the clouds with the same vigilance for enemy aircraft.
We have fired our guns in the still waters of Norwegian fjords and
heard their echoes in the snowy mountains. We have embarked and
landed troops and stores – and we have many times been attacked
by German planes.*

*We were at Dunkirk ... The text books will tell you that
six hundred soldiers can be embarked in a destroyer. On each
of our trips we never had less than one thousand, and we made
six trips.*

*Eight officers and one hundred and fifty men all living very
close together; long periods at sea in all weathers; very limited leave,
moments of acute excitement and stretches of extreme and tiring
monotony; periods when the world and family and friends seem very
far away. That is life in destroyers. But there are very few of us who
would exchange it for the comparative comfort of a battleship, or
the fixed and certain routine of a shore establishment.*

*Come on board any day and you will see our battle-honours
carved in oak on the quarterdeck: 1794 The Leeward Isles; 1854
Bomarsund; 1915 The Dardanelles. There is another which is blank.
We are going to fill that in ourselves.*

Alan told me that he was always seasick for the first three days at
sea, and that it started when he heard the anchor chain winding up.
'But so was Nelson,' he added defensively. He said that one of the
crew, the 'Postie', was always put in charge of the ship's cat, and that
the crew nearly mutinied when, after a plethora of kittens, the ship's
doctor suggested neutering Moggy. 'She's got to have her fun when
we're ashore, same as the rest of us, ain't she?' they told him.

Alan told me the dockers in Liverpool were especially mean, as they stole the rations out of the lifeboats and then buttoned back the covers so that the theft shouldn't be discovered; that a survivor from a North Atlantic convoy could last only five minutes in the water because of the cold; and that he had tried to grow a moustache and beard to avoid shaving in often icy water. (Naval officers, unlike soldiers, have to grow both, if either, and have to ask permission from their commanding officer.) It hadn't been a great success and Alan's captain had sent for him and said, 'You look like a rat peeping through oakum. Shave it off!' – which he did, thank God.

I learnt that the captain of a ship always ate alone in his cabin, but that the first lieutenant messed with the other officers in the wardroom; that the engineer was called 'Chief' or 'Chiefy', and that destroyer officers drank in harbour, but never at sea; that a second Plymouth gin-and-water was 'the other half', and a few other things that every sailor's wife ought to know.

He did not tell me much about the war. Rather, he reminisced about his childhood – holidays in the British embassies in Vienna and Berlin, a happy prep school at Summerfields, in Oxford, and a less happy Dartmouth. Then a riotous time at Greenwich with like-minded tearaway young officers, who played as hard as they worked; and then his first posting as a duly brevetted midshipman or 'snotty' to the battleship *Queen Elizabeth*, the pride of our Mediterranean fleet and the flagship of Admiral Fisher, who was Maurice Baring's great friend. In particular, he told me how, when Mumble was the Admiral's guest on their summer cruises, his birthday would always be celebrated by a party for the young officers, which invariably ended with MB diving overboard in full evening dress and shouting, 'Help!', to be instantly followed by the entire wardroom, in mess kit.

It was for the *Queen Elizabeth*'s young officers that Uncle Mumble wrote this ballad:

> *I can't drink whisky with a grin,*
> *And soda cocktails make me sick,*
> *And bitters neat has too much kick.*
> *I think this ship is far too quick,*
> *But since you summon me to quaff,*

For once I don't mind giving in –
I think I'll have the other half.

I have drunk Han-Shen at Pekin,
And shandy-gaff at Eton Wick;
Deep draughts of Pilsner at Berlin
And Viking's Head at Reykjavik,
And Benedictine made from brick
And vodka with a Russian staff.
You say there's something in the bin?
I think I'll have the other half.

My head will soon begin to spin;
My utterance is growing thick;
I've sprained my thumb and bruised my shin
And broken someone's walking-stick;
I cannot see the fingers flick,
I cannot read the barograph,
But just to drown the taste of gin,
I think I'll have the other half.

Envoi

Prince, though I hate the taste of gin,
I can't think why that makes you laugh.
I'm feeling very well within,
I think I'll have the other half.

Alan also told me that when his mother had become a Catholic he had followed her happily into the Church, as it had seemed to him the obvious and natural thing to do, and that he had fitted very comfortably into the Catholic faith. It was really what he had always believed in, and he had needed no theological argument to convince him. Many of the clever people he admired, like Hilaire Belloc and Archbishop David Mathew, were Catholics and he felt completely at home with the ordinary people who heard Mass in the beautiful churches of Vienna, or Malta, or the Mediterranean ports of Italy and France.

On our way back to Inverness, we stopped again at the Inverailort Inn. Archie MacFarlane, who was a Lovat Scout reservist as well as head stalker at Stronelairg, my cousin Bill Stirling, my brother Shimi and

Commander Geoffrey Congrave were training officers on hill and sea for future Combined Operations and the Inverailort Inn had become the famous centre of their off-duty activities. Shimi and Rosie were living there during the week, but they had also rented a cottage nearby for Napoleon Tansy, who had by then side-stepped from Moniack, and their baby son. A few mornings before our arrival, Tansy had looked out of her window at about six a.m. and had seen a large black submarine that had surfaced in the bay below the little house. At first she thought it was part of a commando exercise, but when the conning-tower opened and some very German-looking submariners emerged to take the air, she decided that caution was the better part of valour and crept downstairs and locked the door. She had no telephone or other means of communication, and it wasn't until evening that she was able to tell her story to her amazed and at first incredulous employers. But there were physical signs of the submarine's visit – oil and beer cans – and finally she was believed.

'I wish I'd had a gun,' she said. 'I would have shot the lot.'

'Thank goodness you didn't,' was the official verdict.

We spent the last week of our honeymoon with my new in-laws at West Stowell, their pretty Queen Anne farm-turned-manor-house in unspoilt country at the foot of the Wiltshire Downs. Frances Phipps had made it into a pleasant and comfortable home, to which Eric had retired – rather sooner than he had expected – the previous year.

Pike had been successively British Ambassador in Vienna, Berlin and Paris, until in 1939, shortly before war was declared, he was somewhat brusquely replaced by a much less experienced diplomat. That this had something to do with Sir Robert Vansittart, Pike's brother-in-law and head of the Foreign Office until he resigned, must be an obvious conclusion, for the two men and their wives, who were sisters, disliked each other intensely, and had been on opposite sides during the Munich crisis. In Berlin Pike had seen how formidable Hitler's Wehrmacht and particularly his air force had become, and his dispatches had argued for caution and immediate re-armament at home; but Van saw this as appeasement, and did much to sully Pike's reputation.

Eric was the son of Sir Constantine Phipps, a cadet of the Normanby family, who had been Ambassador in Lisbon, and his beautiful and neglected wife. Rumour had it that Eric's real father was the Portuguese

Don Juan and Edwardian man about town, the Marquis de Soveral, although others hinted, over the port, that in fact it had been the Bourbon King of Portugal himself who had seduced the beautiful and lonely Lady Phipps. Eric certainly did not look like Sir Constantine, who was tall and blond, with magnificent whiskers, being small and dark and neat, 'like a Hungarian fly', as he once described himself over the telephone to a stranger who asked how he could be recognised.

His mother died when he was still a small child, and he was brought up by a conspicuously indifferent father, who would take him to his London clubs, tell him to wait with the porters at the door until collected, and then forget all about him until night fell, when the poor little fellow, who had gone to sleep on his hard mahogany bench, would be wakened, piled into a hansom cab and returned to the care of his father's domestics.

Yet little Eric was clever and scholarly, and eventually passed into the Foreign Office with top marks. Almost his first posting was to the Paris Embassy, during which he fell in love with, married and devotedly cared for a beautiful but consumptive French lady who was twelve years his senior, and died two years after their wedding.

His second spell in the French capital was a great deal happier. In 1909, once more *en poste*, he met three unconventional young brothers whose father, Herbert Ward, was an equally unconventional Irish artist, sculptor and anthropologist with a studio in Paris and a house outside it on the River Seine. He had led an adventurous life in Australia and Africa, and had married an American heiress against her parents' wishes. The Wards' elder daughter, known as Cricket, was eighteen, exceptionally attractive and already on the lookout for a husband; and when the bright young diplomat from the British Embassy began to call, she thought he was courting *her*. In fact it was her younger sister, who had large grey eyes in a heart-shaped face, played practical jokes and boisterous games with her brothers, and espoused romantic causes and underdogs, who captured his heart. He proposed to her, rather unsteadily, while skating round the Palais de Glace, and she accepted immediately. 'He seemed so nice, and I thought it would be rude to say no,' she told her astonished parents and rather cross sister.

The Phippses had six children, spread over twenty years and born in different countries: two boys, two girls, and then two more boys, the youngest of whom, William, had been my only attendant at our wedding. He had been born in Berlin, on – to my mother-in-law's chagrin – Hitler's birthday. The Führer had sent a bunch of red roses round to the Embassy, which Brown dutifully acknowledged and threw straight into the nearest dustbin.

While we were honeymooning at Morar, Mumble had been moved from Rottingdean to Scotland by my mother and Nurse Neill, for the stress of the air-raids on London and the south coast had become unbearable. In spite of leaving behind his home, his books and his belongings, including innumerable scrapbooks and the small picture-gallery of inspirationally beautiful women that stood on his mantelpiece or hung on the William Morris-papered walls of his writing room, he settled with relief into the quiet tempo of life at Eilean Aigas. There I found him at peace and relatively comfortable; but from then on he was bedridden, and except for the occasional moves of the whole household back to Beaufort, five miles away, he never left his room.

I, too, settled down to wait, but the call from Alan came sooner than we had expected. 'Marvellous news!' he told me on the telephone one evening at the end of September. 'Come down to Hull at once. I've booked a room in The Ship Hotel and I'll see you on Sunday. Champagne and hugs for dinner.' And so, after a difficult journey, I managed to arrive at The Ship, a pleasant small hotel outside Grimsby, in good time and was shown up to a chintzy, old-fashioned bedroom with a very large brass bed.

It was the first time I had ever stayed in a hotel on my own, and I felt very grown-up, but also a bit shy of starting conversations with the other naval wives, the predominant guests. There was a scribbled note from Alan, written the same day as he had telephoned. 'I'll explain everything when we meet, but it looks as if we'll be here for a bit and I can sleep ashore quite often, darling, so dig in. See you at eight on Sunday.'

I decided not to go down to dinner till he arrived, but left a message at the reception desk. Eight o'clock came and went. The clock in my bedroom ticked away. At nine thirty I went down and asked, 'Any messages?'

'No, madam.'

Fancy being called 'madam'! It looked as if all the wives had finished their dinners and turned in, and the waiters were busy laying up for breakfast. I retired to our bedroom, telling myself that this was probably the usual form and I must get used to it. Hungry, but philosophical, I got ready for bed.

Half an hour later there was a knock at the door and a matronly naval wife came in with a glass in her hand. 'Drink this, dear, and you'll feel better. Then I'll tell you what's happened.'

Obediently I gulped it down and choked. I hate whisky drunk indoors, especially with soda, but she paid no notice and began: '*Ivanhoe* was laying mines off the Dutch coast, but early this morning something went wrong: she hit a mine and is out of action. I don't think there have been casualties, thank heavens, but she's drifting and, as she mustn't fall into enemy hands, the captain has left a demolition party on board to blow her up and sink her. Your husband's in charge, and he'll follow as soon as they get her to sink. Don't worry, my dear; I expect he'll be here by morning. Try to get a little sleep.' She patted my shoulder, made a wry face and left.

Sleep was impossible, but it was not until much later that I discovered the full horror of the situation. Despite all efforts, brave old *Ivanhoe* refused to sink, and when morning came, and the mists lifted, she was spotted by the Luftwaffe and became a sitting target. But before my imagination could conjure up anything worse than what was actually happening, there was another knock on the door: 'You're wanted on the telephone.'

My heart leapt, but it was Moo, not Alan, on the line, and her voice kept breaking as she told me her unbelievable news. Rose, darling, sweet, holy little Rose, had died that evening.

'But how?' I cried. '*How* did she die? She was quite well when I left.' I was almost angry with my mother, and with the shock.

'We don't know. It must have been her heart. An aneurysm, they think. You know how she always said the Rosary before supper in Kiwi's bedroom? Well, about seven o'clock this evening she suddenly said to Kiwi, "I feel so tired, Koggs. I think I'll lie down on your bed."

'She closed her eyes and lay very still. Kiwi thought she'd fainted and rushed for Mumble's nurses, but they couldn't revive her. Her heart had simply stopped beating, and she was dead.'

There was a pause, and then my poor mother asked, 'Will you come back? Alan will understand.'

When I told her some of what was happening to Alan, she immediately empathised. Moo was always at her supreme best in moments of crisis.

'Then of course you mustn't come. Ring me as soon as you hear, my poor darling. We love you, and we'll all pray for you both.'

Early next morning Alan's captain rang and told me to go to London and wait there. He didn't seem to have any solid news, or couldn't tell me if there was any, over an open telephone, but I gave him the Tite Street number, hired a taxi to Grantham, and caught a train that seemed to take for ever.

It was in Tite Street, in that beautiful studio drawing room where we had been so happy only three weeks earlier, that something very strange happened: something I cannot explain. I had been praying as I'd never prayed before, and telling Rose that, since presumably she'd only just arrived in heaven, she must do something quickly, and ask God personally to bring Alan back to me.

Suddenly there was a clear, loud noise of singing all round me, inside me and outside me, and a very bright golden light shone in the room, as if the sun was rising over a hilltop and illuminating a dark landscape. I have often tried to remember what that heavenly host, if such it was, was singing, and I think it was the hymn we used to sing at my convent school at Easter, 'Christus vincit, Christus regnat, Christus imperat', especially the last line, which seemed to resonate triumphantly.

It lasted less than half a minute, but I was now convinced that all would be well. Not long afterwards, a redirected telegram from Alan arrived, saying he was on his way, and to wait for him where I was.

The full story of the loss of Ivanhoe and its aftermath was wretched. On the night of 30 September, she and two other destroyers had blundered into a newly laid German minefield. There were two explosions, which killed many of her sailors, and one of them started a fire. In the dark there was much confusion. In spite of the damage, Ivanhoe went to the help of HMS Esk, which had also been hit, and picked up many of her survivors as she was sinking. HMS Essex was also badly holed but was able to limp home.

Ivanhoe managed to put out the fire, but her back was broken and she could not get up enough steam to make port. She was also drifting dangerously towards the enemy coast. Philip Haddow, Alan's captain (and his best man at our wedding), decided he must abandon her and save the lives of the *Esk*'s men and his own remaining crew, so the next day he transferred them to another destroyer, leaving Alan, a petty officer and two ratings to blow up *Ivanhoe* and sink her. But despite all their efforts she wouldn't go down. They were spotted by enemy aircraft, which came out of the mist and strafed them, and it was only a torpedo from another of our own destroyers which finally achieved her end.

Alan later received a Mention in Dispatches for 'coolness and resource' when *Ivanhoe* was sunk, but there was an inquiry, and poor Philip was reprimanded for not making greater efforts to bring his ship home, which his own officers knew was grossly unfair. The criticism blighted his career, and though he eventually was given another command, he never recovered his old spirits, and he was killed in 1944 during the Algiers landing.

Alan lost all his possessions, except for the sea-stained commonplace book we had started together at Morar, which opens with Lear's ballad, 'My aged Uncle Arly', and its refrain, 'But his shoes were far too tight.' We went down to Chatham together to say goodbye to Philip, and Alan started his second 'survivor's leave', which we spent this time at West Stowell.

Moo had asked me to write Rose's obituary for *The Times* – though she doubted whether the newspaper would print one for a mere child – and so I travelled up to London by train with Pike one morning and nervously showed him what I had written. He read it slowly, and then, before handing the sheet of paper back, took out a white handkerchief and dabbed his eyes. In that moment I knew that my words were all right, and that *The Times* would print them. I knew, too, that I loved my father-in-law, who was a kind and good as well as a wise and clever man.

My piece appeared in the obituary column a few days later:

The Hon. Rose Fraser

'Et Rose, elle a vécu ce que vivent les roses
– l'espace d'un matin.'

She was called Rose; she died quietly and gently on Saturday

*evening, like a shy flower closing its petals after the brief glory of
a summer day. Everything that she had found time to do during
that too-short day was gentle and flowerlike in quality; and she was
well named. Her fragrance will only be remembered by the very few
who stooped to discover it, but to them the world will seem bleaker
and less kind. She was unconscious of the qualities that made that
fragrance, for she was completely unconscious of herself. Her world
was filled by people she loved and by her nearness to God. There was
no time or room for herself. She was always the shy and sheltered
one of the family. 'Rose cannot travel by herself,' it was said. But she
has gone now, on that journey that we all fear, without a qualm or
a hesitation, alone and unafraid.*

My father-in-law had a quick, irrepressible wit, and many real or
apocryphal stories based on his *bons mots* went the rounds in diplomatic
circles. When Goering arrived late for lunch at the British Embassy in
Berlin, and excused himself on the grounds that he had been shooting,
the Ambassador murmured drily, 'Animals, I hope?'

Life at West Stowell was run at Pike's tempo, and was as orderly
as one would expect in an ambassadorial household in war-time. We
changed for dinner every night, the food was delicious, the beds
were turned down and had hot-water bottles in them. Also staying
in the house was old Countess Kudenhove, a refugee from Austria,
together with her equally aged lady's maid Betti, and we would listen
enthralled to the *Gräfin*'s tales of Imperial Vienna: how in his youth
her husband had waltzed with Maria Vetsera at a Court ball (she had
eyes pale as woodland violets, he remembered), and how, when her
body was discovered at Mayerling with Crown Prince Rudolph's, after
their joint suicide, she, or rather her stiffened corpse, was brought
back into the city in an open carriage, sitting bolt upright between two
ladies-in-waiting, who held it so.

The Fire Ships

Alan had admitted to me that before our wedding he had volunteered
for Special Service assignments, which were supposed to be for young

bachelor officers only, and that he had forgotten to take his name off the list when we married. It was therefore no great surprise when he returned from London one evening with a beaming smile. 'I've been given my first command!' he announced. 'It's wonderful. She's an *enormous* ship, a converted oil-tanker. We're to go down to Rochester immediately – so get ready, darling, to pack, pay and follow.'

I soon discovered that the wonderful new job was in fact a semi-suicidal mission dreamt up, no doubt, by Professor ('the Prof.') Lindemann, Churchill's Chief Scientific Adviser, and approved by Winston (an Elizabethan at heart) in one of their wilder and more desperate moments of inspiration. Three fire ships – tankers filled with petrol and high explosives – were to sail across the Channel at night and be aimed at the ports of Boulogne and Calais, where Hitler was gathering his invasion fleet for his attempt to land in England once the battle in the air had been won. Having lit fuses and set the engines at full speed ahead, the skeleton crews and captains (Alan included) would jump into the sea, and, if not machine-gunned by the enemy, would *hope* to be picked up by a lurking British Motor Torpedo Boat. All this could only happen on a moonless night and at high tide, with the RAF cooperating by bombing the defences at the entrances of the ports.

The scheme sounded crazy to me, but Alan was delighted, and telephoned to say that he had already rented a small house on the Pilgrims' Way near Ashford, in Kent. This turned out to be a whitewashed, rose-embowered dwelling, clinging to a wooded hillside, which pilgrims once passed by on their way to Canterbury. Before we moved in, we stayed at the Bull Hotel in Rochester, and my mother came down from Eilean Aigas for a brief respite and joined us there.

There were almost continual air-raids over the port, for the Battle of Britain was at its height, and one evening she returned to her bedroom to find a piece of shrapnel and lumps of plaster on her bed, a hole in the ceiling, and feathers from her pillow everywhere. This, curiously, was the only thing that seemed to cheer her up a little, and she went back to the Island feeling satisfied: she, too, had been in the front line of the war which her children were fighting.

I settled into my new role of cook and housewife with a certain amount of success ... except for the shirts. Those dreadful white, stiff-collared naval officer's shirts! Alan expected a clean one every day, and I spent hours washing the beastly things in an old-fashioned sink, and then ironing them on the kitchen table, for there was no ironing-board. The moment the front looked good, the back looked terrible, and vice versa. He came back one evening to find me in tears of rage and frustration, swearing I would cook for him and clean for him, pack for him and if necessary die for him, but never, *ever* wash his clothes again. I kept my vow, and the next day we found an excellent laundry in Ashford.

We stayed in Pilgrim House for nearly a month, while the terrible and heroic Battle of Britain raged in the sky above us. Alan and his fire ship left harbour four times; but each time, thank God, their mission was aborted – once because the RAF had been diverted and failed to bomb their targets; twice because weather and tides were unsuitable; and the last time because the destroyer commanding the operation blew up on a mine just short of Calais. Alan's tanker, fully loaded and with a much deeper draught, had been in the lead, on the same course, but by some miracle missed the mine.

In between our blissful reunions and stoical goodbyes, life was exciting enough. One day we watched and then heard a German fighter plane crash into a field near our house, exploding in a cloud of smoke and flame, but not before its pilot had baled out. A bright-orange parachute floated lazily above our chimneys, and we rushed down to the orchard gate, thinking it had landed there. We ran across one field, then another, then a third, and found a dazed and frightened young man sitting on the ground, still attached to his chute, surrounded by four or five angry farmers armed with pitchforks. Alan took over, reassured him in German and calmed the vengeful Home Guard in English, until the village policeman arrived on a bicycle and led the pilot away, apparently unhurt and obviously immensely relieved.

Another day we had been shopping in Rochester and stopped on the hill above the town to look at the view. We knew an air-raid was beginning, for we had heard the distant wail of sirens – and all at once a squadron of our own fighters zoomed and snarled up into the sky above us. They looked like angry dragonflies as they attacked the German invaders, with sunlight flashing on their wings as they turned and twisted. We had got out of the car and were watching the contest

NATIONAL GALLERY

Sargent's portrait of my grandfather, Lord Ribblesdale – the 'Ancestor' – which hangs in the National Gallery, London

The 'Dolls', Laura and Diana Lister, at Gisburne

My father, Simon Lovat, as Colonel of the Lovat Scouts, 1914–1918

My mother, Laura Lovat, circa 1920

Rose, in her bridesmaid's dress for Magdalen's wedding

Shimi and Rosie get married in London, 1938

LONDON & COUNTY PRESS

Alan Phipps on the bridge of HMS Ivanhoe

PORTMAN PRESS BUREAU

Our wedding reception, August 1940. Pause for the photographers: 'Pike', my father-in-law, in the doorway with Alan's sister Mig; Alan's little brother William was the page boy

ANDREW PATERSON

At Jeremy Julian Joseph's christening, Eskadale, July 1942

During the General Election, 1945: Hugh, Magdalen, Moo, Shimi and me

Hugh wins Stone for the Tories and is carried in triumph by his supporters. Mr Moore, his agent, is in the raincoat and flat cap on the left

A new life: learning to type and be married to Fitz

Making friends in 'The Marsh'. Fitzroy holds his Lancaster constituency in the 1951 General Election

PICTURE POST

MIRRORPIX.COM

The family, 1950. Fitz with Sue-Rose, Jeremy and Charlie plus Fury, the first family dog

Chartwell: Winston sporting pigeon feathers and (below) playing me at bezique (I won)

M. CAMPBELL COLE

Strachur House from Fitz's 'second best pier'

Rhoda and Cockerill in the 'Bear Pit', Strachur

Macleanery: a ceilidh on Mull with our chief, Lord Maclean of Duart

INTERNATIONAL NEWS PHOTOS

In the Caucasus: Fitz on Mt Kazbek, at the top of the pass

The new Captain setting off to plant his standard on Dunconnel, 'in the Isles of the Sea'

Which way? Fitz filming in Siberia

as if mesmerised when Alan suddenly brought me down in a flying rugby tackle and lay on top of me. For a few seconds the sunlight was blotted out as, with a terrifying roar, a stricken aircraft passed a few feet above our heads, planing downwards, with smoke pouring from its tail. Down, down, down it went, across the estuary and over the docks, until there was a flash of orange and we realised it had crashed into some little houses on the other side of the river. 'It was a Heinkel,' said Alan quietly. 'One less for London.'

HMS Bulldog

After the last aborted attempt, the fire ship scheme was finally deemed impracticable and abandoned. Alan, though disappointed, was quite glad to be alive – and to receive a letter of congratulation from Captain Agar, VC, who had been in overall command. It was then the first of too many goodbyes, and I travelled sadly back to Eilean Aigas. On the inside of my wedding ring Alan had asked the jeweller to engrave: 'A – V *Toujours*', and I would now read the message every time he left me.

In the late autumn of 1940 he was appointed to the destroyer HMS *Bulldog*, and on 1 November he joined her in Scapa Flow as second-in-command. She and her captain, Commander Neville Currey, already had a high reputation in the navy, having rescued Mountbatten's destroyer HMS *Kelly* after she had been torpedoed in the North Sea and towed her back to port. *Bulldog* was a newer ship than poor old *Ivanhoe*, and a happy one. Both Alan and I made lasting friends with Neville, and even managed to get him married to Rosemary, the girl of his dreams, during one of the ship's refits.

All that winter *Bulldog* was engaged on convoy duty in the Atlantic, escorting and defending the merchant ships which were bringing us acutely needed munitions and food from the USA, under the Lend-Lease programme which Churchill had managed to set up as soon as he became Prime Minister. It saved us from starvation and enabled us to rebuild our shattered war machine, but the losses in ships and lives were appalling – over three thousand ships went down between 1940 and the end of 1943, when we finally won the Battle of the Atlantic, and there were never many survivors.

On convoy duty in the Western Approaches, *Bulldog* sometimes sailed from Liverpool, sometimes from the Clyde or Orkney, and sometimes from Poolewe in Wester Ross, where the 'iron ships' now gathered exactly as, in the seventeenth century, the Brahan Seer had foretold they would, before the Mackenzies burnt him to death as a witch.

When *Bulldog* came into the Clyde, we generally put up at the Bay Hotel in Gourock, whose proprietor, Two-Ton Tessie, was a delightful character, of broad proportions and wit, who bred poodles and mothered half the junior officers in the Fleet. Sometimes, as a wonderful treat, we stayed with Sir John Stirling-Maxwell (Uncle Archie's elder brother) at Pollok House, a beautiful early-Georgian building in the style of a French *château* which still stands in the middle of Glasgow. Uncle Johnnie was one of the city's greatest benefactors. He had built the Stirling Library, and he gave part of his park to the Burrell Trust, which, after many years of procrastination, at last built a magnificent museum-cum-art gallery to house its great collection. He also presided over a hundred organisations which ameliorated the harsh lives of his neighbours, the citizens of Pollokshaws.

Shimi's No. 4 Commando and the newly formed Combined Operations headquarters had moved their base from Troon, in Ayrshire, up to Inveraray, in Argyll, preparing for the raid on German bases on the Lofoten Islands, off northern Norway. Churchill had overridden the advice of the General Staff and was pressing ahead with his plan to land small raiding parties in occupied Europe before the eventual opening of a second front. The men who had persuaded him that only specially trained forces could do the job were Admiral Sir Roger Keyes, the remarkable First World War hero who had fought at Zeebrugge, and General Adrian Carton de Wiart, an equally distinguished warrior, who had only one arm and one eye, and, in the words of the author Peter Fleming, 'rather more surprisingly, only one Victoria Cross'.

Sir Roger was the first director of the new Combined Operations Force, and the men he picked to shape and lead it were mostly chosen from those who had passed through the training establishment at Lochailort. Although no longer young, the Admiral was an inspiring figure, who, as Shimi wrote in his autobiography *March Past*, 'believed in leading from the front. He took part in all our operations, in all weathers, in all conditions, nor did he quit until the last man was back aboard his ship.' Sometimes, after twenty-four-hour sorties in winter gales and icy seas, Shimi would have to help him change his clothes, as his feeble old hands were too cold to undo the hooks and buttons of his duffel coat. But, Shimi wrote, 'time spent in his company made one feel twice one's size, and that, of course, is what leadership is all about . . . To let him down was unthinkable.'

The Admiral had a firm place in Shimi's gallery of great war-time leaders, alongside Churchill, Smuts, Alexander, Slim and Carton de Wiart – but, significantly, there was no mention of Mountbatten or Montgomery.

The commando raid on the Lofoten Islands, carried out on 6 March 1941, was a great success, and later there were others, about which we would know nothing until they were over. Occasionally Shimi would come on leave, visit us on the Island, and spend a few happy days with his family in the private part of Beaufort; but mostly he was away, training his brigade.

The main part of the Castle was now occupied by the military, and much of the estate, around Beauly and Kiltarlity, by the Canadian Forestry Corps, who had arrived in 1940–41 to cut down and log my brother's plantations (and to capture the hearts of half the local girls, many of whom returned with them to Canada when the war ended).

Alan's telephone calls from ports became fewer and fewer, and our trysts in crowded stations and gloomy docks further and further apart. *Bulldog* never seemed to need a refit, and was constantly at sea. Then one day he wrote to say that they were now to be based on the Island of Hoy, in Orkney, and that he might occasionally get a night or two's shore leave. That was enough, and I immediately started plotting.

I had fifty first cousins scattered round the country, all willing to put me up or help. Fanny Fraser, eldest of the Moniacks, was running a Catholic Women's League canteen at Kirkwall, in Orkney, and I soon persuaded her to take me on as temporary assistant, and to let me share her rented bedroom in the local priest's house.

There were no civilian aeroplanes flying to Orkney, so I crossed the Firth in a small ferryboat, and I shall never forget it. I am not usually seasick, but the sight of other people suffering sometimes makes me feel ill, so when it's rough I always try to sit on deck. This time I was sternly ordered below, and I soon realised why. When the waves are as tall as three-storey houses, the ship climbs very, very slowly to the top of each one, and it is really better, *far* better, not to look, for one knows that once over that white-foamed crest there will be a vertical plunge down, down into the trough, and *thump, bang, crash, shudder,* while one clings desperately to anything that is solidly bolted down, and thanks God that she is climbing again and still the right side up. Then, after a respite of only a few seconds, the whole dreadful process begins again.

'Is it always like this?' I asked a sailor when we docked.

'Och aye, when there's a gale – and there's gales most times in winter.'

'And what about the North Sea and the Atlantic?'

'Oh, yon's worse.'

Only then did I start to realise how awful convoy duty in the Atlantic and Arctic must be, and how crews had to face the unending battle *with* the sea, as well as the one against mines and torpedoes and air attack, not once, but every day and night, for weeks on end. Later, in another article, Alan captured some of the ocean's menace and violence:

Side by side with this battle on the Atlantic there continues the unceasing battle with the Atlantic. For it is no blue stretch of water as the maps portray, but rather a great, savage and temperamental animal. There can be days of unruffled calm while the beast lies dozing in the sun, days upon which the feather of a periscope or the track of a torpedo can be quickly observed. There can be days, and nights too, of fog and mist and driving rain that blot out completely any ships that are in company; such weather can be useful on occasion to both sides.

There are also those days when the wind passes the stage of noble violence and becomes a furious, screaming thing that knows no bounds, and, having roused the anger of the sleeping beast, sustains it with a mocking howl, urging the waves to more and more stupendous efforts. The flat plain of blue becomes a great mountainous inferno populated with a thousand screaming devils that whip the spray into men's faces, blinding their sore eyes and numbing their whole bodies. And sometimes there will come one wave far larger than the rest, a wave that men may see approaching as a huge, indomitable and unavoidable thing that towers for a lingering moment above their heads before it breaks upon them with

a deafening roar. And when the ship, still staggering from the blow,
slowly shakes off the draining tons of water that have poured upon
her, the immense power of the sea can be judged from the damage
that is left behind.

As the sailor predicted, there were gales every day of my month's
stay on Orkney. I got quite used to seeing hen-coops fly through the
air, and to shouting downwind to my closest companion and not
being heard. But it was enervating: tempers flared easily, and I could
understand how a dram or two, or even three, could soothe taut nerves.
Whisky consumption in Kirkwall and Lewis is three times greater than
in the rest of Scotland, and one soon realises why.

Before long I learnt to my chagrin that no civilian was allowed
anywhere *near* Hoy, off which most of the Fleet lay at anchor,
tantalisingly close and yet unapproachable. I also discovered that
passes for officers to Kirkwall were rarely given, and wholly unpre-
dictable. But there were compensations. When the wind dropped
and the rain stopped lashing, the town and countryside were very
beautiful, and the inhabitants, with their funny *di-dah, di-dah* Norse
voices were most friendly. The ruins of the magnificent cathedral
and bishop's palace, the finest Romanesque buildings in the United
Kingdom, rose majestically above the heart of the little town, an
incontestable statement of faith and fortitude, and contrasted wildly
with the breeze-block and tin-roofed huts now grouped around the
newly expanded naval base, opposite which, out to sea, one could just
make out some of the grey, ghostly ships of the Home Fleet, riding
at anchor in the waters of Scapa Flow.

There were several canteens for the sailors and soldiers stationed
on the mainland, or who could occasionally come into town on liberty
boats when off duty. Ours, run by the Catholic Women's League, made
the best tea and baked the best scones in all Orkney, and we were a
penny cheaper than the Church of Scotland canteen, our nearest rival.
Fanny was a great organiser and cook. She taught me many tricks and
useful disciplines – for instance, that tea-leaves were not just the rather
revolting mess left in the bottom of one's pot and immediately dumped
into the nearest trash-can, but rather the residual buds of aromatic
bushes that had simply been softened by boiling water. At the end
of each day we would have a dozen buckets full of the damp brown

leaves, and we would plunge our hands into the pails and sprinkle the wooden floors with them, then brush them into neat heaps and rows awaiting the dustpan. It was a wonderful way of keeping our canteen smelling fresh and clean.

At the end of a month I had not seen nor even heard a squeak from Alan, and so, abandoning hope, I re-crossed the Minch, this time, thank God, in calm, frosty weather. Before I left, I witnessed the unforgettable spectacle of a British battle fleet leaving Scapa Flow for North Africa, where they were to take part in the first Algerian landings – but I knew that *Bulldog* was not among them.

I returned to base on Eilean Aigas, waited for the telephone to ring, and rubbed olive oil into my gradually swelling tummy. At last, in February 1941, a call came. Alan's faint voice, from a Liverpool dock, told me they were in port for a long refit, and to come south immediately. He had booked me into rooms in the dock area.

Great ports were scary places in war-time, and on that first visit to Liverpool I felt very small and ignorant. Alan had booked us into strange but highly entertaining theatrical rooms recommended by his old friend and shipmate, Christopher Philpotts, who had recently married into the Redgrave family. Most of the other rooms were occupied by the cast of a musical, who were trying it out before taking it to London. I made friends with Pat Kirkwood, the nightingale who sang about nightingales in Berkeley Square. Through the paper-thin walls we could hear her practising, ending with a scale or two, until someone banged on the floor or threw a book. She was very pretty and excited about this, her first starring role.

After depositing my bag in our rather seedy bedroom, I went downstairs to ask the brassy-haired owner if there were any messages.

'Yes, ducky,' she said. ''E says 'e can't get away tonight. Too bad!' A mascara'd eye winked lewdly. 'But you're to go down to the King George V dock, and you'll find his ship in Berth E. 'E'll be looking out for you, and 'e'll leave a pass at the gate.' Then she added kindly, 'If you want my advice, luv, you'll take off them glad-rags and dress simple. No jewellery, mind – that's asking for trouble. Tramcar No. 67 at the end of the street will get you near enough. Don't talk to anyone round the docks, and hold on to your purse. They're a thieving lot, them dockers – not that they need it, with *their* wages.' And with a withering snort she returned to adding up the day's sums in her ledger.

Everything was on a much bigger scale than I had imagined. As the tram dropped me off a long way from the docks, the conductor pointed to a rough asphalt road with mean houses on one side and a high, sooty brick wall on the other. The road's surface was pitted with puddles, for it was raining, but soon I could see the forest of funnels and grey gun-turrets of the ships that lay on the other side of the wall. I walked for what seemed miles, desperately hoping I was going in the right direction.

Finally I came to a wide double gate with spikes on top of it, above which a name had been painted out. Beside it was a little postern gate, and a man in a sentry box reading a comic. He looked me up and down and handed me an envelope on which was written 'Mrs Alan Phipps'. 'That'll be you,' he said.

A dozen or so destroyers, looking surprisingly small beside the enormous battleships, were berthed alongside each other. To my inexperienced eyes, all were exactly alike, and, oh God, I had no idea *which* was *Bulldog*! But then, as I havered, there was a shout, and Alan came leaping down a gangplank, to envelop me in an enormous bear-hug. The sun came out and shone for the rest of the day.

Towards evening we decided to risk naval discipline and take a look at one of the Royal Navy's only two battleships, which were berthed a little farther down the dock. Alan told me she would be sailing for the Far East next morning. 'She's enormous, and so spick-and-span you could eat your dinner off her decks. You'll love her.'

It took us a good ten minutes to walk along the dock from stern to bow of the great gleaming hulk, and just as we reached the end, the wretched air-raid sirens went off, accompanied by a barrage of shouted commands, searchlights sweeping the sky and anti-aircraft guns clattering.

'Oh blast!' cried Alan. 'It's my watch, and I'm not on board. There'll be a hell of a row if Neville finds out. Run, darling! Run like you've never run before!'

He set off along the quay at a cracking pace, with me panting behind. As we heard the horrid drone of bombers overhead, we both knew what their target was, and that we were running smack into the middle of it; but the peril of Alan's absence being discovered by his captain seemed much more alarming than that of obliteration, and we got back to *Bulldog* just as the first stick of bombs fell, fortunately wide of their mark. His captain never found out, and his coxswain covered for him. Beautiful *Prince of Wales* sailed out of Liverpool in triumph next day, bound for Singapore and her ultimate doom.

The second half of *Bulldog*'s refit we spent in much greater comfort, in Sir John Shute's home on the other side of the Mersey. Our host was a shipping magnate, a friend of Uncle Johnnie and a Member of Parliament for one of the Liverpool constituencies, as well as being one of the kindest men on earth. I had developed a persistent cough, but we did nothing about it except to buy bottles of Campbell's Cherry Cough Cure, which tasted good and gave me temporary relief, and it was a delight to be warm again, and cosseted by Sir John's Liverpudlian hospitality.

11

ALAN II

I OUGHT TO HAVE KNOWN BETTER. THE RESULT OF THIS CARELESS and unhygienic behaviour was not very surprising. By the time *Bulldog* went back to convoy duty under a new captain and I returned to Eilean Aigas, I had developed double pneumonia, or congestion of both lungs, and had to stay in bed or near it for nearly two months, devotedly nursed by Uncle Maurice's wonderful Jean Neill and her New Zealand colleague Zoe, but chafing to join Alan at the Bay Hotel in Gourock. It was especially frustrating because *Bulldog*'s base was now the Clyde, but Dr MacGregor and the nurses were adamant and would not let me travel; and as the baby might arrive any time in April, I stopped arguing and, for once, behaved. I never even met Alan's new captain, Commander Baker Cresswell, whom he liked and admired, but we both missed Neville, who had been transferred to another command.

Meanwhile, as the nurses continued to look after their two invalids, I got to know my godfather much better. The war could be said to flow through Mumble's bedroom. He had the only reliable wireless in the house, and we would congregate in the large, sunny room with its cheerful log fire and inviting club fender to listen to the news bulletins at one, six and nine p.m. He would ask Nurse Neill to dispense sherry and whisky, when it was available, and we would discuss endlessly the various campaigns.

If the news was bad, he would begin talking about something else, or make Dempsey, his turquoise-blue budgerigar, sit on his bald head and recite, 'Maid of Athens, e'er we part . . .' Here Dempsey would stop and, in spite of intensive tuition, never get any further. It was generally agreed, however, that this was far enough. Or Mumble would recite by heart the Derby winners from 1778 to 1939, a feat of memory which delighted him, or go off at a tangent on some nonsensical story or youthful recollection. 'But of course everyone knew that Winston was really Gambetta's son! The dates fit exactly, and it happened like this . . .' If a day lacked any real drama, he would embroider and elaborate on the mini-dramas of the household, for which he had an uncanny sensitivity and sympathy.

'*Bonjour, Suzon,*' he would greet me as I came in to say good morning. 'Did you know that Kitty [our ancient parlourmaid] nearly broke her ankle on the back stairs last night because Margaret [the kitchenmaid] *will* leave the coal bucket on the bottom step?' Or, 'I hear that Mrs Kennedy's sister in Portree has had a vision that the war will be over by Christmas.'

The most frequent visitors to his bedroom were the Catholic chaplain of the Canadian Forestry Corps, a Redemptionist missionary priest called Father Austen Maguire, and our Viennese Jewish refugee, Dr Stefan Zeissl, who had been deported to Australia as an enemy alien (in spite of having spent six months in Dachau at the time of the *Anschluss*), but who had now happily returned to us, a year later, in the guise of a forestry worker in the Pioneer Corps.

Mumble loved them both, yet you could not have found two more contrasting characters. The Canadian priest was always cheerful and happy, a spruce and confident soldier of God, whose childlike faith – no, I think the right word is 'certainty' – shone out to such an extent that it made an instant impression on everyone who met him, but who never talked about religion. Dr Zeissl, on the other hand, was a nervous, stooping and often deeply introspective intellectual, highly cultured and civilised, who talked endlessly about ethics and the problems of faith. Yet he too had great charm and, as well as his moments of doom and gloom, a deliciously Viennese sense of humour and frivolity.

From his sick-bed Uncle Mumble continued to correspond with friends and literary colleagues. Nurse Neill and I would take down his jerkily dictated answers. Rupert Hart-Davis, Logan Pearsall-Smith, Hilaire Belloc, Eddie Marsh, Ronnie Knox, Enid Bagnold, Diana Cooper and Dame Ethel Smythe were some of the people who wrote to him for elucidation, or from love. He had made, before his illness became acute, four small, light volumes of his favourite poems (in at least six different languages), and these reposed at his bedside in a white vellum binder called simply *Das Gepäck*; he was able to hold them in his hands and they were of great solace, as were the four Gospels that he read in French, Latin and the Authorised Version.

Pushkin was a poet he never tired of reading, and thought the greatest. His translation of *The Prophet* was dictated hesitantly and with much effort to me at the Island. It was the last poem he published. His love of Russia and of all things Russian was very deep, and it awoke in me a curiosity about the country and people that much later in my life was amply rewarded. I remember his once telling me that Russians were the most naturally religious people in the world, and that atheistic Communism could not last: the Russian character would one day overwhelm it.

Then at the beginning of April, by a wonderful piece of luck, Alan succumbed to an attack of jaundice, was given sick leave, and arrived at the Island looking happy but as yellow as a sunburnt Chinaman. To speed up the baby's arrival, he took me out in our first car, old GNO 540, for the bumpiest possible drives, which I supplemented by taking daily doses of castor oil, sandwiched between orange juice, which some misguided soul had told me assured early labour. We were determined to have the baby at home, and while Alan was still with us; so, in spite of my gynaecologist's reservations, Moo engaged a local gamp, Mrs Grant, whose nursing credentials were rather vague, but who had 'brought hundreds of babies into the world'. Dr MacGregor anyway was skilful and charming (and the brother of the Beauly butcher), so we felt sure that between them all they would cope.

'It's a great, great honour, Miss Veronica,' said Mrs Gamp-Grant, when my pains started, spreading towels in front of the fire, presumably to sterilise them, 'to be here and to assist you at your lying-in, because my great-great-grandfather carried your ancestor, the MacShimidh, back from the Battle of the Shirts two hundred years ago and mair, a' the way from Lochaber to the Aird, where they buried him – a' the way, and him a heavy man, too.' It was a cheerful but not exactly reassuring thought.

My labour took thirty-six hours, partly because I was weak after the pneumonia, and partly because it stopped halfway through; and the baby, a girl, had to be 'turned' and eventually pulled out with forceps, but Dr MacGregor was brilliant and no damage was done except for two tiny bruises, which soon disappeared, on either side of the downy little head. 'Never,' said the good doctor to Moo, when it was all over, 'never ask me to work with that incompetent fool again.' Two days later I developed cystitis, and he tore yet another strip off poor Mrs Grant.

I had expected a boy, but Alan was delighted. 'She'll keep all the others in order,' he predicted, and he was right. We called her Susan Rose – Sue-Rose for short. Later we shortened it to Sukie, but at the time it seemed to me the prettiest name for the prettiest baby the world had ever seen.

Soon there was more good news. Alan had asked, and had been recommended by his captain, to train as a signals officer, and in May word came through that he must proceed to Portsmouth for an interview which, if successful, would mean his joining the Signals School at Leydene, near Petersfield, in the autumn. The course would last six months, and if he passed the final exams, he would be promoted to signals officer of a flotilla of destroyers, and sail on its leader with its captain.

It was promotion; it was a challenge. It meant six glorious months together, away from the beastly sea and bombs and mines and torpedoes. We couldn't believe our luck.

Alan sailed through the interview and we immediately began making plans. Young Rhoda Stone, the daughter of Shimi's head keeper on Farley Moor, who had trained as a nurserymaid at Moniack, had already taken over Susan Rose and shown that she had a way with babies. She was immensely conscientious, and the routine of the temporary nursery at the Island was quickly established. Chrissie Fraser, Willie the Moon's daughter, also promised to come south and cook and clean for us. Now all we needed was a house in which she could do so.

This time Alan went back to sea in good spirits and good health, before his leave started in July, and it seemed no time before I began packing up and saying tearful goodbyes to Moo and Mumble, the nurses and all our friends in the north. He stayed with *Bulldog* for another two months, and when she made landfall in the Clyde he left her with mixed feelings of sadness and relief. His shipmates treated him to a touching goodbye ceremony – they hoisted a signal and made speeches, and the ratings all lined up and cheered, and then his chief petty officer piped him down the gangway and we drove away.

We spent that leave with the Phippses at West Stowell and in London, and in touring the West Country on Jack Eldon's highly temperamental motorbike, which Alan had to run beside to start, with me riding pillion and a last-minute bag clutched between us. Both at the Island and West Stowell, everyone was dismayed by the news that the British Fleet had fired on the French Fleet in Oran harbour, in case they might go over to the Germans: we all felt that the action was not just wrong, but an unmitigated disaster. Admiral Dudley North sent a strongly worded letter to *The Times* protesting against this betrayal, and in response to a letter of congratulation from Alan, wrote back to say that he and Admiral Somerville had tried hard to prevent 'this mad and bloodstained crime'. Indeed, he wrote, they had perhaps been too outspoken in their opposition, as a result of which he, formerly an admiral, now was obliged to sign himself: 'Dudley North, Major, lst Battalion Dorset Regiment, Home Guard'.

In August we all stayed with my sister Magdalen at Ropley, near Alresford. She soon found us a house, West Tisted Manor, which belonged to Jack Scott, the 'Gentleman Bookie', who by then was a prisoner of war in Germany. It was far too big for Ruth Scott to live in on her own, and of course far too big for us, *and* far too expensive at five guineas a week, but it was a beautiful, impractical, rosy-brick Tudor manor with a Great Hall (icy), a small sitting room only slightly warmer, and six bedrooms.

'We'll take in lodgers,' we said, and promptly signed the lease. Once term began, we moved into West Tisted Manor and collected three other trainee signals officers, to whom we fed breakfast and supper, and who owned a variety of motor vehicles, which made the daily 'school run' to Leydene very easy and allowed me to keep GNO 540 to visit the village shop, six miles away.

Sue-Rose was a model baby, and by the time she was six months old liked nothing better than to be played with, cooed at and doted on by four handsome naval officers every night before bath-time. We were tremendously proud of our first home and asked all our friends and family to come and stay, which they did; and as it was war-time, one never knew who or how many would turn up next. We also gave dinner parties and finally, just to show off, a small ball.

Our first visitor was Hilaire Belloc, who arrived in his black cloak, with a bottle of claret and a hunk of bread in his pockets, 'in case of emergencies, my dear'. His visit was a blessing, albeit a mixed one. I had been summonsed by the local ARP (Air Raid Patrol) wardens for not sufficiently blacking out our twenty-foot-high windows in the Great Hall, and I had to appear in court and was expecting a fine, probably a small one, just to teach me a lesson.

Unfortunately, Hilaire decided to accompany me and said he would try to 'get me off'. Wholly ignoring cries of 'Order! Order!' he made an impassioned speech from the floor of the tiny court house about liberty and citizens' rights. The astonished magistrate, unable to quell him, fined me £5 for the blackout and £25 for contempt of court. Mr Belloc was delighted. 'You see, my dear, it's always right to stand up and challenge these petty bureaucrats who bedevil our system. I found it very amusing to see how her arguments collapsed.'

Alan did not find it quite so amusing when I asked him for £20 extra for housekeeping money.

Evelyn and Laura Waugh were our next visitors, Evelyn having what he called 'army business' to attend to somewhere near. He was in uniform and looked, I don't quite know why, rather ridiculous. The days when he would be evacuated from Crete, sacked from Shimi's commandos and causing Fitzroy headaches in Jugoslavia were still a long way ahead, but I suppose I shared the original Pixton prejudice against the poor man. He was in aggressive mood, truculent with Laura and barely polite to his host or to the other sailors, whom he treated as dimwits. That night we heard sobbing from the Waughs' bedroom, and I clutched Alan and thought how awful it must be to be married to someone who makes one cry.

Just before our party, Jakie Astor turned up with Stagg, his soldier-servant. Having joined Phantoms, a newly formed reconnaissance unit, he had been on an exercise in the English Channel and was still shaking.

'You've no idea what it's like having live ammunition fired at you. They have these great things called "Chicago pianos", with real bullets. I didn't like it. I didn't like it at all. I think I'll resign or go AWOL. How about us all stealing a plane and flying to the Bahamas?'

He was, as always, very funny and lovable. Stagg was getting on well in the kitchen, where a romance with Chrissie seemed to be blossoming. Anyway, Stagg managed to sneak back for the party night and gave great *ton* to the entertainment, manning the bar and bustling in and out of the kitchen.

We treated fifty uniformed young friends and their girls to a sit-down dinner of dressed crab, chicken risotto and strawberry fool, and we danced until dawn to what would now be called a disco, which the about-to-become signals officers rigged up from spare bits and pieces they had 'borrowed' from Leydene. Tookie and Jack Eldon provided the champagne, and my fingers smelt of crab for days afterwards.

When exam time approached, Alan and all the lodgers got the jitters. There were such reams of high-tech data to memorise. Yet in the event Alan and two of the lodgers passed, but of the four of them, only one survived the war.

The signals course ended in March 1942, and in April Alan was appointed signals officer to HMS *Faulknor*, leader of the 8th Destroyer Flotilla, and told to join her at Scapa Flow. His new captain would be A.K. Scott-Moncrieffe, one of the best-looking and smartest officers in the Royal Navy, an extremely efficient commander who was well liked and respected by his sailors. He also happened to have been a signals officer himself, so the new boy soon realised there would be no opportunities for bluff.

After a few more days at Ropley, we packed up and set out on a horrendous twenty-hour journey from London to Inverness. Having survived it, Rhoda, Sue-Rose and I settled comfortably into the Home Farm cottage at Beaufort. Alan flew up to Scapa, Zelle came to stay, and I began rubbing olive oil on to my tummy once again. Then it was back to the Island to wait for the arrival of our second child, due in June.

From now on, for Alan and *Faulknor*, it would be Arctic convoys, which were far worse than the Atlantic ones. Only a handful of the ships they escorted reached their destination at Murmansk, and a Russian docker at Polyana once gave Alan a three-rouble note, which I still have, an irony which was probably not lost on either of them, however cheaply lives were valued in the USSR.

That summer I made friends with Joan Wyndham, a pretty and curvaceous WAAF officer who was making or breaking codes for the air force in Inverness. She had adopted and cared for the incredibly brave young pilots of the Free Norwegian Navy, whose mess was a converted steamer on the Caledonian Canal, and who flew old-fashioned, heavily armed sea-planes to protect our North Atlantic convoys on their way to Russia. They could not carry enough fuel to make the return journey, and had to ditch in the sea, hoping to make landfall alive or to be picked up at sea by a friendly ship.

They were a big, blond, noisy and extrovert band of heroes, who told tall stories and drank as if there was no tomorrow. For many of them there wasn't. We never dared ask about the one who was suddenly absent, for fear of breaking their cheerful façade.

The other heroes of the Atlantic convoys were the destroyers and the merchantmen themselves. Altogether Alan and *Faulknor* survived five Arctic convoys, and he received a second Mention in Dispatches, but the hardship of those terrible journeys took its toll, and the next time I saw him he looked thin and drawn and years older.

Jeremy was born on 30 June 1942, much more easily than his sister and without the help of Mrs Gamp-Grant or even his father, who arrived from his ship on compassionate leave five days later. That leave was a short one, but full of happiness and jokes and stories, the best being one Alan had brought back from Scapa Flow.

'You see, there was this rather dim able seaman who appeared before his commanding officer on a charge of buggering a sheep.

'"Any defence?" the prosecution sternly demanded.

'"Please, sir, it was a dark night and I thought it was a Wren in a duffel coat", was the perfectly reasonable reply.'

The story went the rounds of the Fleet, and thereafter every time a ship passed HMS X, which shall be nameless, a bevy of sailors would lean over the rail and chorus, *'Baa-aaa, baa-aaa!'*

Alan soon returned to his ship and yet another Murmansk convoy, but this time he was armed with a long leather motoring coat, lined with soft fur, that someone had given Moo way back in 1912. 'I'll be the envy of the Fleet,' he told us. 'It's so cold sometimes that moustaches and beards freeze solid. Luckily I don't have either, and this will keep me very cosy.'

Moo was delighted, but I was apprehensive. 'If you get torpedoed and try to swim in it, it will sink you.'

'That,' he answered soberly, 'might well be another of its advantages.'

One evening in September, Moo and I had, as usual, gone to Uncle

Maurice's bedroom to listen to the six o'clock news, which always began with the first bars of Beethoven's Fifth Symphony, followed by the solemn *dongs* of Big Ben's clock and the calm voice of Stuart Perowne: 'This is London calling, and this is the BBC news.' That night his voice was not as calm as usual as he read an Admiralty communiqué about a battle that was raging in the North Atlantic and a convoy that was fighting its way through to Russia.

We looked at each other, aghast and puzzled. We knew that *Faulknor* and Alan's flotilla would be defending that convoy, but we also knew enough to wonder why the Admiralty was disclosing details of the engagement when nearly every other convoy's progress was shrouded in secrecy and censorship. Of course I worried more than ever, particularly when next morning's papers repeated the German claims that a large British convoy carrying arms to Russia had been smashed and forty-five warships sunk.

That convoy had in fact become involved in one of the major sea battles of the Second World War. The fighting had lasted for more than a week, the enemy aircraft using torpedo bombs for the first time and attacking in waves, in line abreast, even though, also for the first time, our own auxiliary carriers were giving protection. One of the most frightening descriptions was that of Arthur Oakeshott, a brave Reuters correspondent on one of the warships. He talked of 'the extraordinary sensation of looking *down* from the bridge at the Heinkels and Junkers as they roared past banking steeply sideways to launch their torpedoes'.

Admiral Burnett, in the report that the Admiralty finally published, wrote of 'the reckless gallantry' of the Fleet Air Arm fighter pilots and their success in counter-attacking, despite the fierce defensive fire they had to brave from our own ships' guns to get at the enemy.

I thought of Alan on the bridge of *Faulknor*, in his long fur motoring coat, keeping watch and keeping steady among all the noise and chaos, the death and fear. Four days later the Admiralty announced the battle was over and the convoy had got through to Murmansk. The total number of our ships lost was not divulged. We were only told that one of our destroyers, HMS *Somali*, had been sunk, as well as one of our minesweepers; but forty enemy torpedo-carrying planes had been shot down, two U-boats had been sunk and many more damaged. The Luftwaffe had suffered in morale, too, for until then they had thought they were invincible. Alan told us later that *Faulknor* had accounted for two aeroplanes and one U-boat. In the long list of awards that were eventually gazetted, her captain, Scottie, was given a DSO for 'gallantry, skill, and resolution in HM ships escorting an important convoy to North Russia, in the face of relentless attacks by enemy aircraft and submarines'.

After it was all over, the ship's company was given a brief leave, and in November *Faulknor* steamed up the Tyne to Newcastle, to 'show the flag'. Scottie and Alan gave talks to the dockers, who had been threatening to go on strike for more pay, and Alan gave an account of the battle on the BBC which, of course, none of us heard. I rushed down to Newcastle to join him, but it was only for a couple of days.

Faulknor's next duty was to take Winston Churchill and Sir Stafford Cripps up to Scapa to review and congratulate the battle fleet. 'I nearly lost him,' Alan wrote in a smuggled-out letter. 'I was escorting the great man up to the bridge when the ship gave a sudden lurch and he near as dammit went over the side!' Then Randolph Churchill, a member of the party, leant over the upper deck in a cream-coloured duffel coat and a jaunty yachting cap, and was hailed, 'Hi! Taxi!' by one of the ratings. Otherwise there were no contretemps.

More, but less dramatic, convoys sailed all through that winter, the long Arctic nights giving them at least short respites from air attack. Yet when Alan came on leave in January I knew he was dreading another one. 'It's bad enough reaching Murmansk,' he told me, 'with the few ships we do manage to get through, but when you see most of the cargo you brought on the last trip still lying on the docks, untouched, my sailors get angry. They think it's all political humbug, for what can those small amounts of supplies, half of which have been sunk, do to help a country the size of Russia? The men don't like the restrictions we're put under when we dock; they don't like the surly dockers, and it's all I can do sometimes to prevent a fight.'

This time it was the saddest of partings, and his last words, *'Partir, c'est mourir un peu,'* sang in my head as I watched his train steam out of Inverness station.

But before he left me, we had come to a happy and momentous decision. As we now had two babies, our Eilean Aigas quarters seemed a bit cramped, and since leaves were so precious and so rare, we wanted to spend them on our own, in our own home. Recently, by great good fortune, I had been offered the rental of a lovely old farmhouse called

Clunes Mains, at Kirkhill, near Beauly, and after we had inspected it and found it perfect for our needs, we told the owner, Mr Cameron of Clunes House, that we would take it and I would move in as soon as possible, and Alan would join me on his next leave. It had a pretty garden, which separated it from a working farm, and was equidistant from Eilean Aigas and Inverness, where I had already started working in the Raigmore blood-transfusion unit.

Alan loved it, and though he could not join me there until the spring of 1943, we managed to spend our last days together in our own home, with our own little family, and they were perhaps the happiest of our married life.

Early in 1943, with the campaign in Africa effectively won, the war theatre was changing. The Allied armies began their assault on Italy by capturing Pantelleria, then attacked Sicily to secure air bases and jumping-off places. I do not know exactly when *Faulknor* sailed into the Mediterranean to join the invasion fleet, but it must have been soon after Alan's last leave, for on 7 May he wrote to say that I would not hear from him for some time, but that when I did it would be from a sunny place, far better than those cruel Arctic waters. One of his rare letters told me that the Fleet had been ordered to camouflage their ships by painting them splotchy lilac, and that he had not resisted the Phipps family's penchant for puns. *'Mauve qui peut!'* he had signalled to his flotilla, and was delighted with his own joke.

These sporadic communications told me little, and we tried vainly to reconcile their scant information with the BBC news. Looking back, I am amazed at how little we knew of the land and sea battles raging at the time, and how complete the censorship was. We did not hear details of the disasters or successes (precious few) until long after they had happened: the evacuation of Greece, the enemy's recapture of Crete, the huge Allied losses on the Sicilian and Italian beach-heads – all that passed us by. Not until much later did I learn about Crete from Paddy Leigh Fermor and David Sutherland, about Sicily from Shimi's book *March Past*, and about the Anzio beach-head from my cousin Ian Fraser's brilliant account of it in his *The High Road to England*. But Alan's destroyer flotilla was involved in most of those actions, and he got his third Mention in Dispatches when *Faulknor* was supporting the landings, 'for devotion to duty, and constant cheerfulness ... he set a high standard to his men'.

Then, in order to divert the German bombers from the Italian front, the Allies attempted to occupy Rhodes and garrison the islands of Kos and Leros, which lie off the west coast of Turkey. This, the politicians hoped, would bring neutral Turkey into the war on our side, which would have been of inestimable value, for it would have given us the air bases we so desperately needed in the eastern Mediterranean and the possibility of attacking the enemy's southern flank.

All I knew at the time was that Scott-Moncrieffe's squadron of destroyers had been moved to Alexandria, to supply those islands, and that soon afterwards Scottie had been recalled to the Admiralty in London to start planning the real 'second front'. He had promised Alan to send for him as soon as possible, but meanwhile a new captain was appointed to the squadron, whom few on *Faulknor* seemed to like. She ceased to be a happy ship, and the spirit of the letters I now received became steadily lower. The run between Alexandria and the garrisons on Kos and Leros was deadly, as German bombers from bases in Greece and Crete continuously harassed the convoys, sinking – in only a few months – a cruiser, four destroyers and various support vessels, as well as the merchantmen they were escorting.

Alan's occasional weekend leaves in Cairo were hectic, especially if enjoyed in my cousin David Stirling's flat, but then the return to sea and the pitiless enemy strafing seemed by contrast almost worse than before. In late October came a letter that showed between its lines how near he was to breakdown. It was different from any he had written before, full of longing and love and faith, but very little hope. It was almost as if he knew he would not see me or his children again. But then, only two weeks later, came another, just the opposite, full of excitement and bounce and all his usual happy optimism.

'I've got a shore job at last!' he announced, and it was true. He had decided to make a break, and had volunteered to be temporary liaison and signals officer to the army's headquarters on Leros. 'It will only last about a month,' he wrote, 'and by then Scottie, with any luck, will have sent for me. I may even be home for Christmas!'

Filled with joy and new hope, I decided to go to London, to ring up Scottie and to wait for Alan's return. Moo was also coming to London, and we were to meet in the flat, but it was my sister Magdalen who opened the door to me, drew me inside, and put her arms round me, just as I began excitedly telling her the good news.

'There's been a telegram,' she said. 'From the Admiralty . . .'

It was as if a steel shutter had clanged down between us, blotting out the light. The message was brief. 'Regret to inform you that Lieutenant Alan Phipps, RN, has been reported missing, believed killed.' I read it over and over again without taking in the words. Then I sat down, for my whole world had suddenly disintegrated, and I could see only blackness all round me – and ahead.

The first days in London I now remember as a jumble of frantic, futile enquiries, telephone calls and interviews. For a family who were usually good at pulling strings, cutting through bureaucracy and getting to the top, we were singularly unsuccessful. The battle for and the fall of Leros, the muddled and too-slow reaction of General Jumbo Wilson to the crisis in the Dodecanese, the predicament of the Admiralty, who had lost so many ships in its defence – indeed, the tactical weakness of the operation as a whole and the feeble performance of some of the military garrison – all these factors kept official lips tightly closed.

Alan had been, uniquely and temporarily, a sailor working in a soldiers' HQ. His official commanding officer was miles away. We didn't know anyone in the regiments that were garrisoning the islands, or in Special Operations Executive (SOE) in Cairo, an organisation which was regarded by friends as immensely secretive and unreliable, but which might well have told us more. By then David Stirling was in Colditz, Shimi was practising commando raids in preparation for D-Day, and no one, *no one* could tell us about the last days and hours of the Leros battle.

I returned to Clunes, to the babies and the Island and the blood-transfusion unit in Inverness. For months I went on searching for news, for I would not and could not accept that Alan was dead. Had we not eventually heard that after the battle our brave friend George Jellicoe had managed to reach the headquarters cave, and that he found no body, no trace of him? I imagined, therefore, that he had perhaps been only slightly wounded and had somehow smuggled himself out to mainland Greece, where he would be recovering or working with the Greek guerrillas and freedom-fighters.

I followed up every clue, wrote to all the wounded prisoners who had been repatriated early in exchange for Germans, in case they had heard anything in their camps. I contacted Louise Argyll, who was working for the Red Cross in Portugal, as her husband, Ian Argyll, was a POW with the Highland Brigade. I also wrote to Donald Maclean, who was at the British Embassy in Washington. I visited the underground offices of the Admiralty in the bunker off Horse Guards Parade, where our own High Command sat and deliberated. One hopeful lead took me on a long, weary, cross-country railway journey to a remote village in north Wales, only to find that the poor, nerve-shattered Tommy I interviewed couldn't remember anything about Leros, or even where it was, and didn't want to talk about it anyway. An agonised look from his mother made me stop harassing him and leave.

Then, when hope was barely flickering, something occurred which re-lit its flame.

One Sunday a spruce young soldier with an unusual shoulder-flash on his uniform appeared at Clunes and asked to see me. He took from his notecase a crumpled press cutting – a picture of Alan and me on our wedding day – and began pumping me with questions. I was so eager to hear what he could tell me in return for my answers that I probably disclosed far too much about Alan and his presumed fate.

My visitor, who called himself Jacques, then launched into a strange story: how he belonged to a Free Czechoslovak Unit, attached to a secret British organisation (presumably SOE) that was working with the underground resistance movement in Greece; how he had met Alan some weeks after the fall of Leros; how Alan was being well looked after and recovering from wounds; how Alan had told him he hoped soon to be strong enough to join the local EOKA guerrillas; how he himself had made his way back to Alexandria to report and had been flown out to Scotland.

It all sounded so plausible and confirmed my wildest dreams. Dizzy with joy and relief, we stuffed the Czech with scones and chocolate cake, took details of his unit (which he was rather loath to give) and begged him to return the following Sunday. I spent the next two hours telephoning every friend and relation I had, to tell them the wonderful news.

Uncle Alastair at Moniack did not, from the start, find it so wonderful. In fact he sternly insisted that he should be present when I saw 'Sergeant Jacques' again. 'The man may be an impostor,' he said. 'He could even be a deserter on the run.' But when they both turned up the following Sunday, and Jacques brought some unreadable Slovak papers with him, and gave a credible description of Alan, the dear Alligator admitted he was baffled. He left, shaking his head and telling me not to be too hopeful.

Of course I disregarded his good and kind advice, and it was only when I later met my friend Gavin Maxwell, who had had dealings with SOE, that I began to view the exotic stranger with greater suspicion.

'SOE is full of crooks,' Gavin told me blithely. 'I wouldn't believe a word he says, but I'll make enquiries for you.'

The enquiries drew another blank. Gavin disappeared back into his regiment, and after a couple more visits Jacques, too, passed out of our lives. After the war we learnt that he was a psychotic character who had preyed on other anxious wives before me.

Looking back on those dreadful days, which I can do now more or less objectively, I believe that the revival of my hopes before their final extinction gave me time to accept my loss in, as it were, small stages. 'It's only through time and the grace of God that you will find peace and comfort,' a wise old priest had told me, and time is what I was given.

The other thing that I understood only later is that necessary war-time security creates virtually impenetrable barriers between the various branches of the services, and the fact that Alan was a sailor temporarily attached to a short-lived military headquarters made his fate much more difficult to ascertain than it would otherwise have been.

It wasn't until the summer of 1944 that I knew for certain that he was dead, and not until August of 1945 was his name gazetted by the Admiralty as having received a posthumous Mention in Dispatches. This did not mean a great deal to me at the time, but thirty years later it did to Jeremy, our soldier son, who knew that posthumous MiDs are exceedingly rare, and who, spurred on by this anomaly, tracked down the facts that I had so desperately wanted to hear.

He found that his father had joined the staff on Leros on 6 November 1943. The entire headquarters was living and working in a narrow, dark tunnel at the top of Mount Meriviglia. The cave provided good cover from German air-raids, but conditions inside were extremely cramped. Outside, the defences consisted of a series of sangar positions (low stone walls) and sandbag emplacements.

In their onslaught on Leros, the Germans put in more than a thousand air attacks, mainly with dive-bombers, concentrating on the coastal defences and the anti-aircraft gun positions. The final battle started on the evening of 12 November, with a large airborne assault on the waist of the island, followed next morning by a seaborne assault on the north-east coast. For three days the British infantry fought valiantly, repelling attack after attack, all the time under fire from the Luftwaffe's ground-strafing Stukas. Although outnumbered, out-manoeuvred and totally exhausted, they yet managed to stay their ground.

On the morning of 16 November the headquarters on the mountain came under attack. The steepness of the ground made a concentrated assault difficult, and pockets of German infantry crept up to seize various gun emplacements. When things were looking dire, Alan volunteered to take a small group to recapture a particularly important position, and, clutching an enormous Webley pistol, he led them across open ground exposed to fire, forcing the enemy to withdraw. But shortly after the objective had been re-taken, he was hit by small-arms fire and killed instantly. The Germans made no further attempt on the headquarters until about four p.m., when, after a concentrated attack, they overran the position, leaving Brigadier Tilney, the force commander, no alternative but to surrender.

Later, in a statement to the Admiralty, one of the officers who had been with Alan, Lieutenant Horton of the Royal Signals, wrote this personal appraisal:

> I would like to comment on the outstanding bravery of this officer, who initiated and led the attack. It was due to his leadership only that the position was taken and thus prevented the enemy from further advance until much later in the day. At one stage in the fighting, when the supply of grenades had been exhausted, he stood at the parapet hurling rocks upon the advancing enemy below.

Next morning the German commander, Lieutenant General Müller, allowed the British to coordinate the collection of their wounded and, where possible, the burial of their dead. George Jellicoe, an old friend of our family, who had been reconnoitring the island with some troops of the Long Range Desert Group and the Special Boat Service, but had been captured, asked permission to look for Alan. Exhausted as he was, he climbed Mount Meriviglia and searched the area in front of the cave, not knowing that Alan had died some distance away. Having drawn a blank, he went down again and, true to his word, surrendered. That evening he escaped, making away with some SBS colleagues, stealing a caique and sailing it to the Turkish coast. My whole family has always been enormously grateful to him for his dedication and courage in trying so hard to find out what had happened.

The British survivors were shipped across to Athens and taken by train to prisoner-of-war camps in Germany. For various reasons they were split up, with the result that details of the battle for Leros took a long time to reach London. In March 1944 the Naval Department received an initial account of Alan's action, and a recommendation for an award, from Lieutenant Commander Frank Ramsyer, RNVR. The Naval Honour and Awards Committee were of the view that his action had been so outstanding that it merited the award of a Victoria Cross, but they called for confirmation from Commander Baker, who had been the senior British naval officer on Leros, and was then still a prisoner somewhere in Germany. It took the Naval Secretary's office eight months to locate him, and when he replied via the Red Cross in December 1944, he gave a fairly bland account of Alan's performance as communications officer, but failed to describe the battle – no doubt because, being inside the cave, he never saw it. With hindsight, he should perhaps have recommended an approach to the army, in particular to the Chief of Staff at Force Headquarters, to obtain a full account.

After another six months' deliberation, the Honours and Awards Committee finally awarded Alan the posthumous MiD, which was gazetted on 14 August 1945. By an extraordinary fluke the letter from Lieutenant Horton arrived at the Admiralty that very day – too late for the Committee to change its decision. Inter-service muddle, lack of communication and the fog of war all contributed to the outcome.

I am glad that Jeremy found all this out, but it only confirmed what I already knew: that Alan was not only immensely brave, but always cheerful in impossible situations, and that he had a gift of inspiring others to follow him with equal courage.

*   *   *

The next few months passed very slowly, though I was now working nearly full-time, collecting blood for our blood-transfusion unit from all over the county, but mostly from the soldier volunteers at the Cameron Barracks depot in Inverness. The Jocks used to march into an empty ward of Raigmore Hospital and line up in a queue, with a sergeant-major shouting at them: 'Step forward, lad. Roll up your sleeve and look the other way. It won't hurt and it won't take a minute. If your blood's blue you're no good for the ******* army, but if it's tartan you'll do for the regiment.'

With such words of encouragement, in would go the thick needle connected to the plastic bottle, which took at least five minutes to fill. If one soldier fainted at the sight of his neither blue nor tartan but very red blood, the others waiting behind him would all go down like ninepins, and we would lay them out on emergency beds which stood waiting all round the ward.

In the villages we would arrive by ambulance and take over a school or the village hall. There was enormous demand for full blood and plasma, both from the Royal Army Medical Corps and the civilian hospitals, and Dr Kirkpatrick, a fiery Ulsterman who was head of pathology at Raigmore, never thought we worked hard enough. Eventually he sacked my boss, poor Mrs Fraser-Simpson, who was wimpish and a bit of a moaner, and appointed me in her place, which was rather awkward as we had become friends. I got on quite well with Dr Kirkpatrick, as I stood up to him and could make him laugh, but as D-Day approached the demand for blood became so great that a professional unit was formed with a medical man at its head, and I retired.

The Lovat Scouts, just as in the First World War, had been given a highly unsuitable and wasteful role, guarding the Faroe Islands from possible Axis invasion. Shimi had left them for Combined Operations, but Sandy Fraser of Moniack and Hugh had been stuck on those barren rocks for over a year. When Rose died, Hugh applied for a compassionate posting nearer home and was eventually transferred out of the Scouts to the newly formed Regiment of Forward Intelligence, which worked with the SAS and was called 'The Phantoms', an outfit which was much more to his liking.

In December 1943 something went wrong with the Eilean Aigas

boiler, and as Hugh and Shimi were both on leave, we all moved to Beaufort for Christmas. Stefan was now happily lodged in a crofter's house near Daviot. Most weekends he came to the Island, and his music and funny stories brought life and light into all our lives. I spent many happy hours at the Island with him, learning and singing German *Lieder*: Schubert and Schumann, and Hugo Wolf, and some of Moo's favourite Reynaldo Hahn songs, like *'D'une Prison'*, the setting of Verlaine's poem *'Sagesse'*:

> *Le ciel est, par-dessus le toit,*
> *Si bleu, si calme.*
> *Un arbre, par-dessus le toit,*
> *Berce sa palme.*
> *Un oiseau dans le ciel qu'on voit*
> *Chante sa plainte.*
> *Qu'a tu fait, O toi que voilà, pleurant sans cesse,*
> *Dis, qu'a tu fait, O toi, de ta jeunesse?*

I loved that song and gave it all I'd got.

Lighter entertainment included Lucienne Boyer's *'Parlez-moi d'Amour'*, with a picture of a glamorous vamp with dark red lips stretched out on a piano on the cover of the music-sheet; while upstairs in his bedroom Uncle Maurice enjoyed 'Coming in on a Wing and a Prayer', which Nurse McDonald fancied because of a relation in the RAF, and played to him on her wind-up gramophone.

Father Maguire dropped in as often at Clunes as he did at Eilean Aigas. He adored the babies, and nicknamed Jeremy 'Ferocity' Phipps, as he always yelled loudly for more porridge (his grandfather Eric once told me, 'All Phippses are savage when hungry'). To Sukie he would sing a special tune, 'Sue, Sue, I love you, I love you, I do', and she picked it up and would sing it back to him.

I paid periodic visits to the Deep Purple flat in London, where one or other of the family would be sure to turn up, for it had become our unofficial HQ in the south. I had often been asked by the Scott-Moncrieffes to visit them and decided simply by chance to do so on the weekend of 4 June. They were living in a lovely house near the Hampshire coast, and when Scottie, in old corduroys and a bush shirt, met me at the station, we talked briefly about Alan. He seemed tired and preoccupied, but he was just as elegant and handsome and had just as commanding a presence as ever. I didn't like to press him about the forthcoming invasion, but its imminence became ever more apparent as we drove down side lanes and took byways to avoid the main and secondary roads, which were choked with lorries, trucks, personnel carriers, jeeps and tanks – all the frightening might of a great army on the move.

I knew Alan's old captain, Neville Currey, would be aboard his gunnery command ship, a floating (and stationary) death-trap that would integrate naval bombardments during the landings, because he had written me a touching letter asking me to look after Rosemary 'if anything should happen', in a posting that was probably one of the most dangerous in the whole British Fleet. I also knew that Shimi and his commando brigade would be battened down and waiting in their landing craft, ready to go, and that he would have his personal piper with him.

That Sunday we held our breath but behaved as if it was just an ordinary weekend. Scottie mowed his lawn, but was never more than yards away from the telephones on his desk.

Next morning I was awakened at about five a.m. by a steady roar. Looking out of my bedroom window, I saw the Admiral, already dressed in uniform, gold braid and medals, standing on his newly mown lawn with a cup of tea in one hand, looking up at a pink sky that was rapidly turning into silver, as squadron after squadron of aeroplanes flew over us in close formation, all heading south, towards France.

He shouted up to me, 'It's started, and thank God, the weather looks good!'

A camouflaged staff car with two smart sailors and an ADC rolled up. The ADC leapt out and saluted, Scottie waved goodbye to us, and was gone.

My return journey to London, by slow train which seemed to stop at every station, was unforgettable. Every carriage, every new arrival buzzed with excited rumours and wildly improbable news. The very air at Waterloo and in all London was electric. I rang Moo and tried to soothe her fears. Rosie was out of touch, waiting near his headquarters for news of Shimi. The scale of the operation was so tremendous, so awesome, it was frightening.

*   *   *

Not long after the Normandy landings, Mr Cameron, my gentle landlord, told me that for financial reasons he would have to terminate my lease and put Clunes Mains on the market, so once more I took the sleeper train from Inverness to London to consult Moo about this new crisis in my life. Looking for my berth number, I saw on one of the carriage lists the name of Colonel C.W. Ritchie, King's Own Scottish Borderers, and I suddenly remembered that he was one of the Leros POWs to whom I had written, but who had never answered. I decided to call on him as soon as the train started.

He was drinking a glass of whisky and had it in his hand when he answered my knock, and he looked surprised and slightly alarmed.

'Were you on Leros?' I asked. 'And did you know my husband, Alan Phipps, who was the naval signals officer in the headquarters cave?'

'Yes,' he answered nervously. 'I knew Phipps quite well.'

'He was reported missing, believed killed. Do you know what happened to him?'

'Oh yes, I was in a kind of sangar quite near him. He was throwing rocks at the Germans below us, and then he stood up. He was hit in the throat and chest.'

'Was he badly wounded?'

'Oh no, he was quite dead when I reached him a few minutes later.'

I couldn't speak, and he went on hurriedly, in a kind of rush, 'I got your letter. I'm so sorry I never answered it. I always meant to, but somehow I never got down to it, and by then I thought you must have known everything.'

Still speechless, I started to withdraw, but before I left, the bastard offered me a drink of whisky.

I suppose I had really known and had begun to accept that Alan was dead, but now the fact was concrete, I knew I must make plans for myself and our children. It felt a very lonely task. Moo and I sat up together the following night and talked and talked. As always she was a rock of strength and stoicism, of faith and, most importantly, of practicality.

'You'll have to get a job,' she said. 'You can't possibly live on Alan's pension and your capital, which is practically nonexistent. You'd better come south and look for work, and a flat, in London.

Whatever happens, hang on to Rhoda: she's a treasure.' I had already come to that conclusion myself, and faithful Rhoda indeed stayed with me through all my troubles, sharing the family's joys and sorrows for the next half-century and more.

I had thought of training to become a district nurse. I liked the idea of eventually living in the country, preferably the Highlands, and having a free house and a profession which I would find interesting and rewarding. St Thomas's was offering a course in their maternity unit that took account of VAD experience and might knock a year off training, which would mean I could be eligible for a post in three years' time.

Flat-hunting in London was exciting. There were hundreds of evacuated and often bombed and battered semi-sound houses to choose from, many of which were bargains, many potential disasters. I particularly fancied the Maida Avenue canal and its lagoon, which was within walking distance of the Bakerloo line, as well as being near Moo, the Rosary Church and Selfridges. I liked its romantic literary associations. Wasn't it in the little house on the island in the lagoon that the young hero of Monty Mackenzie's *Sinister Street* had found the dreaded hat in the hall and knew that his green-eyed mistress had betrayed him?

I went to look at the house on the island. It was still there, but its roof had fallen in and it looked more decayed than romantic. There was a sign for 'Flats to Let', however, on the south side of the canal, on a hideous block that was half Pont Street Dutch, half mock-Tudor (how *could* they combine the two?). I pressed the bell and asked to be shown round. There were two empty flats, one on the ground floor, one at the top, which we glided up to in a lift pulled by a rope.

'No chance of your getting stranded when the electricity is cut off,' purred the vendor. He opened the door. I walked to the window and looked out on a view over the canal on which two barges were passing and then, far beyond, to a distant vista of Harrow-on-the-Hill.

'How much?' I asked.

'Two hundred pounds a year, plus fifty pounds ground rent and rates, but you'll have to do your own repairs.'

This sounded a bit ominous, but I said grandly, 'I'll take it,' and then rather spoilt my impersonation of a worldly plutocrat by adding, 'providing my lawyer and guardian approve.'

Of course Mr Money, the Phipps' lawyer and guardian who had been put in charge of my marriage settlement (he lost most of it in Dalton bonds), did not approve. I had to argue my case very hard.

'It's got four bedrooms, a decent-sized sitting room and dining room, a large kitchen with a rubbish-chute and fire stairs, which admittedly don't work, and a very small bathroom. The views on both sides are fantastic. It's dirt cheap. Even if the roof leaks, I won't be there for ever, and I know Alan would have loved it.' This seemed to clinch the argument, for Mr Money was a kind and sentimental old man, even though a rotten lawyer. In the end we packed everything that belonged to me at Clunes into wicker hampers that had once been laundry baskets at Beaufort. I handed my dog Barney over to Calder, my old shepherd friend, who I knew would love him as much as I did, and we moved south.

The story of Shimi and his brigade's heroism on D-Day is well known, and has been told many times, not least in the film *The Longest Day*. He was severely wounded three days after the landings by a piece of shrapnel that tore through the most vital parts of his anatomy without quite killing him. His injuries kept him in hospital for weeks, but he ached to return to Beaufort, and soon he insisted on doing so. The result was that I did not see much of Moo during my first months in London, for she went with him and returned to Eilean Aigas.

I, too, was busy, making curtains and covers, combing second-hand shops and antique stores, begging and borrowing what was missing from my large and generous family, and generally installing my own small one in its new nest.

By then the Allied armies were fighting their way across Western Europe, racing the Russians to reach Berlin first. There were victories and setbacks, terrible fighting in Normandy and at Arnhem, where many friends were killed in action. Hugh was in the Ardennes, in touch with the Resistance there and scouting the enemy's front lines to report back to his battalion. It was a dangerous job, but it must be admitted he had some very congenial brother officers to share it. His cousin 'the Puffer' (Lord Hardwicke), as well as Jakie Astor and Prince Bernhard of the Netherlands, were all expert at liberating the best cheeses, foie gras and champagne, as well as the population, wherever they happened to stop and bivouac.

And then, quite suddenly, the long-awaited moment finally arrived. Hitler committed suicide, the Germans surrendered to the Allies on 7 May 1945, and the war in Europe was over.

My sister Magdalen had become a queen of the Red Cross, and I had half expected her to be marching on VE Day, but because Jack was on duty as a personal lord-in-waiting, and they were close friends with the King and Queen, she chose instead to watch the parades from Buckingham Palace, to which they had both been invited. She told me they were going down to Ropley that evening, and suggested I caught the four fifteen train to Winchester.

That morning I roamed the streets alone, heard the bands, watched the gleaming regiments as they marched down the Mall. I tried to be happy and join in the cheering, dancing, delirious crowds. I told myself there were thousands of widows like me, and now, thank God, there would be no more of us, as the war was *over*, but it didn't help. So I packed a bag and sat on an almost empty platform at Waterloo station, waited for my train, which never seemed to come, and wept.

12

A NEW LIFE

O N 23 MAY 1945 PARLIAMENT WAS DISSOLVED, AND IT WAS announced that a General Election would be held on 5 July. Many of our friends, newly demobbed, decided to fight it, and Hugh was selected as Conservative candidate for Stone, a rural constituency in the middle of Staffordshire and the strongly Socialist Five Towns of the Potteries. He was therefore in London quite a lot and took on the mission of cheering me up.

For the campaign, my mother rented a small gabled villa in the grounds of Trentham Park Gardens, once part of the great Sutherland estate and *château* in Staffordshire. The house she took might have belonged to their agent or head gardener, but now it became the headquarters of Hugh's campaign, and the family congregated there to help.

It was my first General Election – except that of November 1931 when, aged almost eleven, I had heard both Ramsay MacDonald and the twenty-year-old Randolph Churchill speak in Kiltarlity village hall. We had sat in the back row of the platform, and I remember seeing Mrs MacDonald tug at her husband's jacket and whisper, '*Wheesht*, Ramsay, you've said enough.' She was quite right, for he was rambling away and seemed incapable of coming in to land. Randolph, on the other hand, spoke crisply and made jokes, and to my eyes, with his blond hair, bright-blue eyes, cream-coloured duffel coat and all, he looked gorgeous. But just as he did in later contests, he bit the hand that fed, or helped, him, quarrelled with all his chairmen and supporters, and was never asked to represent a seat in Scotland again.

It was very different in Stone in 1945, and Hugh was smothered in loving care by the Tory matrons of the area. He did have a little trouble with the reputation of his Tory predecessor, who was said to have called on the army to 'Shoot the miners if they won't go down the mines.' This was ritually brought up at the beginning of every meeting, but Hugh and Mr Moore, his agent, were quite capable of dealing with it and turning it into a joke.

Mr Moore was a remarkable man. A tailor by profession, he had never been trained by Central Office – nor, indeed, had he ever been paid by anyone to nurse the constituency between elections. He was simply a brilliant amateur who had loved politics and Conservatism since he was a young apprentice sitting cross-legged at the back of the shop, stitching away while his seniors read out speeches from the local newspapers 'to keep the lads amused'. His greatest treat was to attend county meetings and hear those great orators Lord Salisbury and Lord Derby speak. 'That's why tailors and printers are the best politically educated people in the land,' he would tell us proudly. 'They know what's going on.' . . .

Hugh had been advised to replace him with a professional agent, but he wisely refused to do so, for Moorie, with his long, quivering nose and watery blue eyes, never missed a trick, and knew every householder in the constituency. He lived in a small cottage with a small wife, who would cook great Staffordshire high teas for us, murmuring, 'Eat up, now, and don't mind me. I'm just the little oil can.' So she was, and soon both the Moores became lifelong friends.

Quite a few of Hugh's friends came to visit or speak for him. Quintin Hogg drew a large audience, but the most surprising visitor was Jack Kennedy, who was covering the British election as a journalist, and also picking up a pointer or two for his own struggle to win a seat in the House of Representatives. He was as charming and debonair and quick-witted as ever, danced beautifully with all the right ladies at a fund-raising Tory ball, and flirted with all the wrong ones whenever our backs were turned. But if anyone had said, 'Fifteen years from now Jack will be President of the United States,' I would have thought them barmy. To me he always seemed a lightweight character, but I undervalued his unfailing political instinct and faultless timing, and also his ability to communicate and involve. Once in power, he always seemed able to say the right thing at the right moment to the right people. In reality his dream of a better world might only have stayed a dream had he lived a little longer, but nevertheless the New Camelot and its court which he and Jackie created were an inspiration to a whole generation, and not only of Americans.

Robert Cecil was fighting a hopeless Socialist seat in Wigan, Julian Amery a difficult one in Preston; Andrew Cavendish, who had married Debo Mitford, a tricky one in Chesterfield. We decided to take a break from the hustings, have a picnic together and compare notes. One Sunday we drove over to Chatsworth to meet the other candidates.

It was the first time I had seen Robert since I had told him I was going to marry Alan. We wandered off and sat on a grassy hill by a little stream, while the others exercised Debo's greyhounds on the uplands above.

'Would you still like to marry me?' Robert asked. 'The Catholic thing doesn't seem to matter so much, now, and I think there are ways . . .'

It was the kindest, the most generous thing that anyone could have said to me, for it restored my self-esteem and made me feel wanted and perhaps even a little loved, and it gave me hope that there might, after all, be a new life for me, somewhere . . . But as we looked at each other, sadly and fondly across those dividing years, we knew that our future could not be together. It was too late. The passion and the pain of our young love were now only a memory, though one I would never, ever forget.

Hugh won his seat by a majority of over a thousand, the best in the Midlands. Robert lost Wigan, which he had expected to do. Julian squeaked through, but to the Establishment's amazement, the nation rejected the man who had inspired it for five long bitter years and brought it to final victory. It was the returning servicemen's vote that did it. They had been brainwashed by Socialist education units, but also they were tired, dead tired of war, and Winston would always be associated with it.

'It's our turn now,' was the general feeling. 'We've done our bit. We want a new world, and what's more, we *deserve* one.' 'Labour will give it to you,' they were told. So Winston was out and Clement Attlee's government came into power with a socking majority.

Number 40, North Audley Street, Aunt Peg's flat near Selfridges, had become the London headquarters of the Stirling family and their SAS colleagues; and, although Irene and she were supposed to be its primary residents, it was always full of Bill and Peter and David's friends. One evening in August Irene and I were pottering about in there, thinking of a boiled-egg supper, when the telephone rang. It was David, and I could hear Irene protesting mildly to her brother as she answered. When she rang off, she said, 'He's coming round to supper and he's bringing Fitzroy Maclean, one of the old SAS officers. I met him last week, and he's very glamorous. They say scrambled eggs will be fine.'

We looked at each other, and simultaneously revolted. By the time David's key turned in the lock, we had changed into the most elegant clothes we could muster, had curled our eyelashes, rouged our lips, and were ready for them.

'We think it would be much more fun if you took us *out* to dinner,' said Irene sweetly.

Fitzroy looked us up and down and concurred – and that was the beginning.

They took us to a new Polish restaurant, which was very expensive and very good. The Stirlings eventually faded, but Fitzroy and I sat on and on. We talked about how he had first met David and how he admired him, about his travels in Russia during the 1930s, about Italy and Scotland and the election, but not about his own war.

'I haven't seen my parents for five years,' he told me. 'They got caught in Switzerland, and as my grandmother fell ill there, they couldn't leave her, so they were interned. It was awful for them hearing practically nothing from me, their only son, and very frustrating, but I'm flying out to Montreux next month, and it'll be a terrific reunion.'

He was funny and he was amiable and, to me, rather frighteningly grown-up – he was thirty-four to my rather naïve twenty-four. He had a kind of natural authority, beautiful hands and carelessly elegant clothes. When the waiters began folding tablecloths and coughing, he proposed going on to the Four Hundred nightclub in Leicester Square. There we stuck in a corner of the dance-floor as he, lifting one foot, putting it down and then lifting the other, made little progress. I soon realised he was probably the worst dancer in all London.

'It's called the collegiate style,' he explained rather sheepishly as I led him back to our table. 'My mother took me to a dancing class when

I was seven, but unfortunately it was held in a friend's drawing room where there were books all round the walls, and I was more interested in their titles than in my partner. We hobbled round a bit until she hit me, and my mother was so mortified by my behaviour that she never took me back, so I've never learnt to dance.'

'What about all those beautiful Russian ballerinas in Moscow?' I asked.

'Oh, off the stage, ballerinas walk like ducks.'

We left at three a.m. and promised to meet the next day, which was a weekend. Fitzroy considered. 'Lunch may be a bit difficult, but I'll come and pick you up at eight o'clock.' Later he told me he had had to do a bit of disentangling: he had already asked Moira Ponsonby to lunch, and – worse – he had promised to spend the weekend with Harry and Catherine Walston (Graham Greene's unofficial wife), a beautiful and very determined woman.

'I'm afraid she wasn't over-pleased,' he said. 'She's a Catholic, too,' he added, I thought unnecessarily.

We saw each other constantly in the next few days. I drove him to the Maida Vale flat in GNO 540 which, as usual, stalled in the middle of traffic. He seemed practical and determined as he removed his jacket, rolled up the sleeves of his Beale & Inman discreetly striped shirt, and swung the handle. He seemed even more of a handyman when I asked him if he could polish the outside of the flat's windows and carry some of the now empty hampers up to the loft. It was the first and last time that Fitz ever did anything domestically useful in all the years that we were married; but he passed the test, and Rhoda was impressed.

One evening we prepared a delicious dinner for him, which he ate with relish. The babies behaved perfectly, and Sue-Rose, always a flirt, sang, 'You are my sunshine, my only sunshine' to him for the first time. It was also a try-out, but we must have passed his test, too.

Fitz left for Switzerland and didn't come back until the end of the Parliamentary recess. While he was away, I picked up more scraps of information about his background. During the 1930s, while stationed as a young diplomat at the British Embassy in Moscow, he had travelled extensively in the Soviet Union, particularly to romantic destinations like Bokhara and Samarkand in Central Asia, almost always hotly pursued by agents of the secret police, the NKVD, forerunners of the KGB. His efforts to outwit his followers had often been hilarious, but also often dangerous. During the war he had been one of the first to fight in the Western Desert with David Stirling's budding SAS. Then he parachuted into the mountains of Jugoslavia, where, as a brigadier commanding the British Government's political and military mission, he established a unique relationship with the leader of the Partisans, Marshal Josip Broz Tito. This personal friendship, founded on mutual respect, had had, and was still having, a beneficial effect on relations between Jugoslavia and Britain. Since 1941 Fitzroy had been Conservative MP for Lancaster (largely *in absentia*), and had now returned to the House of Commons.

Someone told Uncle Mumble about us, and he had said to Moo, 'I hear Veronica has a follower.' I longed for them both to meet.

When Fitzroy did come back I knew, without wanting to think about it, that I was more than a little in love. There were moments – like when he pulled me back from colliding with a white-collared, wild-eyed man dashing for his bus and said quietly: 'Watch out, it's a clergyman running amok!' Another time, he had put down a Parliamentary Question on the order paper, but forgot it because we were talking so much that we drove right through London and found ourselves on the wrong side of the river. There were times like the night of Sissy Ormsby-Gore's dinner party . . .

David and Sissy were living in a tall, narrow house in Pimlico, and had asked Fitz and me and some other friends to dinner. They included Mary Asquith, who had asked if she could bring Philip Toynbee with her. She and Philip arrived in the middle of dinner, and it was easy to see why. Philip had reached the noisy stage, arguing loudly with everyone and not eating; soon his voice became slurred, his head drooped, and he more or less passed out into his plate of fruit salad. David hauled him to his feet and sat him at the bottom of the stairs in a draught. But he had forgotten that it was the only staircase, the one that their new parlourmaid had to negotiate on her journey from the kitchen up to her attic bedroom. Every time she tried to pass what she hoped was a gentleman's corpse, it would give a groan, open an eye, and make a grab at her little black-stockinged legs.

When it was time to say goodbye, and for Mary to apologise profusely, Philip was still lying there like a sack of potatoes.

'Do something!' I hissed at Fitz.

Murmuring, 'We gotta get out of here,' the brave fellow picked

Philip up and staggered towards my car, but there were new problems. GNO was a two-door model, and neither of us fancied driving with a corpse lolling around beside us. We tried to manoeuvre him into the back seat. 'He won't fold,' said Fitz patiently. 'We'll have to put him in the boot,' and we did, wedging it open just enough to avoid suffocation and hoping an inquisitive bobby on the beat wouldn't stop us.

'Where to?'

'Sloane Square,' I answered confidently. 'It's a turning off . . . Oh God, I've lost the bit of paper that Mary wrote the address on. It's Lawrence Gowing the artist's flat – well, at least it's his friend's flat and I know that Philip usually stays there.' And so we drove round and round Sloane Square before turning into the Pont Street Dutch maze, where I finally remembered the name and number.

Sissy's parlourmaid handed in her notice next morning.

My mind was in turmoil. Surely I couldn't love someone so soon? I was still mourning Alan. I only half-knew this stranger, who seemed in some ways to have come from another planet, in others to be the most intimate, stimulating and cosy companion I had ever met. I kept pushing the idea to the back of my mind, and it was Fitz who brought it to a head. We were driving across Hyde Park towards Speakers' Corner when he suddenly said, 'Stop the car.' I turned it into the little garden beside Marble Arch and waited, knowing what was coming and dreading it.

'Will you marry me, please?' he said. 'I love you, and I think you love me a little too.' The last was said so gently and self-deprecatingly that my heart melted.

I answered unhappily, 'I do love you too, but I don't know . . . I'm not sure. I'm not really ready yet . . . I can't tell.' And then a bright and, I felt, sophisticated idea came into my mixed-up head. 'Couldn't we just live together for a bit, and I be your mistress?'

'Don't be silly,' said Fitz firmly. 'Why do you think I'm asking you? I want to marry you so that we can live happily ever after, and so do you, even if you don't know it yet.'

He hugged me, and I suddenly did know. So we became engaged, and I knew every day from then on that I had made the right decision.

A girly letter I wrote to Joan Wyndham, part of which she sent me forty years later, explains a bit what I felt:

*At first I didn't know if I could really love him, but now I know
I do, it's rather exciting. He won't be an easy husband, as he
gets into rages when not sufficiently exercised, which show up his
terrifyingly good intellect and are difficult to deal with – with my
poor bird-brain – but when taken for daily walks he is angelic, drily
funny, good and cosy.*

*That's what I like best: his never having melted from his great
intellectual and rarefied reserve until he met me; and now it being
a complete* ramollissement *– and even his face changing and
looking foolish and schoolboyish when he looks at me. Next I like
his eighteenth-century elegances – long hands, long legs, perfection
of dress and taste, snuff-taking and wine-holding – and then his
more than Elizabethan courage and resolve, his love of adventure,
and his simplicity. There, you have it all.*

We motored up to Aberdeen to tell Fitz's soldier-servant, Sergeant
Duncan, and to ask him to come and look after us. Duncan was a Scots
Guardsman who had been with Fitz from the moment he joined the
SAS in the desert war, and all through the Jugoslav campaign. He had
ejected Randolph Churchill from a peasant's house and put him in its
pigsty because, he said, Randolph's snoring disturbed his brigadier,
who needed his sleep. He had jumped from aeroplanes, landed from
MTBs, and whenever Fitz asked him what he thought of their new
location, he would answer, 'It's awfu' like Aberdeen.'

Fitz loved him, and was sad when Duncan told him he had just
accepted a well-paid position as a courier for a London bank, and
that it was a job for life with a good pension which his family
said he couldn't refuse. They said goodbye and promised to keep
in touch, which they always did, and when Fitz opened a new
SAS barracks in Birmingham which was called Maclean House after
him, Sergeant Duncan came up for the celebration dinner and sat
beside him.

On our way north, we had stayed with Fitz's aunt, Daisy Whitworth,
in Admiralty House at Rosyth, where her husband, Admiral Sir Jock
Whitworth, was Flag Officer, Scotland. He knew all about Alan and
was especially kind to me as a sailor's widow, and he was delighted by
our engagement and new-found happiness, but he never talked about
the war, or his terrible experience in *Illustrious* which haunted him for

the rest of his life – for when she was sunk by Japanese dive-bombers, he was the only senior officer who survived. It was he who had given the order to abandon ship minutes before she went down, and in his last years – when his mind was failing – he would relive that dreadful moment again and again.

Our wedding was set for 12 January 1946, Moo's birthday. I had dearly hoped Fitz would meet Uncle Mumble before then, but in early December Maurice died of pneumonia at Beaufort, peacefully and gently, with Moo, Father Maguire, Nurse Neill and Salvatore, the Italian ex-prisoner-of-war who helped look after him, at his side. His death changed the whole rhythm of our family's and especially my mother's life, which suddenly became sad and lonely – and I still miss him.

That Christmas Fitz again joined his parents, and I don't think he came north until he moved in for our wedding. When he did arrive, he was immediately at ease with all the family, and he asked Andrew Maxwell, my first cousin, who had been one of his officers in Jugoslavia and the most resourceful of scavenging ADCs, to be his best man.

Yet one evening at Eilean Aigas, just before we married, a dark mood came over him, and it frightened me. I suppose I had chattered on too long about loving the Highlands, and how much Beaufort and the river and the people on the estate meant to me, and how I would love to settle there one day, when he responded fiercely, almost angrily, 'I could never let a house or a place tie me down. It would be a stone round my neck, stopping me from doing things and being free to go wherever I wanted to, any time, anywhere. Families and houses do just that – stop you,' and he stopped himself, looked at me and then looked away gloomily. There was a long silence, until he said, 'Forgive me, *c'est la nostalgie de la boue*,' and got up and went for a lonely walk. I didn't begin to know what he was talking about.

We had discussed endlessly where we should go for our honeymoon, Marrakesh being the favourite choice, but in 1946 foreign travel was extremely difficult, and to that destination almost impossible, so in the end we settled for a skiing holiday in Switzerland, stopping first at Montreux so that I could meet his parents.

We flew out to Zurich, rang my new in-laws from our hotel, and next evening took the crowded commuter train to Montreux on Lake Geneva, where we arrived in a dimly lit station. As Fitz's father limped towards us waving his stick, and his mother stood quietly by, tall, stately and stiff as a Grenadier, my first impression of them was disconcerting. We drove back to the Hôtel Monnaie, an old-fashioned hotel on the lake which had harboured them for most of their long internment, and there, in the candlelight of its grand but rather bleak dining room, I got a better view of my in-laws and they of me.

'What shall I call you?' I asked them. Somehow Christian names didn't seem appropriate, and 'Major' and 'Mrs' seemed too formal. We decided on initials: FIL for Father-in-Law and MIL for Fitzroy's Ma, which is what he always called her.

Fil was very easy to talk to, a typical Cameron officer of the old school, straightforward, capable and honourable, with all the soldierly virtues Shimi admired. He was far from stupid, but probably rather rigidly set in an older generation's mould. Mil was more difficult to fathom and it was not until I saw her in a Florentine background that I really appreciated her wisdom and the breadth of her learning and gentle wit, and, best of all, her complete unshockability and tolerance.

Fil was the grandson of General Peter Maclean, who had married Lord Charles Somerset's daughter when he was that nobleman's ADC. General Peter was the second son of the 16th Chieftain and Laird of Ardgour, and his remarkable wife Lady Margaret Hope, so that by the time the blue blood trickled through to Fil there was a soldiering tradition but no land and even less money.

Mil's ancestry was more unusual. Her father was Captain George Royle, Royal Navy, known to friends and colleagues as 'Royal George'; her mother was Fanny de Longueville Snow, a family of legal and literary traditions related to the Sitwells. George Royle, after serving in the China Seas and taking part in the battle of the Yangtse and many other adventures, left the navy in disgust when dreadnoughts took over from sailing ships, and went to Oxford, where he read Maritime Law. His first case was a brief from Lambert Bros, the company which controlled a large proportion of east–west trade passing through the newly opened Suez Canal.

He won it, and they asked him to stay on and become their permanent representative and barrister in Port Said. So Mil was brought up in an imposing house at Ghezireh, outside Cairo, the only child of devoted parents who were British hosts to just about everyone of interest or importance passing through or spending a couple of idle months in what was then the chosen place for wintering in the sun.

George's younger barrister brother was already in practice in Cairo, and I have a picture in my mind of a happy family, talented, affectionate, full of fun and with a great appetite for travel and adventure. Long before Fitz penetrated the Caucasus or the Oasis of Siwa, his grandfather had been there. A few articles, mostly written for *Blackwood's* magazine, some letters and sketchbooks – both brothers were amateur artists – portray their experiences, but when George Royle died in 1913 his widow and daughter returned to Cairo, sold the house and destroyed all personal papers, which is a great pity. Only a few snatches of the jokes and the fun the 'Gebrüder Royle', as they called themselves, had has come down to me from Mil. Fitz remembered his mother's nonsense jingle:

> *Well, slap the cat and count the spinach,*
> *Aunt Jemima's gone to Greenwich!*

There was also George Royle's witticism about a rich young couple who, someone said, were incompatible. 'Maybe so, but he's got the income and she's very pattable.' But my favourite reminiscence was Mil's story about her grandmother, who, as a young bride, was asked by her husband to keep monthly accounts and given a handsome ledger in which to do it. It had 'Income' printed on one side, and 'Expenditure' on the other, and at the end of the month she proudly brought it to her husband. Under Income she had written, 'G gave me one hundred pounds', and on the opposite page she had written, 'Spent it.' Now that is the sort of accounting I *can* understand!

Mil's youth must have been very agreeable. In the cool early mornings she would go for long rides in the desert with her latest admirer; then the family would sail to favourite bathing-places for leisurely picnics, exploring the classical sites which litter that arid coastline, and she would play tennis, dance with and entertain all the nicest officers of visiting regiments and ships. It wasn't until she was twenty-seven that she finally decided to marry, and then she danced away with the handsomest officer of the nicest regiment: the First Battalion of the Cameron Highlanders.

Fil took her first to Inverness (where they actually called on the Lovats at Beaufort), and then with the regiment's Second Battalion to India, first to Delhi and then to Poona. Mil hated India, especially the snobbery, pettiness and small jealousies of army wives, who she thought treated the natives abominably and were totally uninterested in the culture and history or the traditions of the great subcontinent.

Fitz was looked after by both a sergeant's wife and an ayah, and he sometimes got the cultures mixed up, as when Mrs Brown's unsuccessful efforts at toilet-training produced a kindly, 'Oh, it must have been a false alarm,' and he thought she had said, 'a full salaam'. For some time afterwards he would bow gracefully over his chamber pot with his little palms joined in the appropriate gesture.

When war was declared, the battalion returned immediately to England, so swiftly that the Jocks were still in tropical kit when they landed. For the next four years Fitz lived in a comfortable villa near Bournemouth, to which his widowed great-grandmother, Mrs Snow, had retired. She was a determined and rather eccentric old lady who, after the death of her husband, decided to live out the remaining years of her life prone, like Madame Récamier, in a large sunny bedroom which she never left, and in which she held court contentedly.

Even in war-time it must have been an unusual household for a little boy to grow up in, but a disciplined and happy one, especially when his father came back several times on Blighty leave. Shortly after the war came to an end, so did Fil's military career. He had survived the trenches; had been adjutant and second-in-command of an infantry battalion throughout the war in France; had been wounded twice and won the DSO; had been ADC to General Allenby in Jerusalem, and would probably have risen far in his natural calling – but one serious and neglected wound now caught up with him, and he was invalided out of the army. Fortunately, Lord David Scott, who had been at Sandhurst with him, had just been given the task of reorganising the Foreign Office, and needed people of his calibre to take on honorary (in other words, unpaid) posts and work as consuls in cities of secondary importance. Fil was offered Florence and, encouraged by his enthusiastic and overjoyed wife, he jumped at it.

Florence in the 1920s had a quite small British colony, but it was an eccentric and distinguished one. In those days there was practically no Anglo-Italian trade for the consulate to worry about, and few tourists. It happened to be, in Mil's eyes, the most beautiful city in the world, and she was delighted by the move – as was their small son. Soon the Macleans were settled into the Villa Passerini, above the city but in sight of the Duomo's rosy cupola – which every self-respecting Florentine must be able to see from his window, garden or rooftop. I still have the letter an enchanted seven-year-old wrote back in a clear, well-rounded script to his grandmother in England: 'It is very nice here . . . The sun shines every day . . . One thinks nothing of seeing a lizard.'

Mil was equally happy. She made friends, looked after indigent British subjects, gave luncheon parties, collected antique furniture, studied the history of the Crusades in three languages, and familiarised herself with every picture, statue and building not only in Florence but in most of Tuscany.

Fil would walk slowly down the Viale to the Consulate in the Palazzo Ginori every morning, and work there for an hour or two with Signor Lelli, his chief clerk and personal assistant, and then be driven home, or to a delicious light lunch at the golf club, where he would play a round or two on its steeply sloping fairways, and hear the city's gossip. Apart from two formal parties on the King's Birthday and New Year's – or was it St George's? – Day, from which I have inherited ninety-eight little silver forks and spoons, there was very little official work. His leg held up, though its curve always looked frighteningly like snapping, and he was permanently in pain. When I asked him why he was never operated on and given a calliper, his reply was unanswerable: 'Don't like doctors. Don't trust them,' and I resigned myself to the fact that the Macleans knew nothing nor wished even to learn anything about 'health' (which Fitz would call 'symptoms', and ban from conversation, until almost the end of his life).

The first two villas they lived in were rented from Mr Acton, who had married Hortense, a rich American, and had settled in a beautiful Renaissance villa to the north of Florence, where he gradually accrued a magnificent collection of books, pictures and other works of art. He dabbled as a painter, and had a studio in the city where there were thought to be goings-on with the models who posed for him. The Actons had two sons, William and Harold, who were roughly the same age as Fitz and had been at Eton with him.

In 1922 the Villa Arighetti on the Viale, near San Miniato, came up for sale and the Macleans bought it, and spent the next seventeen years happily restoring, modernising up to a point and furnishing it. There was an olive grove and a small *podere*, which a charming *contadino* and his brother cared for, occasionally donning striped waistcoats with silver Maclean-crested buttons to transform themselves into footmen when there was a large luncheon party.

Fitz had a pony and galloped it round the village above the villa. Fil helped with the haymaking, but unwisely suggested liberating two of the *contadini*'s cows which were permanently incarcerated in a dark hovel. One of them immediately fell over the terrace, broke its leg and had to be put down. The *contadini* happily ate her, accepted full payment and returned to their age-old farming practices.

The plumbing of the villa created problems. Fil had insisted on hot water in all the bathrooms, and the plumber dug up half the garden to obtain it, but one morning the goldfish in the ornamental lily pond lay gasping in a boiling brew while the new brass bath-taps still gushed forth muddy cold water.

On our honeymoon Fitz told me wonderful stories about pre-war Florence and its characters: how Mr Acton had innocently gone up to a pretty girl at a party and asked her to dance, upon which her *cavaliere* had slapped him across the face and challenged him to a duel; how Mr Acton had bravely accepted, even though the man was a well-known champion; how he had taken lessons in pistol-shooting and had pinked his opponent in the arm, thus satisfying honour and British prestige.

He told me how Valdemaro Fiorovanti, whose parents owned an immense medieval castle above the Certosa, kept a tame crocodile which lived in its underground vaults and fed upon rats. It had been quite small when he was given it, but had unfortunately grown so big that it now tipped over huge cupboards when scratching its back on them, and terrified all the servants.

Then there was the penniless Miss Goode, who lived in a tiny flat in St Catherine's house on the Erta Canina. She had seen St Catherine's ghost, and she was used as a convenient tour guide and periodically humiliated by Violet Trefusis, who lived with her sister Sonia and their parents at the large and elegant Villa Ombrellino. Old Alice Keppel (Mrs George Keppel), whom Fitz loved and used often to visit and confide in, told him solemnly that she had never slept with King Edward VII, though she had been his intimate friend and so-called mistress for many years. 'People will always tell you I did,' she said to him, 'but you know it wasn't true. I loved the King, but I never slept with him. I had too much respect for his wife and family, I suppose.'

Now, why would she say that to a seventeen-year-old young man, who by that time was quite well aware of the facts of life, if it wasn't true? Fitzroy said she had the best sense of humour and the greatest fund of amusing gossip of anyone he had ever known, but her stories were never unkind or malicious. She even told him one about herself: When she got into a hansom cab one day, and instructed its driver, 'King's Cross,' the cabby turned round, winked, and replied, 'Sorry to hear that, ma'am!'

The skiing bit of our honeymoon at Crans sur Sierre, above Lake Geneva, ended without serious mishap. There was a small earthquake which tipped me out of the bath and into Fitz's arms, but that was incidental.

13

SETTLING DOWN

WHEN WE RETURNED TO ENGLAND WE IMMEDIATELY BEGAN looking for a house in Fitzroy's constituency, which at that time included the towns of Lancaster and Morecambe, Carnforth, the Vale of Lune, part of the Fylde and the high fell country around Swinnerton. We did this very comfortably from Holker, which Richard Cavendish had inherited on the death of his parents. At the beginnng of the war he had eloped with and secretly married Pamela Lloyd-Thomas, to the excitement and delight of all their friends. Both sets of parents had thought them too young to wed – they were my age – and both were proved spectacularly wrong, for there has seldom been a stronger or more mutually happy marriage. Pamela was the elder sister of Sissy Ormsby-Gore, whom Fitz had loved romantically and watched grow up when he was a young diplomat in Paris, so we both felt they were more than friends, almost family; indeed, they treated us as such, and for three months Holker was our home.

In between reintroducing himself after four years of absence, and presenting me (almost as a war trophy) to the Tory ladies of Lancaster, Fitz and I house-hunted feverishly. We soon narrowed down the options to two – one, in a village called Yealand Conyers, a neat, square Georgian box of a house, with a stone porch, an enormous copper beech tree on its front lawn, plate-glass windows and a lovely view; the other a much older and more pretentious crumbling manor, which included a medieval hall with lancet windows. Fitz was for the Georgian box, I for a knightly atmosphere.

'It's so romantic,' I said, gazing up at the manor's moss-covered roof and elegant chimneys.

'But very dark,' he answered, and lifted me up to look through one of the narrow windows. It did indeed seem almost pitch-black inside, and it was only after we were cosily installed in Beechfield, the Georgian box, that he admitted he had spotted a window in the manor that still had its war-time blackout curtains drawn.

Our first act, when the contract for Beechfield was signed, was to send a telegram to Wallace Cockerill, my aunt Diana Westmorland's butler, who had cared for Uncle Burghie at Lyegrove until he was called up. Newly demobbed from the RAF, he was without a family to whom he could harness his devotion and skill. He answered our telegram by arriving in person, with a small suitcase and in a smart new demob suit. For the first three nights he slept on the floor of our bedroom in the empty house, as 'We can't have people breaking in or nosing around,' he told us.

From that day until he died thirty years later, he was watchdog, valet, butler, groom, gardener, carpenter and friend to all our family. There was a lot of painting to be done, and he and I did most of it, Cockerill taking on the ceiling and difficult bits, whistling Mozart on top of a ladder, a lovely clear sound as he slapped on the distemper. *Eine kleine Nachtmusik* was a special favourite of his, and good to paint to.

Soon furniture was given or lent or acquired, and the house began to look pretty. Fitz was determined that we should stand on our own feet financially, and refused to borrow from any bank or be subsidised by his parents. His parliamentary salary, the letting of his Mount Street flat and two years of a brigadier-general's pay had produced a small nest-egg of £12,000, and we bought Beechfield for exactly that. Things were a bit tight, as back-bench MPs earned a salary of only £600 a year in those days, with precious few emoluments except free travel between the House of Commons and the constituency, wives not included. My father had left me £6,000, and as a widow I had lived off the income from that and a naval pension, which, of course, now stopped. The children's nanny and (later on) schools were paid for largely by their father's marriage settlement and the income of an American trust. No one could accuse Fitz of marrying for money! In spite of these modest finances, which Fitz supplemented with journalism, we could still afford a butler, a lady gardener, and a daily cook and housemaid, as well as keeping on my flat in London, where we also had a housekeeper, and gave many parties.

We began to settle in and settle down, and, looking back on those first days, I suppose there was more to be settled than in most marriages. On my side, I had to adapt to living with the young eagle who had taken over my simple and fairly negative life. I had to learn quickly to assume the duties of a Tory MP's wife, and in a Lancashire constituency, where there are few grace notes and people did not let me forget 'a spade's a spade and not a bloody shovel'. I had to balance the tricky three-cornered relationship of providing my children with a stepfather and my thirty-five-year-old (bachelor) husband with a ready-made family. I had to run two households three hundred miles apart and get to know a host of Fitz's friends, who were at least ten years older than I was, and, coming from the top ranks of the diplomatic corps, the army and politics, seemed infinitely cleverer and more sophisticated. Worse, I had to feed and entertain all of them to the high standard he expected, and at the drop of a hat.

Only lately have I realised that I was also taking on a man whose nerves were still raw from five years of living under tremendous pressure, excitement and danger, who had loved the challenge of those years and was going to have to make huge adjustments in settling down to family life and domesticity, both of which were new and alien to him.

From Fitzroy's side the challenge was also great. He accepted my own faith but, when I bore his children, bitterly resented having Catholicism imposed on them. He took a long time coming to terms with it, and there were related irritations – the Douai translation of the New Testament, for example, instead of the Authorised Version, bad Church Latin, and Old Catholic tribalism and heartiness. Once a neighbour cheerfully greeted him outside the Roman Catholic church in our village with, 'Coming to Benny [Benediction], old boy? It will do you lots of good, you know.' It did him no good at all, and such talk made him feel sick.

His ingestion into my enormous family clan, fortunately, was never a problem as, thanks to David, Irene and Aunt Peg, he already felt himself almost part of it, and I think its diversity and warmth supplied a background he had missed in his own youth, being the only child of an only child, and growing up far away from his father's Highland roots. There had been no territorial imperative in his life, as there had been in mine – that came much later – and while I had fifty-one first cousins, he had only six, most of whom he hardly knew.

I don't suppose, either, that I was easy to live with that first year – ignorant, opinionated, naïve and disorganised, unpunctual and noisy. I still had almost all my teenage faults and had hardly ever read a biography, let alone any serious history.

One of my shortcomings that most irritated Fitz was that our minds worked at different tempos, or perhaps in different gears; and that I could not help, having been brought up in a large, noisy, rumbustious and affectionate family, where one often had to shout to be heard. I was highly articulate myself, and spoke very fast – often, I'm afraid, before I had thought out what I was going to say. I was also adolescent enough to like intimate and introspective conversations on great themes, in which the protagonists instinctively follow and stimulate each other's thoughts, pick up a sentence or mood, and finish in perfect harmony – 'soul' talk, inherited perhaps from my mother's genes.

With Fitz, such speculative dialogue was out. It was not his way at all. He hated introspection and great thoughts. He had never had to battle his way into a conversation like I had. He had never been teased, or laughed at, or interrupted. His own family never argued or quarrelled, never raised their voices in debate, and so he had grown up listening carefully, talking slowly and with consideration. He was extremely articulate on paper but, until he had to become more so verbally ('in self-defence', he admitted), he was a hesitant and very slow speaker, and when there was a measured pause and I fed him what I thought was the next step or word, he would react furiously: 'I wasn't going to say that at all! You've absolutely no idea of what I was thinking,' and, 'If only you wouldn't *interrupt!*'

I'm afraid I always interrupted, and I often got it wrong.

He could react to a situation physically and mentally in a flash, but in speech – and particularly in his speeches in the House of Commons – that measured-judgement process always intervened. He saw all the way round a subject, which slowed him down, and he could never flannel and waffle as others did. He believed that sentences must always be brief, well-chosen and meaningful. A politician's humbug was the thing he hated most and his temperament was not really suited to his being one.

Another difficulty, which lasted through much of our married life, was that I was always able to forgive and forget, or just forget, within hours of a tempestuous disagreement, whereas Fitz was incapable of doing so, and the memory of some hurt I had caused him would not leave him for days, even months. It was only in the last decades of his life that a kind of mellowness took over and our closeness became much closer, most of the edges having been ground down by the bond and the habit of marriage, by his illnesses and their acceptance, and the merging of each other's faith, so that the final love and trust we had in each other eventually became absolute.

At first he found the loss of his bachelor freedom hard to take, for in a diplomatic and military career the occasions for dalliance and possible seduction are endless; and he also missed the camaraderie of men, and their jokes. The ambition and sheer hard work which before the war had singled him out as a front-runner in the Diplomatic Service, and which would have almost certainly brought him eventually to its summit, were now changed for the life of a back-bencher in a rather dull and unfriendly House of Commons, a House which had not cared for the fuss the media had made of his war-time exploits, and in which there was no sure ladder to success. Fitz made things more difficult for himself by not being clubbable in the Members' Smoking Room, and by not accosting the senior figures. 'It's for *them* to speak to me first,' I remember him arguing.

There was also the problem of his stepfather relationship with my children, for, by honouring Alan's place as Susan Rose's and Jeremy's real – and in his view hero – father, and being determined never to usurp it, he created difficulties. He treated them with cautious affection, but with a certain detachment that, sadly, they did not understand and even, I think, may have grown to resent. As they grew older, because of this self-imposed discipline, he left all major parental decisions in their lives to me, never visited them at school, or took on any real *fatherly* role. Nevertheless, there were happy moments. He would drive them on specially bumpy roads to make them squeal with laughter; Sukie would hug him – at knee level – and sing, 'You are my sunshine,' and once, when he was axing down a huge monkey-puzzle on our back lawn and had come to the very last stroke, he gave Jeremy the end of a rope and said, 'Pull!' The little fellow pulled – and the tree fell down – a triumph Jeremy never forgot.

We somehow lived through those first traumatic six months without actually murdering each other, and there was room for jokes and laughter and fun; but the war-time legacy showed in many ways: in Fitz's inability to sleep; in his rolling out of bed at the slightest sound or movement, landing on the carpet with hands clenched in defence; in his mood-swings, and constant changing of plans; in his passionate arguments about the minutiae of life which were not in any way important.

'You see,' he would say, 'I love you so much I can't bear you even to *think* differently from me.' That was both the cause and the comfort of many of our quarrels, just as our eventual adaptation to each other's thoughts, and strong wills, was the way to final maturity and peace.

Once when I was being particularly obstructive a friend asked Fitz if he had ever thought of divorce. 'Divorce, never. Murder – often!' was his answer. Then he told the story of a Maclean ancestor who was about to slay a Macdonald chief, but who desisted at the last moment and replaced his dirk in its scabbard. 'For with The Macdonald gone,' he told his clansmen, 'who would I have to *bicker* with?'

There was also the question of taste, about which we both felt strongly. Jakie Astor remembered a luncheon party which Fitz and I nearly broke up by a fierce argument about where a picture which we hadn't yet bought would be hung in a house which we didn't yet own. My taste in decoration had been formed by Moo's, which I believed to be impeccable, and a modest injection of the Mells, Lyegrove and Holker traditions. White walls, well-drawn and colourful chintzes, crimson carpets or good old Turkey ones, flower prints, pretty china, comfortable chairs, good furniture, subtle colours and faded charm – a gentle background to anything beautiful you might own, which was more important than decorating fashion.

Fitz's taste was much more austere, being formed by the spare elegance and Renaissance classicism of Florence. His admiration was for Greek rather than Roman antiquities, for eighteenth-century symmetry rather than Victorian or Edwardian style. He liked bare boards, good carpets, on which he had been brought up, and of which he had a modest collection, made during his travels in Central Asia, and he hated 'lumpy' Elizabethan and Stuart furniture and all dark oak.

One never-to-be-forgotten early bloomer of mine came with the visit of an old diplomatic friend from the Levant Service, an expert on tribal and Central Asian carpets.

'I'd like to show you two rather nice rugs and camel bags that I brought back from Uzbekistan,' said Fitz before lunch. 'They've still got their rope tails [for tying them to their owners' beasts] on them.' Proudly he opened the door of his study: horror and consternation! I had cut off the tails that very morning, as everyone kept tripping over them. I lamely explained this in the total silence that ensued. Luncheon proceeded in a below-zero atmosphere, and, almost worse, I had ordered oxtail, a Beaufort favourite, which neither Fitz nor our visitor could eat.

It was years before we compromised, agreeing that Fitz was best at architecture, style and good proportions as well as the authentic dating of old furniture, and I was best at soft furnishing – colour, comfort and atmosphere.

When in London Fitz discovered a picture shop in King William IV Street, which he passed on his daily walk to Westminster, and this was a source of much pleasure. Usually he returned with mezzotints or watercolours, but one day he bought a small oil of two Cossacks on plunging horses fighting with lances. He hung it in our bedroom. I did not think it went with my gentle Redoubté flower prints and, while he was away, banished it to the passage outside. The next time I looked it had gone.

'You didn't like it, and didn't understand it,' he told me bitterly, 'so I got them to take it back.' It was indeed an ignorant folly, as the painting was of the Delacroix school, and I soon came to regret it; but no amount of cajoling would make him change his mind, and I realised that I couldn't make that sort of mistake twice.

Our best friends in Fitz's constituency were Colonel Pat and Edith Cowper, who lived in a large, decrepit and inconvenient house on the other side of Lancaster. 'Teedie', a colonel's lady in the very best sense, complete with hat, was the backbone of the Tory Party's organisation and ran it with the utmost efficiency and political nous. It was she who, in 1941, had turned down a local candidate and insisted on selecting Fitz to fight the Lancaster by-election. It was she who had believed him when he admitted he knew nothing about party politics, would have voted against Munich had he been in a position to do so, and had been brought up to regard all politicians except Winston with the gravest suspicion.

'All right,' she had told him. 'I'll arrange for someone to go round canvassing with you who'll tell you what to say, and you'll soon get the hang of it. You may even like it, one day, and Lancaster can wait until you win the war.' And so the bouncy and cheerful Miss Berry, of the neat tweed suit and sensible brogues (with impeccable relations in Argyll), was produced to be Fitz's minder, to tell him how to win votes, and to believe in orthodox Tory policy.

Unfortunately, they had barely started the campaign when, preceding him up an icy path on a council house estate, Miss Berry's sensible shoes slipped from under her and she landed flat on her back, hitting her head on a garden stone or gnome – it mattered not which, for she was out, stone-cold. Fitzroy, who was in kilted Cameron Highlander uniform, picked her up and did the only possible thing – he rang the council house bell. The housewife who opened the door gazed at them both in amazement, but he managed, 'I am Fitzroy Maclean, madam, your Tory candidate, and this is my lady organiser. Please—' before she cut him short.

'Sorry, we always vote Labour here,' she briskly replied and shut the door in his face. It was an inauspicious start to his political career.

Nevertheless, he won the Lancaster and Morecambe by-election for the Tories, and was able to escape from the Foreign Office and remain a soldier. For the duration of the war he handed over the care of the constituency to Jim Thomas, an able and friendly Tory MP, and then, having held on to the seat in the Labour-won landslide of 1945, he had taken up his interrupted political career once more and, by the time we were married, was pursuing it with vigour and his usual steely determination.

In the Commons, he was bad at speaking but good at Question Time, mastering the complexities of his brief and often giving the answering ministers a hard time, and these exchanges were faithfully recorded in the *Lancaster Guardian*, our local newspaper. I remember one, about the size of the herring catch at Fleetwood, appearing under a singularly unflattering photograph of Fitz and the heading 'Immature Fish'. His speeches always read well, but sounded dreary, for he spoke too slowly and in a flat monotone.

After we moved to Beechfield, we sold Fitz's Mount Street flat and installed Mrs Macdonald in my Maida Avenue, or 'Canal Zone' one, to look after and cook for him from Monday to Friday, when he would catch the train back to Carnforth, and spend the weekend in our new home. Many hours of these weekends were spent working with his electors, but at least they were spent together, and it was in the constituency that Fitz really enjoyed politics and came into his own. Everyone liked him, and he genuinely liked meeting people, making friends and trying to help them. In spite of looking 'every bit a gentleman' – quotation from the *Lancaster Guardian* – he was completely classless and equally at ease in the poorest houses of Lancaster as in the middle-class and often snobbish homes of the Lune valley, the country and 'county' part of his constituency.

In the north of England in those days there was a solid working-class Tory vote, which slowly disappeared as council estates grew and unions became more powerful. We were always welcomed into the tumble-down terraced houses of 'The Marsh', the poorest part of the city, whose occupants would talk to Fitz about the two world wars, or about Churchill or, if they were old enough, their other hero, the great Lord Derby, who had been the constituency president for many years. It was in these houses that we made real friends, and that I was brought face to face with urban poverty for the first time.

The working-men's clubs were fertile ground for grass-roots politics. Fitz was an honorary member of the British Legion and the Carnforth ones, and we often visited them on Saturday nights, when ladies were allowed in. Nearly all the best stand-up comics and singers of my generation started their careers touring working-men's clubs in the north of England, and the entertainment on a Saturday night was usually superb.

In the low-ceilinged back room of the Carnforth Club, hazily blue with pipe and cigarette smoke and dark except for two spotlights over a makeshift stage, about sixty to eighty men would be sitting round small iron-legged tables, with wives and girlfriends squeezed in between them, and glasses covering every inch of flat space. We would hover round the door until asked to sit at one of Fitz's chums' or supporters' tables, and then, between turns in the programme, orders would be shouted from dark corners of the room to scurrying waitresses, and glasses would appear like magic in front of us. 'A rum and Coke for Mrs Maclean, with the compliments of the Lune Fisheries,' 'A dram for the Brigadier from a fellow Scot,' and so on.

Sometimes the turns were hilarious, often scurrilous; we all joined in the choruses. We were entertained by singers, saw-players, hypnotists, stand-up comics, impersonators, ventriloquists and others.

One friend, an engine-driver from Carnforth, then an important railway junction and engine depot, would always buy me a shandy and tell me about his much-loved old mother. 'She's a true-blue Tory, she is, always has been, won't ever change, not her. But I'm Labour. Labour looks after me, and I tell her so, though I can't change her. Red-hot Labour, that's me,' and here he would pound a barrel-shaped chest. As election time drew near he would always give me a hug. 'That's from my old mother,' he'd say, 'and may the best man win.'

Fortunately he always did. 'Red-hot' told us about the pride old drivers had in keeping their great steam engines in sparkling, tip-top shape with every piston and knob gleaming, and how the young ones 'didn't care any longer' and were all the worse for that. Certainly the Carnforth trains then ran on time, though they took seven and a half hours to reach London. I became very fond of Carnforth railway station, where we experienced so many wistful goodbyes, joyful reunions and exciting departures. The fact that it was later used as the background of Puffin Asquith's film *Brief Encounter* made it all the more romantic.

That summer, as I was pregnant, I spent more and more time in Lancashire. Fitz would hold surgeries every other Saturday morning in our constituency headquarters, with me and our fat and lazy agent, Mr Batty, as back-up, taking notes. One never knew what to expect: one morning a wild-looking man sat down opposite Fitz and reached into a capacious pocket. 'And what do you think of that?' he asked, pulling out an enormous lump of coal and skidding it across the desk between them.

'Well,' answered my husband, who had recoiled involuntarily, as if the object had been a hand grenade, 'well . . . could it be . . . er . . . a lump of coal?'

'That's what they all say!' roared the man. 'And at five shillings a bag it's a disgrace! I'm not paying that for bloody stones and lignite!' With which he stood up and stalked out of the room, and our lives.

Most of the cases were local government housing problems, over which a Member of Parliament has no jurisdiction, but Fitz always listened sympathetically, and I believe the plaintiffs left feeling slightly happier. When a question for a government minister came up, a personal letter from an MP to the minister involved would cut out a lot of red tape and often worked wonders. I would be the one who wrote the letters, with two fingers, on an old portable typewriter, for Fitz's part-time secretary in London had more than she could deal with.

The baby was due in October. Moo was coming down from Eilean Aigas to be with me, and a monthly nurse, this time recommended by our gynaecologist, was in place when Fitz announced he was leaving on a parliamentary delegation to the Far East. He was only semi-apologetic and obviously raring to go.

'You know, darling, how I like to believe that babies are found under gooseberry bushes? I wouldn't be much good at the detail, would I? You don't mind, do you?'

I pretended I did, just for drama's sake, but in fact I didn't mind at all, being also of the opinion that childbirth was women's work and a very personal act that I could share with my mother but no one else, and that the last thing in the world I wanted was for Fitz to see its indignities and be horrified by its pain.

The baby was three days old when Fitz returned, breathless, bronzed and only slightly guilty, but grateful for what he had been spared. However, his verdict after seeing his son for the first time, still red-faced and puckered, peeking out of a bundle of Shetland shawls, was, 'Very nice, darling. Show him to me again in six months' time – he's a bit crumpled now, isn't he?'

Sukie and Jeremy, however, were delighted with what they thought was a new toy, and Fitz looked quite smug when he was told that Charles Edward was twenty-three inches long and weighed ten and a half pounds. 'A real bruiser,' was how he described him to his parents. I think it was the first time he had ever seen a baby close to.

While I lay in blissful motherhood, Fitzroy and Moo, who got on together tremendously well, went on several raiding parties to a second-hand furniture emporium in Preston, and one day they brought me back a beautiful eighteenth-century inlaid cabinet with Chinese lacquer doors, and two Chinese armorial plates as a present for having the baby.

The parliamentary session that opened in November 1946 was not a particularly happy one for Fitz. In the tumultuous period that followed the capitulation of Germany, there were just as many problems in the Balkans and Eastern Europe as there are today. After his war-time involvement with Tito, the Partisans and the Royal

Jugoslav Government in exile, Fitzroy had left Belgrade in March 1945, handing over his dual roles of negotiating diplomat and retiring head of the redundant military mission to successors. He thus missed two of the nastiest episodes of that period – the forced return of the Cossacks to certain death in Russia, and the vengeance killings of Croatian *Ustaše* by victorious Serbian Partisans in the woods of Slovenia.

In spite of brave words from Ernest Bevin, the Labour Foreign Secretary, about 'Left being able to speak to Left in confidence and comradeship', by 1946 relations between the two countries had reached their lowest ebb. And so they did for Fitz in the Commons. Winston, on the few occasions when Fitz and he met, would growl about 'your Tito'. Then came the arrest of Draza Mihailovič, a former colonel in the Royal Jugoslav Army, who during the war had become leader of the anti-Communist guerrillas, the Četniks, and was known by Tito's Partisans to have made accommodations with the Germans. When he was tried for treason and executed, many people in the House of Commons seemed to hold Fitz personally responsible.

Archbishop Stepinac, who had blessed the Croatian pro-Hitler *Ustaše* troops on their way to commit atrocities, was put under house arrest. Koča Popovič, the brilliant but mercurial Partisan Chief of Staff, now Jugoslav Foreign Secretary, was giving Charles Peake, our new Ambassador in Belgrade, a particularly hard time; and the Croatian seminary of San Geroliamo in Rome was providing a rat-run for escaping war criminals under the very nose of the Pope. It was a bad time all round.

14

MAC-MISS TWO

S EVEN MONTHS AFTER THE CESSATION OF HOSTILITIES, THERE WERE some three hundred thousand refugees from the Jugoslav and Ukrainian armies, who had fled Communism, holed up in temporary British camps in Italy and Austria. No one knew exactly who they were, or what part they had played in the war. The United Nations Refugee Organisation, which was trying to deal with them, appealed to the Foreign Office, who recognised that the British Liaison Officers (BLOs) of Fitzroy's war-time mission to the Partisans, nicknamed Mac-Miss One, were probably the only people capable of interrogating them and sorting them out.

January 1947 came in with major blizzards that swept the country, and with temperatures that dropped low enough to freeze the Thames and burst pipes in every home. At Beechfield we were more or less snowed in, but kept a negotiable footpath to the village street. One night, about nine p.m., the door-bell pealed and Cockerill came into the drawing room where we were drinking coffee in front of a log fire, to announce in his professional butler's tones that two gentlemen were in the hall, asking if General Maclean was at home.

Fitz greeted the damp and shivering strangers and, calling for whisky and glasses, led them into his study. The door closed, and it wasn't until two hours later, after a buzz of goodbyes and promises to meet again next day, that he returned, rubbing his hands and looking pleased.

'What was all that about?' I asked.

'It was about a proposition that's going to change our lives,' he answered, 'and one that I'm going to find very hard to refuse.'

The proposition was that Fitz should lead a new mission, composed of the officers who had acted as BLOs in his war-time one, with the aim of screening the many thousands of men and women still held in displaced-persons or prisoner-of-war camps in Italy and Austria: sorting out who they were and separating the innocent from those guilty of war crimes. Most of his ex-officers needed little persuasion to join. As for myself and their wives, the idea of escaping from England, with all its post-war gloom and shortages, was delightful, and we needed no coaxing at all.

The business of transporting Mac-Miss Two to Rome became known as 'Operation Cow & Gate' (the name of the prevalent baby food), as there were, besides Charles Edward Maclean, aged three months, two other infants and numerous toddlers in the mission's tail. It was put in the capable hands of 'Groupy', aka Group Captain John Selby, DFC and Bar, who had been in charge of the former Mac-Miss's air traffic.

After crossing the Channel on a stormy afternoon, we boarded another train at the Gare du Nord, where Thermoses were filled with boiling water for the babies' bottles and the grown-ups fed sumptuously on Dover sole and Chablis in its splendid *fin-de-siècle* restaurant. Then it was into the *wagon-lits* of the beautiful Paris–Rome–Istanbul Express, and full steam ahead.

Italy was still occupied and under Allied military government, of which we now became a part. Fitzroy had been pipped-up one to be a major-general, so in Rome the Maclean family were given a general's billet, the Royal Suite of the Grand Hotel on the Via Veneto.

It was only in later years, when I worked for the tourist board, that I learnt from bitter experience that royal suites in grand hotels are often the worst, for they are mostly used for weddings or receptions, and can quickly be tarted up in the unlikely event that the ex-king of Transylvania suddenly decides to visit. There is usually something fundamentally wrong with them, and in Rome we soon found out what.

There were six of us: three children, Rhoda, Fitz and me. The manager, who received us with enthusiasm in the very grand foyer, led us up the equally grand marble staircase. Halfway up, on the mezzanine floor, were heavy double doors carved and gilded in the rococo manner. He threw them open with *éclat*, revealing an enormous bedroom which looked on to the Veneto, with a suitably caparisoned royal bed with a crown over it, very little other furniture, and acres of floor space. This led to more double doors, which he again threw open with a superbly Italian gesture of largesse.

'Your drawing room, *Signor Generale*,' he announced, and we gazed with amazement at a late-rococo ballroom, complete with gilded mirrors, angels, chandeliers and about forty stiff-backed chairs ranged round three sides. On the fourth side there were three open windows, through which traffic noise poured so deafeningly that we all had to shout.

The manager, no doubt seeing that things weren't going too well, shut the windows and, returning to the bedroom, patted the crimson-and-gold bedspread. 'Very wide, very comfortable, *un letto matrimoniale*.' Then, dropping his voice to a reverential tone which could only just be heard above the roar of the traffic: 'Our late lamented King Alfonso *died* in this bed.'

'And the children?' I squeaked.

'Ah! *Gli tesori!*' The manager beamed, and led us to a small windowless room off the landing with twin beds in it.

It was no good pleading for five smaller rooms in the attics; this part of the hotel was still in hock to the forces of occupation, and Fitz being a senior officer, a major-general no less, he was not only entitled to a royal suite but firmly designated to it, too.

In the end we managed. The *tesori* were walked to a convent crèche in the mornings by Cockerill, who had joined the mission as both Foreign Office courier and the General's batman. Rhoda perambulated the baby round the Borghese gardens, avoiding flying footballs, and Jeremy discovered the joys of the Grand Hotel's electric lifts, which were run by a teenage bell-boy called Curly, in a smart monkey-jacket with gold epaulettes. He would happily ride up and down all afternoon with Curly, and occasionally be allowed to press a button, but one day Curly brought him to our room in tears. 'I got out at the wrong layer,' the poor little fellow sobbed, 'and you weren't there.'

Before long Miss Jeffreys, Fitz's constituency secretary, who had previously never roamed further from Bolton-le-Sands than Blackpool, and had already shown signs of hysteria on the journey out, succumbed to agoraphobia. She believed that every Roman who eyed her in the street or commented with gestures on her appearance – and they all did, for she had a neat figure – was bent on kidnap, if not rape. She was sent back to Lancaster, and I took to typing Fitz's private and parliamentary correspondence with three fingers, in the ballroom.

Fitz was quite often away from Rome, visiting and setting up the mission's headquarters in the various Italian camps, which left me time for quick cultural expeditions carried out with a guidebook. Whenever he came back, the problem of exercising him was always the most urgent and came first. We eventually solved it by borrowing two police horses from the municipality and cantering round the *Gallipatoio* in the Borghese gardens, a kind of inferior Rotten Row, where perambulators, juvenile football teams and horses fought for space on a narrow sandy track.

What I had not reckoned for was that police horses, though by then well nourished on black-market Allied oats, were seldom allowed out of a sedate walk, and therefore had mouths like leather from being constantly reined in. When encouraged to canter, in spite of the footballs whistling around our heads and prams dashing across our path, they rapidly became unstoppable, and after being unseated once, I gave up the struggle and told Fitz that he must find a cavalryman among his officers to replace me.

Social life in Rome was made enjoyable by Fitz's unbroken links with his diplomatic past. Our Ambassador was Noel Charles, and both he and Grace, his brassy-haired and soft-hearted wife, were wonderfully hospitable and became firm and lasting friends. Noel was not a serious character, but full of charm and quick wit and unconventionality. He understood Italians well, and they understood him, while Grace had a genius for making embassies pretty and comfortable, and for bullying the Office of Works, that dreaded Foreign Office department, and its bureaucratic, tasteless inspectors. She was capable of giving a dinner party in a stable, but was then fighting a losing battle to persuade the Foreign Office and Treasury to buy the only slightly war-damaged Palazzo Barberini, one of the grandest and most beautiful of all Renaissance buildings in Rome, instead of building from scratch a glass-and-steel monstrosity, of which they were strongly in favour. The Barberini would have rivalled the Palazzo Farnese and for once beaten the French at the 'best embassy' game, but it was not to be.

Meals at the Grand Hotel were particularly trying. The children ate in their room, but Fitz and I were assigned a residents' table in the magnificent dining room. I was surprised when a basic menu was presented for our first dinner. I had just seen a beautiful trolley of Italian *antipasti* roll by, while at a table behind us an American couple were tucking into a mouthwatering mountain of *Monte Bianco* and its purée of chestnut 'worms'. Fitz summoned the head waiter and enquired politely why such delicacies were not available to us.

'Ah, *Signor Generale*, they are eating from the civilian menu, verra good, verra verra expensive. This,' he continued, flicking our bit of pasteboard contemptuously, 'is the military menu.' And so, heaving a patriotic sigh, we succumbed to a tedious diet of thinly disguised spuds and Spam.

Roman society – not the black Romans, who one hardly ever saw, but the IWT (International White Trash) Romans, who were fighting their way back into post-war respectability, and especially the *macedoine* of Allied military and civilian personnel who had invaded the Eternal City – was rife with gossip and rumour of every kind. The arrival of Fitz's mission and its somewhat ambiguous role was a nine-day wonder and started a series of new canards, not helped by the huge welcome and six dozen red roses presented to him by the most elegant and conspicuous of all ex-spies in the city, who had recently arrived in Rome with her husband from Belgrade (a Communist capital!).

Actually Dragica, Fitz's old friend, had always been more of a good-time girl than a spy, and when Mac-Miss One had found her in Belgrade in 1944 (one couldn't miss her), she had never failed to declare her devotion to a mysteriously absent husband, as she dallied with almost all of his staff. She looked like a Slavic Marilyn Monroe, sang 'Lili Marlene' in a husky voice, accompanying herself on the piano, and now, in Rome, pretended to those not in the know that she had opened the Victory Ball in liberated Belgrade with Tito on one side of her and Fitzroy on the other. She was both lovable and laughable, greedy for a happy, privileged life, and yet somehow earmarked by fate for exile and tragedy.

Her husband, a psychiatrist, was a very different creature, a good-looking, cultured Jugoslav national who had spent the war as a doctor practising in Germany, where he was regarded by the Wehrmacht as such a trusted anti-Communist spy that he was given the Iron Cross by Hitler. But he also gave information about the Germans to the

Allies, and lived a life of amazing danger and intrigue. Whether he was a triple agent (a Russian one, too) and not just a double was never clear, though Fitz told me he suspected it. What was abundantly plain was that the dubious pair, already involved in treasure-hunting and probably black-market international smuggling, were not good news for Mac-Miss Two, yet I still feel a little ashamed of Fitz's stuffiness in refusing their advances and invitations, for only a few years later poor Dragica was blown up and killed with her husband in an aeroplane he was piloting on some mysterious mission.

As spring turned to summer, and Rome and the Royal Suite became hotter and more claustrophobic, I had further reason to regret my husband's scrupulous correctness. On a rare holiday outing together to Tivoli we had discovered, among the five-hundred-year-old olive trees below the garden's cascades, an enchanting old farmhouse, half hidden by a vine pergola, white jasmine and climbing roses, near which the owner and his sons were carting hay. We asked if we could eat our picnic there (it even had a duck-pond for the children to paddle in), and we quickly made friends with the family. On a second visit it emerged that the owner had a daughter he wanted to educate in England, and he offered us half his house if we would pay for her schooling in Canterbury. This kind of barter was strictly forbidden by the British Government, and in spite of my tears and pleading, Fitz was adamant. We had to live by the rules.

Not long afterwards, however, he moved the children and Rhoda out of Rome to the Villa Lauder in Florence, which Fitz's parents, Mil and Fil, had rented for us from old Lady Dick Lauder, and which had cool rooms, a lovely garden and a very good cook. The raspberry-coloured villa stood near the top of a steep lane, the Erta Canina, or Dog Walk, that led from the broad boulevard of the Viale to the Arno, coming out near the Ponte Vecchio. When Fitz was a child he used to ride up it, avoiding the precipitous descent of a legless old man, who hurtled down on a kind of trolley every morning, depending on the kindness of his neighbours to haul him back up for his siesta.

Gradually I got to know the remnants of the British colony in Florence, whom my father- and mother-in-law had looked after so faithfully in the inter-war years. For the most part they had stayed on, some for reasons of poverty, some from choice; and there were some delightful eccentrics among their number.

Miss Goode, the bony, horse-faced gentlewoman now in her late seventies, still lived in her exquisite little apartment in St Catherine's house on the Erta. As Fitz had told me, she knew more about the city's history than any guidebook. Being lonely, she loved to be dropped in on by me and the children, and she would ply us with home-made lemonade, pressed from the fruit of a tree on her terrace, and complain about the continuing bad behaviour of Violet Trefusis, who lived in the grand Villa Ombrellino at the other end of the city. Violet would smother poor Miss Goode with kindness and cast-off garments when she wanted friends taken on sightseeing tours, and then cut her dead at a cocktail party next evening. 'I never know where I am with Violet,' the poor old dear would confide, 'but I think I'll give her one last chance.'

Valdemaro Fiorovanti still lived in his enormous medieval castle, but alone, as his parents had recently died. He had never found the good English Catholic girl he hoped to marry, and now probably never would. The old Marchese had bravely looked after the Maclean silver during the war, burying it by night in two trunks in his *podere*. To Fil's delight the cases were now returned unharmed, together with two small tortoises which Jeremy and Sukie played with in the Villa Lauder's garden.

In August 1947 Mac-Miss Two was winding up its work in Italy and moving on to Austria, to a new headquarters near Klagenfurt on the Wörthersee. On this occasion we paid and packed but did not follow: instead, we spearheaded the move into Carinthia. Groupy sent an army staff-car to Florence with Fitz's own driver, Corporal George Gregory, to look after us and help us pack. Rhoda, by this time familiar with army parlance, assured him that if anything from the sacred nursery paraphernalia was left behind, she would 'have him put on a charge'! Gregory just grinned and went on loading.

We started off, sardine-packed, in the sweltering heat of a Florentine summer, and headed thankfully for the hills of Venezia Giulia. Our first night stop, though, was by the sea, with General Terence and Bridget Airey at Duino, where he had the particularly tricky command of our border troops, policing three countries which hated each other, but with the compensation of living in the fairy-tale old castle of the Thurn-Taxis family.

After leaving Trieste we were challenged by Jugoslav, American, Italian and British guard-posts before we finally found the castle and drove up to its high, iron-studded gates. Bridget Airey, a cousin of Mary Herbert, was used to invasions. The comatose children were quickly bedded down in a huge brass bed in a vaulted room, while Rhoda boiled up dozens of bottles of Cow & Gate for the next day's march, and showed off Charles Edward, who was by now very handsome and not at all crumpled, to a succession of admirers, including lots of soppy soldiers. I left them to it and joined my hosts for a delicious fireside dinner and all the latest news. Touchy Americans, touchy Italians, bloody-minded Jugoslavs and Russians on their nearest disputed borders, a commander-in-chief way off in Vienna, and incompetent, ignorant politicians in London stirring everything up and not having a clue – it all sounded too familiar.

The castle at Duino is built on a cliff above the Adriatic, and when I went into my little turret bathroom, I found a nineteenth-century loo with no visible plumbing. When you pulled the white china handle on its brass chain, the pan opened and its contents dropped straight into the sea, leaving you staring at a small circle of blue water and the odd crested wave two hundred feet below.

We spent next morning climbing slowly to Udine, then at last to Villach and the foothills of Carinthia. When we halted at the top of a pass, the children gambolled among the heather and bracken, gulping in the pure mountain air and whooping with liberation and delight. Rhoda and Gregory unpacked Bridget's generous picnic, little Charlie beamed, and we all felt a lot happier.

The Gulf Hotel on the shore of the Wörthersee, and later our own villa at Portschach, were both very comfortable, and a paradise for Sukie and Jeremy, who learnt to swim and talk nursery German, and had all the other mission children to play with. The refugee camps were not so distant as those in Italy, and Fitz came home most evenings, often bringing with him his old friends and ex-officers from the Partisan war, like the Vivian Streets and the Keanes, whom I now got to know. The Austrian girls who helped us cook were always delighted when there was a dinner party, and took great pride in laying out on our army-issue dining table lovely mosaics of flowers, berries and ferns that made it look elegant and beautiful. It was a very happy time.

Once we drove up to Vienna, for Fitz to confer with General

Steel, the commander-in-chief. The ruined city looked exactly as it was later portrayed in the film *The Third Man*. Sacher's celebrated café, though battered, still stood, and it was there that I met Stefan Zeissl again and his old father (*der schöne Hans*) and his father's mistress, who was a bit of a disappointment, being in her seventies and looking more like a respectable retired housekeeper than a seductress. But it was lovely to see my old friend once more. He was full of new Viennese jokes, and took us to the Volksoper, which had just begun to function again, to hear Offenbach's *Orpheus in the Underworld*.

Any unlawful expedition outside Fitz's stern military discipline was called 'swanning'. I can't remember exactly when Richard Keane's wife Olivia and I plotted a super-swan to Venice, which neither of us knew. But the next time our husbands were away, we approached Groupy, who was temporarily in charge, to ask if Gregory could drive us, softening him up by promising to bring him back lots of Italian green figs (he being very greedy).

All went well on the road, and we sailed through the frontier, arriving at Mestre about four p.m. As Gregory dropped us off, we promised to return to the rendezvous within twenty-four hours, and caught the bus-boat into the city. Enchanted, we wandered round the dark, mysterious canals and *calles*, gazed at the *palazzi* and crossed over the little stone bridges until we found our way to St Mark's and its great square. We dined in a small restaurant, which took longer and cost more than we expected, and then, it being dark, we began to look for a cheap hotel.

We had not reckoned on Venice being chock-a-block with an international congress. About midnight we gave up searching in the city centre, and, having been told there was more room on the Lido, we took tickets for the last Lido-bound boat of the evening. Soon we were deposited on a dimly lit quayside near the bulk of a substantial building surrounded by barbed wire.

'Oh God!' I whispered. 'This isn't a hotel at all. It must be some kind of military headquarters.'

'It's American,' Olivia whispered back. 'I've just seen some white caps. Go on – do your major-general's wife's act, and don't say which army.'

We gingerly approached the guard-house.

'I wonder if our rooms are ready?' I asked the sergeant, who was adding up sums in a ledger. 'I'm afraid we're hopelessly late – and as my husband, General Maclean, suddenly had to return to headquarters, we came straight through to you on our own.'

'No problem, ma'am. Plenty of room in the guest-house.'

After a brief parley on the telephone, we were whisked off by a chief petty officer and shown into two of the most luxurious rooms we had ever seen, with armchairs, drapes and six-foot-wide beds, and balconies that looked over the sea. Next morning Olivia came into my room while I was finishing my crisp American bacon, English muffins, maple syrup and coffee, served bedside by a smart member of the WAVES. 'Get up, quick!' she said. 'We can walk straight out on to the sand.' We spent the morning on a wonderfully clean beach, with a few American family groups dozing in the sun and watching their children paddle.

Eventually we found an officer who looked kind and responsive, and to whom we came clean. 'We *do* apologise,' I told him. 'The only thing we can offer in return is a visit to the Wörthersee.' He promised to consider it, and then a dozen more officers turned up, who gave us lunch, and we returned in triumph to Mestre in a speedboat. Fitzroy was not amused when he heard of our adventure, and poor Groupy was given a rocket (as well as two kilos of Venetian figs).

I knew that telegrams constantly flew back and forth between London, Vienna and the mission headquarters, and I knew that Fitz was continually harassed and often exhausted; but I heard little of the mission's work, for he kept it and family life apart. I helped him with his constituency letters and entertaining, and tried to piece together from others whether things were going well or badly, but he rarely shared his worries with me.

Clearly the mission's task was herculean. When we arrived in Rome there were eight thousand Ukrainian refugees in a single camp in Rimini, including the Galician Brigade, who had fought in the German army against the Russians, and they had to be dealt with before September, when the Allies' treaty for the demilitarisation of Italy would be ratified and the Italian camps closed. When that happened, any remaining inmates would almost certainly be chucked back to the Russians, who would most likely shoot them.

Other camps in the British Zone of Italy held twelve thousand

Jugoslavs, mostly Četniks and *Ustaše*, who were desperate not to be sent back to Jugoslavia, where the new Communist government would almost certainly shoot *them*. (Before he took on the mission, Fitz had refused to screen the Ukrainians, as none of his officers spoke their language. He did, however, visit their camp, outside Rimini, and found it in a chaotic state, with every detainee armed to the teeth and on the brink of mutiny. In the end the Labour government shipped the lot back to England, where, in spite of earlier promises, they were never screened.)

The Jugoslavs still in camps in Italy and Austria all wanted visas to emigrate to the Americas or Australia, as political refugees, but no country was keen to accept them. The mission's twin objectives were to identify the guilty and protect the innocent – but how guilty was guilty, and how innocent innocent? At first individuals were categorised as black, grey or white. The blacks were those on the 'Most Wanted' lists already agreed by the British and American governments, and if found, they had to be handed over to the War Crimes Authority, whose tribunals would deal with them. But by the time the mission started its screening, a great many had already skipped their camps and melted into the Italian population, or had been clandestinely filtered away to the Argentine by a Catholic 'mafia'.

Later, when someone asked Fitzroy about the endless political chicaneries, the rivalries, the suspicions, both British and international, with which he had to deal, he merely said, 'It was a very funny time.' It was not only the Foreign Office that had two different policies about what to do with refugees: so also did the Special Intelligence Service (SIS), the American State Department and the Italians, while the Jugoslav government and the Russians were naturally suspicious of every British and American move. And then there were the Catholics, who, almost worldwide, regarded assistance to their Croat co-religionists as morally legitimate, however many crimes they had committed in the war – a war, after all, against Communism, the arch-foe.

Father Krunoslav Draganovič, director of San Geroliamo, the Croat seminary within the Vatican, was personally responsible for shipping Ante Pavelič – Hitler's puppet and top-of-the-list war criminal – through the mission's net and enabling him to escape to South America. In the camps themselves Draganovič had set up a highly efficient intelligence network which reported directly to him, and he ran what became known as the Rat-Line, by which hundreds of *Ustaše* and seriously guilty war criminals escaped to South America. But it was impossible to confront him, as he travelled freely through the camps in his 'spiritual' capacity as chaplain.

Faced with so many insurmountable difficulties, and with time running out, Fitz decided that his best bet would be to make use of his personal friendship with Tito, and to try for a negotiated settlement – an ad hoc agreement with the Jugoslavs that he might just manage to pull off if he met their leader face to face. At first, as usual, the Foreign Office dithered and prevaricated, but in the end Fitz got his way and received permission to fly to Belgrade for talks – and this time he took me with him.

15
TITO

ITO WAS NOT IN BELGRADE: HE WAS IN SLOVENIA, IN THE EX-REGENT Prince Paul's small castle of Brdo, near Lake Bled, where he was enjoying a summer holiday with his sons. So it was to Slovenia that we were flown by our Jugoslav hosts, and it was there that I met Tito for the first time. We were lodged in a villa on the shore of the lake, and in the afternoon Fitz went up to the castle on his own. It was the first time he had seen the Jugoslav leader since 13 March 1945, when the Marshal had decorated him with the Partisan Star, and his first mission had come to an end.

Now there was much to catch up on, and it was evening before they parted; but as they did so, Fitz complained that since the Germans had stopped chasing him round the *shuma* (roughly the equivalent of the *maquis*), he never got enough fresh air and exercise. Tito immediately promised that next day he would have plenty of both.

In the morning we were called at six a.m. A quick bathe in the lake at the bottom of the garden, a scramble into improvised riding kit, and we were off. I enjoyed the drive through Slovenia's peaceful green valleys, and at about seven we arrived at the gates of Brdo. There we were challenged by two sentries, raw-boned youths with cropped fair hair, blue eyes and guileless smiles which did not altogether annul the menace of the tommy-guns that stuck out from under their arms.

The next few moments were not my happiest. Dressed as I was in a pair of my husband's khaki drill trousers, hitched up at the waist by a bandanna handkerchief and cut off at the bottom, I did not feel at my best, or indeed equal to facing the group of fifteen or twenty smartly turned-out officers who stood about under the trees in front of the castle. But the moment I was introduced to Tito, I realised he was even more shy than I was, and that although he had no idea what to say to me, his object was to be nice to his old friend's wife.

After a few moments' awkward silence, a faint look of despair came over his face, and I suddenly heard myself chattering in a mixture of nursery German and kitchen Italian, until at last hot milk and plum brandy arrived simultaneously, and the situation was saved by a clinking of glasses, an outburst of *zivio*s and *zivila*s, and general quaffing. Tito looked much younger than I had expected. He had light, almost Irish-blue eyes, smooth, fine-grained skin, good features and a natural dignity of manner, which was increased by a certain stiffness and newly acquired *avoirdupois*.

A sudden clatter of hoofs made me look up, and round the corner of the castle came, in all their glory, about thirty white Lippizaner Arab horses, led by stable-boys and brilliantly caparisoned with blue-and-silver saddle-cloths. Before I had time to put down my cup, every individual in the group around me was in the saddle and off, with a rattle, a prancing and a shout, full gallop down the drive into the open country beyond. Hoisted on to the remaining horse, and on the move before I had time to feel for my second stirrup, I thanked God for a brief hold-up by the entrance gate, which gave me time to collect myself, and also to catch a last yell of advice from my husband as he galloped past: 'If you get run away with, lean back and pull like blazes. Pull for all you're worth!'

After that we were galloping four-abreast down wide dust roads through flat, cultivated land and villages of white, red-roofed houses with deep eaves and balconies heaped with geraniums and golden maize cobs. Little girls with flaxen plaits scuttled to the safety of farmhouse doors, then turned to smile and some to yell, *'Zivio Tito!'* as we hurtled by. Distant mountains loomed on the horizon, blue and remote in the early-morning light.

The indisputable delight of being the only woman among forty men galloping across Central Europe as if leading a cavalry charge, the crisp air and the beauty of the countryside – everything went to my head like champagne. After an hour, however, my thoughts were less high-flown. The mountain range ahead looked scarcely any closer, my behind was sore, and we seemed to have come a long way from base.

My mare, however, was as enthusiastic as ever, so I gave up trying to control her and let her have her head until we joined, at great speed, the group at the head of the column.

'Your wife does like riding fast,' remarked Tito to Fitz as I shot past him.

'Ever since she was a child, Marshal,' Fitz answered disingenuously.

Amazingly, I stayed aboard my flying mare, and somehow I completed the return journey. I was even able to stagger up the castle stairs on legs that felt like cotton wool, to a pretty, English-country-house-style bedroom and a wonderful deep, hot bath. Fitzroy, always curious, was delighted to find a small medicine bottle in the bathroom cupboard labelled, in Russian, 'Kremlin Pharmacy'. 'Ah – that explains it,' he observed cryptically. (He must have been thinking of a rumour that Dimitrov, head of the Cominform, had recently visited Tito, trying to persuade him to tone down his country's anti-Soviet behaviour.)

Breakfast was laid outside, under the elm trees. With the ice broken, Tito and his officers and Fitzroy ragged and joked with each other. I thought the story that Tito had grown soft and pompous in peace-time rather missed the mark. After breakfast we walked round the estate, admiring two artificial lakes, and when I asked the Marshal if he had ever thought of putting swans on them, he replied, 'But naturally,' and sent an officer into the bushes, from which, after a preliminary scuffle and hiss, two beautiful white swans sailed forth majestically.

We came upon a group of three women and three small boys who, with some more officers, were playing volleyball, a game that looked like a cross between netball and deck tennis. Ales Bebler, who was walking beside me, told me that the boys were the sons of Tito, Marko Ranković (the Minister of the Interior) and Edo Kardelj (the Foreign Minister), all eight-year-old school friends who were spending their holidays together. We joined fiercely in the fray, Tito punching the ball with immense vigour, and rugby scrums developing when the boys tackled friends and visitors alike. No one played with greater energy than Ranković.

By this time the sun was blazing, and a bathe in the lake seemed most inviting. But it was no quiet swim: the boys, who all had shaven heads and spider-like limbs, saw to that (Tito had nicknamed his son 'Spider'). With enormous enthusiasm and devilish ingenuity, they pushed their elders into the water, hit them over the head with oars, ducked them, and made the more energetic officers race each other across the lake in leaky boats. Meanwhile Tiggar, Tito's devoted Alsatian, barked and swam after sticks and dived for stones and shook himself dry over everyone.

We sat down to luncheon at the same long table under the elms, with appetites revived, and did not get up from it until four p.m., by which time a great many toasts had been drunk and a great many stories told. Prompted in Serbo-Croatian by my neighbour Bebler, phrase by phrase, I even proposed a toast to 'the brave women of Jugoslavia from the Tory ladies of Lancaster', while still sober enough to do so. After that, whenever my glass was refilled I passed it to Fitz, who was quite able to drink for two.

Then he, Rankovič and I piled into a Porsche sports car with a cream-coloured hood which had once belonged to Goering, and followed Tito's motor up into the frontier mountains towards which we had ridden that morning. Marko sat in front, next to the driver, with a bag of walnuts which he occasionally passed back, remarking, with a wink, 'Very good for the digestion.'

At last we reached a hunting lodge, where the air was cold and sweet, and the thinning pine trees gave way to tumbled screes of grey rock. The snow-line was only just above us. Then, after a short walk to a mountain hut and a viewpoint, we drove back through the evening light, in Tito's car this time, past the white villages with their wayside shrines, their honeycomb brick barns, their drying tobacco leaves, their scattering of geese and children and pigs. Window-boxes flashed by, with streaks of scarlet from the geraniums, white from marguerites. Tito pointed out a village in which many hostages had been shot during the war, a new roof being tiled on a church, a special breed of cattle, a party of children on their way home from school.

It was dusk when we sat down to a simple supper of soup and *kasha*, and dark when a French film was shown on a screen fixed between two elm-boles. I do not remember much of it, for my eyes kept closing, despite every effort to stay awake. Just before the end, someone slipped into a chair behind me, and I was introduced in whispers. It was Kardelj, Tito's Foreign Minister, who had just flown up from Belgrade for consultations (for although we did not know it, relations with Russia were worsening). He sat down beside his son, looking pale and tired in the half-light from the screen, with a drooping moustache, steel-rimmed spectacles, and what used to be called a 'noble brow', like a country schoolmaster in a Chekhov play.

By the time the film was over we had spent seventeen hours in the open air, six of them taking violent exercise; the stars had come out and the moon had risen. Everyone said goodbye in the moonlight, and we drove away, leaving Tito, still my husband's good friend and now beginning to be mine, standing waving to us beneath the elm trees.

We returned to Bled in September 1947 for the official signing of the treaty that Fitz had later negotiated with Tito in Belgrade – a unilateral, almost personal treaty which irritated the Americans, and the Russians even more, showing that Jugoslavia had considerable independence from both super-powers. The Foreign Office was delighted, for it freed the British from their earlier undertaking to repatriate *Ustaše en bloc*, without screening, and set a definite time-limit on further requests for the handover of quislings and war criminals.

For the occasion, Charles and Catherine Peake came up from Belgrade, and General Steel down from Vienna. The ladies of the party were given small and rather tasteful brooches by the Marshal, who was magnificently turned out in sky-blue serge and rows of medals. By the time of the treaty's ratification, the short-list of wanted war criminals agreed by Britain, the USA and Tito had become almost redundant, and there was not a great deal left for Fitz's mission to do. The Ukrainians, still unscreened, had been sent to the United Kingdom; the Jugoslav displaced persons were safe in Allied and American refugee camps in Austria and Germany, awaiting permission to settle in the USA, Australia, South America or whatever country would have them.

In early January 1948 Mac-Miss Two was wound up, and we returned to England. Fitz was officially congratulated for achieving the government's aim, which had been to protect innocent or even not-so-innocent displaced persons from the dangers of forced repatriation. The Foreign Office may have heaved a sigh of relief, but Stalin was not at all amused by the Marshal's latest display of independence, and he said threateningly to Milovan Djilas, who had been sent to Moscow by the Marshal to answer various complaints, 'If I lift my little finger, there will be no more Tito.'

16

BACK HOME

DURING OUR YEAR ABROAD MUCH HAD HAPPENED TO MY OWN family. I returned to find Beaufort at last relieved of its occupying soldiery, and Shimi and Rosie re-established in their own home with their young family. Simon was now eight, Fiona six, Tessa five and Kim three, with Napoleon Tansy still masterminding the nursery and Geggy, who had never left the Castle, once more in charge of the household.

Half the Castle's interior, only basically rebuilt after the fire and left with bare floors during the war, was now complete. Nurseries had been moved to the ground floor, new kitchens with an Aga installed below the dining room. Our old Servants' Hall had become the repository of the Shikar Club's trophies (saved at great expense from London bombs, by Shimi, its president), and our famous Nursery Passage had been smartened up and given over to visitors. I could hardly recognise my old home, but there is no doubt that it was far more practical, and just as welcoming as ever. The great dining room, with its magical view, was still the same, and now Shimi, frail but active, could pace up and down with his porridge bowl at breakfast, gazing at the river below and up to the hills beyond, just as our father had done before him.

It was one evening in 1945, when Winston's caretaker government had been briefly in charge at Westminster, that the telephone had rung outside Nanny Tansy's new nursery, and the following conversation had taken place:

Voice: 'This is No. 10 Downing Street, and I should like to speak to Lord Lovat.'

Napoleon: 'I'm afraid you can't. He's gone to bed and doesn't like to be disturbed.'

Voice: 'This is very important. Who am I talking to?'

Napoleon: 'His Lordship's nanny. Who are you?'

Churchill himself must have overheard and enjoyed the conversation, because now he came on the line.

Winston: 'I am the Prime Minister, and I would like to offer Lord Lovat a post in my Cabinet.' Pause, then a Winstonian chuckle. 'Do you think he'll take it, Nanny?'

Napoleon: 'I'll see that he does, sir! He'll ring you in the morning.'

And so Shimi had been temporarily propelled into the role of Under-Secretary of State for Foreign Affairs in the last stages of Winston's government, which meant winding up a lot of loose ends. He had gone down to London complaining, stayed in the job about three months complaining, and then returned to Beaufort still complaining that it had all been a silly waste of time. But he did travel to Moscow with a delegation and met Stalin, by whom he was not at all impressed, describing him as 'very short and ugly'.

Although Shimi was still recovering from his D-Day wounds, he was also hauling the Lovat Estates back into solvency, selling off the less profitable parts and adopting a new ranch style of cattle-breeding in its glens, a radical experiment which proved in certain areas of the Highlands to be extremely successful. Rosie was a great success as the new Lady of Lovat. Everyone loved her, and she cared for the old and sick and the ancient family servants just as much as my mother had done before her. In London my mother had kept on the Deep Purple flat off the Edgware Road, and when she was not in Scotland she shared it with Hugh, who was now an enthusiastic Member of Parliament, soon to be Parliamentary Private Secretary to Oliver Lyttelton, who became Colonial Secretary in 1951. The flat-sharing was an unsatisfactory arrangement: it caused a lot of tension, and Hugh stayed on only because he knew it would upset her terribly if he should leave.

I soon saw that Moo was exhausted, physically and emotionally, by all the blows she had suffered: the deaths of Rose and Alan, war-time anxiety for her sons, Shimi's long struggle to recover from his wounds, and finally the strain of nursing Hugh through a bout of viral pneumonia. When I went up to Eilean Aigas, I found her on the verge of a nervous breakdown – and this came only a few months later. She developed acute melancholia, refused to eat, and was saved from dying only by the still brutal electric-shock therapy, which was then in its infancy and, though successful, left her much altered. For the rest of her life she was a quiet, gentle, quite contented semi-invalid; all the *chiaroscuro* of her bright, often dazzling personality had gone, and with it the laughter, drama and 'social courage' of the Tennant family. She would now feel confident only within the close family circle, or with Sister Whittock, the sweet Perthshire nurse who came to look after her in 1949 and stayed on as her faithful companion and friend until the day of her death in 1973.

The tenor of Hugh's life inevitably changed. He loved pretty girls – and chased them enthusiastically – but he also loved family life, and he eventually decided it was time to get married. He chose Antonia, the eldest daughter of Frank Pakenham, his old tutor at Balliol, a buxomly pretty, clever and amusing girl. He declared himself head-over-heels in love, proposed and was accepted, and they were married on 25 September 1956, with the bride dressed as Mary, Queen of Scots, or nearly so, and Hugh in velvet doublet and tartan. They rented a flat in Eaton Square near Antonia's employer, the publisher George Weidenfeld; Antonia blossomed, and for the rest of their strange but happy marriage, which no one in our family remotely understood, Hugh settled down to play second fiddle to a famous beauty and successful author, of whom he was immensely proud.

Jack and my sister Magdalen, with their two little boys, Johnny and Simon, had moved to Rackenford, on the edge of Exmoor, so that she could be near her best friends, the Pixton Herberts. During the war she had been a senior officer in the Red Cross, rivalling even Edwina Mountbatten in courage and efficiency, and when peace returned she was put in charge of a campaign to raise funds for the disabled and the aged. A natural speaker, and a very beautiful woman, she could quickly move people to tears. Her meetings filled public and church halls all over the country, and no one left them without wiping an eye and contributing to the cause.

She had also become what one might call a Catholic activist. Her life now revolved round the Church, and she organised many of its lay activities, as well as writing and illustrating several children's books.

Yet sadly these activities never seemed wholly to satisfy her. She was obviously capable of conquering wider worlds; but Jack had no ambitions other than to farm, fish, shoot, hunt and take photographs – all of which he did exceptionally well – and to live the life of a good and placid country gentleman.

I wish I had been closer to my sister, and that I had given her more support; but our temperaments were as different as chalk from cheese, and our lives, after my second marriage, even more disparate. I think her own family never really appreciated Tookie: we teased her too much when we were young, and I was as guilty as the others. The rest of the world treated her very differently, and she had a host of admirers. Duncan Grant saw her one day in a cinema and asked to paint her. Max Reinhardt begged her to succeed Diana Cooper as the Blessed Virgin Mary in his play *The Miracle*. Bobbity Salisbury and King George VI adored her; but though an acknowledged beauty, Magdalen herself was diffident and genuinely modest about her appearance. The 'social courage' and confidence of the Tennants had passed her by.

June, after her long romance with Anthony Chaplin came to an end, had been introduced by him to a talented German musician called Franz Osborn, and to everyone's amazement she had quietly married him. It seemed to me at the time like a stroke of black magic on Anthony's part, for he suddenly found it perfectly easy to abandon his wife, Alvilde – something he had always promised June he would do, but never did – and propose immediate nuptials to Oliver Lyttelton's daughter, a glorious redhead who had been June's lodger at Bletchley. But we were all wrong: June and Franz loved each other dearly and had a happy marriage, producing a single, idolised son, Christopher, who is today a talented musician like his father.

Irene's situation was frustrating and unfortunate, for she had fallen deeply in love with Robin Darwin, the divorced head of the Royal College of Art, and although our formidably Catholic family were, somewhat questionably, pulling every string to obtain an annulment of his marriage, their lobbying was proving fruitless, and it was obvious to me that Robin would not be prepared to wait.

As for ourselves – the constituency had remained faithful to Fitz during his second absence abroad, but there was a lot of work to catch up on, and with another General Election looming, he was fully stretched and therefore happy. Besides, he had started work on his memoirs. Writing for him had always been a release, and now it became a delight. By chance he had met the artist Edward Seago, who had just published a lovely book of sketches of the Italian campaign, and who now said that if Fitz produced a book about the war in Jugoslavia, he would like to illustrate it. The idea found favour, and resulted in the door of Fitz's study, a small room off Beechfield's hall, being firmly closed, with a zone of absolute silence imposed on the whole household for long periods.

My life in London was a complete contrast. Although our Canal Zone flat was not grand, it was certainly different, and all our friends seemed to like it. We entertained a lot, hanging an orchid or some other glamour flower on the door of our rope-powered lift and cramming up to eighteen people into our small dining room. Mrs Macdonald's chicken Maryland and chocolate soufflés were the best in town. Fitz would give us pink champagne, and everyone enjoyed what became known as the Maclean 'small balls'.

Our son Jamie was born in June 1949 at Beechfield, with my mother and the same excellent team in attendance. Charles Edward, now two and a half, had been banished to the gardener's lodge, with Procter, our lady gardener, put on oath to keep him there; but he escaped, and was one of the first to see the new arrival. He reported back to Procter: 'What do you *think*? We've got a new baby! But it's only a very small one, and it can't talk!'

David Stirling was one godfather, but failed to turn up for the baptism, and as we were walking to the church Fitzroy told the other godparent that he wanted 'Aeneas' added to the names we had chosen.

'What on earth for?' I whispered – for we had already reached the porch.

'Good Highland name,' he answered. 'And the man had an excellent record. Aeneas saved his father from burning Troy – carried him out on his back.' And so Jamie was christened Alexander James Simon Aeneas.

While I struggled through my pregnancy, Fitz had struggled with the birth of his book (the idea of cooperating with Edward Seago had fizzled out). 'What shall I call it?' he asked one evening. 'Its three parts have no related theme except myself. I don't want a silly title like *Fitz's Fun*, or anything dull or pompous.'

The navy's heroic war in the western approaches was still resonating in my mind, and suddenly I had a brain wave. 'Why not call it *Eastern Approaches*? After all, your exploits were all east of Brighton, weren't they?'

Billy Collins sat on the typescript for a week (of agony), then told Fitz that though he liked it, it was too long, and would have to be cut in half and rewritten to make two volumes. Fitz immediately rejected this idea, which outraged his literary instincts and judgement; but he was devastated by the implied criticism, and feared his year's work had been in vain. In despair he rang up his old friend Peter Fleming – himself a best-selling author – to ask his opinion. At the same time he wrote to Billy, saying that if he didn't hear from him in a week, he would try elsewhere. Fitz had not realised that Peter read typescripts for a rival publisher, Jonathan Cape, and when, a week later, a messenger came bounding round to the flat with a Cape contract ready to sign, and a charming letter from Jonathan, he was overjoyed.

He rang Peter and said, 'They're offering me a twenty per cent royalty. Is that good?'

'It's what we gave Hemingway for his fourth book,' Peter answered, and they both went out to dinner to celebrate.

Eastern Approaches was a huge success. A classic adventure story, full of exciting action, it fell into three parts – the author's life as a diplomat in Moscow during Stalin's purges and reign of terror, and his travels to the remoter parts of Central Asia; his time with the early SAS in the Western Desert of Libya in 1942; and his experiences later in the war with Tito and the Partisan army in Jugoslavia. The book has never gone out of print since the day it was published in 1949, and it has sold well over a million copies. Today it reads as freshly and easily as it did fifty years ago (easy reading means hard writing, Fitz would tell me), and it has never dated. When that great traveller Freya Stark came to stay, she wrote to her husband Stuart Perowne, 'Fitzroy tells me he is now really happy only when writing, and I think I was right in *Perseus* to say that loving and creating are the only two happinesses that last.'

The book brought an avalanche of requests for lecture tours, articles and speeches. Never one to despise the use of scissors and paste, Fitz soon devised a universal lecture-cum-speech which became known to both of us as 'The Bird', after a quotation in the text: 'A snake slid across the path, a brightly coloured bird flew out of a tree, its wings flashing in the sunlight: I knew that I had left Europe far behind.' The talk always went down well at meetings of the English Speaking Union and in school halls, and he even got away with it at Eton, where he had great fun lecturing to the boys of the First Hundred (the senior section of the school) and answering their questions.

There is no doubt that *Eastern Approaches* made his reputation as a writer, adventurer and traveller far beyond Whitehall and Westminster, and that it inspired several generations of young men and women to seek adventure in exploring remote countries.

Forty years later, we were staying in the British Embassy in Paris and gathered before dinner in the Salon Vert, when Ewen Fergusson, the Ambassador, picked up a copy of the book and read a couple of paragraphs aloud. 'And that,' he told the young Italian and the Third Secretary who were our fellow-guests, 'is why I joined the Foreign Service.' Turning to Fitz, who had gone pink, he added, 'And that is why, Fitzroy, I should like to give a party for you here next year, for your eightieth birthday. Will you come?'

He did; I did; we did; and it was a party that fifty of our family and friends will never forget. At dinner I sat between our host and Monsieur Jacques Chirac, who was then Mayor of Paris, and had a lovely time. The Fergussons had taken enormous trouble and the long table in the 'orangerie', the flowers, the food and the wine – not to mention Ewen's brandy – were sumptuous.

After publication, Fitz's postbag doubled overnight. Jeanne Thomlinson, who had typed and re-typed the book a dozen times, now became his permanent, full-time secretary. As she had long been our best friend and wisest adviser, she became even more a member of the family when she married Stephen Clissold, one of Fitz's former BLOs and a Jugoslav expert who had been with him on both missions and wrote serious books about Jugoslavia and Spanish mystics and saints, a rather different subject!

17

STALIN'S LETTER

I**N 1948 T**ITO'S RELATIONSHIP WITH MOSCOW HAD DETERIORATED sharply. One small factor was undoubtedly the unilateral 'Bled' agreement which Fitzroy had brokered between Jugoslavia and the British Government; but a stream of complaints had been pouring out of the Kremlin for some time – of rudeness and slights to the Soviet military, of failure to collectivise agriculture, of too-great independence in foreign policy, and of 'undemocratic behaviour'; and then, of course, there was the underlying disagreement about the future composition of a Balkan Federation. Through all this Tito had remained calm, believing that Russia's threats were mostly bluster – which is why the letter delivered to him by the Soviet Ambassador on 28 March caused such consternation.

It was eight pages long, and, having repeated Stalin's accusations, it informed the Marshal that Jugoslavia would be expelled from the Cominform, that the Soviets were planning to recall their Ambassador from Belgrade and to break off diplomatic relations with their former ally, unless Tito yielded to Stalin's demands and mended his ways. The letter did not mention Fitzroy by name, but it expressed outrage that the chief negotiator in the 'recent discussions' over Soviet–Jugoslav relations had been *the British spy*, Vladko Velebit.

Vladko – our lifelong friend – gave me quite recently a blow-by-blow account of that fateful morning.

When he went into Tito's office, *Stari* ('Old Man', his nickname among friends) was already at his desk, holding a letter in his hands. Seeing Vladko, he swept aside the papers awaiting signature and cried, 'Look at this! Forget the rest!'

'I was as stunned by the letter's contents as Tito obviously was himself – especially by the bits that referred to me and my so-called defection from the Communist camp! Although there had been many signs of Stalin's displeasure over the last few months, it had never entered our heads that anything so drastic as expulsion from the Cominform and the breaking-off of diplomatic relations could possibly happen.'

After grave deliberation, Tito summoned his four most trusted colleagues and told them what he proposed doing: he intended to rebut Stalin's accusations, refuse his demands and stand by the ideals of the *Jugoslav* Communist Party, whose ideas he believed were more faithful to Marxist-Leninism than those now held by the Soviet leaders in Moscow. It took him a little time to convince them, but he managed it, and later they called a plenary meeting of all twenty-six members of the Politburo's cabinet, who, with the exception of two voices, endorsed this decision.

Their view was then put to every Party Committee in the nation – a referendum that took several weeks to complete, and could easily have toppled Tito; but in the event the Communist Parties of all five Republics stood firmly behind him, and as soon as he had received their positive response, he pulled up the drawbridge and outfaced his attacker.

Refusing to give in to Stalin, he broke off relations with Moscow and withdrew all Jugoslav representatives from the Soviet Union. Most Russians left the country. The Jugoslav Cominform was dissolved, and on 28 June, St Vitus's Day, at a meeting in Bucharest, Jugoslavia was duly expelled from the international Communist body.

In Vladko's view, Tito's robust response changed the world, for it cracked the monolith of Soviet Communism, and things would never be the same again. But it also had far-reaching political consequences in Tito's own country, for it meant that in later years he could never abandon the Jugoslav Communist Party which had shown him such solid loyalty, or allow any opposition party to confront it.

Vladko himself, in order to avoid further criticism, left Belgrade for a high-level job in the United Nations, and although he remained one of Tito's closest friends, he stayed outside the government and the Party.

After the break, which was complete, Tito was ruthless at stamping out dissidents. The several thousand who had opposed his policy were rounded up, dispossessed of their properties and interned for a time in isolated prison camps, including Otok Goli, the most notorious. But considering the bitter divisions that had existed during the recent war, their numbers were surprisingly small.

In the House of Commons Fitzroy continued to lobby for Jugoslavia. He felt the country must now be saved from economic collapse by substantial financial support from the West, which would keep it afloat until the terrible devastation of the war years could be repaired and its new isolation bolstered. In May 1949 he was unofficially sent to Belgrade by the Labour government to meet Tito again, and to find out discreetly what Britain could do to help.

Once more he took me with him, and we stayed at the British Embassy, where Charles Peake was still the Ambassador. A meeting with the Marshal was quickly arranged, and we entered the White Palace unobtrusively, through a side door. An ADC took us up some stairs and down a long corridor to a lobby where, among several uniformed men, Fitz recognised a few old friends, Tito's personal bodyguards Bosko and Preja among them. The room we then entered was large and windowless, and the walls were hung with blue velvet curtains. Tito got up from his desk and came round to clap Fitz on the shoulder and shake my hand. He looked years younger than when I had seen him in Bled, thinner, more alert, and as if he was enjoying life.

The two began talking and laughing, and as I gazed round the room I couldn't help thinking that, if I was in the Marshal's position, I wouldn't want to be surrounded by so much arras (there had already been two attempts on his life). Their conversation lasted no more than forty minutes, but it produced new ideas and opened new doors, and by the time we left Belgrade an agreement had been sketched out. When this was implemented, the British Government approved an £8 million credit scheme, which was of immense value to the emerging Jugoslav Federation, and led to a massive infusion of aid from the United States a few years later.

18

FAREWELL
AUSTERITY

A T THE GENERAL ELECTION OF OCTOBER 1951, WHICH BROUGHT Churchill back to power, Fitz was again returned as the Member for Lancaster. He was still not popular with the Whips in the House of Commons, because he tended to give the impression that he had remained in politics only because the war had ended, and that he knew more about foreign affairs than anyone else – and this, I think, particularly irritated Ted Heath, who was then Tory Chief Whip. Nevertheless, Fitz plodded on, asking acute questions about foreign and military affairs, taking a hawkish line over Korea and Egypt, and making painstaking speeches that still read much better than they sounded.

The House of Commons fascinated me and I used to listen to many debates. I thought the best speaker in the House then was Aneurin Bevan, and in spite of his virulently left-wing views, I admired him, for he had real 'fire in his belly' – and the Welsh fluency to express it. On a good day Enoch Powell could also be inspired, while Nigel Birch, a good friend, was often witty, sarcastic and deadly at the same time, but always principled. Among Fitz's Labour friends were George Wigg, who loved the army, and Tam Dalyell, who, though sometimes obsessive, had no humbuggery and was often very shrewd.

The saddest debate I ever listened to was one on the demise of the Raj. Every seat in the public galleries was occupied by turbaned Sikhs, patrician-faced Punjabis and swarthy Hindus, and downstairs those who had not found places were queueing right out into Westminster

Square. But in the chamber the front benches were thinly occupied, while barely a handful of back-benchers lounged on either side. I suppose the fate of the subcontinent had long since been decided, though the speed of our withdrawal was a disastrous new factor: Winston, who really cared about India, had made an emotional speech, and after that no one seemed interested. Yet, looking at those eager and strained faces around me, many with tears running down their cheeks, I felt deeply ashamed. Six million people were to die in the ensuing holocaust, and British politicians could not even be bothered to hear their death-knell.

The 1950s brought down a shutter between those who had fought or suffered in the war of 1939–45 and those who had not. The period marked a demarcation line that divided, for ever, twentieth-century generations into two, and those who *had* been involved adopted a new yardstick for judging people – a measurement barely comprehensible to the generations who came after.

When peace returned, we talked about people having had 'a good war' – an accolade that had nothing to do with class or money or social confidence or success in civilian life. It meant that someone had been courageous enough to risk or give his own life for others. We had learnt that, in facing danger and death, all men are equal, but that some are capable of extreme heroism and self-sacrifice. 'Oh, he's all right,' we would say, 'he had a very good war' – and not go into details. Survivors of the conflict looked at the world through different eyes, and at each other with mutual respect and affection. How could they not? We were proud of what our countrymen had achieved together, even if we could not agree on what they should do next.

The Conservatives won the 1951 election only by a whisker – a majority of seventeen – but the vote put Winston back into power for the next four years. The old 'Establishment' must have felt happy and safe again, at least for a little while longer, and austerity was banished by a torrent of parties. Balls were given to celebrate a daughter's debut, a child's engagement, a coming-of-age, a mere anniversary. These dances were of two kinds: the spectacular, held in very grand houses and royal palaces, where one wore every jewel one could lay hands on and promenaded through one great room after another, admiring pictures and tapestries, flower arrangements and other people's *parures*, but rarely took to the floor; and the other, more intimate kind, which depended largely on the personalities and inspiration of our hosts and hostesses.

I had not yet inherited my mother-in-law's jewellery, and complained to Nancy Astor that I didn't have a tiara for one of the Buckingham Palace balls to which we had been invited. 'Don't worry,' she replied. 'I'll lend you a replica of mine. I keep it to fool the burglars. It's just a half-circle of false diamonds on an elastic band, very easy to arrrange.' So it was, but every time Nancy passed me on the ballroom floor, she ruined the effect by reaching out and tweaking it, then letting it go with a twang, announcing in a loud voice, 'It looks very good – almost real!'

Later that evening I was brought up and presented to King George, who asked me to dance. Suitably flattered, I accepted, and we hopped around for a bit; but when the music stopped I didn't know whether I should curtsy and move away, or whether that would be *lèse-majesté*. The King went on talking, the music started up again, and so did we. But when this happened for a third and fourth time, and there was still no husband of mine or courtier (lazy brutes!) in sight to deliver His Majesty from me, I remembered seeing Queen Elizabeth across the room, and steered my partner towards her like to a port in a storm.

I later learnt that part of the King's shyness, and charm, was his great difficulty in saying goodbye.

Much less formal dances were taking place in the country, and the hunt balls were relaxed and noisy. There were also fund-raising dances for charity, like the fancy-dress party at the Royal College of Art, where Truman Capote arrived in what we all thought was fancy dress, but turned out to be his normal clothes. It was there that Paddy Leigh Fermor, dressed as a Roman god with a trident, danced with me, in a white nightgown which exposed one shoulder and had cost £7 10s. from Peter Jones. 'You're not Roman, darling, you're Greek,' he told me. 'Yes, definitely Greek.' He was probably a little drunk, but no matter: it was the best compliment I ever had.

Parties at the embassies in London were somewhat intimidating, and nowhere more so than at the French Embassy, in Prince's Gate, during the reign of the Massiglis. One dreadful evening Fitz and I arrived punctually (as we thought) at eight thirty p.m., to find a large and distinguished company waiting impatiently to go into dinner, and the Ambassadress looking daggers at us. It wasn't until that moment that I remembered: there was a four-line whip in the Commons that night, and when I had explained this to the Social Secretary three days previously, the Massiglis had kindly moved the party from eight thirty to eight o'clock for our sake. I had completely forgotten about this, and, worse still, had never told Fitz, who was expecting to have to excuse himself in the middle of dinner to go and vote.

General de Lattre de Tassigny and my great hero Teilhard de Chardin were there, as were Duff and Diana Cooper, Bobbity and Betty Salisbury and about six others. Dinner proceeded, and Fitzroy left in the middle of it. After we had reassembled in the drawing room, I began to apologise profusely to my hostess, but at that moment Betty caught her coffee cup on something and spilt its entire contents down Madame Massigli's new Dior dress. Out came a scream and a hiss of pent-up rage, followed by, *'Ah, mais celà – c'est vraiment de trop!'* We didn't hear the rest, as she bolted from the room and slammed the door. Betty looked at me from under her drooped eyelids. 'What an extraordinary thing to make such a fuss about! After all, it was only a *dress*, and she must have a hundred more.'

The German Embassy, with Fitz's great friend Johnnie von Herwarth (a fellow ex-, pre-war Moscow diplomat) and his wife Pussy presiding over it, always gave us a warm welcome. It cannot have been easy, so soon after the end of the war, to reconcile British society with post-Hitler Germany, and needed tact and sensitivity to do so, but both the Herwarths worked tremendously hard to establish respect for the new, democratic Germany they were representing, and I think they succeeded.

The embassy we both loved best of all was the British Embassy in Paris. It had many associations with my family. The Ancestor's younger brother, Reggie Lister, had been Minister there for several years, and because his Ambassador was frequently ill or absent, he would sometimes act as Chargé d'Affaires. He was a bachelor, and he asked his clever niece, Barbara Lister, who was still single, about twenty-five and strikingly beautiful, to act as his hostess. She must have had a wonderful time, for it was the end of the Belle Époque, and her sketchbooks are full of the literati and *beau monde* of the day – Proust, the Montalembert brothers, Sarah Bernhardt, Yvette Guilbert and (not least) my godfather Maurice Baring, who, as an honorary attaché, had a famous ink fight in the tiny Chancery (the splodges on the walls have been carefully preserved to this very day).

Eric and Frances Phipps, my first parents-in-law, were the Embassy's incumbents from 1922–28, and again from 1937–39. They, Duff and Diana Cooper, Oliver and Maudie Harvey, and even Fitz as a humble Third Secretary, all seem to have spent some of the happiest years of their lives in that beautiful and friendly house.

One day, when we were staying with the Harveys, Maudie told me about an extraordinary drama that took place soon after they had arrived. She and Ol were about to set out for an official engagement. Their car was waiting in the courtyard, and the maître d'hôtel was standing by the heavy front door, holding it ajar, when in dashed a small woman in eastern clothes, shrieking, 'Save me! Save me!', hotly pursued by two thugs in Arab dress. The butler let her slip in, and Oliver instantly ordered him to shut and lock the door. Her pursuers ran back into the street and escaped. The refugee threw herself at Oliver's feet, and when he had raised and calmed her and then asked her name, he found she was the Queen of Jordan.

She and her husband, King Talal, had been living quietly in Paris, while he was being treated for a nervous breakdown. He had suddenly become convinced that she wished to poison him, so he ordered his bodyguards to do away with her. In fear for her life, she had escaped during a shopping expedition and made a dash for our Embassy.

This created a delicate situation. The Harveys had no confirmation of the Queen's story, but they believed her, and in spite of excitable telegrams from the Foreign Office urging 'utmost caution', they stuck to their decision to give her shelter. They found her a bedroom and sitting room that could be discreetly guarded, furnished her with a toothbrush and an emergency trousseau, and gave her all the sympathy she needed until her dilemma could be sorted out.

Its solution took many days and bristled with national and international complications; but in the end Oliver devised a master plan. A brave volunteer veiled like an Arab lady left the Embassy one morning in the official Rolls-Royce. The car was immediately spotted and followed by the King's men, who had been waiting for just such a departure, while the real Queen escaped by the garden exit, from which another car whisked her away through Paris to a private aeroplane, which flew her out of the country.

19

LEARNING
TO TRAVEL

O NE SUMMER RECESS IN THE EARLY 1950S WE EMBARKED ON OUR
first long trip together and drove across Europe and Turkey
to Tabriz, in Iran. Fitz decided to break me in gently to his
version of camping, which was quite austere, and founded on military
experience. It meant sleeping in the open, without a tent, in a
sleeping-bag on a rubber palliasse, with only a ground-sheet to protect
one from early-morning dew. It meant going to bed at dusk and waking
at dawn (or 'sparrow-fart', as the SAS boys called it), brewing up on
a 'desert fire' (a bucket of sand soaked with petrol), and carrying a
minimum of food and utensils – frying pan, kettle, teapot and mess
tins – in a lockable kitchen box. There were also plastic petrol cans
and water-carriers, a book bag, a 'night-bag' each, and a medicine box
containing a small navy-blue ribbed bottle labelled 'Poison' as its most
valuable item. Chlorodine had saved the soldiers of the Queen from
dysentery – or so the bottle's label said – presumably in the Crimean
War, for it was signed 'Wolseley'. 'It's pure opium,' explained my
travelling mentor. 'Just the thing for us.' There was also a case of
spirits, which we replenished on the way with local produce, and a
kit-bag full of warm clothes.

'What if it rains?' I asked nervously.

'It never rains in August, and if it does, we just drive on.'

We piled everything into the new Land Rover which its makers had
kindly lent us, and set out for Paris. When we landed at Boulogne, it
was raining.

'I think we'll look for a little shelter,' said Fitz, 'as it's your first night on the road.'

A nice farmer near Bapaume let us into his half-derelict Dutch barn. I was tired from the excitement of our departure, and Fitz bedded me down expertly and kissed me goodnight. The stars came out and twinkled through the holes in the roof of the old building: it smelt deliciously of new-mown hay – and I could not sleep a wink! It was so *noisy*! Rats rustled, dogs barked, motorbikes revved, and I found my bed, for all its Dunlopillo bounce, supremely uncomfortable. Towards dawn I must have dozed off, because at six a.m. the good farmer's wife brought us new bread and mugs of *café au lait*, which were very comforting.

We spent the next two nights in luxury at our Paris Embassy with the Harveys, who promised to meet us in a couple of days' time at the Grand Hotel in Biarritz, where the Marquis de Cuevas was throwing a grand gala evening to promote his private ballet company and the resort in general. We had planned to spend the next night in Tours, but as we passed Chenonceaux we were seduced by the sound of a *cor de chasse* and a hunt in full cry that seemed to come from the woods all round us, so we stopped – and were enchanted by our first *son et lumière* performance, in front of the *château*. We therefore arrived in the beautiful old town too late to find a bed, and camped out, uncomfortably – between the goal-posts on a football field!

Next morning the coastal road led us south through the pine forests and maize fields of the Landes, but always, maddeningly, a kilometre inland from the sea. At dusk we decided to use our four-wheel drive, and turned off down a sandy track which had *'Défense de Camping'* and a skull's-head sign beside it, but which, we hoped, would lead us to a beach where we could swim. It did, and we soon parked among the pine trees and a little way off the track, looking forward to a dip in the morning.

Fitz had climbed into his sleeping-bag and was reading by the glow of the Land Rover's side-lights, and I was crouched in the back of the car, searching for my toothbrush, when we heard the sound of another vehicle coming down the track.

'Damn!' said Fitz. 'It's probably a *guardien*, coming to arrest us.'

But the dark saloon car passed us and continued down to the sea, where four men got out. I could just make out that they seemed to be dressing or accoutring a fifth man, who had his back against a tree.

Then they all disappeared from my view, and I crawled out of the car to ask Fitz who he thought they were.

'Smugglers,' he answered, suitably smugly. 'Just keep quiet and go to sleep. I'll stay awake and guard camp.'

As usual he had no weapon – he never carried one in peace-time, on the principle that possession of a gun merely increased your chance of being murdered – and soon I heard his breathing turn into a gentle snore. He was fast asleep, the brute, and I was alone, surrounded by villains. But though I tried to stay awake, I too soon dropped off, for the sand was soft and the murmur of the nearby sea deliciously soporific.

Hours later we were both woken by the sound of voices and bumps. The men were loading their car with something heavy. Fitz leant over and touched my hand, meaning 'Keep still'. Then the doors slammed, and as the car turned round for a brief moment our little camp was caught in the beam of its headlights. Fitz's pressure on my hand increased. Then the car accelerated, bumping away up the track. He let go, and I breathed again. In the morning, when we swam, we found the marks of a boat's keel in the golden sand of our little beach.

By the time we reached the Grand Hotel in Biarritz we were covered in dust and dirt, and as we approached a lift, a stout, ugly little woman recoiled in horror when she realised we were to share it with her. It was Elsa Maxwell, the New York socialite and party-fixer, the first of the celebrities we met that evening, but she gave us a searching look when we got out on a floor rather grander than her own.

The ball itself was extraordinary, with a hundred flaming torches lighting the path to an artificial lake, where the Marquis's *corps de ballet* performed on an artificial island and Parisian stars of film and stage appeared in live tableaux, dressed by famous couturiers in sensational costumes – Jeanmaire in sequins on the back of an elephant, Lucienne Boyer in a silver wig and ball dress by Balmain, Josephine Baker in a flower-decked straw hat on a sweet little donkey that refused to move. In the supper tents tables were laden with whole turbots in aspic, boars' heads, galantines and guinea fowl, profiteroles and pastry extravaganzas to make you blink; but alas, the guests descended on them like wolves, and by the time we fought our way to a table, there was hardly a fish-tail left.

Oliver Harvey said we should report our camping experience to the local police, which we did; but they shrugged their shoulders in Gallic indifference, telling us that the coast was well-known for smuggling – guns and Communists into Spain, cheap brandy and Basque terrorists out of it. 'You were lucky,' they said. 'Last year Sir Jack Drummond was murdered.'

So we pressed on southwards. Our next assignation was with Freya Stark, who had invited us to spend a night at the villa belonging to her niece, near Ventimiglia. The house was somewhere at the bottom of the celebrated Hambro gardens, whose terraces had lain semi-abandoned since the beginning of the war, and we knew it would be hard to find in the dark. But at the top of the gardens, just off the main road, was a four-star restaurant, and when we arrived at eight thirty p.m., Fitz suggested we should have a drink and dinner before starting to search for our destination.

'Oh no, we can't,' I told him. 'Freya will have spent all day slaving away to cook dinner for us. It would be just too rude.'

'You don't know Freya,' sighed my husband.

We humped our night-bags down at least half a kilometre of crumbling terraces and overgrown paths towards the lights of a habitation far below us. Freya herself opened the door on to a scene of considerable sophistication. It was a pretty room, and the *nizza* was pretty, too, lying on a kind of chaise longue in a black satin négligée, smoking a Turkish cigarette in a long holder, *à la* vamp, and blowing (or making) rings round a small group of admirers, who knelt and squatted round her slim, silver-sandalled feet.

She looked up, but did not rise: she just gestured towards her aunt and went on with her merry badinage.

'You must be very tired,' said Freya. 'I expect you'll have eaten and want to lie down.'

'No, Freya,' Fitz answered. 'We haven't eaten, and we're ravenous.'

'Oh dear. I'm afraid we all ate earlier. There's only yesterday's bread and some cheese left. But you're welcome to it.'

We champed our way through stale bread and rock-hard cheese. The young men then left, and Freya rose to show us our room – a tiny alcove that looked down on to a dimly lit railway line.

'I know you'll sleep like a log, my dear,' she said warmly. 'It's not a big bed, but Duff and Diana managed beautifully. Goodnight.' She then shut the door quickly and very firmly, and vanished.

'Duff may have managed, but he's half my size and very sexy,' growled my husband. 'I'm going back for my bed-roll. Where's the damned torch?'

At that moment there was a screech and a rattle, and the room shook as an express thundered past our window. Fitz raised a sardonic eyebrow. 'See what I mean?' I gave him the torch, but the battery had died.

Next morning everything was different. There were no more trains, and a path led to a delightful little cove with a sandy beach, two umbrella pines, and not a soul in sight. We swam out in cool, clean water and watched the sun rise over the mountains, then lay on the rocks to dry. There were fresh croissants and honey for breakfast, and Freya was at her sparkling best. We left reluctantly after a happy lunch cooked by the *nizza*, who, deprived of young men, now flirted with Fitz.

At the British Embassy in Belgrade we were regaled by Charles Peake with all the latest gossip, including a splendid story about a French military attaché who decided to liven up the Jugoslav capital by throwing a party in the restaurant of the old Hotel Metropole, to which he asked each of his guests to bring a 'surprise'. He himself booked a pretty Serbian girl from the city's single nightclub, the Lotus, who had promised, after some hard bargaining, to effect an entrance exactly as Mother Nature had made her. At the last moment she lost her nerve, and said she could only accompany him if her head was wrapped in a cardigan. He agreed, and they burst in on the company with a roll of drums and a merry *tra-la* – whereupon a small and balding Belgian diplomat, whose wife was not present, leapt to his feet yelling, '*C'est ma femme!*' and dived at the unfortunate Frenchman, laying him out with a hail of well-aimed blows.

There are only two ways south from Belgrade to the Aegean, and they follow the valleys of the rivers Varda and Morava through the mountains of Serbia to the sea. These are the roads along which countless armies have marched to meet their destinies, the road that the Lovat Scouts took in 1917 during the famous Serbian retreat, the road that led them to Salonika, the Dardanelles and the withering fire of the Turks who lay in wait.

We took the Varda route, through beautiful wild country and past fine Byzantine monasteries. We stopped to admire the great portals and

The Old Town, Korčula

Mama Katarina, the matriarch of 'the family', as we found her in Korčula in 1957

The next two generations: Paula (left) and Ruzica (right) with me

Tito, the Partisan leader, Bosnia, 1943

Marshal Tito drives us round his island. Vera Velebit (head turned) and Tito's wife Jovanka are in the back of the buggy while I sit next to the President in front

DIMITRI KASTRIN

Sukie, on the morning of her wedding

Benjie Marlowe, Sukie's youngest, studies the form

Sukie and husband Nic Paravicini

My grandson-in-law, Harry Boothby (who is married to Laura), and Maudie, my first great-grandchild

Jeremy and Sue's son, Jake Phipps, as a baby

Dogs and babies at Glyn Celin

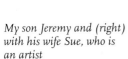

My son Jeremy and (right) with his wife Sue, who is an artist

FREMANTLEMEDIA

The cast (from left): Charlie Maclean (just visible), Rhoda Cockerill, me, Eamonn Andrews, Sue Phipps, Jake Phipps, Fitzroy, Sandy Glen, John Henniker-Major, Rafo Ivancevič, Mary Soames

Fitz and Tito around the time of the President's eightieth birthday

My son Charlie (now Sir Charles) Maclean as a teenager

Charlie's wife Debbie collecting wood for a bonfire, Strachur

Charlie and Debbie's eldest, Margaret Maclean, getting ready to swim in Korčula

Katharine Maclean playing a game of patience, Strachur, 2000

*Jamie and
Sarah Maclean
on their
wedding day*

*Jamie and Sarah's boys,
Alexander Fitzroy and
Johnnie Maclean*

GLASGOW HERALD

*Jimmy McNab and the Georgian
dancers*

Fitz in his library, which overlooks the garden

Talking to Lord Carrington and Queen Elizabeth The Queen Mother, during a weekend at the Royal Lodge

Fitzroy, looking apprehensive, is about to open the Northern Meeting ball with Princess Margaret, Beaufort 1993

medieval frescoes of Peč and Subačič. We camped and drank good beer near Pristina, where some young kittens joined us for breakfast.

Fitz promised to feed me the finest chocolate cake in the world at Skopje, but before we reached the earthquake town, we were sidetracked by a sign pointing to Krpinski Banja, where we found an enchanting little Turkish domed bath-house in a verdant garden, clinging to a rock-face and smelling strongly of rotten eggs.

'Hot sulphur springs!' cried my husband, as if he had discovered gold, and within minutes he had persuaded the medical director of the spa to let us bathe in its therapeutic pale-green water, which meant sweeping aside a disgruntled group of elderly arthritics, who had been waiting their turn for a dip. So we undressed and lowered ourselves, naked and alone, into the stone-rimmed pool, into which hot, sulphur-laden water gushed directly from a fissure in the mountain. The pool had the remains of seventeenth- or eighteenth-century tiles on its floor, and a little stone crescent moon on a pillar at its centre. A large modern clock hung on one wall.

Afterwards we asked the director if there was anything we could do to repay his kindness.

'Well,' he said, 'some of my patients aren't too good at reading the time, and they stay in the pool too long. Could you send me an hour-glass that measures thirty minutes exactly, to supplement the clock?'

We promised, and after our return to London shipped him a fine mahogany-and-brass sand-timer.

In those years there were no draconian rules for campers in the Balkans. We simply stopped, unrolled our bedding and slept. In Jugoslavia peasants and passers-by tended to leave us alone, but in Greece we often woke to find ourselves surrounded by a ring of bright little faces, gazing down at us with intense curiosity. '*Fiye mikro*' – 'buzz off, kids' – were the first words I learnt in modern Greek.

In Greece I caught fleas, which proved hard to get rid of, and we were harassed by large farm dogs. But in due course we passed safely through the Turkish frontier at Edirne, and drove on to Istanbul. It was my first visit to that magical place, and we walked everywhere, the only way of getting to know a city. As we stood under the delicate iron tracery of the Topkapi's Persian Kiosk, looking down into the formal gardens where once Suleiman the Magnificent had watched his tortoises, with night-lights glued to their backs, wander among his tulips, a blue-jay flew up with a shirr of wings. 'The brightly coloured bird!' we both exclaimed. 'We really have left Europe far behind.' But four days were not nearly enough to see Istanbul, and I vowed to return.

My first sight of the Black Sea was from the upper deck of a Turkish boat bound for the romantic city of Trebizond (now Trabzon). 'We are on our way to Persia,' I wrote in my diary. 'We have decided to travel the heroic way, following Alexander's armies and the old caravan routes across the Zingara Pass.' Our boat had three types of accommodation – first class, tourist and steerage. The first morning I mistook the number of our first-class cabin and opened the door on to what seemed like a scene from an illuminated Koran. A venerable Moslem, a *haji* in green turban and silken *khalat*, was sitting cross-legged on what I had supposed to be my bunk, his face turned towards Mecca and his head bowed in prayer. His surprise equalled mine, but ten minutes later the suave Turkish businessman in a dark-blue suit who joined a table next to ours for luncheon showed no sign of it. That was my first experience of the inscrutable oriental.

The many soldiers travelling steerage seemed to be popular with the other passengers, sharing the food and drink of their civilian companions. Suddenly one leapt to his feet and began to dance. Another joined him, and soon several were in line, arms over shoulders, bodies linked. From behind a mountain of sacks a drum began beating out a fast rhythm. At first watching the dancing was exciting, but eventually it became monotonous, for it was simply a contest of endurance that went on and on, hardly stopping for the whole two days and nights that we were at sea.

At Trebizond we were met by a driver from the British Consulate, who took us a roundabout way through the ramshackle old town to a substantial white house overlooking the harbour. Afterwards, our host, the Consul, told me he had avoided the main square because it was a day of public executions, when criminals were hanged and left dangling overnight as a grisly warning to the rest of the population.

I should love to re-visit Trebizond, which retains echoes of its great past in some neglected Byzantine churches and the tumbledown remains of towers, palaces and bazaars. The position of the town is magnificent, the surrounding countryside beautiful, and the coast becomes greener and more sub-tropical with every mile you travel eastwards. The hills are bright with cherry and chestnut trees, with berberis and cornus, azaleas and *Rhododendron ponticum*, whose name and origin are here, *Pontus* being the classical name for the Black Sea.

Above Trebizond a precipitous mountain road climbs towards the Zingara Pass, from which Alexander's armies, returning from Persia and India, had first seen the sea. As we drove higher, the vegetation and climate changed abruptly, and by evening it had become so chilly that we pulled on jerseys and duffel coats. Patches of snow lay among the heather and scrub that covered the rocky escarpments, and it began to rain. I was tired and refused to drive on, so after a heated dispute we parted and I took refuge in a handy stone-roofed shepherd's hut, where I lit a fire of pine branches and cones and prepared to cook some eggs, while Fitz stumped off in a huff. Just as I had the fire going well, I heard a long, low howl, accompanied by a snuffling sound. 'Oh God!' I thought. 'Wolves!' Someone had told me they still existed in those mountains, and this one sounded dreadfully close.

I took a lighted branch in one hand and cautiously approached the door, to be confronted by my wicked husband with his head thrown back, about to launch his second howl. He came in laughing, delighted by my panic, and we polished off the eggs and spent a cosy if somewhat smelly night beside the dying embers of my fire.

It was only after the first thousand miles that we realised the Turkish army knew, and had always known, exactly where we were. We also found they were more than willing to help us on our journey. One afternoon we had a puncture and were struggling with a recalcitrant jack when a jeep drew up alongside and a smartly turned-out officer said in perfect English, 'Let my men deal with that' – which they very soon did, simply by lifting one side of the Land Rover into the air, taking off the wheel, slipping on the spare and letting the vehicle down again.

'I've come on behalf of my colonel to ask you to dine in our mess tonight,' he went on. 'Also, we'd like to offer you a bed in our new guest-house.'

After a pleasant dinner with about a dozen officers, our saviour led us through a dark courtyard to a building that looked newer than the rest, and from which two soldiers were emerging. 'They've been lighting the boiler to heat your bath water,' he told us apologetically.

'We have no gas or electricity here – only wood and oil. But it won't take long.'

Our bags had been taken upstairs to a comfortable bedroom, and the copper tank began to hiss and gurgle invitingly in the bathroom next door. I had the first bath – and oh, the joy of it, after all that dust! Soon the water was really hot, and I lingered happily, until Fitz called, 'What about me?' Pulling out the plug, I wrapped myself in a huge pink towel – and was surprised to see my *pantoufles*, which were also pink, floating gracefully out of the room and down the stairs on a flood of escaping water.

'That's not going to put me off *my* bath,' said Fitz. 'We can always open the front door – and perhaps they'll connect a waste-pipe before they get another visitor.'

It was at the frontier town of Dogubayazit (known to us as 'Doggy-buys-it') that we nearly got shot. We had been held up for hours by a tiresome and pompous policeman, who took our passports and disappeared. It was siesta time, and tentative enquiries suggested he had gone to the cinema, so Fitz drove straight to the flea-pit in the dusty main square and sat there with his hand on the horn until the entire audience, including the embarrassed official, poured out to see what was happening.

'Passports!' Fitz demanded; and on their being handed over, 'You can now show us the way to the Iranian frontier.'

The official may not have quite understood, but he perched on the front mudguard of the Land Rover, whereupon Fitz drove off so fast that he dared not jump off. After a full kilometre he began yelling, 'Stop! Too far! Please, sir, I get off!' and brandishing a pistol. But Fitz carried on relentlessly, laughing, and it was only when we saw the double eagle of the Shah's imperial flag flying above the frontier post that he let the wretched fellow get down.

'He might have killed us,' I complained.

'Not really. I don't believe his gun was loaded – and anyway, it was worth the risk.'

The incident confirmed to me not only that Fitz could sometimes behave outrageously, but that he thoroughly enjoyed the dust-up and danger caused by doing so.

The telegram caught up with us almost as soon as we reached Tabriz:

there was to be a four-line whip in the Commons the following Tuesday. Fitz would have to return immediately. He left me in Ankara to fly home, telling me to drive carefully and, when I reached Paris, to make for the American Residence, where his friends Chip (another ex-Moscow diplomatic colleague) and Avis Bohlen would look after me. Somehow I made it, taking easy main roads and stopping off in small hotels, and in Paris the Bohlens welcomed me with open arms. 'We were getting anxious,' said Avis as she greeted me. 'Fitz has been ringing every five minutes. Come in, darling, and put your feet up.' It was the beginning of a long and happy friendship.

During that first journey I had learnt a little about myself and a lot about my husband: his expertise in conjuring up good food; his stamina; his all-round knowledge and linguistic talents; the fact that he was at his best – his most charming best – in risky situations, and that, if they did not exist, he positively revelled in creating them.

I myself had come to realise that travel was what I had always wanted, and that nothing else could match it for excitement, for adventure, for awakening and satisfying all my senses and intellect. I had immense curiosity, and a burning certainty that there would always be something new and fascinating over the next horizon. Fitz shared this romantic view of travel, and our experiences were always doubly enjoyed and doubly enjoyable. He loved to teach me, and I was eager to learn, and no one has ever had a better or more amusing instructor. Thereafter, whenever a new journey was planned, Fitz would ask, 'Care to join?' and my heart would leap.

Beyond Women

Meanwhile, the children were growing up. In the autumn of 1950 we sent Jeremy to Gilling, the preparatory school for Ampleforth College. It had been suspected for some time that he was becoming BW (the Fraser term for Beyond Women), and when he let off his newly acquired .410 in his bedroom at Beechfield, narrowly missing Mr Cockerill's ear, we felt the time had come. At first he was not particularly happy or unhappy, but when he moved to the Junior

House, under the supervision of a remarkably wise monk, Father Walter Maxwell-Stuart, who understood him, he blossomed.

'Jeremy has not learnt much history this term, but at least he can cast a pretty dry fly,' wrote Father Walter, and it was in the Junior House that the unique synergy between Ampleforth College and the countryside, the unchanged Yorkshire countryside of pre-Reformation monastic times, was perhaps most evident. Jeremy learnt to shoot, fish, sail, pray and get on with everyone he met. He had a happy nature, and even if he was allergic to exams and serious study, the monks never worried about his future. 'Jeremy will be all right,' Father Walter promised – and so he was.

We used to drive over to Ampleforth for uproarious half-term lunches at the Fairfax Arms in Gilling. 'Taking out' Jeremy meant taking out at least half a dozen of the Fraser clan, including little Kim and Simon Fraser, the young Master of Lovat. Simon kept two greyhounds with Mr Amies, landlord of the pub, and he used to escape regularly to watch them race. There was one potentially awkward moment when he and Father Paulinus, an Irish monk who had also taken French leave, came face to face at a meeting at York; but all the good father said was, 'And what would *you* be fancying now, Simon, for the next race?'

The Fraser cousins at Ampleforth practised and perfected all kinds of sport, including that of hoodwinking the much-loved monks. But for the boys the peaceful, unchanging tenor of monastic life that had existed for centuries in those valleys, the beautiful liturgy and plainchant, the rhythmic calendar of the liturgical year – would all become potent memories that would stay with them for the rest of their lives, growing a strong root and perhaps a seed that would one day flourish.

Susan Rose had been longing to join her cousins at their Woldingham convent, but I didn't think this was a good idea, and delayed too long in deciding where to send her. When Fitz and I returned from one of our summer trips, I found to my horror that her grandmother, Frances Phipps, with whom she was staying, had already enrolled her there, bought the school clothes, packed her trunk and sent her off.

That was the start of some very strained moments between me and my mother-in-law, who, after Pike's death, had become inconsistent, panicky and sometimes unreasonable in making arrangements for her own children, as well as for Alan's and mine. She would write long and passionately sincere letters explaining why some new and often lunatic decision must be taken – so much so that I came to dread the pale-blue envelopes in which they arrived.

The ones that dealt with financial matters were the worst, because the provisions that her financial adviser had made in dealing with my marriage trust had been disastrous. He had lost nearly all its capital, and though Frances replaced a good deal of it later with money of her own, the capital had never grown or kept pace with inflation, and there was always a deficit, which I hated having to ask Fitz to make good from our own limited income. Although it was true that we always lived above it, we never travelled (our greatest extravagance) without the cost being defrayed by Fitz's and sometimes my own writing. 'I don't know how the Macleans remain solvent,' Jeanne, his secretary, would grumble. 'It's all done by mirrors.' Alas, after Fitzroy's death the mirrors cracked, but meanwhile life went merrily on.

Sukie was quite happy at Woldingham, but she did little work and in no way developed her potential. The teachers classed her as amiable but dumb, and although I knew they were wrong, I let things drift. I was too preoccupied to take her away and send her to a different and perhaps stricter school. Nor did I write or visit as often as I should have. I can now see that I was a pretty feeble mother, who relied heavily on others to bring up her brood – but the older children were gregarious, and when Fitz and I disappeared on our journeys, they enjoyed happy holidays with the Fraser cousins at Beaufort or Morar or Eskadale, just as I had done with the Moniacks during my own childhood.

The Maclean boys who were still at home fared better. The excellent grounding in French, Latin and the three Rs given them by Chem, our Belgian governess, was now supplemented by lessons from a delightful old schoolmaster, so that Charles was being well prepared for Heatherdown, his father's prep school. In the shorter holidays there were many happy times at Beechfield, with picnics on the shores of Morecambe Bay, where the tide races in faster than a man can walk. There were tunnels and houses to be built in the bracken above Leydean and Leighton Moss, and Fitz constructed a ride with small jumps over which Sukie and Charlie's fat ponies would leap, Charlie dressed like a knight in knitted dishcloths which we had painted silver to simulate chain mail, and a breastplate and helmet specially made by a Lancaster tin-smith for his seventh birthday. He seemed to like walking as much as his father did, and the two amazed everyone by climbing Farlton Knot together when he was only five.

At Heatherdown he did well, and always came near the top of his form in the weekly order; but as Common Entrance loomed he seemed to have fallen behind a classmate called Hotham. When I asked him why, he quite reasonably replied, 'Oh, but Hotham's a genius. You can't possibly expect me to beat a genius!' I have often wondered what Hotham did in later life.

Jamie, two years younger than Charles, was a merry, roly-poly sort of baby, amusing, extrovert, with a strong will of his own. But in 1953, when he was four and a half, I nearly killed him. One of the children had developed chicken-pox, and to get over what I thought was a fairly routine child's illness I decided to let the rest of them catch it. The eldest three ran mild temperatures, came out in spots and were soon convalescent; but one night, to our horror, we found Jamie lying rigid in bed with his eyes turned up, apparently in a coma. Dr Byrne, quickly located, at once diagnosed encephalitis, a condition in which a virus attacks the lining of the brain. He had Jamie taken straight into Lancaster Hospital, where, for the next forty-eight hours, he remained semi-conscious. Because he became hysterical when approached by strangers or anything resembling a drip, Rhoda and I – but mostly Rhoda – spooned sips of water into his mouth for twenty-four frightening hours, struggling to rehydrate him.

Fitzroy rushed back from London in an agony of worry and remorse, for he had agreed that we should expose Jamie to the infection. He brought with him a bright-blue tie with bears on it, and when he put it round the patient's neck, the little boy actually smiled – the first sign of recovery. It was like the sun coming out after an eclipse. Fitz was never demonstrative with children, and not very good with them – and it was only then that I realised how much he cared for his sons.

Camping with the Boys

The boys were still at Heatherdown when we first took them camping in Jugoslavia. We had bought a Ford *décapotable* and hitched it to an old farm trailer to carry our gear, and we sped down through Europe, reaching the Slon Hotel at Ljubljana on the fourth night. '"*Slon*" means "elephant",' Fitz told the boys at lunch next day. 'I've never known if that's meant to show that Hannibal slept here . . .'

At that moment two young army officers approached our table, saluted smartly and asked if they might join us. 'Of course,' said Fitz, who guessed what was in the wind. After some small talk the best-looking one said to Charlie, 'We've come to kidnap you! Marshal Tito wishes you to be his guests on the island of Brioni.'

Charlie looked anxiously at his father, who was smiling, then at me, and I nodded encouragingly. 'You'd better come quietly!' the officer added as he rose to leave.

The drive through Istria was dull; the launch waiting in the harbour at Pula looked sleek and fast. Our abductors handed us over to a naval ADC in immaculate white uniform with gold epaulettes, who led the boys on to its bridge. Until the end of the war Brioni had belonged to Italy, and Mussolini had developed the island, with its lovely pine forests and olive groves, into a kind of country club for the very rich; but now it had become the official holiday resort for senior members of the Jugoslav Communist Party and Tito's personal guests.

After a night in an elegant hotel suite overlooking the sea, we made the short crossing to Herta, Tito's own small island, where he and his wife Jovanka met us, looking very relaxed in casual summer clothes. The President was rightly proud of his island, which he had planted with vines and apricot trees. Winding sandy paths linked his low, rambling glass-framed dwelling-house with the farmstead and various viewpoints and wine cellars. There was a workshop where he could revive his old skills of mechanic and locksmith; there were greenhouses and stockades, and even a small zoo.

Tito and I climbed into an electric golf-buggy, and with Fitz riding shotgun behind, the President drove us round the outlying regions of his estate. Then, after an enormous meal eaten at the edge of the blue Adriatic, our sons joined in singing Dalmatian, Scottish and Partisan songs, and Tito was prevailed upon to recite 'The Owl and the Pussycat', which still was, as in war-time, his party piece.

Continuing our journey down the coast, we were given a magnificent home-cured ham by a war-time friend of Fitz's, now mayor of his village. We hung it over the crossbars of the trailer and draped a kind of sunshade over it; but we soon realised that in accepting it we had made a big mistake, for at any speed less than 40 m.p.h. local insects discovered it, and we arrived at the Hotel Excelsior in Dubrovnik with a three-metre trail of wasps, bees, hornets and flying beetles buzzing behind us.

It was in the mountain passes of Montenegro that Jamie first became mutinous and the trailer a decided liability. It could not take the hairpin bends in one go, and Fitz, never the best of drivers, could not back it accurately, so that we had to manhandle it round the worst corners. When Jamie refused to do this any more, his father told him sternly to unpack and stand guard while the rest of us searched for a campsite. This took longer than we expected, and by the time we returned, the bees and hornets, having eaten their fill of the horrible ham, were buzzing round poor Jamie in swarms. From that day the penitent family have called him 'Bugsy Maclean', for he is 'allergic' to anything that flies or buzzes.

The children would later complain about their parents' habitual (and enjoyable) bickering in the front of the car, but a good deal of fraternal squabbling also went on in the back, where fisticuffs sometimes broke out. Once, near the summit of a particularly steep mountain road, Charlie punched Jamie on the nose, causing it to bleed. Jamie, more of a strategist than an action man, then quietly tipped his brother's night-bag over a precipice – never, we thought, to be seen again. Since the bag had contained his little all – clean shirts and pants, toothbrush, camera, boy-scout knife, books, torch and two tins of Spam for emergencies – it seemed a serious loss. Not long afterwards Fitz backed the trailer over the lip of another precipice. This time we *all* revolted; and, having unloaded the contents, which we somehow managed to cram under the children's feet, we gave the beastly thing a shove and sent it hurtling down the mountainside, to rousing cheers from everyone.

Next day, without mentioning the trailer, we reported the lost bag to the police. Six months later Fitz and I were astonished when it turned up, with contents intact, at our London flat, addressed, 'Maclean, c/o Jugoslav Embassy, London'. In those early days of the Communist regime Tito's country was both honest and watchful.

Yet in Jugoslavia dark memories of the war were never far away. On a later visit that Fitz and I made to Tito, an evening on Herta ended with the first showing of the film *Kozara*, a harrowing and beautiful portrait of one small community's epic defence of their village and mountain during the Germans' fifth offensive. The women were commanded to dig graves for their fathers and sons, who had been cold-bloodedly shot for helping the Partisans. In the film they do so, but in a slow, ritual way that is indescribably moving, singing in hard peasant voices the immemorial mourning songs of their country, sad, slow, fierce and unconquerable.

In the front row of the audience, sitting on either side of Tito and Jovanka, were men and women who had fought and suffered all through that terrible time, now generals, diplomats, politicians, academics. When the film ended, no one moved, and the lights did not go on for a few minutes; but when they did, it was easy to see that everyone there had been in tears.

By then Fitz was gathering material for his projected biography of Tito, and since he had no personal knowledge of the Germans' fourth and fifth offensives, which had taken place before he arrived in Bosnia in 1943, the Jugoslav army were keen to lend him two colonels who had taken part in them, and would show him the route the Partisans had taken to escape enemy encirclement. The idea was that we would all camp for the night in an alpine village above Foča, where horses would meet us. The men would then ride on over the mountain, while I drove round the Dermitor massif to meet them on the other side, near the frontier with Montenegro.

Our hosts told us that the honey (*med*) in that area is particularly delicious, and promised us some for breakfast. But alas, according to the villagers, the bears (*med-ved*, or 'honey-eaters') had come down in the night and gobbled all their supplies – so we had to make do with Spam. Far worse, at dawn there had occurred a tragi-comic event.

Fitz's horse, which had been hobbled near our palliasses, broke loose and, by sheer chance, relieved itself fairly and squarely into his precious night-bag, which lay open at the foot of his bed. He woke to hear the swish of a steady stream and to watch, in horror, as one after another of his intimate possessions floated out over the top of the bag. He yelled and cursed in Serbo-Croat and English, and we both pushed and pulled, but nature had its way. The horse, once started, was immovable, and I, of course, was weak as a kitten with laughter.

When I next saw Fitz, two days later, he had recovered his composure, and some of his toiletries, and reported that the march over the mountain had been gruelling. The paths were too narrow for the horses, which could rarely be ridden, but trod on the men's toes and had to be pushed and pulled up and down precipitous ravines. They spent one night in the house of a shepherd, who brewed tea with water melted from the winter snow which still lay thick on his roof. He lived off hunted game and the produce of hairy pigs, goats and a few hens, but seemed perfectly content.

The officers were jubilant on their return. 'We think he got the picture,' they told me. 'But of course it was infinitely harder in 1943. There were thousands of us. We had nothing to eat but beech-leaves. We were carrying all our wounded, and being bombed all the time, and we had to cross the Neretva.'

That night we camped together above Titograd (now Podgorica). Our companions found mushrooms and taught us how to cook them on the hot stones round our fire: 'Take out the stalk, put a pinch of salt into the hollow, and roast them for just a few minutes, till the juices bubble and the salt melts.' After the mushrooms and several glasses of vodka, they held a revolver-shooting contest, in which Fitz managed to uphold the honour of the British army.

Next morning we drove into Titograd, the small town around which the new capital of Montenegro was fast arising. Among the latest buildings was an ultra-modern steel-and-glass café, into which the neighbouring population poured every evening, mostly on foot or by donkey. We gave a lift into town to some pretty teenagers, who sat on our mudguards and were immediately arrested. 'Ne kulturni,' said the policeman, or words to that effect. Montenegro was being dragged by its bootlaces (if it had any) into the modern world, whether it liked it or not.

20

SECRET JOURNEY
TO THE TURKISH
COAST

ONE MORNING, AFTER I HAD OPTED OUT OF A DINNER PARTY FOR some frivolous reason, I was furious to find that I had missed the chance of sitting next to 'C', the mysterious security chief whose identity Fitz would never disclose to me.

Only a week later my husband told me he had hopes of going on a secret mission arranged by C to explore the southern coast of Turkey, with the aim of seeing which stretches might be suitable for amphibious landings or guerrilla operations in the mountains, in case the Cold War turned hot and Russia crossed the Black Sea. The Americans had just finished building a new road along the coast, and it had opened up new possibilities for MI6. When the trip was later confirmed and Fitz asked, 'Care to join?', he didn't wait for my answer, because he knew it already.

I was thrilled when we collected a 'secret' Land Rover from a faceless garage behind Victoria Street, and I rushed up to Lancashire to bring down camping gear and tough clothes. Our colleagues on the journey, whom we would meet in Ankara, were Dickie Brooman-White, a fellow-MP and a member of C's organisation, and Sergeant Baker, a Turko-British soldier, who would act as interpreter, guide and protector. Fitz and I would travel in our Land Rover, the other two in a Turkish army jeep.

Our first morning in camp was something of a revelation. Fitz's usual assessment of MI operators – 'a lot of silly boy scouts' – sprang to mind as Dickie and Sergeant B, spruce and shaved and *reisefertig*, woke us at dawn.

'What about breakfast?' I asked nervously.

'Oh,' answered Dickie, 'we never eat much breakfast. Takes too long. Just a handful of raisins and some cold chai, and we're off.'

Fitz and I looked at each other. 'Well,' he said tactfully, 'we take rather longer. Tell us where to meet, and we'll RV at dusk. Two opinions of the terrain are better than one, and we can discuss things over supper.'

So it was arranged – but in practice it did not always work out. The Turkish jeep was for ever breaking down, and we often passed our two professionals, or rather their legs, on the road, their bodies nearly always hidden under their wayward machine. Sometimes we would switch partners, and I would ride with Dickie. He knew that I was longing to visit Leros, and to see Alan's grave, and the dear fellow told Fitz it was most important we should reconnoitre Bodrum (ancient Halicarnassus), its little port, and even some of the adjacent islands.

The massive ruins of the great fortress still stand, and we reached it around dusk. I remember sleeping on a wooden drawbridge over its moat because I have a phobia about snakes and hoped it would be adder-proof. There were plenty of caiques available in the port, and the next morning the boys hired a bright-blue one with a great eye freshly painted on its prow. The crossing to Leros took only a few hours, for the wind was favourable, and we put up a rough, tan-coloured sail. It was when we landed that I began weeping, quietly and not unhappily. The tears just streamed and I could not stop them. Fitz and Dickie each put an arm round me and led me to the car in which the British Vice-Consul, who was waiting beside it, drove us to our temporary war cemetery, at the foot of Mount Meraviglia, where Alan had been killed.

It was a wonderfully beautiful, quiet place, among olive groves, and hibiscus and rose bushes had been planted between the rows of white headstones. Fitz and Dickie found the names of men they had served with, and left me alone with mine. I picked some scarlet hibiscus flowers and sweet-smelling herbs and put them on Alan's grave, and felt very close to him and comforted, as if at last a long journey had come safely to its end.

Our return that night, across the wine-dark Aegean occasionally lit by phosphorescent gleams and under a canopy of stars, seemed almost Homeric. The sailors trailed a line behind the caique, and soon caught several strange-looking fish, which we roasted and ate with peasant bread and Greek wine. Later, lying on deck, I looked up at the stars and thought how good and *nice* men are. No woman – neither mother, nor sister nor girlfriend – could ever have behaved like those two had to me that day. Then some words floated into my head: 'All shall be well, and all manner of things shall be well.' Feeling newly at peace with the whole universe, I fell asleep.

Back on the mainland, we found that as the Americans' new road had not yet been officially opened, there was little traffic on it, and no tourists. Sometimes it followed the coast, giving us wonderful views of ruined Crusader castles, and the chance to bathe on deserted sandy beaches; but often it crept inland and threaded its way through rough, mountainous brigand country, with only an occasional village or shepherd's hut. The few-and-far-between *locantas*, or inns, had primitive kitchens, with a dozen copper pans bubbling all day on primitive stoves. Most of the pots seemed to contain the same bright-orange mess, and to order, one simply removed their covers and pointed. But there was always good rice, usually fresh fruit – melons, figs and grapes – and occasionally, best of all, ice-cold beer from a fridge.

In the villages the adobe-and-stone-built houses were guarded from goats by rough stone walls, most of them made from the debris of Greek or Roman buildings – a stele here, a capital there, a Corinthian pillar acting as a gatepost. The Turks seemed to have no respect for, and no knowledge of, the ancient world.

The men in our party were dressed in old army clothes, for the most part khaki-coloured. One evening, as we approached a village perched on a hill, Fitz and I were somewhat surprised when two fierce-looking young men held up our Land Rover and leapt on to the running-boards, pointing ahead with their sub-machine-guns. At first we thought they might be a guard of honour, but their expressions soon disabused us of this theory, and when we arrived in the village square our vehicle was quickly surrounded by a crowd of menacing, hostile Turks.

Fitz had two sentences for use in awkward situations, and he was careful to learn them in the language of every remote country we visited. One was 'I am very, very angry,' and the other 'I am very, very hungry.' This time he stood up in the open car, beamed a confident smile at the crowd, and used the second.

It seemed to work. We were told to alight, led into a house and taken into a room containing a stove, a linoleum-topped table and four wooden chairs. The Turks departed – but when Fitz tried the handle of the door, he found it was locked. Some time later a woman appeared with four hard-boiled eggs and a jar of honey; but when Fitz asked her if we could see the Kommandant, she did not understand him, and left again, locking the door behind her.

'I suppose we're here for the night,' he said. 'So eat up and settle down. They probably think we're spies.'

Something of Fitz's question must have percolated, because about midnight a burly Turk appeared and grinned at us. 'I spik Inglis. I bin Liverpool, Glasgow . . .' He then proceeded to reel off a string of semi-English and semi-Glaswegian profanities, which amazed us but left us none the wiser. Having done his bit, he too soon left, once more locking the door.

At about eight o'clock next morning, a small, peaceful-looking man appeared – the village schoolmaster, who could speak a little Greek. He told us we had been arrested because we had driven into a new Valiate (a region governed by a Vali) without permission, but that the military would soon arrive and sort things out. This they did, and when we apologised for our lapse, they counter-apologised for our uncomfortable night: everyone was happy, and we continued on our way – but not before Fitz had had a useful look round the village.

The next night was equally strange. We were on a road that climbed through wild mountains, bordered by pine woods and banks of myrtle and arbutus. There were no turn-offs or passing-places in which we could camp. It grew inky dark, for there was no moon, and thunder grumbled in the distance. At last I saw an opening, and we followed a steep, narrow track down to the grassy bank of a stream.

'Ideal,' said Fitz, and within minutes we were snuggled into sleeping-bags. Then I heard weird snuffling sounds, that seemed to come from all sides, and an occasional high whinny. Light flickered on the far bank of the stream: there was an occasional shout, and a strange, pungent smell filled the air. This place must be haunted, I thought – but I was too tired to bother, and soon fell asleep.

At dawn, woken by the rain that had threatened all night, we found ourselves sleeping among the recumbent forms of a dozen camels. We had blundered into the wrong side of a caravanserai, and the animals' owners now waved to us cheerfully from the other side of the valley.

Not long afterwards we found Dickie and Sergeant Baker on a clifftop on the coast road, gazing down disconsolately at the remains of their jeep, which had taken upon itself to pack up its steering and had plunged over a precipice, giving them only just enough time to jump clear.

We squeezed them into the Land Rover, gave them clean shirts and exchanged stories. Sergeant Baker had some interesting tales to tell about his former boss, Kim Philby. Baker rated him 'a verra good man, verra good spy', and admired him greatly. He also told us that on one 'test of endurance and strength' he and another soldier had climbed to the top of Mount Ararat from the Turkish side.

'Did you find the Ark?' I asked him.

Apparently the summit was too misty and sulphurous and ghost-occupied to find anything at all, and, overcome by its strange fumes, they had fled down again. It was obvious that, in spite of his British citizenship, Sergeant Baker believed in some sort of presence at the top of the mysterious mountain.

'Did you ever go to Lake Van or into the Soviet Union with Mr Philby?' I asked innocently.

'Oh, no. The boss always steered clear of the frontier. He was scared of what the Russkies might do to him – and so was I.'

That was the only time I knew of when Fitz worked closely with MI6, and it was only as an ex-soldier with guerrilla experience – a useful consultant, in other words – that he consented to do so. He had an ingrained Foreign Office-bred distrust of spies, or 'friends', as he called them, telling me that usually their work consisted of rather squalid but dangerous deception, and that their dodging around and slightly childish melodramatics often got in the way of *real* diplomacy. Nevertheless, he recognised their value, and was fascinated by espionage in general, especially its connection with the Soviet Union. He knew a lot of professional spies, army intelligence officers, members of the Secret Intelligence Service, KGB and CIA agents, and he enjoyed teasing them. (In 1978 he published *Take Nine Spies*, a collection of short biographies of famous spies that he much enjoyed writing.)

Parastaiev, the leading KGB officer at the Soviet Embassy in London during the early 1970s, became a particular friend of ours, partly because he was an Ossetian, and partly because he was clever and amusing and enjoyed teasing back. One day Fitz and Iain Moncreiffe took him to lunch at White's, where they introduced him to the porter as 'the head of the Russian Secret Service', and the porter – an ex-Scots Guards sergeant of impeccable credentials – to 'Para' as 'one of C's most trusted men'. Para wasn't taken in for a moment, and in return he entertained Fitz and me to dinner at his London flat – a real Russian dinner prepared by his wife, who was a lawyer. I left behind my handbag, which had a diary in it (too much vodka?), and Para returned it next day with a note saying that all its entries had been sent in code to Moscow, and he hoped his people there could make more sense of 'Lunch with Moo' than he could.

All the Flemings – Peter, Richard, Ian and his wife Anne (formerly Charteris, and my second cousin) – were friends, and we often enjoyed Anne's lively lunch parties, much more than did poor Ian, who was not at all social, and rarely appeared. Fitz revelled in the canard that he was the original of James Bond, and played up to it by looking mysterious when interviewed on the subject. But he and Ian both told me that the smoothest and most dashing spy they had known was Commander Bill Dunderdale, whose cover was Passport Officer at the British Embassy in Paris before the war and whose beautiful wife worked at Balmain's.

Personally, I think Bond was a composite figure, with elements taken from all his creator's louche friends; but Ian did impress me one day when I lunched with him at the Ritz, along with a charming retired inspector from the CID whom he was quizzing about the latest police gadgets and weapons. Their conversation proved to me how much in those splendid books was well-researched and authentic. Poor Anne hated them, but they gave a lot of pleasure to millions of people, including ourselves.

21

MAKE AND BREAK

ONE AFTERNOON IN 1954, THREE YEARS INTO CHURCHILL'S LAST government, David and Jean Lloyd were staying with us in Lancashire when the long-awaited telephone call came through from No. 10 Downing Street. 'The Prime Minister would like to see Lord Lloyd and Fitzroy Maclean tomorrow morning at ten a.m.'

Jean and I cheered in jubilation, but then looked at the clock. There was barely time for our husbands to catch the London sleeper train from Carnforth. We flung their clothes into suitcases, and piled into our car – but it ran out of petrol just before we reached the station, and we missed their train. Undaunted, the boys flagged down a passing motorist and asked him to drive them to its next stop at Preston, forty miles away. 'Drive like hell!' Fitz told him. Whether from shock or sympathy, the stranger acquiesced, and they caught the train by seconds, arriving at Downing Street next morning shaved, groomed and expectant.

David was offered the Under-Secretaryship for Wales, and Fitzroy became Under-Secretary and Financial Secretary to the Treasury at the War Office.

'I've been wanting to give you a job for a long time,' Winston told him, 'but they [the Whips] wouldn't let me. Now that I'm old and haven't much time left, I've decided to do what I want to. You'll like the War Office.'

Antony Head had been made Secretary of State, and a happier team could not be imagined. Fitz settled into the War Office with ease. Administration was his forte: all he needed in life, he often told me, was a table with a drawer, a chair and a pen, to be perfectly happy. In Whitehall he had all three, and excellent civil servants, too. He and Antony called the War Office 'The Elephant', as it took twenty-three months to gestate, and then gave birth to a ton of paper that few people ever read. Being in charge of the army's Finance and Procurement departments, Fitz had some peculiar duties to attend to, such as stopping the annual purchase of several million horse- and mule-nails, which, as cavalry had not been used since 1940, seemed to him an unnecessary extravagance.

Off duty, we saw a good deal of the Churchills, staying with Winston and Clemmie at Chequers – a gloomy, impersonal house – and at their own home, Chartwell, which was much more agreeable. There Winston and Dot Head were forever painting or sketching. I once opened a door on to the terrace and saw the old man installed at his easel, absorbed in creation, and I was about to retire quietly when I nearly fell over Dot, who was painting the painter from under cover of a large bush. She put a finger to her lips and whispered, 'He hasn't noticed' – whereupon I slipped away, out of the picture.

At Chartwell Winston's warmth was evident in a hundred ways, particularly in his affection for children, family, friends and animals, even for his personal robin, which lived around a small paved garden below the terrace. One morning I went with him to visit the bird. We sat down quietly on a stone bench and waited. Then he called, 'Robin! Robin!', and the cheeky little fellow appeared, puffing out its red breast, to be rewarded with cake crumbs. 'You see,' said the Prime Minister, turning to me and beaming, 'he knows his name!'

Over dinner Winston was usually at his most convivial. One evening we were looked after by a smart and frosty-looking non-commissioned officer from the Women's Auxiliary Air Force, who clearly disapproved of his penchant for Armagnac. Having poured him a thimbleful, she passed swiftly on to serve the other guests. This infuriated our host, who finally removed the bottle from her ungenerous hands and plonked it on the table in front of himself, casting a conspiratorial smile at me beside him. The party grew merrier, and someone persuaded him to sing one of his party songs: 'Coming Through the Dye', a ditty about the wedding night of a gentleman whose bride turns out to be not at all what he expected, starting as a glamorous redhead and ending with her unscrewing her wooden leg and removing a glass eye.

The dinner concluded with me smoking one of Winston's cigars, much to his delight. He was so pleased, in fact, that he promised to 'keep me in cigars' for the rest of my life – a promise which failed to materialise, as so many politicians' promises do. But at least the failure avoided domestic warfare, as Fitz strongly disapproved of all smoking.

When Winston, after his retirement, became shaky and sad, we would sometimes be asked to the small dinner parties that Clemmie gave at their London home in Hyde Park Gate, in her efforts to cheer him up. One evening the 'black dog' cloud that he dreaded would not lift, and my every gambit failed. At the end of the meal he put his hand over mine and said, 'I'm sorry, darling, for being such poor company. You see, long ago "I was one of the singers, and now I am one of the dumbs."'

I felt so sad that I impulsively threw my arms round him in a huge hug. 'Oh, Winston!' I cried. 'You'll always be a singer. You've written "volumes of stuff" that sing *for* you, and you're never, never dumb.'

That did the trick. His head lifted, he beamed, and we now chatted happily, recalling further snatches of the immortal introduction to the Nonsense Poems which begins 'How pleasant to know Mr Lear', and agreeing that our favourite line was 'And chocolate shrimps at the mill.'

Cowley Street, in Westminster, is largely inhabited by MPs, because it lies within easy reach of the House of Commons and its Division Bell; and the Heads' house, No. 45, soon became a second home to me, and Dot Head a best friend. Large and comfortably – even extravagantly – built, her figure reflected her personality. She was warm and amusing, but often alarmingly shrewd and sharp: her artist's eye never missed a shadow or a nuance, and she could smell out hypocrisy, dishonesty and pretension a mile away. Quite apart from her sense of humour and intelligence, she had the best taste, both instinctive and informed, that I have ever known.

As one walked along Cowley Street to No. 45, one could see into the uncurtained dining-room windows of No. 33, the rather more grandiose house of Pam Berry, whose husband Michael (later Lord Hartwell) ran the *Daily Telegraph*. Fitz and Antony, like many of my contemporaries, divided the Berry family into the Goodberries and the Badberries, and poor Pam fell definitely into the second category, as, although clever and witty, she aspired to being the leading political hostess of the day and to holding a salon for the Establishment, which was thought pretentious.

Anyone arriving at No. 45 would be closely questioned by Dot about who was lunching at No. 33 – but often such espionage was unnecessary, as Randolph Churchill, one of Pam's regular guests, would enjoy her excellent food and sparkling talk, and then come on for coffee with the Heads, and regale us with the latest gossip. Randolph, who had accompanied Fitz on one of the SAS's desert raids and been under his command in Jugoslavia, was the most impossible, argumentative and destructive of all our friends: he was not even house-trained for, at the end of some passionate debate, he would throw himself backwards into one of my favourite armchairs, quite often breaking its back. One day he must have acted with typical boorishness at No. 33, for he told us triumphantly: 'I'd accused Pam of being inaccurate and careless (which she is), and I clinched my argument by saying, "What's more, my dear girl, you haven't even shaved today!"'

Suez and the Sack

After Fitz became a minister, I saw less of him than ever. He was happy, but the workload was punishing, especially in the months that led up to the Suez crisis in the winter of 1956, and he often could not come back to Beechfield even at weekends. He had always advocated standing up to Nasser, who was threatening to take over the canal, and he was a founder-member with Julian Amery of the Suez Group, but he had been persuaded by his loyalty to Churchill not to vote against the government in the crucial debate of 1953. This, of course, led to criticism from the right-wingers, and I sympathised with Clarissa Eden's famous complaint, 'The Suez Canal flows through my drawing room,' because it certainly flowed through mine.

In 1955 Eden succeeded Churchill as Prime Minister, but he was already ill, and he dithered for months before finally deciding to launch Operation Musketeer and embark on a campaign to recover control of the canal, which the Egyptians had now seized. Thereafter events moved so fast that they overwhelmed him: on 29 October the Israelis invaded the Sinai; on 6 November British and French troops invaded the Canal Zone 'to part the combatants' – a fiction which no one believed; the USA and USSR made threatening noises; sterling collapsed; our army withdrew; and Eden took to his bed.

When the crisis was over, the ailing PM returned to active office long enough to reorganise the Defence Department. Head was moved up to become the new Secretary of State for Defence (which would now encompass all three services), and this distanced him still farther from Fitz. John Hare – a fence-sitter if ever there was one – took Antony's place as Secretary of State for War and became Fitz's temporary boss.

Antony had asked for Fitz to become his War Office deputy at Defence, and all the paperwork for the promotion had been completed when Eden resigned. I had high hopes that Harold Macmillan would confirm the appointment when he succeeded Eden as Prime Minister in January 1957. But he immediately embarked on a populist policy of abolishing conscription and reducing the manpower of our armed forces, in favour of nuclear deterrence, hoping that this would restore confidence and confirm his position after the Suez fiasco. So Head was sent for by Macmillan, but refused to steer the Defence White Paper abolishing National Service through the Commons, and so was sacked, shortly followed by Fitz, who held the same opinion, equally firmly, that the army could not fulfil its commitment without it.

Afterwards, Macmillan told his biographer, Alistair Horne, that he had reluctantly dismissed Fitz because of his poor performance in the House; but when he visited us only a few years later, he claimed to have thought that Fitz wanted to give up politics because he was moving to Scotland. A likely story!

By December 1956 Fitz's political career had taken a series of blows from which it never recovered. He had just missed becoming Minister of State for Defence; Eden had considered him for Ambassador to Jugoslavia (which he would have refused); he had been short-listed for Governor of Malaya. All this might have seemed rather dispiriting, but for one vital fact: he had been adopted for a new constituency in Scotland, and *we were going home*.

22

STRACHUR

I N 1943 Fitz had promised the electors of Lancaster and
Morecambe that he would represent them faithfully in parliament
as soon as we had won the war. They had waited patiently for that
to happen, and when he returned to the constituency he fought and
won five General Elections for the Conservative Party; but it was not
until the mid-1950s that he felt he could abandon Lancaster, leaving
it gracefully and in good shape, to seek a new base for his political life
in Scotland, where both of us had always wanted to live.

Three constituencies were available to him, for at that time he
was a name in the north, and the Fraser mafia was not unhelpful.
His choice fell on North Ayrshire, with its accompanying islands of
Bute and Arran. The retiring MP, Charlie MacAndrew, Deputy Speaker
of the House of Commons, and Alec Cameron, his chairman, ably
steered the Selection Committee his way, so that he was adopted as
the Conservative candidate for the next General Election, which was
due in roughly a year's time.

It only remained to find a house in Argyll from which we could
work the two halves of the constituency, the islands and the North
Ayrshire coast. We hoped it would be possible to deal with both by
the MacBrayne ferry service, which operated from Dunoon in Argyll to
Gourock on the Clyde coast, and on the longer journey from Ardrossan
further down it, to Brodick on Arran.

Strachur estate and its eighteenth-century mansion house, on the
south-eastern shore of Loch Fyne, in Argyll, were advertised in *Country
Life* and looked promising. We got in touch with Joan Campbell,

owner of the property, received permission to view it, and arrived after a long drive from Beaufort on one of those November nights when south-westerly gales whip the loch into a fury of white-capped waves, and almost horizontal rain lashes anyone foolish enough to walk near it.

We had been told we could put up at a small lochside hotel called The Creggans Inn, which was owned by the estate, but leased to Mrs McKechnie, a cheerful widow who now wished to return to Oban. I remember I was literally blown into its glass-fronted veranda, and then climbed a steep little staircase, with a brass ornament displayed on every step, to a rather bleak bedroom overlooking the loch; and that a few minutes later Fitz upset an anthropomorphic brass bell on his way downstairs, so that it tinkled all the way from the top to the bottom.

Mrs McKechnie led us into a cosy room off the public bar, from which sounds of merriment could be heard. A bright peat fire glowed in its hearth, there were several kinds of malt whisky to choose from, and she told us that 'tea' would be ready 'in just five minutes'. Never had home-made scones and oatcakes, eggs and bacon and black pudding tasted so good (and never had even the meanest bed seemed so inviting).

'You'll never be wanting to visit the Park tonight' – it was more a statement than a question – 'and in such a gale?'

'Oh yes, we would,' answered Fitz for both of us, and on being told there was no transport he added briskly, 'Well, then, we'll have to walk.'

The walk, through a splendid lochside archway and up a tree-lined drive, was short but extremely wet. We were almost blown away by sudden gusts of wind, and the night was so dark that the house, much larger than we had expected, suddenly loomed up on us, huge and high. We had barely knocked on the imposing front door when it was opened for us by a stout, unsmiling woman in a neat parlourmaid's uniform.

'Miss Campbell said you were coming, and I'm to show you round,' said Ethel, opening an inner door into a softly lit, beautifully proportioned hall, with four classical pillars and a gracefully curving staircase. A moment later we were racing up it. Fitzroy opened the first door on the main landing. It was a library, lined with books, with a desk set in a bow window. 'My room,' he said firmly in a tone that forbade argument. Next came double drawing rooms with windows looking out on both sides of the house, parquet floors, mahogany doors and lovely Georgian chimney pieces.

'I'll take the first one, and we'll keep the second one for parties and the piano,' I declared quickly.

Then Ethel showed us the dining room on the ground floor, with another bow window and a door leading presumably into a garden behind the house. This room was lined with a pale-blue Chinese wallpaper upon which exotic birds of every description perched and flew. Entering it was like walking into an outdoor aviary in eighteenth-century Peking – and we gasped. The bedrooms included a 'storm bedroom', also at the back of the house, to which Miss Campbell apparently retired when the gales were blowing too noisily. They were all beautiful and infinitely desirable.

'Of course we don't *begin* to have enough furniture,' I ventured practically, 'or money to buy any.'

'Forget the furniture. It's the bones of a house that matter,' said Fitz, and we both agreed that when it came to bones, windows and proportions, Strachur Park, having been built mainly in 1789, was just about perfect. Even before we had seen the view over Loch Fyne, which we did the following morning in bright sunshine and with a cloudless sky, we had fallen in love with the place and knew it would be our destiny to live there one day, and to become part of it.

Miss Campbell was an eccentric lady, but at first we did not realise quite how odd she was. Her mother, Lady George, a Lascelles and a rich woman in her own right, had married Lord George Campbell, brother of the bachelor Duke of Argyll, who lived at Inveraray Castle on the other side of the loch. She had expected to live in style, and when she bought Strachur, she certainly did so, employing five gardeners and a full complement of indoor servants, who were all in considerable awe of her. But in spite of the gardeners, the foresters, the woodland walks and plantations, she spent very little on actual gardening or plants (as I eventually discovered), and even less on heating the house.

Ian Argyll, the next Duke and Campbell clan chief to inhabit Inveraray Castle, told us that as a youth he had been invited by his great-aunt to lunch at Strachur, and that he had observed her putting one small log, rather grudgingly, on the open fire in the icy drawing room, when his fellow-guest, the local minister, exclaimed ingratiatingly, 'A veritable Vulcan at his forge, your ladyship!' – and Ian, who had been brought up in the nightclubs and sunshine of Miami and Biarritz, thought to himself, 'Some Vulcan, some forge!'

There had been three children, but the Great War had claimed the Campbells' only son, and the eldest daughter, Joan, who inherited the estate, was not interested in men or marriage. She pinned all her dynastic hopes on her nephew, Ian Anstruther, whom she counted on succeeding her; but he disappointed her by preferring the urban comforts and salubrious climate of Petworth, in West Sussex, to the damp West Coast and gales of Argyll. And so Strachur estate was put on the market and, the house being too large for most sensible families and the estate too small for economic gain, the asking price was a mere £12,000, with further small sums for the inn and plantations.

Miss Campbell, who had known my mother, wanted a private sale, with no agents involved. That suited us, but I almost ruined the deal. As my father's daughter, who knew all about trees, I pointed out to Fitz that the softwood plantations were in a deplorable state: you only had to lean on a soggily planted, un-brashed spruce and it fell over, and the woodlands were ridiculously overvalued. Unfortunately, forestry had been Miss Campbell's particular interest. She had deliberately nurtured and cared for her trees in the spirit of Nature Knows Best – and she was therefore outraged by my tentative aspersions. She immediately broke off negotiations, placing the sale in the hands of Messrs John D. Wood and Co., who then proposed to sell the estate by auction, in blocks, and had a client who they said was interested.

We never saw Miss Joan again. The situation became very complicated and disagreeable. Fitzroy retired to bed in our London flat with a recurrence of the high fever and shakes that had laid him low on the Adriatic island of Vis in 1943. We were out of our depth, and sinking fast.

If it had not been for the intervention of Peter Oldfield, an old army friend and head of Knight, Frank and Rutley, to whom Fitz appealed in a moment of lucidity and despair, all would have been lost. 'Leave it to me, old boy,' Peter told Fitz on the telephone. 'I've got something to trade with the old bugger.' And he had – but even so, we had to bid separately for each farm, each house, practically for each tree in the park. We had just enough money to buy the important items. New furniture would indeed have to wait.

Before the removal vans arrived and we moved in, Mr Cockerill, our spearhead, slept – as at Beechfield – on a mattress in an empty bedroom. There were no ghosts but the standing stone in the field in front of the house fell down that night.

He and Rhoda were just as excited about the move as we were and had, by now, got married so they spoke as one voice (usually Mrs Cockerill's).

'Now that's what I call a proper pantry,' said Mr Cockerill when he was taken on a tour of the house. 'A lead apron to the sink, and a silver safe you can walk into.'

Fitzroy had been able to buy only two of the four hill-farms that comprised the Strachur estate: Glensluain and the Home Farm, which included five hundred acres of good arable land, as well as the shinty field in front of the house. The tenant of Glensluain, Duncan Sinclair, became his head shepherd and grieve; and so Duncan, Mrs Duncan and their three daughters moved to one of the four cottages in the Home Farm Square, an eighteenth-century group of barns and small houses separated from Strachur itself only by a burn and a beautiful bridge (designed by the Adam brothers).

Duncan was up at dawn and away to the hill before his young family had wakened, but Mrs Duncan did not stir until much later, if at all. She was always to be found in her felt slippers and comfortable cardigan, sitting in front of her kitchen fire with a pot of tea on the hob and some very good shortbread in a tin. If ever anything active was mooted, she would say, 'Well, I'll just go and put my boots on' – but somehow or other she always managed to avoid such definite exertion, and remained peacefully relaxed and almost permanently unshod. Not so her daughters, who were always busy as beavers, and soon introduced our children to the ways of the village's life.

A significant part of this was shinty – the Highland game known in Gaelic as *camanachd* – and one of the first things the village did was to elect Fitz chieftain of the shinty club, by which cunning move he was deterred from ever ploughing up the field in front of the house, which was sacrosanct, and on which fierce contests took place every Saturday afternoon during the summer months. Shinty was to Strachur what football is to Manchester, and because of the shinty battles at

Beauly in my childhood, and my father having started, with Lochiel, the Camanachd Association, I sympathised with our local heroes, the Strachur team.

Among our eccentric neighbours were the Maclachlan family, whose clan chief, Madam Maclachlan of Maclachlan, a cuddly, teddy-bear person, was fond of a good malt. She lived with her husband and six children in what was known as the 'new castle', the old one, bombarded by the English in 1715, being a romantic ruin. It stood on a strategic point which overlooked the loch and a string of low, rocky islands, where eider duck, mallard and seagulls nested.

The Maclachlans, keen Jacobites, had fought for the Prince at Culloden, on the left of the line and next to the Macleans of Ardgour. Their young chief had been killed, but his horse, a Highland garron, had found its long way home, swimming across Loch Fyne and carrying, by its empty saddle, the fatal news of the laird's death.

Traces of Scotland's history and pre-history lay all around us: standing stones and barrows and astro-archaeological sites, mysterious cup-and-ring designs carved into rocks, early monastic settlements with houses built in the form of beehives, medieval brochs and towers and vitreous walls, iron-smelting bloomers and lime-burning clachans. Even the names of some of Strachur's old families, the Blacks and the Blues, had historical significance, for they were descendants of Cluny Macpherson, the robber-chief who had holed up in Glen Arthur and whose very name had been obliterated after the Union, so that the Macpherson clan (in Gaelic 'children of the mists') were known only by the colours of their tartans.

And then there were the Campbells, and their chief, MacCallum Mhor, the eleventh Duke of Argyll, who lived across the loch at Inveraray Castle. To many Highlanders the Campbells were arch-villains, mistrusted and hated – but in fact, or pragmatic terms, they were the only politically minded chiefs in the west who, though sometimes perfidious, always backed the winning side.

When we arrived at Strachur, Ian Argyll was still married to the former Margaret Whigham, but only just. He had already been married twice before, first to Lord Beaverbrook's daughter Janet, by whom he had one daughter, then to Louise, an American southern belle who bore him two sons before unwisely confessing to a war-time romance with an American colonel. This greatly upset Ian and threw him into the rapacious arms of Mrs Margaret Sweeney, née Whigham, the top professional beauty of the day.

Their marriage was a disaster. Margaret carried on sleeping around and spending more money than she brought to the ailing Argyll estate, and when she failed to conceive a child of her own, resorted to shameful slurs on the parentage of the Duke's offspring. Such was the messy background to the Argyll family when we arrived at Strachur.

Yet Ian brought to Inveraray a dash of continental and transatlantic glamour, and that bit of sophistication that our other neighbours lacked. Parties at the castle were never dull. More importantly, the Duke *loved* his inheritance – the castle and the town, his estates, their history and traditions – and he did a great deal to nurture and preserve them. At heart he was a good man: intelligent, kind, funny and cultured, very different from his public image, but he had appallingly bad judgement about public relations, and about women in general, and when he was with people he didn't know well, he adopted a certain stiffness and pomposity of manner which came, I think, from lack of confidence and belied his real character.

With us he was always at ease, and therefore charming. He let our children fish to their hearts' content on his river, the Aray, and picnic in an eighteenth-century gazebo above its falls, where we could watch the salmon leaping. He also lent Fitz his personal piper, Pipe-Major Ronnie McCallum, for special occasions, and he often came over to dinner on his own, once with a mahogany lavatory seat hung round his neck – for he knew that Fitz was reorganising his bathroom, and was anxious to install a proper, old-fashioned loo, with a plunge handle, mahogany seat and panelled sides. For such a collector's item, the Inveraray attics were the obvious source, so I sent this letter to Ian:

> *The mahogany seat*
> *That you find obsolete*
> *And have banished to cellar or attic*
> *I most humbly aspire*
> *To possess, noble Sire,*
> *And I beg you in verse most emphatic:*
>
> *May I visit your castle*
> *And make a small parcel*

> *Of this erstwhile great nobleman's seat?*
> *For I'm sick with desire*
> *To remove from Kintyre*
> *The loo and the handle, complete.*

A week later Ian came to dinner, wearing part of the mahogany seat like a horse-collar round his neck, and presented me with a *billet-doux* which began:

Le Duc-Plombier à sa Maîtresse

> *Must love be won in such a sordid way?*
> *Could I not to my passion bring a crown*
> *Of daffodils, or hollyhocks, a spray?*
> *Not timber, drab and brown.*
>
> *Perchance, if treasured through the cruel years,*
> *Cobwebbed and broken, gnawed by eager rat,*
> *The Thing be found – an end to all our fears!*
> *Maclean may sit where once great Lorne hath sat.*

The ducal mahogany sides followed a few days later, and a magnificent thunderbox was constructed for Fitz by Archie Cameron, the village's finest craftsman.

At first we did not know what to do about The Creggans Inn, but then Rhoda's sister Kitty, who had been a brigadier in the war-time Queen Alexandra's Royal Army Nursing Corps and was now Home Matron in a hospital outside Edinburgh, decided to retire from nursing and declared an interest in managing it for us. That was what clinched the matter. Fitz and I had always wanted to create and operate the perfect small Highland hotel, and we now had the chance to do so. We jointly decided not to re-let, but to run it ourselves, so we wired to Kitty, 'Come as soon as you can.'

That, it turned out, was not until July, so meanwhile we had to muck in and help the skeleton staff that Mrs McKechnie was leaving behind her. How we got through the spring and early summer months of 1957, I shall never know, except that it proved the adage, 'You're never happier than when you have too much to do.' I, certainly, had never been more content.

Fitz had recently inherited the worldly goods of his uncle Henry Maclean of Ardgour, and also the care of his widow, Aunt Ros, our first dependant. Although Uncle Henry had actually lived in Hampshire, he and his wife were rabid Macleans, even fighting a lawsuit to prove that he was the seventeenth legitimate chieftain of Ardgour. Among his effects were trunkloads of Maclean and Carlyle papers, books, pictures, heirlooms and furniture. One day I was called into Fitz's library by an excited shout. 'Come quick! Look what I've found!'

He had been investigating one of the trunks, which was full of unreadable charts and seals, but at the bottom of which he had struck gold. He sat me down and handed me an envelope. On the outside was written in sepia ink and an antique hand, 'The Portrait'. Inside was a note in the same hand: 'Given to me by a gentleman who did not wish the portrait to be found on his person.' Folded into the note was a very small tissue-paper packet, which I unwrapped with the greatest care. Inside were two small strips of heavier paper, each bearing a carefully drawn and coloured picture of a young man's head, wearing a bonnet with a white plume, and an indication of tartan. On either side of the head were the letters 'PC'. The portrait was no bigger than the pinkie on one of my hands. I looked at Fitz questioningly.

'It was the way undercover Jacobites could recognise each other after the '45,' he said. 'It was highly dangerous to be identified with the Stuart cause, and obviously the gentleman who carried this in his watch or snuff-box suddenly lost his nerve, or was about to be arrested, and unloaded the evidence on to a Jacobite sympathiser . . . my ancestor.'

We both looked up at the not-very-flattering oil painting of himself that Prince Charlie had sent the Macleans of Ardgour before the rising, which occupied pride of place in Fitz's library. That was fine – but this tiny secret paper portrait was miles better. I don't think a million-pound cheque could have pleased Fitz more.

We settled Aunt Ros and Ivy, her devoted maid, into one of the nicest houses on the estate, and after she had chosen such furniture as she wished, the residue arrived at our front door. It was invaluable, especially the beds, which were very soon occupied, but when about twenty murky family portraits of Fitz's and Uncle Henry's ancestors were unloaded and about to be carried upstairs, I burst into tears. I had not yet acquired the genealogical bug that comes with middle and old age, and I felt overwhelmed by so much ancestry. Fitz, on the other hand, was delighted. The arrival of the paintings confirmed his decision to stop wandering and to return to his Caledonian roots, and their careful hanging and labelling occupied him happily for weeks.

Occupying the children was easy. We hardly saw them, except when they returned from fishing or rabbiting or taking hideous risks in boats and home-made canoes on Loch Fyne. Rhoda took over the housekeeping and kitchen, for her mother had once been a professional cook, and that talent, lurking somewhere in her genes, was now given plenty of scope. At the hotel, Mrs McKechnie did everything she could to help and advise before she left for Oban.

'Never employ a barman with false teeth,' she told me mysteriously one day.

'Why's that, Mrs McKechnie?'

'Because he'll ring up fifteen bob on the cash register when it should have been a quid, and hide the note underneath his dentures. Yes – there's many a trick they'll be up to, and you'll just have to have eyes in the back of your head.'

Mrs McKechnie's staff were all local girls and what is known as 'characters'. Annie, the waitress, had an impenetrable Bute accent.

'Yer tea's rready on the verranda, sirr,' she told a visiting Englishman.

No response.

'Yerr tea's in the sun-lounge,' she tried.

Still no response.

'Yerr tea's in the bluidy gless-hoose!' she yelled, and that did the trick.

When we took over, there was only one bottle of wine in the bar, and that had been opened, re-corked, and become vinegar. The menus were minimal and unvaried. 'Soup or juice?' Annie would ask the customers, and when they responded, 'And what's yer afters?' The breakfasts and high teas, on the other hand, were delicious and what people expected. I made the fatal mistake of ignoring this one day, when, as the relief breakfast cook, I got up early to make a perfect salmon kedgeree, only to be told by the customers that they could not eat 'messed-up fish', and would I please fry them some eggs sunny-side up?

After the bars closed, counting the tills, balancing them with the floats and the tab, locking up – all this was fun at first but soon became a nightmare. It sometimes took me two hours to complete, the coins and notes seeming to have a life of their own, whose purpose was to confuse me. Even though Jennie Black, the popular bar-lady, had a sparkling set of her own teeth, the bar percentage always remained depressingly low. We struggled for a couple of months with this amateur innkeeping, and it certainly taught me a lot about hotels. Then Kitty wrote to say she would have to postpone her arrival until the autumn. The situation looked desperate, but a crisis was averted by Jeanne Thomlinson, Fitz's secretary, and a friend of hers from student days agreeing to spend their summer holidays running the pub. They took over from me and, being charming and infinitely more efficient, had no trouble at all with the till, the accounts, the staff, the recalcitrant black stove, or the guests.

Charlie passed his Common Entrance exam easily, and no one can have looked forward to Eton more keenly than he did – perhaps too keenly, for in the event he and the school did not suit each other, and it was his first great disappointment. 'Charlie resists education,' his father would say to me sadly, and up to a point that was true. He immediately fell out with his housemaster, Peter ('Wetty') Lawrence, who had prevented him attending Sukie's wedding ceremony for some petty misdemeanour, and then his best friend was expelled for smoking. He responded by taking refuge in the art school, and there he found congenial company and won many prizes. He also organised the first folk concert ever held at Eton, with Veronica Lyle (now Baroness Linklater, a stalwart of the Liberal Party) and himself as the leading performers; but he missed a great many opportunities, and his work suffered.

Once he left Eton, his horizons widened and brightened. After six months' intensive cramming in Strasbourg, where he was put under severe pressure by Monsieur Livet, a teacher of formidable authority, and making friends with the folk-singing twins, Heine and Oskar Kröhe, he went up to New College, Oxford, for his interview. But there again he came to grief: he insisted on reading PPE (a subject that was already oversubscribed) and that none other would do, so he was told to return the following year and a place would be kept for him. He desperately wanted to visit America, for he had met the folk singer Rambling Jack Elliott, who had invited him to California. So

Fitz fixed him up with a job on the Lazy Shamrock ranch in Colorado, a student's bus ticket and letters to friends. It was then that I had one of my craziest ideas. Instead of flying to America, which was expensive, why didn't he work his passage as a stevedore on a merchant ship – a great adventure, which he would never forget?

He never did forget it. He crossed the Atlantic in ultra-stormy weather and mountainous waves, but he never saw the sea, because he was shovelling fuel in the hold, in the company of rough Lascars, who didn't think much of him, fought all the time and frequently stabbed each other. He was violently seasick, and arrived in Norfolk, Virginia, in poor shape, to be rescued first by our friends the Bemisses in Richmond, then by the Warburgs in Connecticut.

He was happy at the Lazy Shamrock, which turned out to be a real ranch, though most of the work was done from the back of trucks, rather than on horseback. The country was amazingly beautiful. There were turkey shoots and poker sessions, at which he often won, the other 'hands' just not being able to 'figger him out'! On his return, I hardly recognised him. He was inches taller and broader, with a new guitar that Rambler Jack had given him slung round his neck, and a four-gallon Texan hat on the back of his sun-bleached head.

He then followed in his father's footsteps by spending two semesters at Marburg University, in central Germany, where he learnt a little German and did a lot more growing up. Returning to Oxford and New College, and deciding after all to read Modern Languages, he completed his degree course successfully and ended up with a respectable 2:1, just missing a first.

Jamie, meanwhile, was also proving to be rebellious, but more subtly so than Charlie. He, too, worked very little at Eton, and won all the art prizes, but he also became head of his house and abolished beating, without any significant loss of discipline. He refused to join the Combined Cadet Force – a bold step – and took pot-shots at the cadets with a modified gas pistol which I had imprudently allowed him to buy in Germany. He ran an amusing weekly newspaper and produced a really beautiful dramatised version of St Exupéry's *Le Petit Prince*, with his own coloured lantern slides. But he still maintains he hated Eton, and he certainly insisted on leaving as soon as he had passed his exams.

23

A VERY
DAMP DUKE

A T STRACHUR IT WAS NOT LONG BEFORE FITZ AND I BECAME involved in local activities. The Cold War brought the American navy and Polaris, the western powers' ultimate deterrent, to the Holy Loch on the Clyde, and in 1961 about fifteen hundred American families arrived in Dunoon and the Cowal area.

The proximity of the submarines was exciting, but also alarming. There we were, right beside what we believed to be the ultimate deterrent – nuclear missiles that could reach Moscow, and carried warheads with many times the destructive power of the bombs which annihilated Hiroshima and Nagasaki in 1945. At first, as we drove into Dunoon, the only new presence we noticed on the waterfront was the huge grey hulk of the command-ship, USS *Huntly*; but then we saw, lying alongside her like piglets beside a sow, the conning-towers of two or three submarines, which looked quite small, because ninety per cent of their bulk lay under water.

Some people were made anxious by the presence of the submarines so close to their homes, believing that the base would be the first target for a Russian response if nuclear war broke out; but the only time I myself felt worried was when, motoring to Dunoon one morning, I noticed that there were no ships at all in the loch. The open water was innocent of menace, and suddenly I felt strangely naked and vulnerable. That night we learnt from the BBC news that the Bay of Pigs crisis was developing in Cuba, and realised that all the American ships in the Clyde had put to sea, for our safety and their own.

With the nuclear fleet came the sailors and their families, who had good enough allowances to rent houses and flats in the neighbourhood. Within weeks every house in Cowal, from Tighnabruaich to Strachur, was angling to rent out accommodation to the Yanks. Leases brought in decent and (even more important) untaxed income – and everyone salved their consciences by saying it was the least they could do for our new protectors.

The American families needed to be befriended and looked after, and family associations were soon formed. In the 1970s Fitz was appointed chairman of the US Forces' Community Relations Committee – a post which sounded onerous, but in fact entailed very little work, as the administration was done professionally by a delightful young woman called Yvonne Cant, who sat in an office in Dunoon and untangled the submariners' domestic problems. What the job did mean, however, was that we got to know many of the American personnel, and I soon realised that, although they ran things rather differently, they were just as efficient, kindly and brave as our own sailors, whom I had known and loved so much during the war.

When Captain Walter Schlecht – a Catholic – was in command aboard the *Huntly*, he used to have a low Mass celebrated by the fleet chaplain every Sunday in the wardroom, and would invite me to a riotous breakfast afterwards. On one of these jolly occasions I noticed that he was sporting the beginnings of a really splendid black eye.

'What have you been doing, Wally?' I asked. 'Running into a bulkhead in the dark?'

'Naow!' he answered. 'I had an argument with one of the ratings, and he was quicker with his fists than I was. But in the end I laid him out cold!'

When a new commodore took over, we decided to introduce him to Ian Argyll, and one evening a wonderfully mixed company assembled before dinner in my drawing room. Our American guests were on their best behaviour, the Commodore a trifle stiff and formal, his wife young and prim, and both ultra-polite. Our house-guest was an eccentric lifelong friend of Fitz's, Michael Vyvyan, one-time diplomat, war-time Black Watch officer, and now a Fellow of Trinity College, Cambridge.

The Duke's party consisted of his daughter, Lady Jeanie, her lover

Norman Mailer – who had just published the best-selling novel *The Naked and the Dead* – and our mutual neighbour Marguerite, a delightful widow who lived alone in Dunderave Castle across the loch, and to whom the others had given a lift. Ian Argyll was in full West Highland kit: velvet doublet, silver 'salmon' buttons, lacy jabot secured by a diamond brooch, fancy knee-stockings with still fancier garter-flashes. The curvaceous Jeanie had poured herself into a tight black satin sheath, and shone all over, as if she had been rubbed down with the best butter, while Mailer was dressed as a kind of Mexican toreador, with a white frilled shirt, scarlet cummerbund and black patent-leather pumps.

Things started badly when Jeanie enquired of the company: 'Isn't he lovely?', then parted his shirt-front, exposing a veritable hearth-rug of black curly hair, and patted it. Next, Norman showed Michael the latest New York fun-game, which consisted of two contestants hooking little fingers and wrestling each other to the ground. Within minutes they were writhing on the floor.

Dinner was delicious, and a good claret and old Armagnac promoted general bonhomie. About midnight a smart naval car rolled up, and the Americans left us. Soon afterwards we also waved goodbye to the ducal party.

Only next morning did I hear what happened after that. When Ian's car reached Dunderave, he got out in pouring rain to see Marguerite safely into her house. In the castle's inner courtyard it took him a few moments to make the ancient key turn in the lock. But when he returned and made a dash to his car, it had vanished. He could see by a light in a turret window that Marguerite had already reached her bedroom, and would not hear him, even if he hollered, so there was nothing for it but to set out on shanks's pony for the eight-mile trudge to Inveraray, still in his green velvet doublet and lacy jabot, cursing his demon daughter and idiot chauffeur every yard of the way.

After he had gone four miles or so, his car reappeared and stopped beside him.

'What the blazes—?' he began.

'It was Lady Jean, your Grace,' replied the driver. 'She said she was in a hurry and had to get back to the castle *immediately*.'

'Never mind, Archie,' Ian told him. 'But never, *ever* listen to her again.'

Five minutes later, when the great Campbell chief knocked

peremptorily on his daughter's bedroom door and shouted, 'Let me in!', she called, 'I can't, Daddy. I'm busy.' When he insisted, she suddenly threw open the door and smiled radiantly at him: the smile was all she was wearing. Next day Mr Mailer's bags were packed for him, and he was told there was excellent accommodation available at the Argyll Arms, a leading Inveraray hostelry nearby.

Our contact with the submarine crews taught us a good deal about the strain under which they worked. We knew they were closed up at battle-stations for weeks on end, never seeing daylight or breathing fresh air, maintaining radio silence, navigating to within a few yards of their designated positions deep below the surface. The punishing routine inevitably led to breakdowns, both mental and physical, and to my mind the men were all heroes who deserved our endless gratitude.

Yet when the time came for the Americans to leave, how did our politicians treat them? Abysmally. The US Navy planned a ceremonial departure, with a bevy of top naval brass coming over from the States for the occasion; but because of some idiotic row about who was to pay for what in the decommissioning process, the Admiralty decided to scale down its representation to a miserable level. Luckily Fitz had been asked to speak at the ceremony: he gave a ringing account of the service the submariners had rendered to Britain and the rest of the western world, and wished them Godspeed, *and* he invited no fewer than a hundred of them to dine next evening at The Creggans Inn, where he hoped to show them some true Highland hospitality.

Our staff at the pub were taken aback by the suddenness of this invitation, about which they had no warning, but they responded magnificently and gave the Americans a night they would never forget. Our spontaneous unofficial hospitality showed what friends the visitors had made, and how grateful we all were to them. They staggered away in the small hours, in a haze of good will.

My cousin Tommy Arran was the minister responsible at the time, and I berated him when we next met. 'I *was* coming to the ceremony,' he answered rather feebly, 'but then the Treasury told my staff it would be unwise, so it was cancelled.'

'Bloody politicians!' I answered crisply. 'You ought to have known better.' But then he looked so crestfallen that I forgave him. We all make mistakes sometimes, but the Treasury makes far too many, and their errors are nearly always mean and counterproductive.

Macleanery

The only sadness of our first summers at Strachur was that Fil had died without ever seeing the place. He had always hoped we would, as a family, return to Scotland and it would have given him immense pleasure to see us do so, but on one of our many visits to Florence he died suddenly of a heart attack and it was fortunate that Fitz was there to love and support his mother. Much later, after we had made the move, Mil was the first to visit us and, as always, it was a joy to see her; but, alas, Fitz and I were so busy that we did not give enough hours to caring for her. Years later I found a sad little entry in her diary of that year. 'F. back to London, have hardly seen him this week and feel a burden in their busy lives.' She was the best, the most generous-hearted person I have ever known. How could we have neglected her? But we evidently did, and I feel a stab of guilt and unhappiness every time I think of it.

The next spring, on one of our bi-annual visits to Florence, she too fell ill, and died from inoperable cancer. We were both with her at the end, but Fitz never returned to Florence – it simply made him too sad – and he left it to me to pack up the big apartment on the Lungarno, which he then sold.

Only Highlanders can understand the Celtic ache for the home-land, the romantic nostalgia for a past which was never particularly comfortable or glorious, but which nevertheless remains the powerful magnet and the glue that binds clansmen together all over the world, however distant and different their lives have now become from the sad reality of the abandoned croft or crumbling castle. After Fitz's abrupt departure from the War Office, Macmillan offered him a hereditary peerage, which he refused, on the grounds that it would be unfair to his new constituents, the voters of Bute and Ayrshire, who had only just adopted him. Instead, he opted for a baronetage, which we all agreed sounded more distinguished – especially Strachur's version, Sir Futzroy, or Sir Futz – and could also be passed on to his descendants.

He had, therefore, to matriculate his coat of arms – and he put pressure on Lord Lyon to be given 'supporters' (he chose two charming, knowing-looking seals, with whiskers) – and find a place name that would link him with his family's history. With advice from Iain Moncreiffe of that Ilk (or just 'Ilk', as the dear man was always called), who was both historian and a herald, he chose Dunconnel, a royal fort on the main island of the Garvellach archipelago, which lies off Jura, of which the Macleans of Ardgour had once been the hereditary captains and keepers. The name had just the right ring to it, and Fitz lost no time in persuading the generous existing owner of Dunconnel to give him a few stones from its ruins. So my husband became Sir Fitzroy Maclean, Baronet, 17th Captain and Keeper of Dunconnel, in the Isles of the Sea, and matriculated his arms as such.

One day we all set forth from Strachur with a Maclean of Ardgour flag and my historian cousin, Kisty Hesketh, to strike it out on the crumbling ruins and declare the fortress ours. It was a two-hour motorboat run from Cullipool to the Garvellachs, beautiful all the way, and the landfall was not easy, even with a quiet sea. We had to choose our moment, stand up, try not to fall over in a rocking boat, then leap on to a rock ledge, scramble up it on to rough grass, and then make our way up a steep hill to the remains of the fort, which is mostly a collection of mossy old stones lying buried in grass and nettles. But we planted the flag on its most visible remains, pulled out a flask of the 'cratur', and drank the new captain's health in fine style.

With Uncle Henry's legacy came his widow, Aunt Ros, who, though she herself was born into a distinguished Irish family, the de Courcy Hamiltons, once married to 'Mac' (as she called him) went in for Macleanery in a big, almost obsessive way and talked of little else.

Our other dependant was Cousin Marge, an equally trying but more interesting relation of Fitz, a true eccentric, an excellent historian, well read, funny and unbelievably thrawn, who made no concessions to the modern world. We had found her living alone in a beautiful Queen Anne house in the main street of Ashbourne in Derbyshire, with no electricity, and only cold tap-water in the basement. When Kate, her family's devoted servant, retired to an almshouse, she wrote to Fitzroy, telling him, 'Miss Marjorie needs looking after.'

She did indeed, but it took some doing. Moving her to one of the empty cottages in The Square at Strachur was comparatively easy, but clearing, packing up and eventually trying to sell a beautiful but ruinous old house with a preservation order on it, and another order claiming it endangered its neighbours, was a nightmare. Cousin Marge, in her small way, was a born collector, and her house was full of good furniture, books, eighteenth-century tea caddies and rare china, as well as mountains of newspapers and piles of miscellaneous rubbish. There was the only collection of eighteenth-century porcelain dog-heads – really dog-whistles – that I have ever come across, and there were good miniatures, a fine seventeenth-century tapestry, and a splendidly macabre small painting of Lady Margaret Maclean of Ardgour as a corpse, which Fitz immediately appropriated. It was like a treasure hunt, but it took days to clear the rubbish and pack Cousin Marge out of her bedroom, where everything was covered in candle-grease, as she would read in bed by candlelight, wearing a runcible hat (the candle flames had burnt holes in it).

She was an expert on Restoration drama, had a wicked sense of humour and a wonderful memory, and could swear like a trooper – but a seventeenth-century trooper. She hated orderliness and, after we had finally got her and her possessions tucked into a clean cottage, which had electricity and all mod cons, she soon managed to recreate chaos by emptying drawers on to the floor and stirring their contents around with an impatient foot.

Fitzroy, of course, was recruited by Chips (Sir Charles) Maclean of Duart, the superb clan chief of all the Maclean chieftains, to revitalise the various Clan Maclean Associations in Glasgow (a Highland city), Edinburgh and London. He was made their president, which was a dubious honour as it involved committee work, solving internal rivalries and attending a great many formal dinners at which we both had to make speeches. But there were compensations. The ceilidhs on Mull were wonderful, the piping and dancing first class, the trips to Nova Scotia, Canada and the USA memorable, and there was the extra bonus of our friendship with two generations of the Dochgarrochs, or 'Macleans of the North'.

It was largely through clan work that we met them. Old Dochgarroch was an Episcopalian minister of great learning, charm and quirkish wit, who acted as a healthy antidote to poor Aunt Ros, and brought some sense into Macleanery. He and his small son Alan came to stay when we were settling into Strachur and when Alan grew up and followed his father into the ministry he became a great friend and adviser, on matters historical, genealogical and religious. Alan's own faith brought maturity to mine. I never heard him say or preach anything that I could not believe myself, and it built a bridge between Fitz and me which resolved many problems. He also lifted much of the Association's burdens from our shoulders and eventually succeeded my husband as its president.

In Gaeldom, as in many early societies, all clans had their official storytellers, or 'Senachies', who would learn the sagas of battles and heroes orally from their predecessors, and pass them on in the same way, for they could not read or write. One evening Ian Argyll asked us to dinner at Inveraray to listen to one of the last of their kind, a Maclean Senachie from Mull.

The old man had travelled from his croft near Aros by steamer and car, and appeared at dinner in a neat tweed suit. Afterwards, with a little cajoling and a couple more drams of Laphroaig, he agreed to recite. 'And how would you like me to be telling it?' he asked. 'In the English? Because there's never a one of you that has the Gaelic.'

We opted for first the Gaelic, even if we couldn't understand it, and then his own literal translation. Off he started, with his noble head thrown back against a ducal cushion, in that high, nasal whine which Hebridean Gaelic sounds like to non-speakers. There were no gestures, just an occasional flash of an eye or a dramatic pause. And then his own translation into 'the English'. It was amazingly vivid, an account by actual eyewitnesses of the past; for instance, in describing the great sea-fight between the Macleans and the Lords of the Isles at the Battle of the Bloody Bay in Mull in 1480, he told us how the sea's little wavelets foamed red with blood, 'and the next morning, which was fair, the women went down to the beach and collected four herring-creel loads of men's fingers and thumbs' – no doubt hacked off as drowning men clung to the gunwales of boats, and brought in with the morning tide.

Seventy years earlier an Argyll duke, fearing that such stories would be lost for ever, had sent out a Gaelic-speaking ghillie to collect them in their original form and then had them translated by a scholarly minister. These tales, and a few that Fitzroy had collected from The Coddy on Barra, formed the basis of one of his nicest books, *The Isles of the Sea and Other Tales of the Western Highlands*, told with just the right amount of gentle irony. The stories were wonderfully illustrated by John Springs, with a frontispiece drawing of the author as chief Senachie.

Fitzroy was still writing – in his library when there were no visitors and the children were away at school, and in an attic bedroom into which he retired when they were at home. But even from there came frequent eruptions and yells of, 'Can't you keep those children quiet? I can't hear myself think!' In summer he retired to the 'bear pit', a sunken garden on the land side of the house with a slate table and an old wooden bench that Aunt Ros had creosoted for him. 'Nothing like it,' she would tell us, 'for preserving old wood.' And one day, she creosoted herself into the rotting floor of an outhouse at the Old Manse, and had to be rescued by Ivy, and Duncan Sinclair, and ropes.

Fitz's passion for exercise continued, and he would swim in the icy waters of Loch Fyne in all weathers, or march not-always-willing visitors up the nearest hill. Destructive gardening was also his forte, and with axe and saw and billhook he carved his way through the overgrown pathways of our woodland walks, dealing death and destruction to every *Rhododendron ponticum* in sight. We followed on behind him, tidying up, building bonfires and carrying picnic baskets.

24

BIG CHILDREN, BIG WORRIES

S
OON AFTER WE HAD MOVED INTO STRACHUR SOMEONE INTRO-
duced Fitz to Grace Wyndham Goldie, who was then director of
the BBC's documentary programmes. A friendship blossomed;
she came to stay, and we somehow persuaded her that if Fitz could
be taught to use a camera, we could bring back film from remote
corners of the world, which would make good viewing. For starters we
suggested Outer Mongolia and, to my amazement, she agreed to try
him out.

We travelled on the Trans-Siberian railway from Moscow to Omsk,
then by plane to Tomsk, where we boarded a small hedge-hopping
machine which took us to Ulan Bator over mile after mile of empty,
rolling steppe, occasionally enlivened by groups of white yurts which,
from the air, looked like crops of mushrooms in a field.

There was no British representative in Mongolia then, so we were
put up in a vast, Chinese-built palace of a hotel, with the Sri Lankan
Ambassador and his wife its only other inhabitants. We visited the
museum, saw the dinosaur eggs, watched the wrestling and the
horse-racing and met the senior lama in a huge octagonal yurt that
served as temple as well as abode, its floor covered by layer upon layer
of the most beautiful carpets I have ever seen.

Fitz hired a car and driver to take us to the site of Kubla Khan's
palace in Karakorum, or Erdeni Tsu (not to be confused with Karakoram,
the western spur of the Hindu Kush, over which the highway has been
built). 'That will be fifty thousand tubreks,' he was told, which rather

dashed our plans; but after some frantic telegraphing, we discovered this translated into £50 – not bad for a three-day trip. The Chinese-built tarmac road petered out five miles beyond Ulan Bator, just about where I saw a dead man lying beside it, and after that the steppe opened before us – a vast grassy plain with only an occasional gentle hill between us and the Urals. There were dozens of criss-crossing cart- and motor-tracks scarring its surface, but no signs, and a driver needed to be a clever pilot to navigate rather than map-read them.

At first sight it looked almost dreary – dull, flat, colourless. But gradually, as we drove further into it, we became a small part of the vastness; and then slowly, imperceptibly, the steppe itself took over; our eyes and ears became attuned to the tempo of such space and it was then that it revealed its beauty.

The sparse, hay-coloured grass turned out to be a thousand different steppe flowers, tiny saxifrage, pasque flowers, iris, crocus, starwort, artemesia, bugloss; the dark patch ahead that could have been the shadow of a cloud transformed itself into sheets of *Iris siberica*, in scale upon scale of lavender and blue. Hundreds of jumping, hopping, little furry animals looked at us sharply for a second with curious bright eyes and then were gone – did they ever really exist, or did we imagine them? And then the horses ... So much has been written about the herds of wild horses in Mongolia, so often do they appear in Chinese and Mongol art, that we knew what to expect; but the reality of coming over a rise in the ground and seeing them – a thousand horses, moving perpetually like the edge of a restless sea, grouping, re-grouping, kicking up their heels, fighting, galloping, conversing – was quite another thing.

The canals that flowed past Kubla's palace were still there, but all that remained of its pleasure domes were a few huge and half-buried truncated columns and a knowing-looking stone tortoise. It was, nevertheless, very impressive. The shadows of its past lay over the place and the air around it seemed to quiver. Coleridge came to mind and even more Shelley, though he wrote of another tyrant:

> *My name is Ozymandias, King of Kings,*
> *Look on my Works, ye Mighty, and despair!*

I wondered whether it was here that Genghis's dead body was brought after that terrible, murderous march from Indo-China, during which every single soul met with on the way was put to the sword to keep the world-shaking event secret and to ensure the succession. (Where it was buried no one knows to this very day.)

We caught the bi-weekly Chinese train from Ulan Bator to Peking, crossing the Gobi Desert, and stopping only once, at the Chinese frontier, which was just a hut in the middle of nowhere. Frontier guards came on board, spotted Fitz's cans of film and told him they were contraband, and could not be allowed to enter China. Fitz told them he was a journalist and could not be parted from them, and that anyway they were only in transit through China and that (crescendo) if necessary, he would leave the train with them and sit on the railway line until they sorted the matter out.

When the other passengers started to grow restive, I really thought we would be booted out of the train and left in the middle of the Gobi, for I knew Fitz would not give up his film. Finally we were saved by a Chinese businessman who spoke a little English, and who ascertained that if the film cans could be wrapped up in something and sealed, they would be allowed through. We then went up and down the train collecting newspaper, candles, matches and string, and finally, after about four hours of argument and frustration, a clumsy parcel was made and sealed, and the train was allowed to proceed. This edited film, with a commentary by Fitz, was shown on the BBC and was enough of a success for Grace to allow him to make another, this time in the USSR, and with a professional film crew, which led eventually to several more under her aegis, and that of her successor, Alasdair Milne.

At home, another General Election was looming. We found that David Lambie, our Labour opponent, had begun calling Fitz 'the Member for Outer Mongolia', accusing him of taking no interest in the constituency or home politics. It was a clever device and did a certain amount of damage, knocking a few hundred votes off our majority; but Fitzroy fought the Lambie family – of whom we grew very fond – three times, and he beat them on each occasion.

The first of my cookbooks came out that year: an amateur effort, inspired by the wonderful Nancy Cameron, our wonderful constituency chairman's wife, photocopied free of charge by another constituent, and sold at the annual Tory fête to raise money for our fighting fund.

It was a collection of good and simple recipes, mostly from Beaufort, Holker, Florence and Strachur, but also from friends whom I had asked to type or write their contribution on their own headed writing paper. Luckily Collins picked it up, and Mark Bonham Carter was my first editor. We had great fun together and produced an elegant book which remained in print for years, until Collins was swallowed up by Harper & Row. It was succeeded by two more sophisticated collections of recipes: *Diplomatic Dishes* and *Second Helpings*, and finally by *Sauces and Surprises*, which I am still quite proud of, as it was certainly the best of its time, and is still used by students – as my Public Lending Right returns show me. Fitz wrote the introduction to the first book: 'When I married I weighed ten stone. Now I weigh fifteen. Need I say more?' – under a smiling photograph of us both.

By the time Sukie was sixteen I had become exasperated by her convent, where she was doing no work and being taught very little; so I made what turned out to be a disastrous decision. I removed her from the good nuns' care and sent her for a year to a finishing school in Oxford, run by a clever and talented Swiss teacher, Miss Hübler, known to her pupils as 'Cuffy'. Under her direction Sukie blossomed, both intellectually and physically: one could almost see the petals unfurling. The transfer would have been a resounding success had she not there met and fallen in love with Richard, the son of Dick de la Mare, chairman of Faber & Faber, the publishers, and grandson of Walter, the poet.

To Sukie's newly awakened sensibilities, Richard was everything an unsophisticated maiden dreamt of. Having been a member of Pop at Eton, and having done National Service in the army, he was in his second year at Trinity. He was good-looking in a rather heavy, moody way and he was a poet – a budding littérateur and a budding rebel against the established order. He was certainly a child of the time, and love blinded my poor darling daughter, who, after meeting him, could not think of, or look at, anyone else.

After Cuffy's and a few months in Vienna, where she learnt German and had piano lessons, Sukie began to read and to educate herself. She was very musical, sang like a nightingale, had an eye for beauty and *l'oreil juste* for languages. She was also deliciously pretty in a delicate, demure and rather old-fashioned way that melted men's hearts and produced a queue of admirers, any of whom she could have married. Her brothers adored her, and she was very quick-witted and funny, expecially with them. In 1959 she danced her way through the Oban balls, the Skye Gathering and the Inverness Meetings, but she had eyes for only one partner, Richard.

At the Edinburgh Festival that year our cousins the McEwen brothers sang Scottish folk songs and came to stay. It was a time of music and laughter and fun, with all beds full and young people sleeping on sofas and mattresses on the floor. The greatest night of all was the one on which Marnie MacLachlan and Fitz gave a joint party for their children in the ruins of old Castle Lachlan, on its promontory above Loch Fyne.

No one slept that night, for we danced till dawn in its only four-walled room, high up in a crumbling, roofless tower. Fitz and Marnie snuggled into one of the window embrasures with a bottle of whisky between them; Ronnie McCallum, the Duke of Argyll's piper, skirled out the reel tunes from another ledge. Stars twinkled overhead, and every now and then we would climb down the perilous path to the castle green, which looks out towards Marnie's islands, and on which an enormous bonfire blazed, lighting up the night. On the green we ate sausages and cutlets, while Cockerill tried to keep some sort of order in the trestle-tabled bar. Guests had parked their cars on the sandy beach below, but they forgot about tides, and in the cold light of dawn many vehicles were seen floating gently out to sea.

The next summer, in London, Sukie's grandmother and I gave a small dance for her, but all these efforts to distract were in vain: Sukie and Richard were determined to get married and though we knew they were both far too young, in the end we stopped arguing and gave in.

A week before their wedding I went down to Much Hadham to meet Richard's family, and I got on very well with 'Catta', his mother, who was Jack Donaldson's sister. Catta was a large and comfortable and very honest woman, who worried me by saying quietly one evening, 'I suppose little Sukie will know how to deal with Richard? He isn't very grown-up yet, but I'm sure *she* will be sensible enough for both of them.'

Richard and Sukie were married in the Church of the Assumption in Warwick Street, like Alan and I were, and the reception was held in the

Wren Banqueting Hall of the Chelsea Pensioners' buildings, courtesy of Fitz's boss, Antony Head. They honeymooned in Michael Astor's shooting lodge on Jura, and returned to our flat in Maida Vale, the lease of which I had given Sukie, with all its furniture, as a wedding present. (Fitz and I had decided to move to a flat nearer the House of Commons, as the Canal Zone was inconvenient for late-night sittings.)

Their daughter Laura was born in July, by which time Richard had come down from Oxford. They settled into the flat, and within weeks I had my first disagreement with my son-in-law, who told me to mind my own business and showed me the door, while Sukie wept behind it.

She fed the baby, cooked and cleaned, and tried to be sensible, while Richard gave up poetry and founded a film company, called Mithras, with three young and very bright partners: Maurice Hatton, John Irvin and Tim Pitt-Millar. They made several documentaries which were screened, and one which was a great success, and won an award. Family life, sadly, was less of a success – Richard could never settle into regular domesticity. In the six years of their stormy and difficult marriage there were several partings and reconciliations, and whenever one of these occurred, along came another child. At one point, homeless and broke, Sukie brought all four children up to Strachur, where they went to the village school and Norman Parkinson took an immortal photograph of them paddling with their mother in Loch Fyne, dressed in shiny black oilskins, with islands looming in the misty background. Another time she fled to Florence, where a friend had lent her a house, and she saw a lot of Harold Acton and the Florentine 'establishment'.

Over those years Sukie grew a tiny carapace of toughness: she needed to, to survive, and some of her youthful radiance may have dimmed; but, thank God, its flame never quite went out.

A surge of courage came to her one day (much later) when, in desperation, she went to Much Hadham to ask her father-in-law, Dick de la Mare, to contribute something towards his only grandchildren's school fees. Catta had died, but he was still living in a fine house and enjoying his beautiful garden. He had just sold some of his china for a great deal of money but had kept his favourite collection of Japanese porcelain.

Sukie put her case, but her plea was received in silence. As she turned to leave, almost in tears, she picked up a precious vase, one of a pair, and looked at it.

'I believe you care more about this than you do about your own grandchildren,' she said, 'about your own flesh and blood.'

With which, she dropped the vase on the stone hearth, where it shattered. Then with a toss of her pretty head she walked out. The story went the rounds and, I must say, Fitz and I were proud of her when we heard it.

Jeremy was at Sandhurst, and Charlie was at New College, occasionally working, sharing a house with Johnny Grimond and William Waldegrave, and deeply entangled with the landlady, whose little girl (not his) was dying of leukaemia. Jamie had just started at the Edinburgh College of Art, and was not enjoying it, and Fitz and I were grappling with our teenage rebels and all the complexities of life in Scotland and London.

One day we were at home in Strachur, but on the eve of departing for Montreal, where we had been booked to preside at the Canadian Black Watch regimental ball, when the telephone rang in Fitz's library. Charlie went to answer it, and came back with a white, shocked face. 'It's Sukie,' he said, as if announcing a death.

I told Fitz to take a visiting MP and his wife downstairs and start lunch. Sukie's voice was small and childlike. 'Ma,' she said, 'I've left Richard.'

'Oh! Darling! Where are you?'

'In your flat. I had a key.'

'And the children?'

'They're all right. Richard's gone to Much Hadham.'

'Do you want me to come down?'

'Yes *please*.'

That afternoon I finished packing for Montreal, handed over the suitcases to Fitz, told him I would join him as soon as I could, and caught the sleeper to London. Sukie opened the flat door.

'Cup of tea ready?'

'Oh, yes, Ma! *Two* cups.' We both burst into laughter, which soon turned to tears.

We talked long into the night. It seemed to me that things had got progressively worse in the little house near Wantage; and Sukie had realised she could no longer cope. Then one of their friends had held a birthday party, and a man had come up and asked Sukie to dance.

When they sat out afterwards, he said earnestly, 'I don't usually make advances to married women, but I hear you're very unhappy, and I'd love to see you again. I'll be looking at the Turners in the Tate on Sunday.'

With that, he got up and left her. His name was Derek Marlowe. Sukie went to London on the Sunday. She went to view the Turners at the Tate, and she fell into Derek's waiting arms. To begin with they were only protective, for she would never have had the courage to leave and finally break with Richard if Derek had not ridden up, a knight on a white horse if ever there was one.

Sukie had become a canary that had stopped singing. Her self-confidence had gone, and in the next few days there were moments when mine nearly left me, too. Richard came up to London and there was a dramatic confrontation in our flat. But then Richard left and Sukie's best friend, Candida Lycett-Green, and my cousin Junie, took over. In three days they had first whisked the children away to Junie's studio, then found them somewhere to live, then taken advice from a divorce lawyer whom Junie knew (possibly the worst who ever donned a wig), and I was able to reschedule my flight to Montreal.

When I finally boarded the TWA plane in a daze, an air hostess brought me an envelope with something solid inside it.

'Your husband gave me this a few days back,' she said. 'He told me it was most important, and we've been passing it on ever since. Is it jewellery?'

Inside were two sugar-lumps, such as TWA then served with their coffee. They were in the shape of two little hearts, and I liked them better than any jewels.

A long time later, when the children's school fees were really beginning to bite, Sukie had a major stroke of luck. One evening she found herself sitting next to Bluey Mavroleon, the Greek shipping magnate, at a dinner party; and quite by chance, the night before she had watched a television programme about British Petroleum and its super-tankers, during which the point had been made that the company was finding it hard to recruit crew.

'It must be because their quarters are so bad,' Sukie told the startled magnate after his first mouthful of soup. 'If you're having the same problem, you should do something about it.'

'Like what?'

'Like getting me to make them more comfortable. It just needs a woman's touch. A happy crew makes a happy ship!'

This head-on approach paid dividends. Bluey gave her a job, and she became responsible for the furnishing and decor of the crew's cabins and recreation areas in his new tankers. She attended the launches of all the ships she had worked on, and when I was asked to launch a new Jugoslav container vessel for the Dubrovnik company Atlanska Plovidba, she gave me good advice. My ship was to be called *Jadran*, which means 'Adriatic', and would be the biggest bulk-container of the Jugoslav merchant marine. Swan Hunter, of Tyneside, had built her, and I drove down to Newcastle the night before the great event, to be rehearsed by Pero Arsete, chairman of the line.

When British ships are launched, the mantra recited over them combines hopes for the happiness of the men who sail in them with good wishes for the vessels; but things are different in Dalmatia. The words I learnt by heart that evening were to be addressed solely to my ship. A rough translation would read, 'Go down, O beautiful ship, to the ocean, and may all your voyages be happy ones.'

Next day, when I stood on an immensely high wooden platform way above the upturned faces of the crowd below, and proclaimed those words, and set in motion the age-old convention by which the youngest lad in the yard knocks away the last chock that holds her, and watched her slow and stately progress down the ramp, and heard the little slap as she hit the water, I felt an almost sacramental union with my ship.

'Put your hand on her as you speak, and feel her leave it,' I had been told. I did so, and after we had parted, my eyes filled with tears.

Meanwhile Jeremy had left Sandhurst, where he had made many lifelong friends, and had joined his uncle Mervyn Phipps's regiment, the Queen's Own Hussars. He was an athletic and enterprising young officer, a natural leader and popular with his men. Before long he was skiing and playing rugby for his regiment, and sailing whenever he got the chance. But it was on a posting to Sharjah in the Trucial Oman States that he first came into contact with the SAS, who were acting as the enemy on an exercise and impressed him with their skill, cunning, fitness and professionalism. When the exercise was over, our chief's nephew, Lochie Maclean of Duart, then a captain in the SAS, approached him and said, 'What the hell are you doing in the QOH? You should come and join us.' Naturally Fitz and David Stirling (the founder of the SAS) were delighted when he passed the tough selection course and joined the regiment.

Thereafter I heard very little of his exploits, for the SAS operates a strict need-to-know policy; but one day I was surprised to receive a letter from Sir David Hunt, British Ambassador in Brazil, thanking me for having a son who had saved his life! Then in 1973, having returned temporarily to the Queen's Own Hussars, Jeremy was chosen as watch-keeper on the army yacht *British Soldier* for the last leg of the Whitbread round-the-world race. To greet the crew on their return to Portsmouth harbour, we hired a motorboat, borrowed Ian Argyll's piper Ronnie McCallum and bought a hundred balloons. Sukie and her children, Susan Crawford (Jeremy's girlfriend) and I then cheered ourselves hoarse as our two boats met in the Solent.

It was the first time I had met Sue, who had obviously made up her mind that she, among the many competitors, was going to carry Jeremy off – and I thanked God for it. Within a short time they were engaged and married, and what made it especially pleasing for me was that Sue's father had played rugger with Alan at Dartmouth, and then, rather more grandly, for Scotland. Sue was already an acclaimed artist, and now she managed to juggle her painting and her army-wife life with remarkable aplomb, establishing studios, successively, and *faute de mieux*, in a caravan, the quartermaster's stores and even a dentist's waiting room! From the moment she took on Jeremy, she made happy and pretty homes for him, following the flag to seventeen different locations, and bringing up two of the nicest children, Jake and Jemma, both of whom, in different ways, have inherited her talents.

As a rule she was silent about Jeremy's role in the SAS; but when he took part in the siege of the Iranian Embassy in 1980, she confided her anxieties to Fitz, to the extent of ringing him up and saying that Jeremy was 'quite busy' – a coded message that meant action was imminent. Six days into the drama, with the hostages and the heroic bobby-on-the-beat, PC Trevor Lock, still imprisoned in Prince's Gate, Fitz was entertaining two old friends to dinner in our Lowndes Square flat, and surprised them a good deal by insisting on keeping the television turned on, *pianissimo*, throughout the meal. Suddenly he leapt to his feet with a shout of 'That's it! They've started!' – and there on the screen was the amazing live spectacle of black-clad figures abseiling down the back of the Embassy building, accompanied by loud explosions and gunfire.

By the time members of our family had stopped praying, the SAS team had been visited and thanked by Mrs Thatcher, the Prime Minister, and Willie Whitelaw, the Home Secretary. When Jeremy finally reached home, he found the house locked up (Sue wasn't expecting him so soon), so he had to scale a drainpipe and squeeze in through a bathroom window to get to bed, where he slept for twelve hours. Next day Sukie and I drove past the still-smouldering Embassy in a taxi, and chatted to the driver. Simultaneously, we could not resist boasting, 'My brother/son did that!' The cabbie stopped, got out, opened the back door, proceeded to hug us both and refused to accept a fare.

The climax of Jeremy's SAS career came in 1989, when he was made Director, Special Forces. He, and the regiment, were fully stretched during the Gulf War of 1991, when the SAS inserted patrols far behind enemy lines in Iraq in order to destroy Scud missiles, and carried out raids very similar to those mounted by David Stirling and Fitz in the Western Desert some forty years earlier.

After this hectic period, Jeremy was promoted to major-general and again posted to Oman, where he spent three and a half very happy but rather quiet years as the Sultan's senior military adviser. Then, after thirty-seven years in the army, he retired and started work as a civilian.

25

AMERICA

I MYSELF HAD DISCOVERED AMERICA NOT LONG BEFORE CHARLIE'S return from it. Eddy and Mary Warburg had a flat in New York, and after dinner Eddy took me for a spin round Manhattan. There happened to be a warehouse fire at the bottom of Wall Street, which lit up the towering blocks on either side of the straight and now-empty road, turning it into a gorge between impossibly high cliffs and mysterious caverns, with clouds of yellow, sulphurous smoke bursting from the ruby-red of the fire far below us.

'It's beautiful!' I said. 'No one ever told me how *beautiful* New York is!' Then I added, 'But it does look a bit like Hell.' Little did I then realise how horribly prophetic those words would prove.

That weekend we stayed with the Warburgs in Westport, Connecticut, in a lovely old farmhouse with a beautiful wood-and-brick barn they had converted into a living room, with soft, fat sofas and an open log fire, masses of books and magazines, and all the latest records. It opened on to a sunken garden and a swimming pool, with woods of hazel and poplar and pine as a backdrop. It was everything one could possibly dream of for a quiet, peaceful weekend after the frantic whirl and champagne air of New York, where it was still Camelot-time and Fitz had many friends at court.

Next door to the Warburgs lived the actor Paul Newman and Joanne Woodward, and their children would often come over and swim. Next morning a delicious-looking five-year-old turned up as we were having breakfast by the pool. She had pigtails, with a bow on top of her head, and was carrying a walking-stick and a bundle tied up in a spotted red handkerchief.

'I've left home!' she announced firmly. 'They're horrid to me over there, so naturally I decided to come and live with you. That's OK, isn't it?' She looked appealingly at Eddy, obviously the biggest sucker around, who handed her a sausage with a sympathetic smile.

'She's always doing it,' sighed Mary, and went off to make a telephone call. I don't blame little Miss Newman for wanting to live with Eddy, for he was the funniest, most endearing man I have ever met, with a quick, sharp mind, a liberal, though sometimes over-sensitive, conscience and a very tender heart. A torrent of bad but highly enjoyable puns and jokes hid his more serious and aesthetic side. With enormous integrity he would tirelessly and ungainfully fight for the causes he believed in. He liked, but never quite understood, the English.

Fitz had first met FitzGerald and Margaret Bemiss when he was lecturing for the English Speaking Union in Richmond, Virginia. He was billeted on them and, after getting his knees under Margaret and Gerry's dining-room table (followed closely by mine), he kept them there for life, and they became our closest American friends.

On my first visit to them we drove over to Margaret's family home, Oakland, which lies in placid Virginian farmland carved out of the native forests of oak and pine. The hub of the house was a long drawing room of bare pine boards, covered with good Persian rugs, with a fireplace at either end: there were hound-dawgs or old ladies in every battered armchair, a fine library of calf-bound books and some wonderful eighteenth-century furniture. Upstairs, in the bedrooms, white walls, muslin curtains and tufted or quilted bedspreads on black cast-iron or mahogany four-poster beds. The walls were freshly whitewashed, the floors smelt of beeswax and lavender; altogether the house had terrific atmosphere, and when her old father mixed us mint juleps with brandy instead of bourbon, he told Fitz, 'No Southern gentleman ever puts whisky in his julep.' It was the finishing touch.

The Bemiss children, young Madge and Sam, became great friends of our own children, and through them we also met the Bush family when we stayed in Maine, at Kennebunkport, where they all had holiday homes. (The last time we met the Presidential family was at Sam Bemiss's wedding, in 1995, which we flew over to attend. Fitz, by then, was very lame and the tall crummoch he used to support himself caused considerable controversy among the guests. Prescott Bush, who had visited us in Scotland, sent him over a pair of specially constructed bespoke crutches, which my thrawn husband never used but which our family now considers 'historical'.)

After the children grew up, I visited the USSR and America nearly every year, sometimes lecturing on my own, and sometimes with Fitz. The tours brought much-needed income and were always an adventure. One year Fitz and I did breakfast-time TV shows together – and they were of such appalling banality that I never feared a movie camera again. Once, lying on a comfortable bed in the Knickerbocker Club, Fitz also took part in a radio phone-in with three former Presidents who he thought were dead: Monsieur Paul Reynaud, Aleksandr Kerensky, the Bolshevik leader (a very old man by that time), and Kurt von Schuschnigg, whom Hitler had ousted from Austria. It was to be a serious discussion as to why Russia and the West were confronting one another in the Cold War – but after the first five minutes things went wrong when an angry American voice interrupted M. Reynaud in full flow.

'Will you please get off the line and stop jabbering politics!' the woman screeched. 'I'm talking to the White Swan laundry that's gone and lost my husband's longjohns . . .'

'Madam, will you please put your phone down at once!' the frantic producer yelled back. 'This is a serious programme for a university.'

'Don't you dare talk to me like that! It's his only pair, and . . .'

The broadcast broke up in confusion, and Fitz lay back on his V-spring mattress and laughed himself silly.

On my travels I would lecture about Scotland or Russia. The tours took me all over the States, including New Orleans, Texas, Nevada and San Francisco, where Fitz joined me and we stayed with our old friends Signe and Merritt Ruddock. These tours were very hard work, but worth every shrimp cocktail for the joy, when they were all over, of collapsing into Chip and Avis Bohlen's pretty house in Georgetown, swimming with Brooke Astor at Holly Hill and Bar Harbour, or jogging with the Bemisses and Clara, their Golden Retriever, round Richmond's Rothesay Circle.

One never knew what to expect on a tour, and had to be prepared for anything, although lecture circles in the South and on the coast were mostly composed of decorous and conservative blue-rinsed audiences. But once in New Orleans' Old Town, where I was staying to address a typical audience, I happened to notice a poster advertising a Rolling Stones concert in the Golden Bowl, their Olympic sports ground. As I knew Jamie Bowes-Lyon, who was one of the organisers for the tour, I managed to winkle a ticket out of him for Mick Jagger's private row of seats, way up in the gods of the amphitheatre. It was the first time I had ever been to a pop concert, and I was staggered by the sheer size and noise of the audience, for the entire baseball ground as well as the tiered galleries around it was crammed, body to body, with dancing, swaying, shrieking fans.

The band performed on a floodlit platform with raised gangways which jutted out over the audience's heads, and down which Mick Jagger danced and pranced into what seemed the very hearts of his worshippers. The programme was a brilliant piece of theatrical showmanship, perfectly timed and executed, but it seemed to me that the pop star's art lay more in this and his intensely physical yet graceful, almost balletic, dancing than in his singing or his songs. There were ambulances at the exits, security guards in the aisles, and the whole scene was luridly lit. The smell of marijuana, part burnt sugar, part mouldy hay, drifted gently up to us from below in a mesmerising blue haze shot by shafts of brightness from the spotlights.

The next day was entirely memorable. The whole of the Jagger mob, of which I somehow seemed to have become part, was invited by the British Consul to a luncheon party at his grand residence in the Old Town's Garden Suburb, to hear some *real* New Orleans jazz, played by the last of the 'old-timers'.

The Consul was a Creole, whose family had lived in style for many generations, and I don't think I have ever been more elegantly entertained. The cold buffet was set out in a series of post-bellum drawing rooms which led from one to another, a new course in each of them. Silver platters were spread on starched white damask tablecloths, behind which stood black footmen to serve one. The first room served iced she-crab soup from eighteenth-century silver soup tureens that I could have died for, and the last room opened on to a ballroom with French windows that led to the garden below.

There, in a corner, sitting or propped against an old upright piano (their own), was the band. There were only four of them: at the piano a fat old girl with grizzled hair twisted into a bandanna; a tall, lugubrious Negro who played double bass; a man on tenor sax; and another man on a clarinet. The tinkling piano was already jumping, the clarinet sobbing, and oh, the rhythm and the style of those ghosts from the past! No one, but *no* one in that room could keep their feet still, and no one who heard that music will ever forget it.

When I first visited Washington we stayed with Chip and Avis Bohlen on Dumbarton Avenue, Georgetown. Their house was enchanting: it had a mounting-block outside, and had kept its eighteenth-century character inside. They had bought it cheaply when Georgetown was still a crumbling village on the edge of a black ghetto, for it was all that a newly married diplomat could afford; but soon many other bright young couples joined them. The Alsop brothers lived opposite, as did Susan Mary Patton and, eventually, the Harrimans, who, financially and politically, were in a rather different league.

Not that fashion influenced the Bohlens, the least trendy of all our Washington friends. Chip lived for his job, and was probably the best Ambassador that the State Department ever sent to Moscow – and Avis lived for Chip. 'It's no good making eyes at Chip,' she told me one day. 'He's wedded to his job.'

'I didn't know I *was* making eyes,' I replied rather crossly.

'Forget it, darling. Every girl does it. Because he looks like Gary Cooper, they all think he's going to flirt – and the poor dumb chick never even notices.'

I sighed, because it was true.

I had not seen Pam Harriman since she arrived as a debutante in London from a blameless background in the heart of Dorset. As a girl she was plump, freckled and what was considered 'a bit fast', and she had shocked fellow pony-clubbers by wearing silk knickers instead of the regulation navy-blue cotton ones. Although we talked endlessly about our figures (meaning bosoms and legs), we didn't notice anything particularly good about hers, and I was surprised when my brother Hugh told me, 'Pamela Digby has the most exciting body in Britain.' I took another look, and decided that the plumpness was rapidly changing into something else.

Pam lost no time in exploiting her assets, and by the time we met again in Georgetown, she had married Randolph Churchill, entered the highest military and political circles, produced a son (little Winston), got divorced and become the mistress, successively, of Averell Harriman and, more seriously, of Giovanni Agnelli, the Fiat millionaire, and Elie de Rothschild, the French banker. She then decided that safety was the better part of valour, and married Mr Haywood, the theatrical impresario, who died soon afterwards, leaving, as well as several million dollars, the way open for Averell to step in and make her, somewhat belatedly, his bride. He, by then, was the leading light of the Democratic Party, having been Roosevelt's personal representative in London, US Ambassador in Moscow and Governor of New York.

With her usual unswerving loyalty to the man in her life, Pam embarked enthusiastically on an American political career, and soon became the leading hostess in Washington, with a house in Georgetown whose doors were open to film stars, politicians and statesmen, but also, *always*, to her old friends. Like all her careers, she made a resounding success of this one, and I honestly believe that, if her British birth had not precluded it, she might one day have stood for President – for of all the women speakers I have heard, only Mary Soames surpassed her in grace and eloquence on a platform. As it was, she made the last ten years of Averell's life active, fruitful and happy.

It was through the Young Presidents of America – an elite group of tycoons who had reached the summits of their corporations before the age of thirty-five – that we met John MacPherson, a Scot who had emigrated to the States with his parents and made a fortune importing orchids to the West Coast. He had also acquired a beautiful, long-legged wife called Carol, and they lived in a large, elegant house on the 'Bing Crosby' estate above San Francisco.

Fitz had been engaged to lecture to the YPA, who were holding their annual convention in Hawaii, and we stayed with the MacPhersons for a happy weekend before flying out to the islands, and arrived in Honolulu in a torrential thunderstorm. A smaller plane took us on to the island of Maui, our destination, and there, next morning, we swam in the lovely, peaceful waters of a horseshoe-shaped bay, which had a bathing raft anchored a little way out, and beyond it a coral reef. Outside the reef, waves were still thundering after the night's storm, and sending up huge plumes of spray.

After lunch I swam out again to the raft, and shouted to Fitz, 'Don't go any farther – there may be a current.' Of course he did, and the next time I looked, he was a long way out, swimming hard to avoid being sucked towards the reef, on what by then was an ebb tide.

I yelled for the MacPhersons, and miraculously they appeared. John immediately saw the danger, and wanted to go in after Fitz, but Carol and I begged him to run back to the hotel and raise the alarm. Away he went, calling out that he would get a helicopter, if there was one. Carol and I ran to the right-hand promontory of the bay and yelled at Fitz to change course and make for us – but he could not, and every minute showed his dark head and weakening arms being drawn closer to the savage rocks and twenty-foot waves ahead.

A small crowd of onlookers gathered with us on the point, but people seemed to be amused rather than alarmed by the drama. 'Gee, he's a goner,' said one new arrival. 'Now, if I had a harpoon gun . . .' said another. I began praying aloud, first 'Hail Marys', and then in desperation to Rose, using her nickname and asking her to intercede for me once more. 'Go on, Rossie-boy,' I cried. '*Do* something! Tell God we want a miracle. Nothing else will do.'

I could no longer see Fitz's head. It had disappeared into the maelstrom of the reef. I felt weak and sick, and closed my eyes.

Suddenly a cheer went up. 'He's OK!' somebody shouted. 'That big wave – look, it's taking him right across the bay. He's riding it. Jesus Christ, it's a goddam miracle!'

And it was. Carol, whose eyes had also been tightly shut, opened them again. We both raced for the winding path that led down to our beach. But a diminutive Filipino waiter, who owned a home-made surfboard, had already sized up the situation and was paddling hard towards the barely conscious swimmer. By the time we arrived at the water's edge, he was pulling him into the shallows.

Fitz was pale-green and coughing horribly, but, thank God, just as irritable as always when anyone made a fuss. 'Get me out of this,' he growled at us as the well-wishers descended, offering towels, brandy, tissues and, soon, an ambulance. Carol and I hauled him to his feet and back to our bedroom, where he collapsed on to our bed. Five minutes later he sicked up half a gallon of sea water, felt much better, and went fast asleep. Later, at a celebration dinner with the MacPhersons, he said, 'We must find that waiter' – and we did.

Brooke Astor is my step-grandmother's daughter-in-law – a curious relationship which doesn't pay much attention to generations. I remember the first dinner party that Fitz and I went to in her apartment on Fifth Avenue, because there I first witnessed a dreadful New York habit of putting lions through the hoop. As people were tackling their cheese soufflés, she tinkled a little crystal bell. The company stopped eating and looked up expectantly – all except Fitz, who, having just arrived from Moscow, was jet-lagged and hungry. Brooke made a graceful little speech of welcome, then turned to him and said, 'Now I'll ask Fitzroy, who I'm sure you know is an expert on all things Russian, to tell us what he thinks our next move should be . . .' Fitz put down his fork, looked up, and said, 'Er . . .'

For him, this was totally unexpected, agony. He suffered, and I suffered with him. Walter Kronkite was on my right, and opposite was Brooke's son Tony. I looked at them despairingly and, thank goodness, they quickly caught on, and in seconds had turned the pause into a general conversation.

Other memories of Brooke's entertainments are far happier. Once, after a visit to Kennebunkport and the Bemisses, we were bidden to stay with her at North East Harbour. She said she would send an aeroplane to pick us up at Rockland airport. When we arrived at the airfield, there were several hedge-hoppers on the tarmac, and a swaggering, fat man with sideburns came forward.

'Mrs Astor's guests?'

'That's us,' answered Fitz. 'Which plane?'

'The gold one.' Our pilot rolled the word with relish, as if it were a hundred-dollar bill. One of the machines was indeed metallic yellow, shining in the sun. What else?

The only other guest was John Sargeant. One evening after dinner, when we had swum, talked and walked all day, he persuaded Brooke to read aloud to us, and we settled down in front of a fire piled high with driftwood to listen. She chose a story that perfectly fitted the place and our mood. It was about a great white whale, who had fallen in love with the deep, booming voice of a foghorn on some lonely East Coast island, which warned sailors away from the dangerous reefs around it. Every year the poor dope returned from Arctic waters to woo what it believed to be its unseen soul-mate, and every year there was no response except that long, intermittent boom that came eerily across the waves. I forget how the story ended – perhaps the whale dashed itself to pieces in one last, desperate attempt to connect with the object of its desire? But the scene is still fresh in my mind: the sound of Brooke's voice, the flickering firelight, the little silence that followed the end of the story, and her closing the book and smiling before we all looked at each other and laughed, half-ashamed at being so moved by the story of a lovelorn whale.

A few days later Brooke took us to an exclusive country club on an island to which members alone had access. Fitz was about to be lionised by the ladies over lunch, and I decided to skip the cocktails in favour of a skinny-dip in the Atlantic.

'But be careful,' they warned me. 'The sea can be very dangerous.'

'Oh, I'm used to that. I'm a hardy Scot.'

I walked along the coast path until I came to a sandy cove where reefs enclosed pools of quiet water, ice-cold and inviting in the hot midday sun. I stripped off my clothes and lay in one of them, basking with eyes closed, in blissful peace. Suddenly a great green wave broke over me with such force that it dragged me bodily over the reef towards the open sea. I just had time to scramble to my knees and feet before the next thunderer came crashing in, but my poor bottom had been scraped raw by the barnacled rocks, and I was bleeding like a kosher calf.

I had nothing – not even a tissue or a hanky, for I had left my handbag behind – with which to blot my wounds. Within minutes, I knew, I would be expected to sit on some elegant sun-lounge sofa, which I would bleed all over, and have to make polite conversation. Horrors! What if people thought I was having a *mademoiselle voiture* – the Lister phrase for a miscarriage?

A ship's hooter sounded – the summons to lunch. I took the belt off my dress, looped it through knickers and bra to make a kind of pad, then ran all the way back and dashed, with a hasty excuse, into the powder room, where – thank my good guardian angel – I found a wonderfully helpful old black attendant who strapped me up with cotton wool and sticky tape. 'Yo shore gwanna lie on yo stomack tonight, lady,' she told me – and I shore did, *and* for several nights after; but my *amour propre*, if not my bottom, was saved.

Hugh, the Bomb and Antonia

By the time we started to visit the States regularly, my friend Kick Kennedy was dead; but Fitz and my brother Hugh kept in touch with several members of the family, including Jackie (by then Mrs Onassis). When her teenage daughter Caroline came to London for a Sotheby's art course, she arranged for the girl to lodge temporarily with Hugh and his daughters Rebecca and Flora, who were roughly the same age, at his house in Campden Hill Square, where he was still living, in spite of Antonia's having left him for Harold Pinter, the playwright. The arrangement worked well, especially as Hugh could drop Caroline off on his way to work every day in the City.

Then one morning, as they were about to start, a telephone call caught him in his study at the front of the house, so he asked Caroline to go back to her room for a few moments, while he dealt with it. Seconds later his neighbour, a distinguished cancer surgeon, out walking his dog, came past Hugh's car, which was parked outside. The dog sniffed at a wheel, and an IRA bomb exploded, blowing the car, the poor surgeon and the dog to pieces, and blasting Hugh backwards to the other side of his room. But for that call, he and yet another member of the Kennedy family would almost certainly have been killed.

Sukie heard the news on her car radio and rang me up. When I arrived, and shoved my way through the cordon of police cars, ambulances and bomb-disposal experts, he was still looking badly shaken. 'For God's sake, get Caroline out of here,' he told me, 'and hide her from the press until I've made a statement in the House.' He had sent his daughters round to Thomas Pakenham (Antonia's brother), who lived in Ladbroke Grove, and asked Sissy Ormsby-Gore to collect Caroline from there – so I hurried her out by a back door in the garden. Although she knew someone had been killed, I don't think she had seen the horrible mess at the front of the house, and she was perfectly composed.

At Thomas's house we found Rebecca and Flora, but the paparazzi soon picked up our trail and arrived *en masse*. I went out and told them they had missed Caroline, who had gone to the country –

whereupon they nearly all left. Then Sissy arrived, and we plotted a covert exit.

'Stuff all that glorious hair into Rebecca's beret,' I told Caroline. 'Then all three of you come down the steps *together*, and make sure you leap into the car without looking left or right.'

I had not counted on the Kennedy genes. At the top of the steps Caroline halted, pulled off the beret, shook out her hair and made a pretty little speech to the two remaining news-hounds. Her words were reported all over America that evening, as were the surgeon's death and Hugh's statement in the House.

When Thomas arrived, we walked together round his garden while he tried to explain to me why Antonia had left Hugh. Thomas is to my mind by far the nicest and most sensitive of the Pakenham family. He loved Hugh, and was genuinely distressed by the havoc his sister's departure was causing.

'She won't listen to us,' he said. 'She's *fallen in love*, and she believes this great passion excuses everything. Antonia has always seen herself as the central figure, the *heroine* of Great Romances and Romantic Adventure.'

'Why can't she just have an affair with the man, without breaking things up?' I demanded.

Thomas thought that Harold Pinter wouldn't settle for that.

When Antonia left Hugh, in a blaze of publicity, he was mortally wounded, both in his pride and in his heart. To begin with he tried to cover his hurt by diversionary flings with other ladies, but these were a temporary balm, and soon failed.

A great many people loved Hugh, and he was not short of friends at home or abroad, in and out of the House of Commons, in his constituency and a dozen other worlds. Tizzy Gatacre, who owned the house he moved to, was kindness itself, and his children, who loved him dearly, did their best; but the contrast between living at the centre of a warm, noisy, mostly happy and always amusing family, known for its hospitality and fun, and his last years, when he lived alone in a rented flat, was awesome.

Not long before he died I visited him there and found him hobbling round in bedroom slippers. 'I can't get my bloody shoes on,' he told me, 'and I don't know what to do.' When I saw him in hospital a few days later, the sister in charge was indignant. 'How *could* his family have let him get into such a state? The poor man must have been in agony.'

How, indeed, could we have? And how, specifically, could I? The question will always haunt me. After an operation and a brief, hopeless fight for survival, Hugh died of cancer of the lungs in 1984. I don't think he minded dying, and the only person he wished to see during those last days was Antonia. She and the children were with him at the end.

The following year, the Stafford and Stone constituency published a memoir of his life. It was, naturally, hagiographic; but until I read it, I had no idea how much good he had done, how strongly he had fought for the people and the causes he believed in, and how often he had won. Flora's collection of tributes from his friends made me also realise how very special they too had found him.

Most people will remember Hugh for his ebullient charm, his delightful nonsense, his kindness and true goodness, his gaiety and his gift for affection; but for me he will always be the fiery, though cautious, leader of our childhood adventures. 'You go first,' he would say, 'and if it's safe, I'll come too.' I considered that then, and still do, the greatest possible compliment and honour. RIP.

26

THE OTHER
SUPER-POWER

ITZROY'S CONTACTS WITH RUSSIA REACHED BACK TO THE 1930S, when he was *en poste* at the British Embassy in Moscow. He shared a *dacha*, outside the city, with three other bright young diplomats who would later all become notable ambassadors, and on his own initiative he had travelled clandestinely all over the Soviet Union. He spoke Russian and his knowledge of the country was wide and deep; he was therefore a natural choice for the first executive chairman of the Great Britain–USSR Association, formed in 1959 by Harold Macmillan to encourage genuine contact with the Soviets, arrange exchange visits and organise hospitality in the United Kingdom. The job took us both to Russia nearly every year, and put us in contact with numerous Russian visitors to Britain.

Fitz always took a long view about the Cold War, first because he was certain Russia, unless invaded, would never start a hot one, and secondly, because he believed that Communist dogma could not defy human nature indefinitely. 'Russian human nature is more human than most,' he would tell me. 'In the end ideology always fails and biology always wins.'

He never believed in confrontation: in public he was rarely judgemental, and he saw the Association primarily as a bridge-builder, not as a monitor of Soviet behaviour or ethics. He himself was motivated by his deep affection and respect for the Russian people and their extraordinary qualities – something which even Soviet party hacks and high government officials understood very well, and which often paid dividends in tricky negotiations. During our travels we made numerous friends and met *apparatchiks* of all sorts, but Fitz always made it perfectly clear whose side he was on, and what he thought of the horrors that Communism had engendered. After all, he had attended the show trials in the 1930s and had heard Bukharin's last speech before he was condemned to death, so he *knew*, and although he did not talk about such events with the new leaders, they knew that he knew.

He appointed General Tom Churchill, a thoroughly nice and capable ex-soldier, as his first director, and one of the liveliest early events the Association and Tom organised was a reception in London for Yuri Gagarin, who in April 1961 stole a march on the Americans in the space-race by becoming the first man to complete an orbit of the earth. The young cosmonaut's visit to Britain in July that year was obviously a propaganda exercise, designed to underline the magnitude of the Soviet achievement, but it caused frenzied excitement, and when Fitz and I stood at the top of a staircase at the Ritz, to receive the invited guests, we were astonished and nearly bowled over by the crowds of unbidden worshippers who turned up, elbowed, shoved and struggled to shake hands or just *touch* the star of the proceedings, like ravers at a pop festival. One of the roughest was Moura Budberg, Bruce Lockhart's mountainous mistress (commonly known as 'the Bed-Bug'), who swept forward, flattening anyone in her way and shrieking, 'I am *Rrrrussian*! I must be the *first* to welcome our hero!'

At Strachur we entertained many Soviet visitors, including the gentle old poet Marshak, who was so enthralled by Uncle Mumble's collection of best-loved Russian poetry – for I unwisely showed him the *Gepäck* – that he refused to stop reading it and so missed the lunch part of the lunch party we were giving in his honour! Then there was the flamboyant poet-cum-pop-star Yevgeny Yevtushenko, who looked like a cross between Rambo and an American college boy and could fill a football stadium with readings of his own poetry, especially the then daringly subversive *Babi Yar*. On the first night of his visit we invited Anastasia Noble, a neighbour and celebrated breeder of deer-hounds, to dinner. She arrived with a young but very large hound in the back of her car, and when she let it out for a run, beautiful animal and beautiful poet met on the lawn.

It was love at first sight – and in fact the two looked rather alike. Over dinner Yevtu learnt more about the history and habits of Irish-wolf-crossed-Scottish-deer-hounds than 'Tasia did about Russian foreign policy. The two talked nothing but dogs, and when she divulged that she had two more youngsters of the same year in her kennels, and wanted to sell one of them, the Russian was ecstatic. By then his imagination had exploded, and I think he could see himself entering a Soviet stadium in a poet's burka (the long white Caucasian sheep's wool cloak), led by a deer-hound wearing a diamond-studded collar . . . But when he said he wanted to buy both of Anastasia's young dogs, she cut him short sharply, saying it was quite unsuitable for large animals to live in Moscow or any other big city.

Among our friends in Moscow were Ed and Nina Stevens, whose daughter at one stage had desperately wanted to marry Yevtushenko. Ed was the wire chief for Reuters, and for many years he and his temperamental Russian wife had been a Moscow institution. During one visit Nina asked us to a luncheon party, at which the star guests were to be the brilliant young cellist Mstislav Rostropovich and his wife, the acclaimed soprano Galina Vishnevskaya. Nina promised she was going to make us *akroshka*, a delicious cold summer soup, and real *blinis*, with caviar that the Rostropoviches would bring with them.

The soup and the *blinis* were superb – caviar appeared anyway – but the celebrated couple did not show, and it became clear that something had gone wrong with their plans. Then, after an agitated telephone call, Galina swept in alone, looking every inch a diva, in a long cloak, carrying an outsize handbag and two silver fox-furs.

There followed an urgent, *sotto voce* conversation between her and Nina, of which I could pick up scraps, for they were talking in English: 'Have you got them? . . . The bank manager refused . . . Just the emeralds.' After only a few minutes Galina stood up and said, 'I'm so sorry. You must forgive me, but I have a plane to catch.'

Only when she had gone did the penny drop. She and her husband were doing their bunk to the West, and she had got the emeralds.

Another veteran newspaperman was Leonard Shapiro, head of the United Press bureau in Moscow. At a dinner we gave for him on the eve of his retirement, I asked him what had been the most exciting moment of all his years in Russia.

'Oh,' he said quickly, 'Stalin's death, without any doubt.'

'Tell us.'

'Well – it was in 1953, and Moscow was seething with rumours that Stalin had died. Every correspondent in the world had descended on us, waiting for the official announcement, and knowing that when it came, communications with the outside world would instantly be cut.

'I had a leg-man in Vienna, and I got him to ring me up every half-hour with some innocuous question – just to keep my line open, until the announcement finally came.

'The last time he rang, he said, "How's tricks?"

'"*Stalin's dead*," I said.

'Two words, and my line was cut. But I'd brought off the coup of my life, and was the first to tell the world that a terrible era had ended.'

On another memorable visit to Moscow, we accompanied a cultural delegation headed by Jennie Lee, our Minister for the Arts (and wife of Aneurin Bevan). There was a gala performance at the Bolshoi Theatre, and we watched the Old Vic touring company's production of *Hamlet*, with Laurence Olivier as the Prince. After it I felt shamed, not because it wasn't a superb production, but because the Russians who were entertaining us knew so much more about the play, its significances and its interpretation than I or any of the other British delegates.

Next day I sat quietly in a corner while Jennie and Madame Furtsova, her Russian counterpart, confronted each other over a green baize table to work out the terms of a new cultural agreement between our two countries. They were roughly the same age: both powerful and beautiful women, highly articulate and determined. Madame F. was a cat-faced, sophisticated blonde with *sandréed* hair, a creamy complexion and almond-shaped green eyes which could suddenly harden and narrow. Jennie Lee was the exact opposite: dark-haired and dark-eyed, high-coloured and buxom, but very good-looking in a friendly, Welsh-country-girl way. They argued long and fiercely, while the Ambassador, Fitz and various male officials looked on in wonder. I am glad to say that when the agreement was finally signed, Jennie had won every point.

That same trip took us once more to Georgia, for it was to the Caucasus, and especially to Georgia, that we nearly always returned. It was not only the warmth and fun-loving characteristics of its larger-than-life people, or their fabulous hospitality, that struck a chord in my Highland heart, it was also the beauty and wildness of their country and the interest of discovering and photographing the ancient monuments and half-ruined churches of its past. It is said that in Armenia alone there are some two thousand ruined buildings of architectural interest.

From the legendary Mount Kazbek on the Georgian Military Highway to the monastery caves of Vardzia on the Persian frontier we travelled, sometimes filming, but mostly taking snaps for Fitz's books and enjoying ourselves. The quest was always an adventure, for the ancient monuments were rarely marked in our Intourist march-route papers and we were frequently turned back at road blocks by the police.

Often, we found evidence in some of the empty churches that Christianity, or perhaps more primitive faith, still flourished in spite of the Kremlin's policies, but mostly they were simply inhabited by the ghosts of the past.

Djvari was one of the churches Fitz liked photographing the most. It stands on the pinnacle of a hill above Msket and is the perfect example of the Georgian genius for choosing architectural sites. It has enormous historical significance, being the place from which St Nina, a Cappadocian Christian, first looked down on the city and decided to convert it and its king from their wicked, pagan ways in AD 303 (which she did in a remarkably short time, thus establishing Christian rule several years before Constantine managed to do so in Rome).

Peggy Trevelyan told me a strange story about Djvari. She and her husband Humphrey, who was then our Ambassador in Moscow, and two other diplomatic couples, were sightseeing in Georgia and walked up the long, grassy hill that leads to the little seventh-century church, but the doors were locked and a notice said 'Fetch the key from the guardian in Msket'. It was hot, and the women went on strike, opening their picnic basket and sending their husbands down the hill in search of the key. The long lancet windows of the chapel are above head height and you cannot see through them, and the door is of solid oak.

Not long after the men had left them, they heard Russian church music coming from inside the chapel, and when the lightest of the wives was heaved on to Peggy's sturdy shoulders she could see candles flickering within, but when the men returned with the key and opened the door, there was no one there . . .

I shall always remember Easter in Etchmiadzin. It was Good Friday and the Patriarch of the Armenian Church, who was then a Romanian, asked us if we would come to the Easter service next day in his great cathedral, and whether we would go to Communion. Fitz said he would, but I demurred. 'I am a Roman Catholic, your Holiness, and I don't know if my Church is in communion with yours.' He answered: 'I don't know either,' then, looking wily, 'but perhaps the *Celtic* church was? Or shall we just leave it to the good Lord? I am sure He would be pleased if you went to Communion with your husband.' And so the next day we both knelt together in that great church, with its wonderful music and ancient liturgy and we felt very moved and happy, and at peace. I believe it is what is called grace.

Religion in Armenia is perhaps more international as well as ecumenical than in the United Kingdom. It is certainly the cement that holds their scattered nation together. When we were filming in Etchmiadzin and Fitz was interviewing the Patriarch, their conversation was twice interrupted by his secretary bearing a telephone: 'New York on the line, your Holiness. They say it can't wait!' And when I noticed the magnificent electric organ in the cathedral I was told it had been sent from England as a special present from Mr Gulbenkian.

This time we would stay in Tbilisi, where we knew we would be royally entertained by our two groups of friends: the Sukhishvilis, creators and directors of the Georgian State Dance Company, whose hospitality was world famous, and Robert Sturia, director and founder of the Rustaveli Theatre Company. Once, having been delayed by rehearsals, he arrived late at his own dinner party, slid into the empty chair beside me, took my hand and started his apology by saying, 'Veronica, my soul . . .' You can't ask for more than that! Later we tried to return some of their hospitality by inviting Ramaz Charkviadze, the principal and star actor of the Rustaveli Theatre Company, for a weekend at Strachur. Thelma Holt brought him north and the first night's dinner was a success. Ramaz took a bottle of Fitz's special McPhunn malt whisky to bed with him; but in the morning he seemed none the worse for it, and as it was a sunny day, though cold, I proposed a spring picnic up the glen.

We drove to our favourite beauty spot, where a burn tumbles down a thirty-foot fall into a deep, peaty, Guinness-dark pool. I told Thelma that we sometimes swam there in summer, and turned away to unpack the food. Suddenly there was a splash, a shriek, and two more splashes.

I looked round, and there was Thelma swimming, stark naked, round the pool and there were Ramaz and Fitz, who had dropped their trousers and dived in after her. We built a huge bonfire and dried them off with handkerchiefs and dishcloths, before tucking in to a lot more whisky, hot grilled chops and sausages.

Yet perhaps the most enjoyable of all our Georgian visitations was the one on which, after a performance in Glasgow, we invited the whole State Dance Company – two bus-loads of them – to lunch at The Creggans Inn. It so happened that Fitz had been negotiating for weeks with the SAS Territorials for a detachment to come and blow up the rotting and obsolete wooden pier which jutted out into Loch Fyne opposite our pub. For the soldiers, it would be an excellent demolition exercise, and it would make an ideal objective for a raiding party of SAS, acting as guerrillas.

We were well into a splendid lunch, and Fitz was on his feet as *tamada*, or toast-master, making the twelfth welcoming speech of the day, when BOOM! CRASH!! BZOOM!!! The world outside the windows exploded in a sheet of flame and falling timber. I must say, the Georgians took it very calmly. Some young women shrieked and rushed into the arms of their protectors, and others sat there stunned and open-mouthed; but the men simply loved it, and thought the whole thing had been contrived in their honour.

We all trooped out to congratulate the soldiers, who by then were speeding back across Loch Fyne towards Inveraray in a camouflaged rubber boat. Fitz was delighted. It was the sort of double coup he loved to bring off. 'Well,' I said, 'I do think you might have warned us,' but it was a lone voice, and by then the Georgians had pushed back the tables and begun dancing.

We retained The Creggans Inn until the end of Fitz's life, and in the early days, under the cheerful management of Camilla Hunter, it even made a little money. Activities were non-stop: ceilidhs, weddings, wakes, film-shows, dances to raise money for good causes, meetings of a youth club which I ran. But success had the fatal effect of encouraging Fitz to double the place's size by building on a wing with twelve new bedrooms and bathrooms and enlarging the bar and dining room.

This really meant becoming professional, which we were not, and the development needed a lot of capital, of which we had none. We also happened to choose exactly the wrong moment for expansion: a flood of new regulations had just hit the hotel industry, and we found to our horror that our wonderful new bedroom passage was three feet too long for the new safety rules, so that it required a second staircase. Our new dining-room ceiling was ten inches too low, and our doors were too narrow for wheelchairs to pass through. We had also seriously underestimated the growing sophistication of our customers.

In spite of its problems, and the low margin of profit, Fitz loved seeing his name above the front door of The Creggans – 'Sir Fitzroy Maclean, Publican and Licensee' – and the inn made a happy bridge between ourselves and the village. Almost all the staff were local, and so many pretty young girls began their working life there that it became a kind of village finishing school – especially while it was being run by Laura Huggins, or 'Laura-the-Hug', as we called her in private, a rare jewel of a manager, who came to us in the 1970s and was intensely loyal, obsessively hard-working, with standards even higher than our own. She and her colleague Betty Finney treated guests (they were never 'customers') as if they were cherished patients entering a convalescent home because they were in need of loving care.

With two such safe pairs of hands installed, we were able almost to forget the worries and dramas of running a hotel, and enjoy simply having it there to entertain in and be entertained. The third person who made this form of escapism possible was Jimmy McNab, the maverick member of a very respectable Perthshire family, who had drifted from being an under-keeper to Lord Bute to a safari park in Spain, where he had been mauled by a lion but had learnt to cook. When Fitz took him on – against his late employer's advice – we found he could turn his hand to anything: he doubled as kitchen help, chauffeur, gamekeeper, breeder of prize-winning goats and bantams, tour guide and personal bodyguard.

Physically, he was enormous: larger than life in every sense, and with a commanding presence. Guests frequently mistook him for (a) the manager and (b) the owner of the hotel: once they had seen him, they never forgot him, and sporting visitors from Germany and Texas would beg him to return with them, all expenses paid, so that they could show him off to their friends at home. Though he was the greatest wangler I have ever known, he became a true friend, who could always be counted on to keep the kitchen out of the consommé when the latest temperamental chef had left in a huff.

If it had not been for my continual extravagance in upgrading furniture and interior decoration, The Creggans would certainly have made money at that juncture; but after Laura-the-Hug retired, it went slowly downhill, becoming a constant worry and a drain on my fading energy, so that I longed to sell it and quit. Many a time I resigned from my position as (unpaid) superintending manageress, but Fitz always managed to talk me round into a new burst of enthusiasm by dreaming up some brilliant initiative which he was certain would succeed. Only after he died did Charlie and I face the inevitable (and the overdraft) and sell it.

27

KORČULA

I N SCOTLAND THERE WAS NOW THE CONSTITUENCY, FITZ'S FIRST
priority; then the hotel; then the farm and the estate; and then
the Clan Maclean Association. For me there was also the garden,
time-consuming, expensive and a joy; the estate cottages, which we
repaired, upgraded and let as holiday accommodation; the dependants,
who were getting older and needed more care; the American wives and
families based on the Holy Loch; the club I had started for our village
teenagers; and last, but not by any means least, *the family*.

In London there was the House of Commons, the Great Britain–
USSR Association, the British–Jugoslav Society (of both of which Fitz
was president), inspections for the British Tourist Authority, and worry
about my mother and sister, who were both ill. There were lecture
tours, articles and books to be written about the latest journey to pay
for the next one, and for Fitz there was filming and photography.

It would seem to most reasonable people that we had enough on
our plates; but then, in the late-1960s, we suddenly decided to buy
a house in Dalmatia. Depressed by a particularly wet and miserable
spring in Scotland, we both felt the need to dry out somewhere in
warmth and sunshine. After several false starts searching up and down
the Adriatic coast, we agreed to take a second look at the island of
Korčula, which I had visited as a girl, collecting wild flowers, and Fitz
had discovered in a more dramatic way during the war.

After a long and exhausting walk from Tito's headquarters at Dvar
over wild mountains and through German lines, he had found a Partisan fishing boat waiting for him on the coast at Boska Voda, which

took him across the Kanal. He fell asleep on its thwarts, and he never forgot waking in the early morning to see the rosy roofs and sturdy towers of the old city, lit by the rising sun.

Finding a house there was not easy; but Fitz's war-time friend Rafo Ivancevič told us that a large, slightly ruinous property, the Palazzo Boschi, might be available in the heart of the Old Town, just behind the cathedral. It belonged to a woman who had emigrated to America and married a Californian, and her lawyer told us that she would indeed be willing to sell – though it would be tactful if the Church and the civilian museum, which both had an interest in the building (though no money to buy it), were allowed first pick of its contents. We agreed to this, sent off a telegram asking for an inclusive price, were given an ancient key, and hurried off to view.

The palazzo was a tall building, mainly on three floors, but rambling downhill in line with the underlying rock of the promontory, and including numerous cellars, outhouses, store rooms and finally three more houses, roofless and ruined, with gloomy gardens in which hens were kept. On the ground floor of the main house, in a large kitchen-living room, we found an old lady sitting up in bed, sobbing into a red cotton handkerchief.

'Why are you crying?' asked Fitz.

'Because I and my family do not own these rooms. We've been allowed to stay here by the kindness of the Commune, and now you'll buy the house and turn us out.'

Fitz, who had already made up his mind to buy, and had been told the story of the old lady's family, and what good people they were, quickly said, 'No, no. We'll do nothing of the sort. I hope you'll stay as long as you wish to, and look after the house for us when we're away. We'll try and make it more comfortable for all of us, and the ground floor will *always* be yours.'

The handkerchief dropped, and Mama Katarina was herself again: one of the most cheerful, intelligent and enterprising characters it has ever been my privilege to know. Once installed, we always had our Sunday lunch with her and her family, and on anyone's birthday there would invariably be a party, with a cake and dancing round the old lady's bed.

When we bought the palazzo, it had no electricity, hot water or modern lavatories, and the roof leaked; so it took us some time to put the place in order and to extend our terrace so that it roofed over one of the ruins and gave us two more bedrooms. As for furniture – little could be bought in Dalmatia, so we decided to import some of the beautiful early Italian pieces, including an eighteenth-century painted Venetian cupboard, which Fil and Mil had owned in Florence. For the past few years they had been at Strachur, but they had never looked quite right against the smooth walls of an eighteenth-century Adam house, and after being moved from room to room they had ended up in the attics.

Now was their chance to shine again, and in ideally congenial surroundings. Once more the poor things were packed up, but this time they were loaded on to a Jugoslav cargo ship, which delivered them to the quayside in Korčula some two months later. They arrived safely, but there was no bill, and when Fitz made enquiries, we heard from the director of the shipping company that they refused to charge us, as they considered it an honour that Fitz had chosen Dalmatia as his second home!

We would never have managed to settle in so quickly without the help of Ambroz Kapor, one of our many kind new neighbours, with whom we became close friends. Ambroz was intellectual, eccentric and very proud of his ancestry. 'Not Venetian, not Austro-Hungarian, not even noble,' he would tell us, 'but from good peasant stock of a far earlier *Croat* civilisation.' His own house was beautiful, with many medieval features, including a kitchen on the top floor (so as not to burn down the whole building when the fat caught fire), a sweet-smelling and peaceful garden and a private chapel.

Ambroz had been a tobacco merchant for part of his life, but his basic passion was the history of his home town and his island, and he wrote many learned articles and books about them. He was delighted to find a fellow-historian as his neighbour, and to know that we would cherish the old house, and he did everything he could to help us, not least by solving the problem of the Venetian cupboard, which was too wide to turn a corner on our staircase. He saw that the only way to get it into the *salone* was to haul it up on ropes, over the parapet of the terrace, from the street below. He and another strong fellow pulled, while Fitz and Janez, Mama Katarina's son-in-law, stood in the street shouting directions and trying to stop it swinging. I was so sure of disaster that I hid with a cushion over my head until I heard their shouts of triumph – and lo and behold, there was the cupboard, in place against the long wall of the drawing room, looking as if it had grown there.

Ambroz and Maria had a lovely, gentle and grave teenage daughter, Nila, whom Fitz photographed every year, until eventually she graduated with honours from Zagreb University and left home. When we asked her parents what subjects she had studied for her degree, they said, rather primly, 'Languages and psychology' – and then told us that the subject she had chosen for her doctorate thesis would be 'the sexual deviations of characters in English novels of the nineteenth century'! Korčula is full of surprises.

The remarkable man who dominated local life, indeed all Korčula, in those days was Dr Juro Arnerič, who lived with his tiny, half-Italian wife Anka in the only habitable part of the Palazzo Arneri, an immense Gothic ruin in the centre of the Old Town. His family had been chieftains, hereditary mayors and leading citizens for generations. Tall and lumbering, like one of the Babar elephants, Juro was as big-hearted as he was large, but had an alert, intelligent mind and a kind of wily elephant's eye that missed nothing. He, too, was passionate about his island kingdom: his whole life was dedicated to preserving its beauty and ameliorating the life of its people. When we arrived, he took us on a tour, stopping at attractive houses here and there to introduce us to the owners, and coolly picking half the flowers in their gardens to present me with bouquets. 'They don't mind!' he answered when I protested. 'They're only too glad that you've come to live here.'

The other pivotal family in our lives was that of Rafo Ivancevič. A former Partisan and ex-merchant-navy officer, he had greeted Fitzroy with a clenched fist when he first landed on Korčula, only hours after the Italians had left. Fortunately, he had also vouched for the newcomer's authenticity. 'My God!' he had said to his comrades. 'This man is British, and if he isn't, you can shoot him first, and then you can shoot me.' Rafo always recounted this story in English, but with a strong Indian accent, for he had ended his career as Jugoslav Consul-General in Bombay, and had learnt most of his English there.

Tourism and civil war had not yet adulterated Korčula's population, which was smaller, more cohesive and much more fun-loving than, alas, it is today. People worked hard all week, but Sunday was a holiday, and one evening as we passed friends in the *corso* – that age-old, ritual evening walk along the sea-front, when all the town turns out to see and be seen, and courtships are started and plans made – they called out, 'Come for a picnic tomorrow – a *Partisan* picnic! We'll fish together in the morning, and cook what we catch for lunch. We'll swim and eat and drink and perhaps even sing, and we'll remember old times together.'

'We'd love to,' we shouted back, before the soft, warm darkness swallowed them up.

Our hosts took the precaution of sending out a boatload of striplings to fish seriously through the night, so that our party of veterans – *stari Partisani* – did not need to start until after sunrise. At seven o'clock next morning a trim little fishing boat chugged up to the landing stage: she was island-built, with the traditional rounded prow of all Korčulan boats, and had a tiny Union Jack fluttering from the stern. She also had fifty litres of wine on board, two straw hats (one with a blue ribbon for a lady passenger), quantities of fishing gear, a box of bait, oilskins in case of rain, and a great round slab of new bread, still warm from the oven and smelling of heaven. The thoughtful provider of all this luxury was Captain Niksa Lozica, our host and comrade, chief organiser and Grand Admiral of the picnic fleet; he was the biggest and best of a family of eight brothers, who all looked alike and between them weighed – it was said – twelve hundred kilos. (When their mother made an omelette, she used a hundred eggs.) Six of them were Partisans during the war, and one was killed. The five survivors came on our picnic, bringing a boat apiece.

All morning we pulled up night-lines, nets and marvellously intricate rhomboid structures that looked like modern sculptures and turned out to be lobster pots. All morning we were hailed by other boats doing the same thing. Shouts of 'Any luck?', 'Nothing yet', 'Leave it to the young ones' and 'Nonsense – we've got six fine red mullet' floated across the water as the sun rose higher.

We reached Badia, the island of our choice, at midday, and Dr Juro set off with us to climb its little mountain and admire the view from its summit. Then, while the boat parties assembled and compared catches, and tables were being laid up under pine trees, we wandered away on our own and swam off warm rocks in a quiet little bay, in water so clear that we could see the bottom five fathoms down.

The catch had been enormous and varied: *barbuni, arbuni,* St Peter's fish, skate, ligne, mullet and so on. Altogether twelve different kinds were roasted on the charcoal grills and eaten with home-grown lemons, olive oil, herbs and home-baked bread. The fragrant pine trees overhead and the blue sky above them completely removed the feeling of claustrophobia that banquets usually give me. And when the fish had been reduced to a pile of bones, and most of us were heaving sighs of repletion, a large, fat, surrealist roasted sucking pig appeared from nowhere, with an orange in its mouth and a bay-leaf crown, just to fill in any empty corners.

The wine had travelled well. There were toasts and speeches which began, 'Comrade Brigadier, I have the honour to have been . . .' and ended in personal reminiscence. And there was singing. A local saying goes, 'When three Dalmatians get together, it's a choir', for it is as natural for Dalmatians to sing as it is for birds to fly, and, like the Welsh, they always sing in chords. There were three score and more of us on that picnic, and I have never heard singing like it: sad island folk songs, rousing Partisan marching songs, bitter Communist political songs and, of course, in our honour, 'Tipperary', belted out with more enthusiasm than accuracy. For our part, we explained about England and Scotland, told them about our own partisan songs of the '45, and taught them 'Come o'er the stream, Charlie, and dine with Maclean'. They loved that, and sang it in parts with real Jacobite ardour. What feasting, what singing, what company!

Of course, the moment we were installed in our palazzo, friends and family began pouring in. Between the two houses we had six spare beds, and they were seldom empty. Our ex-Free French and now diplomat friend, Count Victor de Lesseps, and Diana, his English wife, were the first to arrive, and they liked our island so much that they came each summer for several years, renting a house and widening the scope of our activities, for 'Totor' bought a very fast motorboat, which he never learnt to control or pilot, Diana or Pero Tedeschi (the Mayor) always just managing to save it from shipwreck and disaster. But it took us to all the outlying islands and was a great asset.

Another summer John Bute came out in his rather slow steam yacht, suitably called the *Dodo*, bringing his wife and children, who fitted in well with ours. He came for fun, but also as the official representative of the Island of Bute, with which Fitz had 'twinned' Korčula, and he was soon invited by the Mayor of Orebič, on the mainland, to visit his town and maritime museum.

'What should I wear?' he asked Fitz.

'Oh – just your bum-bags and sandals,' my husband answered carelessly. 'It's only an afternoon visit, and it will be very hot.'

None of us had met the Mayor, or knew the story of his life. We learnt later that in the general euphoria and confusion at the end of the war, the Partisans had unfortunately shot his father as a collaborator and spy, which he certainly wasn't. Realising their mistake, and wishing to make amends, they had installed his son, a rather eccentric character, as Mayor, and his dreadful old widowed mother as Mayoress.

When John's yacht went alongside the Orebič pier at four p.m., he found, to his horror, the whole town turned out to greet him – the Mayor in a frock coat and decorations, a band, a platoon of Young Communists, another of Old Comrades; and as he stepped ashore, the enthusiastic local youths let off dozens of fire-crackers round his feet, making him hop about and causing him further indignity. We teased him about it for weeks – and with his usual magnanimity, he forgave us.

Once Fitz asked Jack and Dru Heinz to fly out with him to Dubrovnik, and arranged a transfer to bring them on to Korčula by car and boat. Sukie had rented a house near us, at Lumbarda, with the writer Piers Paul Read, his wife Emily and their children, and they persuaded me to give a party in the palazzo for their age group the night before the Heinzes' arrival, with babies too young to dance bedded down on mattresses in the guest room.

The trouble was that it turned out *not* to be the night before. Just as the party was reaching its zenith, I heard a familiar voice call from the street below our window: 'Here we are, darling, just in time for dinner! Jack and Dru are exhausted, so we've left their luggage at the bottom of the steps.'

Panic and consternation! Three small children were sleeping on mattresses in the Heinzes' bedroom. There *was* no dinner. Sukie and I held a rapid consultation.

'There's just enough supper left,' I said. 'We'll get them to join the party . . . I'll say it's being given in their honour.'

'Feed them lots of *rakia* while I get rid of the little ones,' said Sukie, '*and start the singing again.*'

'Won't you have to bring the mattresses through the drawing room?'

'No, no – we'll throw them out of the windows.'

'And the children too?'

'Don't ask . . .'

Jack and Dru reacted splendidly. Their bedroom was immaculate by the time they reached it, and they believed (I hope) that the party was indeed in their honour. Fitz smelt a rat, but he was too beguiled by all the pretty girls to worry.

Another visitor who came to Korčula, soon after we did, was Nancy Brown Negley, the daughter of an American philanthropist. She fell in love with the Old Town, and was so concerned for the future of its near-derelict Arneri Palace that when we met at dinner, a few months later, she turned to Fitz and uttered the memorable words: 'Care for a million dollars?' Fitz replied that he very much did – and so began the 'Save the Palazzo' project.

28

TITO'S
LAST YEARS

TITO'S EIGHTIETH BIRTHDAY CELEBRATION IN BELGRADE WAS probably the greatest party that any country has ever given its head of state. By 1972 the Jugoslavs called him *Stari*, 'Old Man', and in a way it was a doom-laden name, for no one wanted to upset the 'old man' with demands for political reform. 'He'll soon be dead,' said the yes-men and cronies who now surrounded him, 'so why not wait?' But on that day, seeing and feeling the great waves of affection and pride that filled the huge stadium in which the birthday bonanza was held, one partly understood their reasoning.

This was no Nuremberg rally, but an intimate and happy crowd, with a mind of its own, bent on celebration: forty years of Tito, forty years of peace, forty years if not of actively loving, at least of putting up with one's neighbour.

The hundreds of small children, who between events rushed down the gangways, scampering pell-mell across the arena to the edge of Tito and Jovanka's box and hurling in their bouquets; the stadium announcement board, which, when it had nothing better to do, just lit up with a thousand Xs; all this, and the cheering, laughing, yelling crowd, must have brought comfort, however illusory, to the old man who had endlessly preached 'brotherhood and unity' to the disparate parts of his nation.

Not long afterwards, when Tito explained to Fitzroy his long-term ideas for a presidency which would rotate between the Republics, he asked sombrely, 'Do you think it will work?' Fitz answered, 'I hope so, Tito' – to which the President replied, 'So do I . . .'

For many friends of the old Jugoslavia, Tito's last years now seem disastrous, the seedbed of quarrels to come, and the nursery of Tudjman's and Milosevič's dictatorships. Why could he not have allowed a multi-party system, as Djilas and other liberals had long suggested? Why were all those national emotions, ambitions and jealousies bottled up, so that one day they would explode? Why, as the economy was known to be in deep trouble, did no one do anything about it? Why was the army commanded by Serbs – and the National Bank in Belgrade?

To outside analysts the answers to such questions may have seemed complex; but to Fitz, who knew the Marshal well, and understood the ideology that had nurtured, then inspired and finally saved him, the reason for his inertia was simple. For Tito, a child of two revolutions, to dissolve the Communist Party was not only unthinkable; it was *impossible*.

Fitz saw a lot of Tito during his last years. He accompanied first Mrs Thatcher and then Prince Charles on official visits to Jugoslavia, and sat in on their interviews with the President. In 1976 he travelled with Tito to Dalhousie University in Nova Scotia, where they were both given honorary degrees, and then flew back to London with him and Jovanka in their private plane, for lunch at Buckingham Palace.

'What were your university degrees in?' I heard Prince Philip ask them.

'In law, sir,' said Fitz, answering for both.

'I don't believe it!' exclaimed the Prince. 'You're two of the most *illegal* people I've ever met!'

The next year, when Tito got rid of Jovanka because (he said) she got on his nerves, it did not entirely surprise us, for she was curiously untactful with him, and a great nagger – even though she worshipped him. Much later, Vladko Velebit told me the truth about what had happened.

In the last years of his life Tito had become forgetful and indiscreet. Underneath the government's supposed unity, factions were building up, and the Serbian army, which had been infiltrated by the UDBA (the secret police), were worried. Tito had told his wife things he probably should not have – and who knew how she might use them?

The plotting generals, becoming alarmed, decided to get rid of her, and Tito was not in good enough shape to resist. Jovanka was offered a decent retirement house in the centre of Belgrade; but, desperately hurt, angry and miserable, she refused it, and was settled instead in a much less nice apartment in an army 'hospitality' block on the outskirts of the city, where she lives quietly today, and is occasionally visited by Vera Velebit, but few others.

In 1980 Tito died at the age of eighty-eight, and world leaders, kings, princes, presidents and dignitaries flew into Belgrade for his funeral. The occasion was somewhat marred by an unseemly game of bluff and counter-bluff between the USA and the USSR, which the USA lost. Thinking that the Russians did not intend to send their top brass, the Americans decided to send Jimmy Carter's old mother to represent the only other super-power in the world; but at the last moment President Brezhnev changed his mind and turned up himself in full dress uniform with medals.

The American arrangements had been taken out of the hands of the State Department and passed to the President's office, which mishandled them sensationally. Mrs Carter was dressed in white, with dark glasses obscuring her pudgy face; but her friends and supporters were mostly in rainbow colours, including scarlet (all except the Harrimans, who were impeccably correct in funeral black). Still worse, they had cameras slung round their necks as they joined the solemn procession up a flight of steps to salute the bier on which Tito was lying in state. The scene was televised all over Jugoslavia and round the world, and next day Laurence Eagleburger, the first-class American Ambassador in Belgrade, told Fitz that the Carter performance had cost him 'three years of hard work in five deadly minutes'.

Fitz and I flew out from London with the British delegation, which was led by Prince Philip and Mrs Thatcher (then Prime Minister). We were all suitably dressed and comported ourselves correctly – though for us it was, inevitably, an emotional day, which Fitz described brilliantly in a BBC broadcast. I myself wrote an eyewitness account of an event which, amazingly, during Tudjman's presidency became unmentionable in Croatia, Dalmatia and a large part of Croatian Bosnia, even though most of the young people who took part in it are still alive.

There were no foreigners in the procession that followed Tito to his grave, only Jugoslavs. It was a long way, but the old generals who carried his medals at the head of the column looked as if they would go on until they dropped, as did the National Heroes, a touchingly heterogeneous collection of elderly men and women, distinguished only by the pink-and-white ribbon of the nation's equivalent of the Victoria Cross. ('Two million dead, and only two hundred heroes,' one said to me thoughtfully that evening.)

These were the veteran *stari Partisani* of Tito's own generation; but the forest of scarlet banners that came next, representing the war-time Partisan brigades, were borne not by the old, but by young people, signifying – and no one could miss the message – that if necessary the next generation would carry on the fight for their nation's independence with equal courage and determination. It needed a bit of both, for the next contingent of young people carried, singly or in pairs, huge wreaths, some weighing a hundredweight, from every Party centre and organisation in the country. They did so without faltering – and it was all of a three-mile course. The guard of honour round the gun-carriage was also drawn from the 'nation of the future', and included, besides soldiers, men in working clothes and factory overalls.

Immediately behind the coffin came the family. Jovanka was supported by Tito's two sons. She was only just under control, and it was hard to look at such naked grief. Her escorts were treating her with obvious affection, and in the bearded young man on her right I recognised Miso, the long-legged boy we had nicknamed 'Spider' all those years ago when we met by the lake at Brdo.

Last came the dignitaries and representatives of every town and Republic in the Federation.

It was not a very long procession. The kings and princes, the heads of state and delegations from a hundred and twenty-five countries waited for it at the place of interment – the garden behind Tito's own villa, to which they had been driven by a different route.

As the coffin was lowered into the simple tomb, a volley of shots rang out. Guns boomed in the distance, church bells tolled, and all the factories in Belgrade let off their sirens. The crowd knew it was the end and began to disperse. The grave is marked by a plain marble block which reads: 'Josip Broz Tito, 1892–1980' – that is all.

What my account did not mention was a hilarious moment, when Fitz opened a door of the building in which the waiting VIPs were assembled, and found it solely occupied by two unlikely and disparate mourners: Prince Philip in naval uniform and gongs, and Yasser Arafat in khaki, with a dark-blue chin. The Prince looked at Fitz despairingly and asked, 'Any chance of a drink? There seems no one around . . .'

Fitz rummaged, and returned with a bottle of whisky, which was gratefully received, no questions asked.

29

LETTING GO AND
TAKING ON

I N 1974, WHEN IT LOOKED AS THOUGH EDWARD HEATH'S NEW
government would be re-elected, Fitz decided – under considerable pressure from me and the family – to retire from politics.
He had been a Member of Parliament for nearly thirty years, and had
won five elections for the Tory Party; only a few friends or people he
admired remained on his side of the House, and its atmosphere had
changed. Not only did he disagree with Heath's foreign policies, he also
disliked what he saw as the pettiness of the man, and he was dead tired
of the weekly slog down to London and back. He had had enough.

His life, in any case, was full to bursting with interests and activities
outside politics, which still involved him in the affairs of the world.
There were books to be written, films to be made, journeys to be
planned and executed. He was president of four international societies;
chairman of the military committee in the European Parliament; we had
two domiciles, and had recently acquired a third, in Dalmatia. We had
a hotel and a farm to run in Scotland, children and grandchildren to be
loved and cared for. When he decided to quit Westminster, I heaved a
deep sigh of relief, and so did all the family.

Fitz's withdrawal from the House of Commons did not mean
that party leaders no longer consulted him: on the contrary, they
continued to depend on his experience and contacts in the Soviet
Union and the Balkans, which were greater than those of most
sitting MPs. Foreign Secretaries and Foreign Office officials quietly
conferred with him about key issues like that of *glasnost*, which he

supported. He urged Mrs Thatcher to meet President Gorbachev, and he chaired a successful meeting at Kelvin Hall in Glasgow when the Soviet leader first visited Scotland. Because he despaired of the government's handling of the impending break-up of Jugoslavia, he visited all the heads of the Federation's Republics on his own initiative, and reported his findings. Through journalism and film-making he kept in touch with old and new Balkan regimes, and even as late as 1990 he founded the St Andrew's Society to encourage trade between Russia and the UK and helped launch Haklyat, a similar organisation. I accompanied him on many of his forays, and agreed with the family that he had become, in a quiet way, an undercover elder statesman.

He had always been a skilled photographer, and what started as a hobby soon became an obsession, and very much part of our journeys. The resulting books, if not literary masterpieces, were always interesting and visually beautiful. They sold well enough, anyway, to pay for the next trip, and keep Strachur afloat.

The Filming Bug

After Grace Wyndham Goldie had sent us to Outer Mongolia, she had enough confidence in Fitz to furnish him with a BBC camera team whose director spoke excellent Russian, and in the 1960s we made two or three films in Jugoslavia, and one with Slim Hewitt in Georgia, then several in Russia and Central Asia in the 1970s and 80s with Tony Isaacs, John Purdey and Michael Gill.

Fitz insisted on presenting and narrating the documentaries himself; but, as in the House of Commons, his style of speaking to camera came over as rather stiff and wooden and not in the least like his natural self. As they said, he needed 'a lot of producing'. But it did not deter him.

I believe that what I called 'the film bug' that took over most of Fitz's life and ambitions after he had retired from the House of Commons was partly a result of what he thought of as his failure in politics. He dreamt of success in this new field, of producing one day 'a real block-buster', but even when he managed to get the financing of a film off the ground, his ideas for it always seemed to run into sand and the final result was nearly always a disappointment.

I am afraid I did little to support him in his struggles with the film world. I knew he wrote beautifully and I thought he should concentrate on that. But there were other reasons why filming and photography so fascinated Fitz: he was nostalgic for the past and wanted to show me the scenes of his early travels; and he had a boundless curiosity about the present – what was really happening on the ground in those remote and seldom-visited places and what had it to do with present Soviet policy and the Cold War?

How strange that nearly fifty years on so many of the places we travelled to should be headlines in the latest news: Merv and Duchambe, Askhebad, Termez, the Fergana valley, Uzbekistan and Tajikistan. (Fitz's destination at the end of his very first journey was Mazari Sharif and he crossed the Oxus in conditions similar to those of today.) Then our later journeys with Robert and Mollie Salisbury up the Khyber Pass and over the Karakoram Highway at the time of the Mujaheddin–Soviet war . . . A 'Replica of Circumstances', or 'La Ronde', seems in my life to have been almost a law of nature!

At first we found enough excuses and enough money for me to be taken along on some of the longer documentary trips, but budgets were all the time becoming tighter, filming more professional, and before long I realised that sooner or later I would be left behind. This irked me dreadfully, and I began to fill the gaps of Fitz's absences by lecturing for Serenissima, the holiday tour company, first in the Soviet Union, which was not difficult, and then in China. Because I had visited the country briefly and only twice, this was more of a problem, but I kept a few pages ahead of everyone else through the books Fitz lent me, and worked up my talks when the clients were sleeping, so that I managed somehow to make a little money and satisfy my wanderlust without total disaster. In this I was aided and abetted by Clare Wickham, Fitz's latest secretary in the House of Commons, who acted as my courier. Clare was an amazingly enterprising and adventurous character who had more experience than I had in working for Serenissima, and just as much chutzpah, and we had great fun together, improvising, commandeering, *bullying* our way through the tangle of red tape and making the most unlikely friends and allies in the process.

In 1990 our Montenegrin friend Bato Tomasevic, a remarkable man and one of the best literary fixers in the business, put to me a suggestion: was I game to travel round the world and interview its last reigning monarchs?, for he and Philip Wilson thought they could make a book out of it. Encouraged by the family I took up the challenge, but unfortunately Bato and Philip's plan foundered and it was for another publisher that I started on my travels.

The worst part of this trans-global project was juggling dates and logistics, but in the end I managed to talk to twenty-three out of the twenty-six kings, queens, grand dukes and emperors who were still reigning in countries as diverse as Sweden and Swaziland.

Fitz joined me for some of the most enjoyable excursions, like those to Bhutan and Nepal, where King Birendra flew us up to Mustang, which lies behind Annapurna, in the ancient kindom of Lo, and is one of the remotest places on earth – but he complained that so much solo travel made me bossier than ever in airports, and by that time it was probably true!

When I finally returned friends quizzed me:

'Which monarch did you find cleverest?'

'King Bhumipol of Thailand.'

'The nicest?'

'Grand Duke John of Luxembourg.'

'The most royal?'

'The King of Spain. He signs his letters: *Yo, El Rey*. You can't get more regal than that!'

'And who did you like the best?'

'Our own Royal Family, of course. What do you *think*?'

This Is Your Life

I had already taken part in an Eamonn Andrews *This Is Your Life* programme, for he had once targeted my brother Shimi. So when I was quietly approached one evening in Dalmatia by two strangers, who turned out to be Eamonn's spies, I was not surprised. They suggested that Fitzroy would make another great subject, and when they asked if I thought he would play, I said, 'Yes,' for I knew he would love it.

The programme-makers were extremely tactful, and the researchers had done their homework most throughly. They chose a date when I knew Fitz would be in London, and soon we had booked all the participants, which was great fun. Then – horrors! Fitz told me he had chucked his engagement and proposed to stay that week in Scotland, after all.

The only thing that could save us was a royal command – and I got one. I rang Martin Gilliat, the Queen Mother's private secretary, and explained the situation. He put it to the Queen Mother, who promptly sent Fitzroy a message insisting that he should be present at a farewell luncheon party she was giving for Chips Maclean, her retiring Lord Chamberlain and Fitz's clan chief, on the day before the programme. Evidently she let quite a few of her guests into the plot, because when we arrived at Clarence House there were many double entendre greetings and jokes, as well as a wink from Her Majesty – none of which Fitz noticed.

The filming was to be done at a studio outside London, and the participants had been bussed there to rehearse. They included Sandy Glen, David Stirling, General George Berger, Vladko Velebit, Rafo Ivancevič and 'Persona' from Korčula, Sergeant Duncan, our piper Neil Campbell and the Strachur pipe band, Rhoda Cockerill, Jimmy McNab from The Creggans, the family (four children and seven grandchildren) and me. To add what the producers called 'glamour', they brought in that still highly seductive actor Douglas Fairbanks Junior.

The cover plan for capture was simple. Fitz was rung up by the BBC and asked to take part in a literary programme with Mark Bonham Carter (one of the plotters) and other authors. Iain Moncreiffe ('Ilk', another plotter) was to delay him at White's, where Mark would pick him up in a taxi supposedly on the way to the studio. I told Fitz I was going to a film with Irene. In fact, as soon as he left our flat, I quickly prepared a drinks party for all the guests we had invited to watch the show, and then dashed to the studio, leaving Jeanne Clissold and Pamela Egremont to host the gathering.

To Ilk's horror, Fitz suddenly decided to ring me up. 'She won't have left yet,' he told his decoy. 'I'll just catch her.' But it was Pamela who answered the telephone, suppressed a shriek and had the presence of mind to cut the line.

The taxi in which Mark and Fitz were travelling drove straight on to the stage in the studio. Fitz got out, *backwards*, wearing his dreaded 'Lord Forecaster', the ancient Burberry I had begged him to leave behind, and gazed around in amazement as Eamonn presented him with The Red Book.

We had asked twice as many friends to watch the performance as were usually permitted, and Eamonn most generously agreed to let them all join in the post-show supper in the studio – which was the best party ever.

Happily Ever After – The Children Wed

Sukie's life continued on its bumpy road. There were highs and there were lows, but Derek and his white horse eventually stumbled. He was a dear, kind man who had never quite grown up; his professionalism as a writer was absolute, but his romanticism was not equal to the rough-and-tumble of a growing family. He gradually retreated from it, first into a quiet writing room, then into a quiet writing annexe, then into a separate writing flat, and lastly into Hollywood and another world. He left behind Benjie, well-named, for everyone loved this happy little fellow, the outcome of a talented father and a good deed in a wicked world. But Derek kept in friendly touch with Sukie, and with his son, and Benjie visited him several times in California, where Derek died, suddenly and unexpectedly, in 1996, at the age of only fifty-seven.

Alone again, Sukie struggled on. Now she had four children to educate, and another to nurture. She was kept afloat by her decorating business, her ships and an explosion in the London house market, for besides fixing up Bluey Mavroleon's tankers and people's houses, she began to buy, do up, gentrify and sell property in outlying suburbs that were becoming fashionable. Soon she and the children were able to move into a large and pretty old house in Lansdowne Gardens, in Stockwell, which she had bought for a song. Her work was gruelling, but, attractive and witty as ever, Sukie had begun to sing again, and Fitz could once more quote the music-hall ballad:

> She's Mary,
> My canary,
> My laughing cockatoo!

All the family celebrated my seventieth birthday in her hospitable kitchen. She produced a brilliant conjuror to entertain us, and a wobbly pink jelly rabbit *couchant* as the centrepiece of the spread. 'Press the je'el – it'll nae keep,' I quoted, and the friendly ghosts of Willie the Moon and Mrs Willie hovered gently round the table, making me feel quite young once more.

Inevitably, Sukie fell in love again, and this time she married Nic Paravicini, the best husband in the world. They live together now in a beautiful old vicarage below the Black Mountains in Wales, a house which seems permanently full of family, his and hers, and friends and laughter. Nic has become quite my favourite son-in-law. 'You've only got one!' he reminds me – and, having been first a soldier, then a banker, he knows how to count; but in that cheerful mêlée of children and grandchildren, great-grandchildren and dogs, it is often difficult to tell which is what.

After Jeremy and Sukie, Jamie was the next to marry. He announced his engagement to Sarah Janson (hereafter known to Fitz and me as Sarah Mark I), a hard-working and successful *trompe-l'oeil* artist whose party-giving mother and financial-wizard stepfather threw an exceptionally large one to celebrate the event.

Jamie insisted on being married on Korčula. A hundred guests were flown out for the wedding, a hundred Korčulans joined in, and the islanders put on a three-day celebration, as only they know how. But in spite of this auspicious start, the marriage foundered, and ended in a painful and bitter divorce.

Jamie's pride and pocket suffered greatly from their parting – yet it had one good result. He began to take life more seriously and to work, perforce, much harder, finding a gap in the depressed art market and founding the Erotic Print Society.

Five years later he found Sarah Mark II, and if ever there was a case of living happily ever after, this was it. I only worry that they both work and play too hard. Sarah paints, cooks and whizzes through life at a pace that leaves me breathless; she is clever, tells good jokes, is a talented artist, loves people, and has (besides two children) the best legs in London. Alexander Fitzroy Maclean is Fitz's double, and the most-travelled six-year-old in his kindergarten. He used to worship the moth-eaten Korčulan cats and long for a kitten of his own; but after visiting Bali and Luxor, he told me he would settle for a small crocodile. I hope that one day he may be an artist, too, or an explorer, or a vet.

And Charlie? After his journalistic start on the *Ecologist,* he wrote a book about the island of St Kilda, which was a success, and then a more ambitious one called *The Wolf Children,* which he researched from Calcutta, and which is still in print. He then went to live in the United States, and landed the job of American gossip columnist for the London *Evening Standard,* while working seriously on his first novel, a psychological thriller of immense complication and horror, which he still hopes will one day make his fortune as a film.

During our annual trips to New York we would sometimes stay with Arthur Ross, our hospitable friend whom Fitz had first met in Strasbourg, and sometimes with Charlie on Long Island, and there we met Debbie, the Afro-American model with whom he had fallen in love. She was tall, beautiful and gently dignified, with a wonderful figure and a way of making everything she wore look wonderful too. She and Charlie were already living together and wanted to marry, but they were aware of our prejudices and fears, and respected them.

I suppose our fears of a mixed marriage stemmed from the inherited attitudes with which we had both been brought up – though they did us no credit. Charlie would chide his father: 'Dad – you of *all* people! You've got friends from every part of the world!'

Yet Fitz's anxiety was not for his own son or descendants; rather, he was afraid that Debbie's exoticism would not fit in or be accepted by old-fashioned Strachur – and I worried that mixed-race children might be bullied at school, and would have fewer options in marriage and careers.

How wrong we both were! Having waited a painful year, they got married quietly in New York, and sent us a telegram to say so. I now think our greatest stupidity lay in not recognising the flair that Charlie has had, all his life, for seeing true goodness in people. When Debbie came home with him and settled seamlessly into Argyll life, she proved to us once and for always that that is what matters most.

30

OUR LAST GREAT
JOURNEY

FITZ LOVED FRONTIERS, AND IN 1989, WHEN HE WAS A SPRIGHTLY seventy-eight, we made our last great journey together. We decided to explore the most famous of them all, the North-West Frontier of India (now in Pakistan), and then travel on the newly completed Karakoram Highway, the great military road which now crosses the Western Himalayas and connects Hunza and Gilgit in Pakistan with Tash Kurgan and Kashgar in Sinkiang. We would continue our journey by car and train across the vast deserts and plains of China, sail down the Yangtse gorges of the Yellow River, to arrive at Kwelin and our final destination, in what was still the British island of Hong Kong. En route, we hoped to make a diversion which would allow us to visit the great monastery of Kumbum and the southern shore of Lake Koko Nor in what used to be Greater Tibet.

The Pakistan part of our trip was organised by Robert and Mollie Salisbury and their eldest son, 'Little Robert' Cranborne, who had made us a splendid itinerary. He was then in his early forties, and had abandoned British politics for the time being to take up the cause of the Mujaheddin, who were fighting the Soviet army in Afghanistan.

Our adventure started brilliantly with a banquet in Islamabad, at which Mollie and I sat on either side of Yakub Khan, the Pakistan Foreign Secretary, who told me more about my Tennant grandmother and the Souls than I ever knew, then switched to Sartre and the Existentialists, before leaving us to catch a plane for an international conference in Geneva.

Yakub, having been trained at Sandhurst, was familiar enough with the British aristocracy to treat Robert like a visiting Grand Vizier. We were given an army jeep, a driver and sometimes outriders on motorbikes; officials and army posts were appraised of our route, and government rest-houses prepared to receive us. We paid a visit to the 'gun-makers' village' near the Afghan frontier, where one could buy anything from a fountain-pen pistol to a Kalashnikov rifle, and the drug-dealers hang sheepskins outside their shops to advertise their trade. In one hill village we happened on a funeral, and heard its elders proclaiming the deceased's virtues, just as a Senachie would have done in Mull a hundred years ago, while women wailed in chorus over the corpse in its open coffin.

Fitz tried to photograph the shy inhabitants of the Bumporpet valley, whose graceful women wear red-and-black *kalaishes* and necklaces of cowrie shells, even though they live hundreds of miles from any sea; they are pagans, and their ancestors are supposed, by some philologists, to have spoken the very first primitive language, just one up from grunts. At the bottom of the Khyber Pass we read the sad inscriptions on the gravestones of the English church, and were touched by the youth of so many brave young men who died before they had time to live, some still in their teens, whose sacrifice is now no longer honoured in their homeland, and whose once-proud regiments are now barely remembered.

Our most exciting encounter was with a celebrated Mujaheddin leader who had been wounded in the fighting and was lying up secretly in a village near Peshawar. Young Robert had taken special care to make sure that our Land Rover was not being followed, for the British were supporting different groups of guerrillas from those backed by the Americans. We therefore approached the rendezvous by a roundabout route; but suddenly, with a horrid thud, one of our wheels dropped into a ditch, and no amount of shoving could shift it. Before long half the hero's village had turned out to help, and many of them, guessing to which house we were heading, showed us the way on foot.

Robert had warned us that Mollie and I must wear our veils, and that his father and Fitz, when seated, must on no account show the soles of their feet. We were ushered into a room with low divans and cushions ranged along one wall. Opposite them lay the wounded young hero, who received us graciously and waved an invitation to sit down.

I shall always treasure the moment when the Marquess of Salisbury and Fitz lowered their slightly creaking six-foot-plus bodies on to the bosomy cushions of the divan, struggling to contort themselves into sustainable positions that would not commit the ultimate solecism of showing the soles of their feet to our hero-host. I used to think he was Ahmed Moussad; but now I know it was Abdul Haq, who had been severely wounded and lost a foot in the fighting. However today it is perhaps of little consequence, as both heroes have been murdered by the Taleban.

The Salisburys had to leave us at Karimabad, the last little town on the Pakistani side of the border with China. The place is dominated by two ancient forts, whose rulers were once at war with each other, and its houses cling to the sides of the valley over which they fought. There are garnets in the rocks and in the rushing river, and children peddle handfuls of crimson lumps in the narrow cobbled streets, which climb higher and higher, to apple and apricot orchards, and then to the bare mountainside. The forts, Baltit and Altit, crouch like sleeping lions in defence of the pass; reminders of the permanent struggle for dominance in those fierce mountains that continues to this very day.

I have never suffered from altitude sickness before, but as the road climbed ever upwards towards the frontier, I felt first a little, then decidedly queasy. But at 4,750 metres above sea level and one final hairpin bend, the land at last flattened out, and there, immediately in front of us, were the two frontier posts. Our kindly driver dumped us with our luggage on the Pakistan side and, quickly reversing his jeep, was away in a flash, leaving us to face China wheel-less and on our own.

The trouble was, we were by no means sure we had valid permission even to enter the Chinese Republic, let alone travel across it. In London, all our attempts to obtain visas had been met with inscrutable politeness and prevarication, even from the Ambassador; the Chinese Consulate in Islamabad had been closed, and we did not know whether word had been sent ahead or not.

We humped our luggage to the Chinese post and sat down on a bench; but there was no transport in sight, and the guards seemed half asleep, so we settled down to wait. After an hour Fitz asked in dumb crambo if he could telephone, but his request was refused. Showing them our papers was futile, as they could not read English.

Just as our future was looking really bleak, I spied a small black beetle scurrying towards us, a long way out across the plain. Deliverance came at last in the shape of Ali, a young Tajik interpreter, small and neat, with dark cream skin, black eyes and good, Indo-European features, and his serviceable little jeep, which he seemed to drive like a horse – for, as he soon proudly told us, all Tajiks are horsemen.

We piled our luggage aboard and were off down the road to Tash Kurgan, with Ali chattering away in his version of English as he explained how he had been hired and sent to meet us – something we never really understood. We began to go downhill, and after a few bends emerged on to a far larger wide plain of astounding beauty.

The road across the savannah that lies between the Chinese border and Tash Kurgan must surely be the most beautiful in all the world, and the high Pamirs that march alongside it the most exciting of all mountain ranges. Fitz made Ali stop every five minutes so that he could take photographs; then the camera froze, and my poor husband was in a frenzy until I had a brain wave and thawed it with my hand-warmers (extra kit I had bought in the Euston Station Survival Shop, in spite of much protest!). We arrived in Tash Kurgan, the Stone City, that night, and slept in its only hotel.

Next day we headed for Kashgar and followed, in reverse, the route along the ancient Silk Road that Peter Fleming and his Swiss companion Ella Maillart took in 1935 on their three-and-a-half-thousand-mile trek to Kashmir – the same road route that the indomitable Mrs MacCartney, the young bride of the British Consul in Kashgar, rode, and that 'Blue Poppy' Bailey followed a few years later.

Kashgar is the most romantic and remote of Central Asian towns. The Embassies of the two countries that once competed for supremacy in the nineteenth-century Great Game both survive, after a fashion. We stayed in the Russian one – by then transformed into a ramshackle hotel – while the British Consulate, the Chini Begh, or Chinese Garden, was almost derelict, and occupied only by the scruffiest of backpackers. Fitz had been asked by the British Council to find out if its once well-known library of books on Central Asia still existed – but alas, it did not, except for a few mutilated pages I found blowing about the overgrown garden. But the Aidkari Mosque, the carpet bazaar, the markets, the fort and the rabbit warren of streets in the old citadel still flourished, as did the famous 'Sunday market'.

Every week several thousand Tajiks, Uzbeks and Tartars ride into town from the surrounding countryside to sell their fat-tailed sheep, their young horses and camels, their poultry, fruit and vegetables, and to buy the city's manufactured goods. They shout 'Hoosh! Hoosh!' ('Make way! Make way!'), a piercing cry which rises above the general cacophony of bleating animals and braying donkeys as they pour down the hill towards the marketplace in an unstoppable flood of lumbering carts and loaded wagons. Ignore them at your peril! The Sunday market is still one of the most exciting and exotic sights in all western China, and I hope it will never change.

From Kashgar we drove for four days across the Taklemekhan Desert (a continuation of the Gobi) to Urumchi, a hot and horrid modern town with no redeeming features. There we were met by Mr Lei, representative of the Chinese Writers' Guild (who were our hosts and responsible for our journey), a rather shy, gentle man, quite uneducated, who had somehow climbed to the higher echelons of the Party's educational bureaucracy and had written one book (about hydraulic pumps) of which he was inordinately proud. He had been born in Peking, and until he came to meet us had never left the city – so this was the greatest adventure of his life. He may have had faults, extreme nervousness being one and blind obedience to rules another, but we learnt to love him, and when we finally parted at the end of our trip, he and I both cried.

The next part of our journey was eastwards, by train, to Xining, for Fitz was determined to visit Kumbum and then take a loop back to what was once, and should still be, greater Tibet. Xining was described by my guidebook as the ugliest and most polluted city in China; but nonetheless a welcome party was waiting for us on the platform, and after our fourteen pieces of luggage had been hurled at them through the carriage window (Fitz and Mr Lei fighting a duel for custody of the camera bag, which each thought too heavy or too precious for the other to carry), we descended and were introduced.

The round-faced editor of the local daily newspaper made us a pretty speech before presenting, with reverence, our host. He was a Tibetan, a Party member, high up in regional government, and it was obvious that everyone was honoured by his presence. Short and square, he dominated the group, and his laugh – a deep yo-ho-ho chuckle, rumbled confidently from his chest, in sharp contrast to the nervous smiles and polite twittering of the Han Chinese. His Chinese ADC, tall and lean, wore a Humphrey Bogart-type mackintosh and a Bogartian expression of deep melancholy. There was also a driver, an unexplained youth and a quiet Tibetan girl with glasses, the only one who could speak or understand a smattering of English.

On our way to the hotel, the chairman proudly explained the amazing phenomenon of Xining, and its transformation from small garrison town on the end of a caravan route to India, to a thriving provincial capital of some two million inhabitants, whose economy is based on oil refineries and heavy industry.

Surprisingly, our Soviet-style hotel turned out to be one of the cleanest and most comfortable we stayed in, with excellent, friendly service. The dining room was majestic, and divided by walls of lacquered screens into zones for foreign tourists, visiting dignitaries and local officials. The chairman, Mr Lei and Bogart disappeared behind one of the screens and we sat down in almost solitary state at one end of the tourist enclave.

The food was moderate; but in the lobby one could buy beer and biscuits, sweets and bubble gum, as well as amber beads, carved ivory kitsch and other tourist temptations. We settled for a bottle of Mai Tai, the Chinese grain spirit which, drunk as an aperitif, helps one face the food, and, as a digestif, assists in keeping it down.

Next morning we drove out in two black Japanese limousines to Taer and the great Tibetan lamasery of Kumbum. The city faded abruptly into countryside: straight roads edged with poplars; adobe-and-brick farmhouses with flat roofs on which crops were drying. Newly threshed corn lay in yellow pools on winnowing floors of sun-baked earth; little putt-putt tractors were pulling huge loads, and now and then there was a flash of distant snow-capped peaks on the horizon.

Soon the road narrowed and started to climb. We overtook battered lorries crammed with Tibetan families and shaven-headed young monks, with bundles and parcels piled round them. Were they pilgrims bound for Kumbum and Lhasa, or detainees being moved to the labour camps in which the province was said to abound? Since they looked happy enough, and waved merrily as we passed, we hoped the former.

As we passed through the outer wall of what is in effect a monastic city, we were transported back four centuries, for the lamasery of Kumbum was founded in 1560: at the height of its power, as the summer residence of the Panchen lamas, it sheltered three thousand monks beneath its gilded copper roofs, and wielded enormous influence in both China and Tibet. When we visited it, between two and three hundred lamas still lived in and operated from Kumbum, with many more vocations occurring than could be accepted.

Questions fizzed in our minds, but politeness and respect, as well as the language barrier, made it difficult to ask them. We could only observe – and what was easily observable was the faith and fervour of the pilgrims, who had come in their hundreds from all parts of Qinghai and from Tibet itself. The good-humoured kindness of the lamas and novices made a great impression on us.

The architecture of the prayer halls and dormitories was restrained, and more Chinese than Tibetan, but inside them the Buddhas and Bodhisattvas and other heavenly company ran riot, while prayer wheels spun, pilgrims prostrated themselves and huge copper gongs clanged. There were hundreds of beautiful and wildly strange artefacts, but it was the pilgrims who delighted me most: a toothless old woman with long grey hair divided into a multitude of elaborate plaits; young girls with high cheek-bones and rosy, wind-burnt complexions; children with cheerful faces caked in grime but still innocent of pestering ploys – all possessed a natural robustness and confidence that were completely beguiling.

And then the clothes! There were marvellous padded robes of dark brown or purple cotton, banded with turquoise or viridian green, of cobalt-blue silk, of damask and velvet and plush. Nearly all showed somewhere a glint of gold or a flash of ancient brocade. A few matriarchs wore torques and plaques of embossed silver, and necklaces of turquoise or amber. Some women and many men sported high-crowned, broad-brimmed felt hats that were a cross between Navajo Indian and the Australian outback.

The men had a wild ruggedness that could defy any Himalayan blizzard. Their felt boots had barbaric, upturned toes, and a few carried daggers or sheathed knives. The faces of men and children were burnt deep brown by wind and sun, and everybody had two features in common: extreme dirt, and a strong smell of rancid yak butter.

The ultimate goal of our journey was Qinghai Lake, once called Lake Koko Nor, where we hoped to find white-lipped deer, wild asses, a kingdom of birds and unexplored mountains. But we had hardly left the perma-smog of Xining, in our two saloon cars, when the first splodges of sleet hit the windscreen. Before long the sleet turned to snow, and in the end the weather – backed by the determination of Bogey and our driver not to go anywhere near to Golmud and the high passes which lead to Tibet – defeated us. After a cold and pretty miserable night in a small hotel on the shore of Qinghai Lake, we turned back, getting stuck in a snowdrift on the way. The morose and inscrutable driver seemed to take this as a personal insult: I am sure he blamed his loss of face on the foreign devils in his vehicle, and there was little chat on the way home. We took a different route back into town, past the long brick walls of a barracks or prison, whose watch-towers were manned by soldiers with mounted machine-guns facing inwards. This made a deep impression, and we too fell silent as we re-entered the capital of that strangely beautiful and still mysterious province.

31

MERCY MISSION TO
KORČULA

IN THE WINTER OF 1991 FITZROY HAD TWO SERIOUS OPERATIONS. The first, in London, was not a success, and it had to be done all over again by a Scottish surgeon in Glasgow. Until then he had always disregarded illness but this time he had to be nursed, and then spend a few months convalescing.

In February we flew out to the Canary Islands, and then moved to Korčula for the summer. Fitz could no longer walk easily on his own, and needed the physical support of my arm, as well as a very tall *cromach* and a folding chair, which now accompanied us everywhere. Igor Lozica – who, as well as being a director of the Moreska Folk Dance Company and the finest baritone on the island, was also in charge of Korčula town's cleaning department – built him an iron ramp on the rocks from which we always bathed so that he could get down, by easy steps, to the sea. He could then swim, and did so every day, and together we watched for the little red fish that hid underneath one of our rock steps and greeted us every year when we returned to the island. Sheila MacPherson came out to help me, and did so devotedly, hauling Fitz in and out of the sea and pushing a Red Cross chair up the only street in the Stari Grad which has no steps.

In spite of the worsening political situation, we still had plenty of visitors. Tudjman was still a long way off from obliterating forty years of his country's history, and Milosevič from trying to re-establish a Greater Serbia which would embrace Kosovo and all its potential dynamite. Fitz had somehow remained an *ancien régime* hero, who looked for solutions rather than quarrels, and, because he refused to take sides, a guru who was sometimes listened to – as well as being known throughout the country as a friend. On one occasion we flew into Dubrovnik airport and were queueing with the other passengers at passport control when the older man in the immigration booth reproved the younger one who was studying the crowded pages of Fitz's passport, growling, 'Don't be stupid! Can't you see? That's *our* Maclean!'

In late 1990, after the collapse of the Communist governments in Eastern Europe, Serbia, Slovenia and Croatia held elections in which the Communist Party lost votes and the nationalist and pro-independence parties triumphed. In June 1991, after a ten-day war between the nationalistic Slovene militia and the professional Jugoslav Federal Army (ninety per cent of which was Serb), the Feds were soundly beaten, and first Slovenia and then Croatia seceded from the Jugoslav Federation. Tito's dream of a united and peaceful nation had disintegrated.

In August the Croat government blockaded all Federal Army installations in their new country, and General Mladič, in revenge, besieged Vukovar. There were massacres and reprisals, torture and rape, and tragic, hunted refugees. The Security Council dithered ineffectually. Milosevič and Tudjman met and agreed to carve up Bosnia. In October the Dalmatian coast was blockaded by the Federal Navy, and Dubrovnik was attacked by the Jugoslav Federal Army, with the help of the Montenegrin militia. Korčula was not involved directly in any of the fighting, but suffered severely from the blockade, and before long we received an urgent appeal from its cottage hospital.

The Jugoslav navy had cut off the island from the outside world, and their beds were overflowing with wounded, as well as with ordinary cases of sick Korčulans who could no longer be sent on to Split or Dubrovnik for major surgery. They were rapidly running out of drugs, and their small theatre lacked the equipment to perform the necessary operations. Medical and surgical staff were desperate. Could we help?

We certainly could. We at once launched an emergency appeal for funds. We wrote hundreds of letters and, with the help of our constituents – Rothesay and Bute were twinned with Korčula, and were particularly generous – the Wellcome Foundation, various ex-Korčulans and friendly millionaires, including Paul Getty, we collected in a very short time nearly £50,000. For the next stage of the operation I relied on the advice of Mollie Salisbury, as for years she had been driving mercy missions to Polish convents and hospitals practically single-handed. Korčula sent us lists, and she told us to shop at a remarkable charitable and non-profit-making institution called EKO, which supplies almost new but redundant hospital equipment to good causes at ridiculously low prices.

The worst problem was renting a van, for many other charities were also scouring around for vehicles and frequently losing or writing them off on their trips. However, a generous firm, Mitchells of Aberdeen, finally produced an almost new two-tonner, but as no one would insure it, we simply had to hope it would survive and return with us to Glasgow. Packing it, in an empty bay at the Vale of Leven Hospital, took nearly six hours, for we had little expertise, and there was much controversy about where to put the morphine – underneath or on top of everything else?

Jamie and I set off in a thunderstorm, with Jamie driving, for, although I had had several hours of tuition at Hatfield, he didn't trust me, and it wasn't until we picked up our third driver, Major-General Bob Loudon, who was head of the British–Jugoslav Society, at the SAS barracks in Chelsea, that I was allowed to take the wheel. Bob, the best of men but the worst of drivers, was so dangerous that Jamie promoted me to be his deputy. Fitz, meanwhile, flew out to Italy.

We arrived at our rendezvous, the Atlantic College of Duino, on the appointed day and more or less at the appointed hour. There we found Fitz, being entertained in a delightful quayside restaurant by our hosts, David Sutcliffe, the rector, and his wife Elisabet.

It was impossible to get reliable news of sailings down the Dalmatian coast, and the next evening, when we reached Rijeka after a hairy drive in stair-rod rain, there was only one ship on the quayside. It was the old ferry-boat *Ilirija*, and she was loading. We left Jamie and Bob in charge of the van, and evading the dockside police, stepped on board.

A wild-looking young man was obviously in charge. You couldn't miss him: he was six inches taller than Fitz or anyone else, and he was laughing and yelling and heaving boxes and crates around. Fitz approached him with some trepidation and asked if the ship was sailing for Dubrovnik and, if so, could it give us a lift? He took us into a corner between a stack of plastic coffins and a mountain of powdered baby milk and, after introducing himself as Jacob, or Yasha, he explained the situation.

After several weeks of negotiations with the Federal Army, the Council of Croatian Jews in Zagreb had received permission to charter the *Ilirija* and sail her to Dubrovnik with two hundred tons of food and medical supplies. She was sailing under Yasha's own version of the Jewish flag – a Star of David with a few artistic embellishments – so that his mission represented neither Serbian, nor Croatian, nor Catholic, nor Orthodox, nor Moslem loyalties, and could be perceived by the authorities only as purely humanitarian. He made it clear to Fitz that if he was to take us, we would have to do our own negotiating with the Feds and receive separate permission.

This was only fair, and we proceeded up the gangway to the captain's bridge, where we were warmly greeted – we had sailed to Korčula with him dozens of times – and offered slivovitz and liqueur chocolates in silver paper. He said he could not give permission himself, but would try to raise the admiral in charge of the blockade, then disappeared with his wireless operator into a cubby-hole. After a nerve-racking wait, he re-emerged and beckoned to Fitz, and in between the squeals of the little wireless I could hear the following conversation. 'Is that you, General?' and, when Fitz admitted it, '*Draga Maklin!* We haven't met for ages, but do you remember . . . ?' The squeals then took over *fortissimo* and the communication was cut . . .

We were once more on tenterhooks, and I ate three more maraschino chocolates out of sheer nerves. Then the voice came back, and after Fitz explained our urgent but separate mission, the admiral not only granted us safe passage and a fair wind, but said he would give orders for the *Ilirija* not to be stopped and searched before it reached Dubrovnik (which was the usual procedure) as Fitz's presence guaranteed its honesty. Wow!

We clattered back to the hold, and Yasha hugged Fitz and said he had just been elected to honorary membership of Zagreb's Jewish community. Bob drove our little blue van on board. It looked very small compared with the rest of the cargo, but we were proud of it. My Fraser tartan scarf, which I had tied on to the mirror bracket in Glasgow, still fluttered damply.

Our three nights and two days at sea were surreal. The captain invited us to dine with him at his table, and when we arrived in the ninety per cent empty but still elegant dining room, we found that the other dozen or so passengers were all dining at the Captain's table, as well as the rest of the ship's officers. There was only the one table, and a kind of everlasting Slavic meal seemed to be served on it all day. We were a merry company and, like people on a pleasure cruise, took snaps of each other and vowed to keep in touch.

As soon as we left port, a fierce storm arose, forcing us to take overnight shelter in the lee of an island just south of Rijeka, so we did not enter the Korčulan canal until three p.m. two days later. We docked in front of the Hotel Korčula, and the few people on the quayside seemed at first bewildered by our Star of David flag, but soon word got around and a small crowd gathered to shout greetings, only for us to tell them we were under captain's orders and could not disembark.

Our own 'family', Ruzica and Janez Napotnik, were among the crowd, along with our old friend Aljosa Mljet, who was then Mayor, and the Mother Superior of the Dominican convent. We could see her black-and-white habit flapping in the wind, and we shouted, 'Yes, we'll be back tomorrow,' and, 'No, we don't know for how long,' but that we had brought them all the things they had asked for. We stayed only fifteen minutes, but someone had time to run up to the cathedral and ring its bells as we sailed out again.

We reached Gruz, Dubrovnik's harbour, as dusk was falling. The Serb guns outside the town had pounded it the previous night, and a warehouse near the quayside was still burning fitfully – a ruby eye and little flickering flames in the dark. It must have contained sacks of sugar, because the sharp, acrid-sweet smell of burnt molasses lay heavily on the air. There was rubble and broken glass where the Jadralinja ticket office once stood, but I could not make out much else. Dubrovnik had no electricity, so the rest of the harbour and town was in inky blackout. A convoy of lorries with dimmed lights passed, and then there was eerie silence, occasionally broken by distant thuds.

Later the Mayor of Dubrovnik came on board, and gave an excellently clear press conference, promising to take us on a tour of the town the next day. We duly toured the city in a formal and rather embarrassing procession, down the Stradun to the steps in front of the Gradski Kafana, where the Mayor, Fitz and Dr Bernard Krushner, the founder-member of that admirable organisation Médecins sans Frontières, were to address the cameras and the crowd.

Suddenly I saw a familiar face and jumped down off the platform. It was Fitzroy's war-time friend Mato Jaksič's son Srdan, who told me that the lovely old sea-captain's house in which we had stayed so often had received a direct hit, and that he was working day and night to repair the roof so as to save Mato's books. Indeed, his hair was full of concrete dust and he looked exhausted.

The destruction around Lapad, Gruz, and the outskirts of Dubrovnik was infinitely worse than that within the city walls; but the real victims were the refugees and homeless who had poured into the town. Their lack of communication with their families and bewildered isolation was dreadful, and we returned to the *Ilirija* in outrage and gloom. That afternoon we heard on the radio that Vukovar had fallen.

The unloading of Yasha's cargo was so desultory that our captain threatened to leave before it was finished, but at last we weighed anchor and headed north again. We did not reach Korčula until ten p.m., but this time all our friends were waiting on the quayside, and we were wafted up to the Stara Kuc with the green door on a tide of goodwill and affection. Dear old ladies in padded dressing gowns and *pantoufles* came out of their darkened houses with electric torches and waved them at us, and Ruzica had prepared a mountain of *keks* and gallons of wine to sustain us. The guests did not leave until midnight, and then Fitz and I climbed up the old wooden stairs above the kitchen and fell into our clean cool linen sheets, on our very own beds, in our very own bedroom, and slept.

Next morning we disembarked the van and drove it to the hospital. The whole staff had turned out to meet us and could hardly wait to unpack the treasure. We had brought all the equipment they had asked for, including a complete small operating theatre with table and lamps and anaesthetists' paraphernalia and, best of all, a new type of battlefield splint, which stretches and wraps round a shattered limb, making it immovable and saving many amputations. For the next four years, the little hospital and its devoted staff and team of surgeons flourished and performed many operations on our table. After the war, when Dubrovnik had built a huge new hospital with foreign aid, most of the Maclean Emergency Fund equipment was absorbed into it, to everyone's chagrin. But that's life!

The Moreska

A decade earlier, helping to save the Palazzo Arneri (our friend Nancy Brown Negley gave the town a million dollars to start the rebuilding project) and taking the Moreska Dance Company on a tour of the United Kingdom, in 1980, had been gestures of solidarity that had made us many friends in Korčula, and closer members of its community. This was confirmed when, in 1984, Fitzroy was made an honorary citizen of the town, the first foreigner to be so honoured.

The Moreska is a sacred institution in Korčula. It is a dance that used to be performed on many small islands in the Mediterranean, for it is basically a sword drill, woven round a legend, designed to keep garrisons in good fighting order. Korčula is now the only island that dances it and is rightly proud that its company has preserved the tradition, and so was I when I accompanied forty of its members to dance in a dozen cities around Scotland and England.

Zivan Filippi and I performed a stylish double-act in introducing the company to our audiences, and Igor Lozica managed to produce great performances, but the biggest problem was feeding the hungry Korčulans when the show was over, and explaining to them that a loaf of bread and a bottle of wine *per person* would present certain difficulties in our benighted country.

Geoffrey Wooler, however, entertained the lot of us in his home to a plenitude of bread, wine, Wensleydale cheeses and good home-baked Yorkshire hams after they had danced at Leeds in its famous town hall. We ended the tour in London (David Dimbleby introducing them that time) with a tremendous party which every Dalmatian, Jugoslav, Fraser and friend in the capital attended, and danced 'Kolas' and Highland reels with wild abandon, irrespective of ethnic difference, till the sun rose and it was time to pack up and say goodbye.

32

SARAJEVO

IN THE SUMMER OF 1994, HANS FELS, HEAD OF A SMALL DUTCH television company called Diogenes, which made documentaries, decided to shoot another in Jugoslavia, and asked Fitz to be its narrator, contrasting the present conflict with his own experiences in 1943. Hans was producer, director, cameraman and editor, so held all the important elements of film-making in his control. There was no dubbing in his documentaries: people talked naturally to camera in their own language and time, and subtitles were put in later to suit the countries where the film would be shown. The music and editing were first-rate, and the three other Dutchmen who made up the team had all worked together previously.

We joined them in Zagreb, where Fitz had set up an interview with the newly elected President Tudjman. Cold-eyed but polite, he put his extreme nationalist views succinctly, in a part-academic, part-imperial style. Fitz listened to him equally politely, and then skilfully changed the subject.

We then called on our British Forces Headquarters in a vast NATO camp outside Zagreb, where he was briefed by our intelligence officers about the war, and asked to present some campaign medals to brave British tommies. Evidence of fighting lay everywhere. We drove through abandoned villages with roofless, smoke-blackened houses that had only weeks before been the homes of innocent Serb families. We visited Colonel Mark Cook, who had organised the rebuilding of a bombed orphanage. This was a massive task, entirely carried out by the voluntary work of his soldiers when they were off duty, and directed by his own enthusiasm and that of Mladen Grbin, an old Korčulan/Glasgow University friend of ours.

Hans's film begins with a conversation between Fitz and a man on a ladder who is repairing his roof. He is not particularly interested in the last war, or the Partisan battle that took place in his village in 1943. He has his own troubles, and they are immediate. The camera then pans to the village war memorial, a fine monument on which are carved many similar names, whole families who were almost certainly shot in the Wehrmacht's reprisals. We read them aloud, and then see that new bullet-holes have pierced the bronze tablets – this time, shockingly, from the guns of the villagers' own countrymen.

That night we slept in the windowless dormitory of what used to be an old people's home. It was so cold that we kept our clothes on. The ancient refugees talked to us at breakfast the next day. '*Bice dobro*', 'it will get better', was on everyone's lips, accompanied by a long sigh. For them it could hardly be much worse, for many had lost both their families and their homes.

Split, in a horribly evil way, was by then *much* worse. The town had been taken over by gangsters and warlords, who often became overnight millionaires from protection deals or sales of black-market armaments to fellow crooks. If one drank or dined under the old Roman arcades of the central square, most of which had been built by the Emperor Diocletian, one could see German marks and US dollars changing hands and hear drunken toasts being given to celebrate the murky deals. All the men wore camouflaged fatigues, and one could not tell which army they belonged to, legitimate or otherwise.

With the film crew, we waited for several days outside the town in one of the once-elegant hotels near the airport that had been taken over by NATO. It was brimming with soldiers and kitbags; cheerful, friendly faces and clackety boots that reverberated down the passages at night. But it was well run by an amazingly patient and kindly civilian staff, and we had with us Boris Marelic, our Korčulan friend, who had bravely volunteered to accompany Fitz as chief 'minder', interpreter and organiser.

The French aircrew who finally flew us into Sarajevo were charming, and the dispatchers settled Fitz as comfortably as possible on the floor of the plane between pallets of soup tins and nets of babies' nappies. At Sarajevo only fifteen minutes were allowed for an aeroplane to discharge its cargo, turn round and depart. As we taxied to a halt, lorries instantly rolled up and the unloading proceeded with tremendous speed and efficiency.

At the perimeters of the huge empty expanse of tarmac we could see Portakabins, jeeps and lorries. Beyond them rose tall apartment blocks, scarred with patches of missing concrete where shrapnel had hit. It seemed a very long walk across the airfield, and I am sure my pulse rate doubled during it, but soon we made out that one of the waiting vehicles had a British flag on it. A cheerful British sergeant saluted smartly and hurried forward to help. 'General Rose's compliments, sir,' he said to Fitz. 'I'm to take you to the Holiday Inn, and then he'll get in touch.' (His expression added, 'God help you.')

We drove down 'Snipers' Alley' and drew up in front of a battered-looking 1950s-style hotel, with its entrance heavily sandbagged and half its windows missing or bricked up. It was rumoured that this Holiday Inn had been condemned by the parent company as not up to scratch long before the war, and it had certainly deteriorated since then!

We were given keys for a double bedroom and bath on the fourteenth floor, and as there was no electricity that day, we toiled up the concrete fire-staircase to a room facing the mountain from which the Bosnian Serb gunners bombarded the town. This side of the hotel had been hit so many times that no one felt it worthwhile clearing up the rubble, so the passages were littered with plaster and glass debris, difficult to negotiate at night, and our bath tub was full of bricks and mortar from a chunk of ceiling that had collapsed above it.

'So much for the *en suite*,' I said.

'Glad you joined?' asked Fitz, and we collapsed on our quite adequate bed and hugged each other.

For all its shortcomings, the Sarajevo Holiday Inn was a cheerful place, as long as one's holiday was short and the ceasefire lasted. The dining rooms buzzed with rumour and ribaldry as the media of the world met, fed and prepared to do each other down. Meals seemed to go on all day, as in Russia, and the hard-pressed waiters, who were perhaps glad to find someone able to speak their own language, could not have been nicer.

I spent a good deal of the next few days sitting in the lobby, with its grandiose sweep of royal-blue carpeting, watching human nature. Fitz was busy filming with the boys, and when the watching finally became tedious, I decided to do a little sightseeing on my own.

I had hardly crossed the roughly mown grass in front of the hotel when a noise like an angry mosquito, followed by a sharp crack, came from somewhere quite near – near enough, anyway, to send me scurrying for the shelter of the church towards which I had been heading. It was shut and locked, but as I got my breath back I felt rather smug about being sniped at and missed. Fitz and the team rolled up soon afterwards and airily dismissed my brief tangle with a marksman. 'He was probably aiming at that goat that's munching thistles over there,' they concluded. 'Goat stew is infinitely preferable to dog.' But Fitz forbade any more forays on my own.

Later we set out together to visit the old Turkish quarter, which we knew from previous visits. It had always been a picturesque town within a town, with steep, narrow streets of artisan booths selling beaten copper objects, filigree jewellery, hand-carved pipes and embroidered slippers, all gathered round a little white mosque at the bottom of the hill, from which at midday the muezzin called the faithful to prayer. There were not many faithful even then, but always a crowd of dark-skinned gypsies milling around its courtyard, so brightly dressed they might have gone straight on stage as the chorus of the *Zigeunerbaron*. Now the booths were mostly closed and there were no gypsies, but the mosque had not been hit or wrecked. We made friends with the owners of a little shop that sold films, drank good Turkish coffee with them, and talked about happier times.

I went with Fitz when he interviewed Sirj Izbegovič. I did not feel there was much hope or indeed faith in the West's Balkan politics in this small, neat, scholarly-looking Moslem, only sadness and perhaps despair. I knew he had pleaded with Peter Carrington for the United Nations not to grant Bosnia independence, when it was still just possible to preserve Jugoslavia as a nation of confederated republics; but Bosnia's neighbours had been too powerful, Europe (including our own Foreign Office) too weak, and Germany too strong. Izbegovič talked with emotion about the destruction of the great library of Moslem books and manuscripts that had been one of the glories of his town. We parted cordially, but I did not have the impression that the President was a leader of men, or even a very astute politician – merely a sad and disillusioned one.

Our meeting with Lieutenant-General Michael Rose, DSO, was much more positive and upbeat, but disappointing for the film crew who, cameras and furry sound-wands at the ready, were firmly barred by the General's ADC from even entering his headquarters.

Mike Rose, as large and dynamic as poor Izbegovič had been small and unimpressive, was on top of his form. Like all ex- and serving SAS officers when they get together, he was gossipy, informative, talking freely 'off the record', as well as being highly prejudiced about the British Army's merits, especially those of his own (and Fitz's) regiment. He was utterly dismissive of other NATO troops and also of Mladič's reputation as a commander.

'Anyone can win a battle or end a siege if you surround an unprotected town with hundreds of tanks and pound it to bits,' I remember him saying, his blue eyes filled with contempt. At the end of a happy hour, with only telephone interruptions and orders barked to ADCs, we rejoined the team, and General Mike consented to be snapped briefly outside the building.

Leaving Sarajevo proved more eventful than arriving. Normally passengers were driven by bus to the airport via a long tunnel, thus avoiding the small bit of Serb territory which overlooked the city. Unfortunately, that day the tunnel was closed for repairs, and we had to take the long road round, which entailed driving through a few kilometres of Serbia. There were, naturally, unfriendly guards at the frontier post, and one of them stomped aboard our bus, and shouted for passports, without the 'please'. Poor Boris, our interpreter, went green, for he had a Croatian one and was therefore illegally on Serbian soil (as well as a roll of film which he had foolishly snapped in the city). Fitz leapt to his feet and took the brute firmly by his arm and asked to be led to his commanding officer whom, he told him, he knew, and who would take it amiss if their reunion was prevented.

By a miracle it worked. The dazed guard led Fitz out and introduced one ex-Partisan, retired British general to a fierce-looking, moustachioed active colonel in the Serb army, and they fell on each other's necks with cries of *'Draga maklin!'* and *'Stara priatelli!'* ('Old friend!'). After a couple of quick shots of slivovitz and promises to get together when the accursed war was over, Fitz returned. No passports were looked at, and we drove on.

'I doubt if I've ever seen him before in my life,' said my husband. 'He was almost certainly a Četnik.'

When we visited Tito's grave in Belgrade, I put a small bunch of spring flowers on his tombstone's marble slab.

'You are the only people who have come here this month,' said its guardian, 'except for poor Jovanka, who comes every week.'

In the mausoleum – a museum of Tito's life and times – we looked at its archives, which are of high historic interest. It was closed to the public, but Milosevič had not dared destroy it. 'Some people wanted to, but then there was an outcry and the idea was dropped,' its director told us. In the photograph albums that Jovanka had kept we found many happy pictures of ourselves – an eerie experience in that sad place.

In the lobby of the Metropole Hotel we met Tito's old colleague Milovan Djilas, who talked about the final chapter of his career. No one could ever stop Djilas talking, or telling everyone his ideas for a solution to Jugoslavia's problems. But it was a different, elderly and down-at-heel Djilas who, rather pathetically, asked for an immediate down-payment for the interview, and then haggled over the deal. While he and Fitz were talking, I noticed that one wall of the lobby was covered with a montage of photographs of Tito, in the war and after it, in his glory days. When I went nearer to look, I saw that every picture of my old friend had had its eyes put out by some sharp instrument. Tito was there, but he was desecrated and blind. Such crude hatred deeply shocked me, and brought the realities of this unhappy country even closer.

Altogether our Belgrade visit was a sad one, and we left feeling pretty certain there was worse to come.

Hans's film was shown in Holland that summer and bought by many countries, but not by the BBC or ITV. I thought it was very good, the best that Fitz had ever made, and so did all the friends to whom we showed it.

33

BONNIE PRINCE CHARLIE

B ACK IN SCOTLAND FITZ AT LAST GOT DOWN TO WORK ON THE BOOK he had always wanted to write – a life of Prince Charles Edward Stuart. The project, soon christened 'BPC', took him two years and entailed much enjoyable travel in the Highlands and Outer Hebrides. Our research into the Prince's time on South Uist was made easy by the local priests, whom Fitz learnt to respect and then to love: their Catholicism reminded him of Florence in his childhood, for their faith and that of their scattered crofting parishioners was as natural as the gentle air blowing in on the westerly winds.

We first visited Father John Campbell, an expert on the Jacobite Rising, whose parish was Loch Boisdale. He gave us many details of the Prince's sojourn on the islands and of the time, after Culloden, he spent in the heather, hiding from the Redcoats, before the schooner *l'Heureux* finally arrived and spirited him away to France, and his sad end in Florence and Rome. We stayed with Canon Angus McQueen at Bornish, and experienced close-up the magic of that extraordinary man.

With him we visited Eriskay, and on 'The Prince's Strand' I collected the little pink convolvulus which grows nowhere else in Scotland, and whose seed is supposed to have fallen from BPC's pocket when he landed. In such a beautiful place it seemed strange that the large, stone-built house on a headland overlooking the bay was standing empty, its windows blind and boarded up, but on our boat trip back to South Uist, Canon Angus told us the reason.

Years ago, as a young curate, he heard that no one would live in the house because it was haunted, and he decided to demonstrate to his parishioners that this was silly nonsense by sleeping there alone. Arriving tired after a six-mile walk and a swim, he had no difficulty in dropping off, but during the night he was woken by the noise of something heavy being dragged up the stairs. *Thump, thump, thump,* it went. It could have been a rolled-up fishing net, whose floats were catching on the stair treads, or something worse. Then the door swung open, and the bedroom seemed to be full of cold air – but the noise stopped, and nobody came in. Next night, the same thing happened again, only the dragging, bumping noises seemed louder and heavier.

'I can tell you,' said the Canon, 'I never tried a third time, but took my people's word for it. The house *was* haunted, and I felt I was the fool, not they.'

'But Father,' I said, 'what was the reason? Had something dreadful happened there?'

He looked at me in that other-world, island way and answered quietly, 'Oh no – no reason at all. You see, it hasn't happened . . . *yet.*'

Fitz really enjoyed working on that book – and people said that his account of the battle of Culloden was the most vivid and accurate ever written.

Our BPC tour ended at Morar Lodge, where we found my cousin Irene upside-down in her garden, planting specimen rhododendrons. When Robin Darwin's annulment failed to materialise, and he finally ran out on her, she was devastated and humiliated, and could not bear commiserations. Deciding to lick her wounds privately, as far from family and friends as possible, she took a job as a children's help in Mexico; but her employers turned out to be hellish, and after bravely sticking them for a year, she returned to the United Kingdom and moved from London to Morar, where her mother, my Aunt Peg, had come to rest.

The two soon made the ramshackle old house the most delightful place to stay in all the Highlands, and every summer relations and friends visited by the dozen, enticed by the fishing in the estuary, the highly dangerous boating on the loch (piloted by Irene and her guardian angels), the icy bathing, and above all by Aunt Peg, who remained undaunted and indomitable and *fun* till the end of her life. As long as she could manage it, she went on travelling round to supervise the Highlands and Islands marketing scheme she ran for the islanders, with Irene providing the transport and local priests the hospitality.

After the war Irene had worked as an editor for Harvill, an offshoot company of Collins, the publishers, which was founded by two remarkable intellectuals, Marjorie Villars and Max Harari, and specialised in publishing art books and Russian *Samizdat* literature from behind the Iron Curtain. Being childless, they became devoted to Irene, and when they died they left her not only some money, but the entire contents of their house, including their library. This wonderful stroke of luck enabled her to transform Morar, overnight, from a basic fishing and shooting lodge into a pretty and comfortable home, without losing any of its charm.

Irene was greatly loved, both by the people of Morar and Mallaig, who were her intimate friends, and to whom she devoted much of her time, and by the select group of visitors who came to stay every year. Many of these were young people, for she attracted children and teenagers as a magnet attracts pins. She was tolerant and supportive of them; she listened to them, and understood. She was also intensely loyal to her own family and her spiritual heritage, and to the faith which she had inherited, to which she added the most human of heavenly virtues – courage and kindness.

I have never quite been able to analyse her magic. She was witty, wise, warm-hearted but never sentimental, forthright and positive, and, above all, like her beloved mother, *fun*. Surely those are enough superlatives to describe anyone – yet they still miss the mark. Irene was uniquely herself.

35

LOSING
BEAUFORT

IN 1965 SHIMI HAD A HEART ATTACK ON THE LONDON-TO-INVERNESS sleeper train, and his convalescence was complicated by the severity of his war wounds. His doctors told him that another attack would almost certainly be fatal, and that, although only fifty-four, he was unlikely to make old bones.

Remembering the death duties the Lovat Estates had paid when his own father died, and realising the ones on his own demise would be very much heavier, he followed the only course open to him. He slowly made over the Castle, the Beauly river, the sporting rights, Morar and ninety per cent of the Lovat lands to his eldest son, Simon, the Master of Lovat, who was only twenty-five at the time, and working in a bank in the City of London.

Had Shimi but known it, he would live for another thirty years, the last three as an invalid; and sadly, the decision he had been forced to make created much bitterness in a family that until then had been happy and united.

Young Simon, who had recently married Virginia Grose, now moved into the Castle, and Shimi and Rosie took over Balbair House, a much smaller and prettier home than Beaufort, which was easier to run, and to which they both became devoted. Shimi had kept his valuable woodlands out of the arrangement, and he had also retained a few acres of pastureland on which he could indulge in his favourite hobby and greatest expertise – the breeding of champion bloodstock (now from a mixed mini-herd of six shaggy Highland heifers).

woman whom he did not meet again until many years later. The girl child that was born as its result was brought up without her true parenthood being revealed to her; it was only when her mother's husband had died and she herself was happily married and had a son that she was told.

Our own children were the first to know they had a stepsister, because they had already become her close friends. They told me, and then, while Annabel and her family were staying with us, we agreed that she and Fitz should talk and then announce their relationship. He, as usual, was writing and I remember holding my breath outside the library, where they were closeted. I gave them fifteen minutes, and then went in – to find the two of them sitting side by side, holding hands and looking very happy. Hardy, her little son, then arrived to hug his grandfather, and I think all three felt equally proud of each other. I, too, was overjoyed to have a stepchild whom I already loved and admired.

And there were other surprises . . . Fitz at last agreed to take a group of friends with him on one of our journeys. A dozen of them travelled with us *in a bus* to Svanetia, the most remote, romantic and least visited region in all Georgia. The party included Gina and her daughter Sasha Abercorn, who were direct descendants of the last Tsar's brother, the 'Viceroy of the Caucasus'; Laurence Kelly, the Georgian historian, and his wife Linda; Jean and Laura Lloyd; Jeanette Maxwell; the Cazalets and the Dunnes. To lead us came our old friend from Tbilisi, Gela Charkviani, and his son Eraklia, whose ancestors, we discovered to our delight, were 'Swans'.

The expedition was a great success and we repeated it with much the same group and flew with them from Nepal into Tibet, which I found far too high, too cold and too sad for pleasure. But Fitz, supported by Henrietta Dunne and Camilla Cazalet, managed to take a splendid photograph of Mount Everest which, with his article, was published in the *Sunday Times*, and he was immensely pleased when the picture editor rang to say it was so good that he had pinned a copy of it above his desk against the office wall.

36

VALE

WE CELEBRATED OUR GOLDEN WEDDING ON 12 JANUARY 1996, in Glasgow's Gartnavel Hospital. Fitz was just beginning to recover from a knee-joint replacement, and was still in pain and a little muzzy, but I brought to his bedside a small jar of caviar and a bottle of champagne, and the nurses produced a surprise cake. He managed a few mouthfuls and the other patients in his small ward finished up the rest. We held hands and thought back, in great contentment. There is a time in long and happy marriages when one doesn't need to say much.

From then on Fitz gave up resisting help, and it was a joy and a comfort for me, at long last, to supply it. He was determined to regain his mobility, and no doubt pushed himself too hard in trying to do so. That spring he wrote another book – *Far Frontier*, a picture-travel book which Bato Tomasevic edited with his usual skill – and started work on his autobiography.

I flew to Korčula in May for a brief visit and there was a joyful reunion in June. The future looked bright.

But there was to be no future, for Fitz died suddenly of a heart attack only one week after my return.

Unfortunately, Simon, the recipient of so many new responsibilities and great opportunities, was by nature and inclination an entrepreneur who enjoyed taking risks. Whereas Shimi was a traditionalist and a romantic Highlander, Simon was a pragmatic one, and he had not inherited my father's or my brother's affection for and dedication to their clansmen, or their closeness to the people who lived on our estates.

Although he got on very well with those who worked for him, and they, in turn, became devoted to him, Simon realised the world had moved on and that the welfare state, unionism and financial independence had largely removed that devotion and trust on the one hand, and the inborn sense of duty on the other, that had been at the heart of our family's chieftainship. Besides, his father, though ailing, was still very much alive – and awkward.

I suppose it was inevitable that the transfer wouldn't work. Shimi, who hated to be idle, could not stop interfering with Simon, and Simon, who had perhaps been over-strictly brought up, resented it. He wanted to go ahead with his own ideas and take the advice of his own friends, who were very different from his father's – and Shimi resented that. Indeed, in the eyes of my generation, some of Simon's friends were not very attractive, and I thought his desire to emulate and impress much richer tycoons dangerous, for he took risks in order to do so and, although our family has always thrived on taking risks (which makes them such good soldiers), these were of a different kind.

Some of Simon's schemes were imaginative and successful, like when he flew the first nucleus herd of champion Charollais cattle to Canada in a jumbo jet. Others were disastrous, like when a thousand head of cattle specially bred at Beaufort were exported to his client, the Shah of Iran, whose regime collapsed before payment could be made.

He seemed pursued by ill luck – or was it poor judgement and timing? I do not know; but, fearing interference with his projects, he became more and more secretive, and neither his parents nor his brethren, nor even his cousin, Giles Foster, his business and estate manager, had any idea of the true extent of his borrowing or his debts, until he died.

One evening at Beaufort I had a serious conversation with Simon, whom I loved. He said he was convinced that large agricultural and sporting estates in Scotland were doomed, that privately owned land would soon be expropriated by socialist governments 'for the people', and that the rights of farmers and landowners would be ignored by the urban and political majority. It was a strangely prophetic speech, and he concluded it, passionately, by telling me he was interested only in preserving financial security for his children, and to hell with tradition and out-of-date methods which impeded his efforts to do so. This, too, was prophetic, for in spite of all our family's anxieties and fears, it was in the end what he more or less managed to do.

Simon was the best and most generous of hosts, and I like to remember him and his beautiful half-Italian wife Virginia before *le déluge* hit, entertaining us all at Beaufort, laughing at himself and filling our glasses with wine which, he told us, was the worst that had ever come out of Australia – grown in his own vineyards, which faced 'the wrong way' – in a house full of flowers and people and laughter.

Simon loved the Australian property he had bought in the outback. He would fly out to it, always alone, and revel in the rough life of an ordinary jackaroo, sweating out the worries and stress of his financial anxieties by sheer hard work. In this I could recognise my father's genes. They surfaced, also, in his love of stalking and of taking family and friends for great walks across the marches of the estate, from Braulen at the top of Glen Strathfarrar to Patt and by the Sgurrs till they finally reached the western seaboard of Loch Maree.

Fishing bored him, and he had no love for my beautiful river, which during his lifetime he sold in time-share slices. He also sold most of the non-profit-making parts of the estate to stem the ever-increasing tide of debt which he knew would eventually overwhelm him. Some of the enterprises he started succeeded after his death, but that was largely due to the devotion and determination of Giles, who has spent all his life looking after our family, and to Kim, Simon's brother, who both worked tirelessly to save what could be salvaged from the wreck.

I don't want to write much about the tragedies that befell the Fraser family in the last years of my brother's and Fitz's lives. In 1994 Shimi and Rosie's youngest son Andrew was killed in a shooting accident in Africa, and barely a week later Simon died from a heart attack, aged only fifty-four.

Thereafter Shimi's health deteriorated. I would visit him at Balbair, and find him chair-bound, but just as good-looking as ever, with his white hair and the still marvellous tilt of that proud head.

'How are you feeling?' I would foolishly ask.

'Failing, failing,' he would answer, in the tones of any old crofter, and then switch to more entertaining subjects – but never to news of Beaufort or its fate. In his last years he became gentler in spirit, and closer, if that were possible, to Rosie, who never left his side, and in whose arms he died in the spring of 1995.

That summer Beaufort and the greater part of the Lovat Estates were sold to cover the enormous debts which had built up since Simon took over their management from his father. At first I minded this acutely, for I had been brought up to believe that the land was our family's heritage, to be cared for and held in trust by each generation for the next. It was more than an idea: it was an almost physical relationship – the one I had felt so strongly as a child, when I said goodbye to our river in the little summer-house above the Cruives Pool. Not only had we owned and loved the land for more than six hundred years: my attachment to it enshrined, also, everything that I felt about Scotland, the Highlands, their people and the good lairds, of whom my father had been such a shining example.

But only recently have I come to realise that I was wrong: the Lovat heritage I so valued is *not* dead; it has merely metamorphosed. In this new century I have been happy to find our family still deeply entrenched and committed to their inheritance. Kim and Hughie, Shimi's other sons, and sweet Virginia, Simon's widow, all now have permanent homes within a few miles of the Castle, and several of Shimi's grandchildren are buying into the old estate and planning new ones. The Moniack Frasers are flourishing, and led by my great-nephew, young Simon Lovat, the new Fraser of Lovat clan chief and twenty-fourth MacShimidh, we are still, thank God, a fighting force, and one, dare I say it, 'to be reckoned with'.

34

SURPRISES

THERE WERE TWO SURPRISES IN THE LAST YEARS OF FITZ'S LIFE that illuminated them and brought a happiness he never expected or dreamt of.

The first was a letter from David Airlie, the Lord Chamberlain. Fitz shouted for me to 'come quick' into his library, and showed it to me. Would he accept the honour of being made one of Her Majesty's Knights of the Thistle?

I don't think I had ever seen him so pleased since the moment he discovered Bonnie Prince Charlie's portrait at the bottom of Uncle Henry's tin trunk! The Thistle is a knightly order even older than the Garter, and is in the Queen's gift. It has nothing to do with merit, which makes it all the nicer.

The Thistle wiped away all the disappointments in Fitz's life at a stroke, and even though he enjoyed its privileges and glory for only a short time, it was enough. We both participated in his audience at Buckingham Palace, to which Sukie drove us. He couldn't kneel, so the Queen knighted him on a comfortable chair in a drawing room, and I was allowed in to watch. In Edinburgh we loved the gossip and the dressing-up in the Signet Library, the pageantry of the parades in St Giles's Cathedral during Assembly week and on St Andrew's Day, and the lunches at Holyroodhouse afterwards. The fifteen other Knights were nearly all old friends and very welcoming.

The second surprise brought happiness to *all* the family. Its origins went back to a time in the war which Fitz had almost forgotten, when, on leave from Jugoslavia, he had a brief romance with a married

ENVOI

I N OUR JOINT WIDOWHOOD ROSIE AND I HAVE DRAWN CLOSER. I have not yet achieved her courage and detachment from things temporal, and perhaps I never shall; but I *have* reached a stage at which I can look backwards with gratitude and forwards with composure, and a little hope.

I know I am lucky to have lived in a privileged world in its heyday, when a code of honourable behaviour, good manners, a belief in excellence and a deep love for our country were all accepted as standard; I am lucky to have had such a wonderfully happy and carefree childhood, lucky to have loved and been loved so deeply and so well, lucky to have shared so many adventures and made so many friends. And I am lucky, now, to have such devoted children, who worry about me as much as I worry about them.

My regrets are ones of omission. I could, and in a long life should, have often done better, and more. But at least I have learnt, through the sadness and joys of all those turbulent years, one certain truth. The only things that really matter are faith and a close, loving family. Only they can sustain one to the end of one's journey, and only they can start one on the road to eternity.

Index

Note: 'VM' denotes Veronica Fraser/Phipps/Maclean; 'FM' Fitzroy Maclean.